MONEY MATTERS IN MIGRATION

Migration, participation, and citizenship, are central political and social concerns, are deeply affected by money. The role of money – tangible, intangible, conceptual, and as a policy tool – is understudied, overlooked, and analytically underdeveloped. For sending and receiving societies, migrants, their families, employers, NGOs, or private institutions, money defines the border, inclusion or exclusion, opportunity structures, and equality or the lack thereof. Through the analytical lens of money, the chapters in this book expose hidden and sometimes contradictory policy objectives, unwanted consequences, and inconsistent regulatory structures. The authors from a range of fields provide multiple perspectives on how money shapes decisions from all actors in migration trajectories, from micro to macro level. Taking an interdisciplinary approach, the book draws on case studies from Europe, the Americas, Asia, and Africa. This comprehensive overview brings to light the deep global impacts money has on migration and citizenship.

TESSELTJE DE LANGE is Professor of European Migration Law and Director of the Centre for Migration Law in the Faculty of Law, Radboud University Nijmegen.

WILLEM MAAS is Jean Monnet Chair and Professor of Political Science, Public & International Affairs, and Socio-Legal Studies, York University, Toronto.

ANNETTE SCHRAUWEN is Professor of European integration at the Amsterdam Centre for European Law and Governance (ACELG), Law Faculty, University of Amsterdam.

MONEY MATTERS IN MIGRATION

Policy, Participation, and Citizenship

Edited by

TESSELTJE DE LANGE
Radboud University, Nijmegen

WILLEM MAAS
York University, Toronto

ANNETTE SCHRAUWEN
University of Amsterdam

CAMBRIDGE
UNIVERSITY PRESS

University Printing House, Cambridge CB2 8BS, United Kingdom

One Liberty Plaza, 20th Floor, New York, NY 10006, USA

477 Williamstown Road, Port Melbourne, VIC 3207, Australia

314–321, 3rd Floor, Plot 3, Splendor Forum, Jasola District Centre, New Delhi – 110025, India

103 Penang Road, #05–06/07, Visioncrest Commercial, Singapore 238467

Cambridge University Press is part of the University of Cambridge.

It furthers the University's mission by disseminating knowledge in the pursuit of education, learning, and research at the highest international levels of excellence.

www.cambridge.org
Information on this title: www.cambridge.org/9781316517505
DOI: 10.1017/9781009042505

© Cambridge University Press 2021

This publication is in copyright. Subject to statutory exception and to the provisions of relevant collective licensing agreements, no reproduction of any part may take place without the written permission of Cambridge University Press.

First published 2021

A catalogue record for this publication is available from the British Library.

ISBN 978-1-316-51750-5 Hardback

Cambridge University Press has no responsibility for the persistence or accuracy of URLs for external or third-party internet websites referred to in this publication and does not guarantee that any content on such websites is, or will remain, accurate or appropriate.

CONTENTS

Notes on Contributors   *page* viii

1 Money Matters in Migration: A Synthetic Approach   1
   TESSELTJE DE LANGE, WILLEM MAAS, AND ANNETTE SCHRAUWEN

   PART I **Migration**

2 The Changing Landscape of Multilateral Financing and Global Migration Governance   19
   ELAINE LEBON-MCGREGOR AND NICHOLAS R. MICINSKI

3 Digging a Moat around Fortress Europe: EU Funding as an Instrument of Exclusion   38
   CATERINA MOLINARI

4 The "Refugee Hospital". Aid Money, Migration Politics, and Uncertain Care in Neoliberal Morocco   55
   LORENA GAZZOTTI

5 Cash Rules Everything: Money and Migration in the Colombian-Venezuelan Borderlands   74
   CHARLES LARRATT-SMITH

6 Recruitment Fees, Indebtedness, and the Impairment of Asian Migrant Workers' Rights   93
   PEDRO DE SENA

7 Pushing Out the Poor: Unstable Income and Termination of Residence   112
   ANNETTE SCHRAUWEN

8 Follow the Money: Income Requirements in Norwegian Immigration Regulations   130
   HELGA EGGEBØ AND ANNE BALKE STAVER

   PART II   **Participation**

9 "This Is Affordable!" The Role of Money Matters in the Use of Live-In Migrant Care Arrangements   149
   ANITA BÖCKER, MARÍA BRUQUETAS-CALLEJO, VINCENT HORN, AND CORNELIA SCHWEPPE

10 De-magnetizing the Market: European Integration, Employer Sanctions, and the Crackdown on Undeclared Work   169
   KIMBERLY J. MORGAN

11 Women as EU Citizens: Caught between Work, (Sufficient) Resources, and the Market   188
   SANDRA MANTU

12 Migrant Financial Inclusion versus the Fight against Money Laundering and Terrorist Financing   205
   TESSELTJE DE LANGE AND ELSPETH GUILD

13 Migrant Remittances and Money Laundering in Africa   223
   CRISTIANO D'ORSI

   PART III   **Citizenship**

14 Millionaires and Mobility: Inequality and Investment Migration Programs   247
   KRISTIN SURAK

15 Are Citizenship by Investment Programs Legitimate? Suggesting Some Assessment Methods   263
   ELENA PRATS

16 Wealth as a Golden Visa to Citizenship   279
   AYELET SHACHAR

17 Divided Families and Devalued Citizens: Money Matters in Mixed-Status Families in the Netherlands   297
   JUDITH DE JONG AND BETTY DE HART

18 Money in Internal Migration: Financial Resources and
    Unequal Citizenship   317
    WILLEM MAAS

Index   336

NOTES ON CONTRIBUTORS

ANITA BÖCKER is Associate Professor of Sociology of Law at the Law Faculty of Radboud University, Nijmegen, the Netherlands. She has published widely on the social and legal status of immigrants, the effectiveness of anti-discrimination law, and the regulation of migration and immigrant integration in the Netherlands and other European states. Her recent research focuses on migration and return migration in later life and on live-in migrant care arrangements in Germany and the Netherlands.

MARÍA BRUQUETAS-CALLEJO is Research Fellow at the Center for Migration Law, Radboud University, Nijmegen, the Netherlands. Her work deals with migration and welfare state policies from a comparative, multidisciplinary, and multilevel perspective. She has published widely on immigrants' access to healthcare and to the welfare state, immigrant integration policies, and transnational eldercare arrangements. Her recent research examines the migration–welfare state nexus, emphasizing the contribution of migrants to retrenching welfare states in the field of long-term care.

BETTY DE HART is Professor of Transnational Families and Migration Law at Vrije University, Amsterdam Centre for Migration and Refugee Law (ACMRL). Her legal, empirical, and historical research focuses on gender and migration, citizenship, mixed (status) families, and law in everyday life. She is the recipient of an ERC Consolidator Grant for her research project EUROMIX: Regulating Mixed Intimacies in Europe, addressing the question of whether, how, and why 'mixed' relationships are regulated in Europe.

JUDITH DE JONG is a PhD candidate in political science at the University of Amsterdam. Her interdisciplinary research focuses on how intersections of ethnicity/race and gender affect citizens' assessments of their political representation, comparing France, Germany, and the Netherlands. She is interested in postcolonial studies, intersectionality, and people's everyday encounters with and understandings of politics and law.

TESSELTJE DE LANGE is Professor of European Migration Law, Director of the Centre of Migration Law (CMR) at the Faculty of Law, and a member of the Radboud University Network of Migrant Inclusion (RUNOMI), all at the Radboud University, Nijmegen, the Netherlands. She has worked as an immigration lawyer, honorary-district judge in immigration cases, and, until 2020, vice-chair of the Dutch Advisory Committee of Migration Affairs, advising the Dutch government. Her research interests are labour migration law and governance in Europe as well as globally, and migrant worker rights.

CRISTIANO D'ORSI is currently a senior research fellow and lecturer at the South African Research Chair in International Law (SARCIL)/ University of Johannesburg. His research interests mainly focus on the legal protection of asylum seekers, refugees, migrants, and IDPs in Africa, on African human rights law, and, more broadly, on the development of public international law in Africa and in the so-called developing countries all around the world.

PEDRO DE SENA is a legal adviser with extensive experience in legislative affairs. He is a PhD candidate at the University of Amsterdam, researching norm creation processes in the context of labour migration. He has a particular interest in migration in Asia, where he lived for over two decades. Currently he is a senior adviser to the State Secretary for Home Affairs in the Portuguese Government.

HELGA EGGEBØ is a senior researcher at the Nordland Research Institute in Bodø, Norway. She holds a PhD in sociology from the University of Bergen (2013), and her thesis explored the regulation of marriage migration to Norway. Her recent work on migration focuses on family migration, integration, immigration regulations after the refugee crises in 2015, and living conditions among queer migrants. Eggebø's recent projects also include research on ageing, gender equality, and climate change.

LORENA GAZZOTTI is the Alice Tong Sze research fellow at Lucy Cavendish College and CRASSH, University of Cambridge. Her research explores the expansion of security and racialized regimes of containment at the Euro-African border. Her research has been published in the *Journal of Ethnic and Migration Studies*, the *American Behavioral Scientist*, the *Journal of North African Studies*, and the *Sociological Review*. Her first book, *Immigration Nation: Aid, Control, and Border Politics in Morocco*, is forthcoming with Cambridge University Press.

ELSPETH GUILD is Jean Monnet Professor ad personam, Emeritus Professor of Law at Radboud University, Nijmegen, the Netherlands, and Professor of Law at Queen Mary University of London. She is also a partner at the London law firm Kingsley Napley and a visiting professor at the College of Europe, Bruges. Her interests and expertise lie primarily in the area of EU law, in particular EU Justice and Home Affairs (including immigration, asylum, border controls, criminal law, and police and judicial cooperation in criminal matters). She also researches EU privacy and data protection law and the nexus with human rights. She is also co-editor of the *European Journal of Migration and Law*. She is co-editor of the book series Immigration and Asylum Law and Policy in Europe published by Martinus Nijhoff.

VINCENT HORN is a postdoctoral researcher at the Institute of Education, Johannes Gutenberg University Mainz, Germany. His expertise includes transnational ageing, transnational migration in old age, old age and transnational families, old-age care migration, and migrant care migration as well as older refugees. He was involved in the research project 'Emergence and Significance of Transnational Old Age Care Arrangements in Germany and the Netherlands', financed by the German Research Foundation (DFG). He is currently conducting a study on older refugees in Germany.

CHARLES LARRATT-SMITH is currently a visiting research fellow at the Observatorio de Dinámicas del Conflicto Armado en el Caribe (Universidad del Norte). His research focuses on counterinsurgency, armed non-state actors, organized crime, and forced displacement and migration, with a regional focus on Latin America.

ELAINE LEBON-MCGREGOR is a postdoctoral researcher at United Nations University-MERIT and the Maastricht Graduate School of Governance, Maastricht University. Her main research interest lies in the area of global migration governance with a particular focus on international organizations and policy coherence. Her doctoral research focused on the role of international organizations in the evolution of global migration governance. She is currently working on the MIGNEX project (www.mignex.org/).

WILLEM MAAS is Professor of Political Science, Public & International Affairs, and Socio-Legal Studies at York University, where he holds a Jean Monnet Chair. He writes on EU and multilevel citizenship, migration, borders, free movement, and politics focusing on Europe and North America.

SANDRA MANTU is Assistant Professor at the Centre for Migration Law (CMR), Faculty of Law, Radboud University, Nijmegen, the Netherlands and co-managing editor of the *European Journal of Migration and Law*. Her research focuses on EU citizenship, free movement of persons, implementation of EU law, social rights, equality and access to the welfare state, and nationality law.

NICHOLAS R. MICINSKI is Libra Assistant Professor of Political Science and International Affairs at the University of Maine. His research interests include immigration and refugee policy, global governance, development, and human rights. He is the author of two books: *Delegating Responsibility: International Cooperation on Migration in the European Union* (University of Michigan Press, 2022) and *UN Global Compacts: Governing Migrants and Refugees* (Routledge, 2021).

CATERINA MOLINARI is a PhD candidate at the Institute for European Law of the KU Leuven since September 2017 and an FWO doctoral fellow since October 2018. Her research focuses on the EU's external action in the area of migration. More particularly, she has worked on the constitutionality of the EU's return and readmission policy, on its fundamental rights implications, as well as on the progressive informalization and externalization of EU migration management.

KIMBERLY J. MORGAN is Professor of Political Science at George Washington University. Her work examines the politics shaping public policies, with particular interests in migration and social welfare. She is the author of Working Mothers and the Welfare State: Religion and the Politics of Work-Family Policy in Western Europe and the United States (Stanford 2006) and The Delegated Welfare State: Medicare, Markets, and the Governance of American Social Policy (Oxford 2011), and co-editor of several volumes, including The Many Hands of the State: Theorizing Political Authority and Social Control (Cambridge 2017).

ELENA PRATS is a qualified lawyer and a PhD candidate in philosophy of law at both Uppsala University and Pompeu Fabra University. Her research interests lie in the fields of legal theory, migration, and citizenship policies. Prats' dissertation provides an approach to the assessment of the legitimacy of programmes granting citizenship for investments in the EU from the perspective of legal philosophy.

ANNETTE SCHRAUWEN is Professor of European Integration at the Centre for European Law and Governance (ACELG) at the University of Amsterdam. She is one of the theme leaders of the research theme 'Diverse Europe' of the Amsterdam Centre of European Studies (ACES), an interdisciplinary Centre of Excellence for research, education, and public debate about Europe, the European Union, and its member states. Annette is chair of the editorial board of *Legal Issues of Economic Integration*. She has published widely in the field of EU free movement law and EU citizenship.

CORNELIA SCHWEPPE is Professor of Social Pedagogy at the Johannes Gutenberg University Mainz, Germany. She was the director of the doctoral research programme 'Transnational Social Support' financed by the German Research Foundation and was awarded a fellowship at the Gutenberg Research College. She has published widely on transnational ageing, retirement migration, and old-age care. Her current research includes projects on retirement migration to Kenya and Thailand, care migration to Poland and Thailand, and transnational care arrangements in Germany and the Netherlands.

AYELET SHACHAR is Professor of Law, Political Science, and Global Affairs at the University of Toronto, and Director of the Max Planck Institute for the Study of Religious and Ethnic Diversity. Her research spans the fields of citizenship theory, immigration law, new border regimes, elite migration and global inequality, combining insights from law and political theory with innovative institutional design. Shachar is a fellow of the Royal Society of Canada and the recipient of numerous excellence awards, most recently the Leibniz Prize – Germany's most prestigious research award.

ANNE STAVER is a senior researcher at the Norwegian Institute for Urban and Regional Research at the Oslo Metropolitan University, Norway. She holds a PhD in political science from the University of Toronto (2014). In her dissertation she examined the development of stricter family reunification rules in Denmark, Norway, and the United Kingdom. Her recent work addresses asylum and integration policies in Scandinavia.

KRISTIN SURAK joined the London School of Economics in 2020 from SOAS University of London where she was an associate professor of Japanese politics. Her research on international migration, nationalism, and political sociology has been translated into a half-dozen languages. In addition to publishing in major academic and intellectual journals, she also writes regularly for popular outlets, including the *London Review of Books*, *New Statesman*, *New Left Review*, and *Washington Post*. Her next book *Citizenship 4 Sale: Millionaires, Microstates, and Mobility* will be published by Harvard University Press in 2021.

1

Money Matters in Migration: A Synthetic Approach

TESSELTJE DE LANGE, WILLEM MAAS, AND ANNETTE SCHRAUWEN

Migration, participation, and citizenship are central political and social concerns in democratic societies and beyond. From the 1948 Universal Declaration of Human Rights (UDHR) to the 2018 Global Compact for Safe, Orderly, and Regular Migration, international agreements portray individuals and communities in terms of worth and value, seeing human diversity as an asset rather than a threat.[1] The UDHR extols the dignity and worth of the human person and declares that everyone has rights to social security, just and favourable conditions of work and remuneration, rest and leisure, free education, and an adequate standard of living; individuals have the right to freedom of movement and residence within the borders of each state, the right to leave any country, including their own, and to return to their country, and the right to seek and to enjoy in other countries asylum from persecution. The Global Compact reminds us that 'migration has been part of the human experience throughout history' and declares that signatories 'recognize that it is a source of prosperity, innovation, and sustainable development in our globalized world'; a key objective of the Compact is to 'mitigate the adverse drivers and structural factors that hinder people from building and maintaining sustainable livelihoods in their countries of origin', while the Compact 'promotes the well-being of migrants and the members of communities in countries of origin, transit, and

---

[1] UN Secretary-General António Guterres stresses how human diversity is 'an Asset, Not a Threat' and the Global Compact on Migration can play a crucial role in the world's recovery from COVID-19. UN Secretary General Press Release SG/SM/20459, 1 December 2020.

destination'.[2] Tying migration to the language of human worth, rights, and prosperity reflects the varied contributions of this book.

The role of money in migration – tangible, intangible, conceptual, and as a tool of policy design – is understudied, overlooked, and analytically underdeveloped. Money matters in curbing the arrival of migrants at borders or facilitating access for certain migrants over others. It is key in non-humanitarian entry policies (e.g. through income requirements, salary thresholds, or fees), for participation in wider society for the migrant and loved ones left behind (e.g. through the payment of remittances, access to the labour market, and fines for those not participating 'properly'). And money matters when obtaining and exercising citizenship (fees, costs of language training) but also when including the rich in citizenship programmes or excluding poor and unwanted citizens. Why not take money as our point of departure in our critical study of migration, inclusion, and citizenship law and governance?[3]

This book starts a reappraisal of migration laws and policies' 'worth' for sending and receiving societies, migrants, their families, and their employers. The in-depth analysis of financial barriers to migrate, to participate, and to remain refreshes our thoughts on migrants' (lack of) money. The selected chapters all use money as the lens of inquiry into regulatory structures. Money is defined very literally and very practically: money in the bank, a salary, a fee, a subsidy; in short, money in the narrow sense of financial resources and as such a 'migration management' tool often overlooked in academic research. In line with the common lay understanding of migrant and by lack of a definition under international law, this book defines a 'migrant' as 'any person who moves away from her country or state of origin either temporarily or permanently and for a variety of reasons'. Migration refers to the process of such movement.

This book does not force an overarching theoretical framework, as the individual chapters each engage with migration theory in their own fields. Our aim is to facilitate overarching engagement and to 'launch

[2] Objective 6 of the Global Compact is to facilitate fair and ethical recruitment and safeguard conditions that ensure decent work; objective 20 is to promote faster, safer, and cheaper transfer of remittances and foster financial inclusion of migrants; objective 22 is to establish mechanisms for the portability of social security entitlements and earned benefits. The rest of the Compact also echoes the language of investments and sustainability.

[3] This observation by Tesseltje de Lange inspired this project on money matters in migration, resulting in a panel session at the 2018 Council of European Studies annual conference and a follow-up workshop at the University of Amsterdam featuring early drafts of many chapters.

new ships' in terms of new research on the subject of money in migration, rather than predetermining their path through a single grand theory. Theoretical notions engaged with by the contributors include Sassen's 'logics of expulsions',[4] addressed by De Jong & De Hart (Chapter 17), Schrauwen (Chapter 7) as well as De Lange & Guild (Chapter 12), and build on it by providing new insights into the meaning of participation, citizenship, and the role of financial instruments in these 'expulsions'. Feminist theory on economic and cultural norms about what constitutes (productive) work informs the chapter by Mantu (Chapter 11); Böcker et al. depart from the Baumol effect, which explains why many countries have a demand for migrant care workers. Their contribution addresses 'irregularity' or 'semi-legality' as a (non)compliance with labour and social security law. Theorizing labour market–related immigration enforcement and (non)compliance with immigration law is the topic of Morgan's contribution. Speaking of markets, Surak (Chapter 14) on investor citizenship theorizes how inequality rather than equality defines the worth of citizenship, while Maas (Chapter 18) explores the ways in which financial disparities and conditions exist in tension with ideas of equal citizenship even for internal migrants.

All contributions to this volume convincingly discuss money as an instrument of border drawing. Shachar sums it up eloquently in Chapter 16: 'States have proven more enterprising than most theories would have predicted in finding new ways to control migration and mobility, developing a sophisticated kaleidoscope of territorial, cultural, and economic line-drawing techniques that can be deployed selectively against different target groups, and according to different baselines, including means, privilege, and power.' She continues:

> In recent years, important strides have been made in revealing the impact of considerations of race, culture, ethnicity, gender, sexuality, and, increasingly, religion too in de facto shaping the prospects of migration and integration – despite being formally prohibited and discredited. [. . .] While enriching and nuancing previous accounts, surprisingly little attention has been paid to the persistence of wealth in creating, or replicating, unequal admission to territory and membership.

The contributions to this volume engage in closing this gap. This book aims to encourage more multidisciplinary and interdisciplinary research into the role of money and resources on migration. Given the different disciplinary perspectives included in this volume, each chapter uses

[4] Sassen 2014.

different research methods, each appropriate in its own field. The sum of the chapters is stronger than the parts, as readers from different disciplines can compare the ways in which money is conceptualized and utilized in research on migration from various disciplinary perspectives. The balance between empirical and theoretical work advances the debate on how (not) to manage migration. The book will hopefully inspire new research on the topic of money in migration.

The selection of the chapters is based on three elements: first, the inspiration they offer for future research into money as a tool to manage migration; second, the multiple methods used by the chapter authors; and third, the basis offered for theoretical as well as policy debates based on the findings presented in the chapters. Such a wide range of cases adds value to this volume.

Aims, Actors, and Instruments Engaging Money

Throughout the chapters, three important elements of analysis return implicitly or explicitly: policy *aims*, sometimes unexpected *actors* and subjects of money-driven migration 'management', and the variety of *instruments* used, such as financial incentives or sanctions ('carrots or sticks').

Money as a Tool to Achieve Policy Aims

The first analytical element is the *aim* that financial instruments seek to achieve. Money matters as an instrument to select migrants in order to protect the welfare state, a policy discourse addressed by Eggebø and Staver (Chapter 8). It matters in the design of labour law enforcement instruments aimed at combating illegal participation of migrants in the labour market. Analysing the role of money in migration management requires exposing the explicit or hidden objectives. The *aim* of policies on remittances can be framed as a development tool or as a way to prevent terrorism, meaning the aims collide.[5] This is precisely the dilemma that entangles migrant workers, as D'Orsi (Chapter 13) discusses in his chapter regarding Africa and De Lange & Guild (Chapter 12) discuss for the UK and the Netherlands. The governance of remittances serves a socio-economic interest of countries of origin. For this reason, countries of origin may not aim to curb migration, as remittances might decrease.[6]

---

[5] Lindley 2011.
[6] De Haas & Plug 2006.

Likewise, as Molinari discusses in Chapter 3, the increased EU expenditure on migration management outside the EU can be understood as an alternative source of income for countries of origin. Gazzotti (Chapter 4) discusses yet another alternative source of socio-economic funding, notably donor-funded projects of NGOs and IOs. The chapters indicate how these alternative financial sources each have their drawbacks that may not immediately become clear if one ignores the 'aim' or structuring role of money. Furthermore, as Lebon-McGregor & Micinski (Chapter 2) show in their analysis of the funding of IOM, a variety of financial sources results in a fragmented global migration policy where aims are mostly prioritized in a way that reflects existing power structures.

Diverging policy aims when taking money as an analytical tool allow for a critique of the dichotomy between forced and unforced migration, between 'refugee' and 'migrant'.[7] We also see this distinction in the UN Global Compact for Safe, Orderly, and Regular Migration.[8] Traditionally, asylum and refugee law, understood as human rights law, tended to develop along other lines than the law on voluntary migration.[9] The right of asylum is primarily understood as a human right.[10] As yet, forms of voluntary migration such as labour migration and family reunification are generally subject to the right of states to deny entry to foreigners on the basis of financial requirements.[11] Legal categorization of foreigners according to nationality, skills, income levels[12] (e.g. Eggebø & Staver, Chapter 8 in this volume), or according to the investments they can make (see Shachar, Chapter 16; Prats, Chapter 15; and Surak, Chapter 14 in this volume) aims for more, or less, migration, participation, or citizenship. Such legal categorizations are often contested. Larratt-Smith's Chapter 5 on money and migration in the Venezuelan-Colombian borderlands forms a painfully clear example that the

---

[7] For a critique of the construction of the dichotomy between 'refugee' and 'migrant', see Crawley & Skleparis (2017). On categorization in general: Schrover and Moloney 2013. For an example of financial consequences, e.g. employer sanctions for mis-categorizing student migrants as workers, see De Lange 2015.
[8] Guild & Grant 2017.
[9] Boeles et al. 2014, p. 3.
[10] Boeles et al. 2014, p. 244.
[11] De Lange & De Sena 2019.
[12] On border drawing through salary requirements, see Paul 2015, p. 111. An example of extremely high income requirements set for family migration in the United Kingdom is discussed by Wray et al. 2015. See also Court of Justice EU *Chakroun* [C-578/08] and *Kachab* [C-558/14] on how income requirements should not become barriers hindering family life indefinitely.

distinction between forced and unforced migration is not clear-cut. EU citizens in contrast form a privileged category because they have a right to enter member states of the EU of which they do not have the nationality.[13] Even for them, the right is subject to financial conditions: EU citizenship allows member states to refuse admission to those who may become 'burdens' just as national constitutions usually guarantee rights to free movement but often also limit these rights.[14]

Actors and Subjects

It is useful to distinguish between *actors* who decide on the use of money as an instrument of migration governance and those who are *subjects* of the rules. In general, governments qualify as actors setting finance-related instruments in migration policy. However, they can also be subjected to financial obligations such as having to bear the costs for the reception of asylum seekers. Migrants and sponsors qualify as actors when they make money-related decisions on where to migrate or whom to hire. They are subject to rules that impose financial conditions on access to territory or family reunification. Employers or passenger carriers are generally seen as actors in the enforcement of migration rules. In fact, they are subjects of penalties included in rules on combating illegal immigration.

The exploration of the role of money in migration in this book uncovers a diverse range of actors, regulatory structures, and impacts which allow investigating the value of money across a myriad of migration laws, policies, and practices. The book includes chapters that address actors and the role of money at the macro level (does the EU budget on migration management reflect an exclusive or inclusive migration policy, Molinari, in Chapter 3) as well as chapters that include research on micro level (e.g. Böcker et al., Chapter 9, describe how money structures decisions of individual households and private employment agencies to hire migrants for in-house care; De Jong & De Hart, in Chapter 17, picture the 'expulsion' of individual citizens with a migrant partner in social policies). The book also includes analyses of intermediary actors such as recruitment agencies (De Sena, Chapter 6), employers of illegal immigrants (Morgan, Chapter 10), or households recruiting migrant workers (Böcker et al., Chapter 9), non-governmental organizations (Gazzotti, Chapter 4),

---
[13] Maas 2007; Schrauwen 2021.
[14] Maas 2013.

intergovernmental organizations (Lebon-McGregor & Micinski, Chapter 2), or banks as service providers (D'Orsi, Chapter 13; De Lange & Guild, Chapter 12), all involved in shaping migration, participation, and citizenship. An emphasis on migrants and governments shows how wealth and income affect movement even within states, facilitating migration or making it more difficult (see Maas, Chapter 18). The focus of the book is on the role money plays in these actors' policies and practices, rather than on these actors as an industry.

Instruments

The *instruments* used can serve as incentives or barriers to migration, participation, or the enjoyment of citizenship rights; they are 'carrots or sticks' to manage migration. Income thresholds are an obvious barrier (Eggebø & Staver, Chapter 8). Less conspicuous barriers to participation are employer sanctions (Morgan, Chapter 10) or the 'unbanking' of sometimes long-time residents (De Lange & Guild, Chapter 12). Multiple chapters demonstrate money-related barriers to full citizenship (De Jong & De Hart, Chapter 17; Maas, Chapter 18; Mantu, Chapter 11; Schrauwen, Chapter 7). Investment citizenship, on the other hand, can incentivize migration, as can subsidies (Molinari, Chapter 3; Gazzotti, Chapter 4). In this volume, Lebon-McGregor & Micinski (Chapter 2) examine the role UN funding played in the origin and evolution of the International Organization for Migration (IOM), an organization with great impact in the field of migration management, supporting diaspora communities but also prominent actors in many return programmes. Böcker et al, Chapter 9, show how cash-for-care schemes (providing allowances instead of services to people dependent on long-term care) incentivize the recruitment of care workers from lower-wage countries.

Migration, Participation, and Citizenship

This introduction mirrors the book's tripartite focus on migration, participation, and citizenship. Following David Abraham's theoretical framework as presented in the seminal work of Brettell and Hollifield *Migration Theory: Talking across Disciplines*, the chapters are grouped under the three subthemes of migration, inclusion (which we rename 'participation'), and citizenship.[15] This structure allows us to offer an

---

[15] Abraham 2015, pp. 289–317.

overarching engagement with migration theory and research. Migration, participation, and citizenship broadly reflect different stages in a migration trajectory, from movement to initial settlement and entering into another context to incorporation in that other context as citizens. Whereas migrants may not perceive their movement as taking place in stages, legal systems do take these stages as point of departure by setting rights and obligations per stage, requiring different sets of rules: rules on border controls and admission, rules on equal treatment and constitutional protection on non-migration matters for those allowed in, and rules of naturalization and access to citizenship for full incorporation.[16] Each policy stage can be perceived as more, or less, 'welcoming'.[17] As already discussed earlier, the authors in this book theorize these stages, again, each from their own disciplinary background.

Part I – Migration

Many actors are relevant in the study of a migration trajectory, be it sending/source states, local sponsors, or intermediaries and recruiters facilitating or restricting migration. And there are actors whose position is in between departure and arrival: not only migrants but also human traffickers, NGOs, states of transition, and transport companies. A focus on the role of money leads to sometimes overlapping analytical fields of study on a single migration trajectory: financial considerations that influence a person's decision to migrate or determine the availability of migration options; employers', agents', financial institutions', or sponsors' costs and benefits in relation to facilitating or restricting migration; decision-makers' financial considerations when governing or managing migration, where decision-makers can be states, international organizations, the EU, or their delegates.

Chapters 2 to 8 address one or more of these actors and their roles, their impact on migration trajectories, and their (ab)use of financial power (e.g. of receiving states over sending states or other institutions). These chapters also cover financial instruments in making, influencing or using migration law, policy, or practice such as financial obligations as conditions or practical obstacles for migration, costs and benefits of the type of migration they are involved in, or the categorization of the people or actors they impact.

---

[16] Abraham 2015.
[17] De Lange 2018.

Chapters 2 to 4 address funding of migration. Elaine Lebon-McGregor and Nicholas Micinski show how voluntary earmarked funding has an impact on the position of IOM, the governance of migration, and contributes to a growing fragmentation of migration regulation through informality and non-binding agreements. Caterina Molinari analyses changes in the EU budget and links them to various areas and objectives of the EU migration policy. She concludes that the EU uses money as a privileged tool to manage migration and that funding decisions post 2015 are mainly directed towards exclusion and return of migrants. Lorena Gazzotti zooms in on the funding of welfare care for migrants in Morocco. Her chapter on donor-funded projects lays bare how this may lead to states outsourcing care and the decision on who does (not) receive care. With that, responsibility has shifted, but without any accountability mechanisms in place other than the conditions of the donor-funded project.

Chapters 5 and 6 turn to the migration trajectory and migrant strategies. Charles Larratt-Smith provides the reader with a more internal perspective of the Venezuelan exodus. His chapter gives an inside and detailed illustration of how economic collapse may lead to people being forcibly displaced without having the protection the international community provides to refugees from war zones. The chapter shows how lack of money results in not being able to access temporary visas because of the fees a home state charges for official documents. With that, illegal border-crossing, dependence on the informal economy, exposure to crime, and exploitation follow in the Venezuelan-Colombian borderlands. Pedro de Sena's chapter brings us to labour migration in Asia. He shows how (lack of) protection of migrants starts at home, hence the importance of sending countries. Where recruitment fees are determined by a supply-and-demand system in both sending countries and destination countries, improvement of working conditions and access to work visas are hindered. The recruitment industry opposes regulation from sending states aimed at protection of migrants. Resulting recruitment-induced indebtedness thus can lead to dependence on the informal economy and exposure to crime and exploitation – also of migrants whose border-crossing was legal.

Chapters 7 and 8 focus on receiving states and their regulation of admission and residence via financial conditions. Income requirements are commonly used across the globe to manage migration, often with a high level of discretion for the receiving state to design the level of income it deems sufficient.[18] In Chapter 7, Annette Schrauwen looks at

---

[18] De Lange & De Sena 2020.

policy and practice on income, or the lack thereof, in three receiving states in the context of internal EU labour migration. Her chapter shows how these states manipulate the internal EU regime on the free movement of workers via financial thresholds and turn to a policy of exclusion of EU citizens with a low or unstable income. Financial conditions are used to blur the formal distinction between the legal categories of EU citizens and migrants from outside the EU. In Chapter 8, Helga Eggebø and Anne Staver identify an economic drift, meaning the use of economic criteria seeps into the non-economic immigration policies, and stratification of migrants' rights in their chapter on restrictive amendments in Norwegian immigration policy on family reunification and access to permanent residence. These chapters signal a more general political development across the high-income states in Europe where money is key in regulating migration.

Part II – Participation

In *The Ethics of Immigration* Carens describes how, as a 'landed immigrant' in Canada, his rights and duties did not seem to differ from those of Canadian citizens for almost all practical purposes. He admits he was a privileged immigrant in many ways but still considers his position to be equal to other permanent residents in Canada and typical for permanently residing immigrants throughout Europe and North America.[19] The focus on money as facilitating participation[20] in the economy and society of the receiving state results in a different perspective. Money is an analytically overlooked tool of creating categories or of 'border drawing' between categories of migrants, citizens, between people eligible for rights and benefits, fit to belong, or not to belong that has a far wider impact than initial admission to the territory. Money has similar effects to the much more extensively mapped border drawing through time and space.[21] The chapter by Morgan provides a clear example of how attempts to control economic transactions replace formal border controls in the EU and how penalties turn employers into guardians of the formal economy who must block accession for certain migrants living in the host society. Financial rules or regulatory structures with financial

---

[19] Carens 2013, p. 88.
[20] We prefer to speak of participation as the term links more to transnationalism instead of inclusion (one-dimensional).
[21] On border drawing and concepts of time and space, see, for instance, Della Torre & de Lange 2018; Mezzadra & Neilson 2013.

implications determine participation in the society and economy of the receiving state, at macro-, meso- and micro-levels. Money-related instruments may impact migrants in ways that are not foreseen, as the example of the contradicting EU rules on access to payment accounts and combating terrorism financing shows, discussed by De Lange & Guild in Chapter 12. Money may influence the choice of migrants for a possible country of destination. It may also influence the choice of sponsors or employers for certain migrants, as a result of balancing affordability and legality. From a transnational perspective, financial regulations aimed at combating money laundering may have unforeseen consequences for remittances – even though the value of remittances for poverty alleviation and development is widely recognized, and facilitation of remittances is included in objective 10 of the global sustainable development goals and objective 20 of the UN Global Compact on Migration.

Chapter 9 describes how policies aimed at containing the costs of long-term care incentivize families with dependent elders to hire migrant care workers; it also shows that differences in national policies translate into different levels of law compliance in the families' arrangements with the migrant carers. Next, Morgan analyses in Chapter 10 how a similar template of financial instruments targeted to prevent unauthorized migrant work in European countries developed. The aim of these instruments seems to be deterrence and making it difficult for unauthorized migrants to sustain themselves by barring their access to the labour market. Access to the labour market is not barred for EU citizens, but financial criteria determining free movement rights do impact that access in particular for women. Mantu shows in Chapter 11 how seemingly neutral financial criteria and definitions present in EU free movement legislation and upheld by the European Court of Justice are not gender-neutral and deny or ignore the impact on EU free movement and citizenship rights of women.

The last two chapters under Part II turn to financial rules to combat money laundering and terrorism. Both chapters show how financial rules aimed at securitization have negative consequences for financial regulation of aims that are recognized as valuable and directed at inclusion and participation. D'Orsi takes the reader to the African continent in a very insightful chapter on the value of remittances. He explains the regulatory framework and the main actors related to remittances and provides case studies on three African countries. He argues that the impact of rules against money laundering should better take into account the position of migrants and the value of remittances. De Lange and Guild demonstrate in Chapter 12 how the EU rules aimed at migrant inclusion in payment system infrastructure are frustrated because of rules against terrorist financing and money laundering. Banks become border guards of formal financial participation of migrants. With the increasing abandoning of cash payments, not having a bank account may result in wider social exclusion.

Part III – Citizenship

Money should not just be understood as a means to pay for migration enforcement, border control, labour market access, or, on the individual level, a means to pay for food, travel, or education. Money is analytically disentangled as the normative value it stands for, the wealthy are not seen as a burden, having an income proves economic ties, having a profitable business is proof of taking 'responsibility', being trustworthy, and deserving a fast-track citizenship. Part III addresses the effect money may have on our understanding of citizenship as an equality-centred notion. In general, the theoretical focus in citizenship literature is not so much on migrants, but on transformation of the host society.[22] The ability of states to determine who their citizens are is a core element of sovereignty, yet EU citizenship creates new rights and a common status transcending the member states and requiring shared governance.[23] At the time of writing, this is motivating EU authorities to scrutinize member state policies on investor citizenship (discussed below), as well as subjecting member state policies on naturalization and denaturalizing to EU law. The chapters in part III address the link between money and citizenship and show how both citizenship and financial instruments can be used as a stick or carrot. Governments' use of citizenship to attract the wealthy has seen a revival at the beginning of the century, to such an extent that a whole industry of investment migration emerged, allowing private actors to make money out of the relationship between state and prospective citizen. On the other hand, governments' use of financial incentives or conditions to protect the welfare state may block access to citizenship even for those 'migrants' who are born on their territory. Furthermore, the use of a financial 'stick' to protect the welfare state may result in taking away or denying the protection of their citizenship to the 'undeserving'. The

---

[22] Brettell & Hollifield 2015, p. 14.
[23] Maas 2016; Schrauwen 2018.

link between money and citizenship results in inequality, both internationally and within states.

The first three chapters under Part III focus on investment citizenship programs. Kristin Surak investigates the increasing concentration of wealth owned by a small group of elites, showing how high net worth individuals generally seek improved mobility rather than immigration, motivated by risk management, business opportunities, and visa-free travel. She argues that fortunes are made within states (caused by mass privatization, marketization, and increasing economic inequality) even as wealthy investor migrants seek to escape the same borders that enabled their wealth. Elena Prats' aim is to bring conceptual clarity to the debate on investor citizenship programmes. In her chapter, Prats provides a solid definition and investigates the legitimacy of the programmes by doing the theoretical exercise of deploying a method of assessment – contract law – grounded on the mainstream characterization of the programmes as commodifying and selling citizenship. Initiating her text with a conceptual distinction of the meanings of legitimacy, the author illustrates the use of the mentioned method with the case of the Maltese programme. Finally, Ayelet Shachar reminds us that the conditions of access to membership reveal much about a society's vision of citizenship and the power dynamics inherent in admission. She finds that money matters in shaping entry, settlement, and naturalization prospects, generating tremendous opportunities for the wealthy while closing doors for everyone else; wealth as a criterion for citizenship, long discredited in light of the ideal of political equality, is being revived.

The final two chapters focus on the relationship between money, migration, and citizenship within societies. Judith de Jong and Betty de Hart investigate the social and financial consequences of being a mixed-status family, focusing on the case of the Netherlands. The exclusion of illegalized individuals from certain benefits for housing, health, or child care extends to legal partners and family members, especially those who depend on social benefits to make ends meet, who also lose their rights to benefits. Because of their relationship with an illegalized migrant, they find themselves relegated to the margins of society as 'failed citizens'; financial instruments of the welfare state thus draw borders within mixed-status families, dividing families and devaluing citizens. Finally, Willem Maas investigates the role of money as facilitator and barrier to internal migration, and its resulting effects on democratic equality. As the previous chapters elucidated for international migrants, rich migrants are generally valued while poor migrants are generally shunned; Maas demonstrates that money matters even when the prospective migrants are internal migrants with shared rights and citizenship.

References

Abraham, David. 2015. 'Law and Migration: Many Constants, Few Changes'. In Caroline B. Brettell & James F. Hollifield, eds., *Migration Theory: Talking across Disciplines* (3rd ed.). Routledge.

Boeles, P., M. den Heijer, G. Lodder, and K. Wouters. 2014. *European Migration Law*. Intersentia, 2nd ed.

Brettell, Caroline B. and James F. Hollifield. 2015. *Migration Theory: Talking across Disciplines*. Routledge, 3rd ed.

Carens, J. 2013. *The Ethics of Immigration*. Oxford: Oxford University Press.

De Haas, H. & R. Plug. 2006. 'Cherishing the Goose with the Golden Eggs: Trends in Migrant Remittances from Europe to Morocco 1970-2004'. *IMR* 40(3), 603-604.

De Lange, Tesseltje. 2015. 'Third-Country National Students and Trainees in the EU: Caught between Learning and Work'. *International Journal of Comparative Labour Law and Industrial Relations* 31, 453–471. www.kluwerlawonline.com/document.php?id=IJCL2015025.

De Lange, Tesseltje. 2018. 'Welcoming Talent? A Comparative Study of Immigrant Entrepreneurs' Entry Policies in France, Germany and the Netherlands'. *Comparative Migration Studies* 6:27(1).

De Lange, Tesseltje & Pedro De Sena. 2020. 'Your Income Is Too High, Your Income Is Too Low: Discretion in Labour Migration Law and Policy in the Netherlands and Macau'. *The Theory and Practice of Legislation*, 1–17. doi/full/10.1080/20508840.2020.1729559.

Della Torre, Lucia & Tesseltje de Lange. 2018. 'The "Importance of Staying Put": Third Country Nationals' Limited Intra-EU Mobility Rights'. *Journal of Ethnic and Migration Studies* 44(9), 1409–1424. doi/full/10.1080/1369183X.2017.1401920.

Guild, Elspeth & Stefanie Grant. *Migration Governance in the UN: What is the Global Compact and What Does It Mean?*, Queen Mary University of London, School of Law Legal Studies Research Paper No. 252/2017.

Lindley, A. 2011. 'Remittances'. In Alexander Betts, ed., *Global Migration Governance*. Oxford University Press, pp. 242–265.

Maas, Willem. 2007. *Creating European Citizens*. Rowman & Littlefield.

Maas, Willem. 2013. 'Free Movement and Discrimination: Evidence from Europe, the United States, and Canada'. *European Journal of Migration and Law* 15(1), 91–110.

Maas, Willem. 2016. 'European Governance of Citizenship and Nationality'. *Journal of Contemporary European Research* 12(1), 532–551.

Mezzadra, Sandro & Brett Neilson. 2013. *Border as Method, or, the Multiplication of Labor*. Duke University Press.
Paul, Regine. 2015. *The Political Economy of Border Drawing: Arranging Legality in European Labor Migration Policies*. Berghahn Books.
Sassen, Saskia. 2014. *Expulsions: Brutality and Complexity in the Global Economy*. Harvard University Press.
Schrover, Marlou & M. D. Moloney. 2013. 'Introduction: Making a Difference'. In M. Schrover & M. D. Moloney, eds., *Gender, Migration and Categorisation: Making Distinctions between Migrants in Western Countries, 1945–2010*. Amsterdam University Press, pp. 7–54.
Schrauwen, Annette. 2018. 'Citizenship of the Union'. In P. J. Kuijper, F. Amtenbrink, D. Curtin, B. De Witte, A. McDonnell, & S. Van den Bogaert, eds., *The Law of the European Union* (5th ed.). Alphen aan den Rijn: Wolters Kluwer, pp. 611–638.
Schrauwen, Annette. 2021. 'Citizenship and Non-Discrimination Rights in the Area of Freedom, Security and Justice'. In Sara Iglesias & Maribel Pascual, eds., *Fundamental Rights in the EU Area of Freedom, Security and Justice*. Cambridge University Press, pp. 394–412.
Wray, Helena, Eleonore Kofman, Saira Grant, & Charlotte Peel. 2015. Family Friendly? The Impact on Children of the Family Migration Rules: A Review of the Financial Requirements. Project Report, Children's Commissioner.

PART I

Migration

2

The Changing Landscape of Multilateral Financing and Global Migration Governance

ELAINE LEBON-MCGREGOR

NICHOLAS R. MICINSKI

Introduction

In 2018, newly appointed Secretary General of the United Nations (UN) Antonio Guterres called for a funding compact to improve the 'predictability of resources'.[1] As part of UN reforms, Guterres aimed to reduce the reliance on voluntary contributions, which since the 1990s had increasingly taken the form of earmarked contributions.[2] Since the concept of voluntary contributions was absent from the UN charter because the founders were concerned it would undermine multilateralism, current funding trends raise concerns about the functioning of the UN as a multilateral system. Earmarked contributions are viewed as both a challenge and an opportunity for the UN. On one hand, voluntary funds have allowed the UN to grow beyond levels sustainable by mandatory financing, as well as expand into areas that do not garner unanimous support.[3] Conversely, earmarked funding allows donors to exert influence over the practices of international organizations (IOs), which results in institutions that reflect existing power relations.[4] Voluntary funds are more vulnerable to fluctuations due to political and economic factors and can lead to reactive, short-term interventions.[5] Reflecting these concerns, a limited but growing body of literature examines the relationship between money and global governance.

---

[1] United Nations 2018.
[2] Graham 2017a.
[3] Graham 2015; 2017a.
[4] Browne 2017.
[5] Ege and Bauer 2017; Seitz and Martens 2017.

Global governance, meaning the rules and institutions that govern state behaviour, consists of many elements, including international law, UN agencies and operations, and multilateral funding. Resources – whether from mandatory assessed contributions, or voluntary earmarked contributions – are at the centre of how decisions are made in global governance and how policies are implemented.[6] Money is only one example of a resource; however, one can think about resources as the authority to establish and enforce norms or to define the contours of global policies.[7] While it is beyond our scope to deal with these wider issues, this chapter contributes to the literature by first outlining the theoretical linkages between funding and governance before applying these ideas empirically to the multilateral funding of the International Organization for Migration (IOM) using a new dataset of earmarked contributions to IOM between 2000 and 2016 (n = 13,306).[8] Specifically, we ask: what role has money played in the history and practices of IOM and what do thematic and temporal patterns of funding reveal about the priorities in global migration governance?

It may appear counterintuitive to select IOM as a case study, given that it has operated outside of the UN for most of its history, only joining as a 'related agency' in 2016. However, the establishment of IOM outside of the UN system reflects the role that money has played in the fragmentation of international cooperation on migration.[9] This chapter also responds to the repeated calls for a more critical examination of the role of IOM in migration governance by providing new empirical evidence about trends in multilateral funding of IOM.[10]

Money and Governance

Governance within international institutions is described as multilateral because member states have voting rights and collective decisions are made through formal governing bodies.[11] Scholars argue that the UN's increasing reliance on voluntary funding has changed its multilateral character by creating new relationships between funders and IOs that circumvent formal governing bodies.[12] In a pure multilateral model, the

---

[6] Dingwerth and Pattberg 2009, 42.
[7] Bourdieu 1991.
[8] McGregor 2019.
[9] Betts 2011.
[10] Andrijasevic and Walters 2010; Elie 2010; Pécoud 2018.
[11] Browne 2017; Keohane 1990; Ruggie 1992.
[12] Browne 2017; Graham 2017a, 2017b; Seitz and Martens 2017.

governing body of an organization has the ability to allocate its revenue as it see fit. By earmarking funding for a specific purpose, donors reduce the ability of governing bodies to make these decisions. Thus, voluntary funding creates multiple channels of responsibility, forcing IOs to be directly responsive to donors, undermining the IO governing body and its multilateral character.

A large academic literature supports the finding that increased earmarked funding from diverse sources undermines multilateralism.[13] However, the implications of these shifts are viewed differently. On one hand, the disruption of multilateralism through changing funding patterns can result in institutions reflecting existing power relations.[14] Powerful member states that make substantial earmarked contributions can exert pressure on an organization to reflect their own national interests. Sridar and Woods coined the term 'trojan multilateralism' to describe the effect that earmarked funding has in allowing bilateral interests to enter the multilateral system.[15] Similarly, Kahler writes of 'minilateral "great power" collaboration within multilateral institutions';[16] and Seitz and Martens warn that the UN is in an 'era of selective multilateralism' where voluntary funding arrangements undermine democratic global governance.[17]

On the other hand, others frame these shifts in more neutral or even positive ways. Naím described minilateralism as 'the magic number to get real international action'.[18] Peter Sutherland also drew inspiration from Naím, viewing minilateralism as a solution to an impasse among member states on certain aspects of migration governance:

> That is why I suggest tackling problems at the lowest level where they can be solved. Sometimes that means the local or national level, but on some issues States need to work together, bilaterally, at the regional or even the global level – seizing on the initiatives of pioneers and champions, and working through what has been called 'minilateralism', whereby small groups of interested States work together to develop and implement new ideas that can then be debated, and perhaps adopted, in more formal settings.[19]

---

[13] Goetz and Patz 2017; Graham 2017b; Seitz and Martens 2017.
[14] Browne 2017.
[15] Sridhar and Woods 2013.
[16] Kahler 1992, 862.
[17] Seitz and Martens 2017, 46.
[18] Naím 2009.
[19] United Nations 2017, 30.

However, others suggest that a broader set of funders and more flexible funding rules can reduce the influence of traditional funders and democratic governance.[20]

While the theoretical arguments regarding the relationship between funding and governance are well developed, the empirical examination of these links is a relatively new area of research. Empirical studies on this relationship fall into two broad categories: (1) state preferences for funding type (mandatory or voluntary); (2) the impact of mandatory and voluntary funding on the functioning of the recipient organization. The evidence generally suggests that voluntary funding is used by states to further their interests. Gray draws attention to the relationship between voluntary funding and organizational growth, particularly in areas that go beyond the original mandate, but also argues that these endeavours often fail at the level of implementation because they are pushed by specific donors and lack legitimacy in the eyes of target states.[21]

Especially large donors can also influence an organization through withholding funding. For example, when the United States withdrew its funding for UNESCO in response to the admission of Palestine, the organization witnessed a significant drop in the number of permanent core staff.[22] Focusing on the US contributions to the UN between 1945 and 1980, Bayran and Graham find that the United States was more likely to provide voluntary contributions to an organization if its interests and preferences were not in alignment with those of the IO governing body.[23] Smaller donors also use voluntary funding to press their interests in contexts where stronger states resist a course of action. For example, UNESCO saw a subsequent increase in voluntary funding with the number of temporary staff increasing – albeit not to the same level as prior to the US withdrawal. The United Nations Development Programme (UNDP) was created because states wanted to move beyond the impasse between the United States and the Soviet Union on industrial development policy.[24]

Research has also focused on the influence of voluntary funding on the composition of IO staff and the functioning of the IO, presumably as a proxy for influence. Thorvaldsdottir finds a positive correlation

[20] Heldt and Schmidtke 2017; Michaelowa 2017.
[21] Gray 2014.
[22] Hüfner 2017.
[23] Bayram and Graham 2017.
[24] Graham 2017a.

between the amount of funding given by a specific donor and the number of staff from that country.[25] The assumption is that staff from a particular country will be more likely to pursue that country's interests within the IO. However, voluntary staff also impact the functioning of the organization. As the example of UNESCO shows, earmarked funding was used to fund temporary staff positions. IOs struggle to retain staff because earmarked funding supports time-bound technical cooperation projects, forcing IOs to hire fewer permanent staff and rely on a higher proportion of temporary staff. Using financial and human resource data of fifteen UN agencies, Ege and Bauer find that higher levels of voluntary funding are positively correlated with a higher proportion of temporary staff.[26] The challenge of having more temporary staff is that it creates a culture of short-term thinking. More temporary staff can lead to IOs that are more likely to be swayed by the interests of their donors, and result in fragmentation and incoherence in their portfolio. It also adds more bureaucracy, as organizations face the additional burden of reporting to multiple funders with different requirements. These effects are expected to be particularly pronounced when resources are scarce and competition is high. Staff themselves may also behave differently in the face of job insecurity, which has implications for building trust between IO staff and their government contacts, affecting project implementation and the achievement of longer-term strategic goals.

However, the relationship between funding and influence is not unidirectional. Funders exert influence over the activities of IOs, and IOs influence funding patterns.[27] IOs influence donors' agendas by creating narratives and defining policy problems to which the organization can respond.[28] Research on IOM confirms this dynamic: 'the projects put into practice correspond to the expectations of their sponsors, in other words the wealthiest countries, although these expectations are in turn strongly influenced by the IOM'.[29] Wunderlich argues that IOM's field presence, combined with its close relationship to the European Commission, allows the organization to act as a 'communication broker' translating EU priorities into project ideas for local authorities that are based on local knowledge and networks, while simultaneously

---

[25] Thorvaldsdottir 2016.
[26] Ege and Bauer 2017.
[27] Michaelowa 2017.
[28] Broome and Seabrooke 2012.
[29] Brachet 2016, 275.

establishing IOM as the ideal implementer.[30] The influence of money on governance is clearly a two-way street.

Migration Governance and Funding

Migration is an interesting case for understanding the relationship between money and governance because migration governance is fragmented and competitive. Graham argues that contentious topics are more likely to be funded through voluntary contributions, in part because voluntary funding does not require widespread support among member states.[31] Migration governance is fragmented because there is no overarching IO, treaty, or normative body to govern how states treat migrants; however, different aspects of migration are governed in different ways.[32] For example, the 'refugee regime' is the area of migration that exhibits the most multilateral characteristics with 145 states party to the 1951 refugee convention and United Nations High Commissioner for Refugees (UNHCR) as the supervisory body. Migration has been a difficult area to reach consensus on within the UN: member states struggled throughout the 1990s to garner support for an international conference on migration[33] and repeatedly failed to get signatories for binding legal norms on migration.[34] As a result, migration governance has evolved within this fragmented context through informal, non-binding, and state-led initiatives, largely operating outside of the UN, and funded through earmarked contributions.

Migration governance is a crowded and competitive field. Within the UN system, there are at least four entities with mandates related to migration: the United Nations High Commissioner for Refugees (UNHCR); the United Nations Relief and Works Agency for Palestine

---

[30] Wunderlich 2012, 493.
[31] Graham 2017a.
[32] Aleinikoff 2007; Koser 2010; Thouez 2019.
[33] The idea for a UN conference on international migration can be traced to UN Resolution A/RES/48/113, six months prior to the International Conference on Population and Development (ICPD) in Cairo in September 1994. At the ICPD, the topic was broached but proved too divisive. States were surveyed on four occasions about hosting a conference (Chamie and Mirkin 2013) eventually agreeing in June 2003 to hold a High-Level Dialogue in 2006 (A/RES/57/270 B).
[34] Attempts to develop normative tools for migration have failed to receive broad support. Discussions regarding the 1990 UN Convention on the Rights of Migrant Workers and their Families (MWC) started immediately after the adoption of ILO's 1975 Migrant Workers Convention (No. 143), but it took almost three decades for the convention to become an enforceable convention (2003).

Refugees (UNRWA); the International Labour Organization (ILO); and the International Organization for Migration (IOM). Michaelowa argues that the effects of earmarked contributions are likely to be greater when earmarked funds represent a high proportion of the income of the organization and when funding is limited forcing organizations to compete for resources.[35] This is clearly reflected in migration governance: in 2016, voluntary earmarked contributions were the main source of revenue for IOM (90.5%) and UNHCR (80.7%), just under half for UNRWA (47.1%), and just over one-third for ILO (37.7%).[36] Labour migration represents only one element of ILO's overall portfolio, and has historically played a marginal role in migration governance, presumably reflecting the lower proportion of earmarked funding in its overall budget.[37] The number of UN organizations that were members of the Global Migration Group (GMG) went from six members in 2003 to twenty-two members in 2018.[38] In response to this crowded field, the UN Network on Migration was created to coordinate activities amongst this growing cohort.

While many IOs work on migration, it is challenging to track multilateral funding within this field for several reasons. First, there is no existing source of data on migration-related expenditure for all GMG members. Migration is not necessarily a strategic priority for most GMG members reported in annual budgets and, even internally, tracking migration-related work is not a priority. Alternative sources of data, such as national reports on financial contributions to IOs also have limitations. For example, the United States has only recently started publishing its contributions to IOs at the project level. Furthermore, since migration 'straddles public and private resources, domestic and external spending, and development, humanitarian and security cooperation', databases on 'bilateral aid'[39] such as OECD's Aids Activity Database also only provide a partial overview of migration-related contributions.[40] Given the shrinking core budgets within the UN, organizations without a mandate on migration are less likely to allocate

---

[35] Michaelowa 2017.
[36] Chief Executives Board for Coordination (CEB) 2018.
[37] Siegel et al. 2013.
[38] The GMG was an inter-agency mechanism through which IOs met to coordinate on migration issues. The GMG was replaced by the UN Migration Network when the Global Compact on Migration was adopted in December 2018.
[39] The OECD defines earmarked contributions by member states as 'bilateral aid'.
[40] Rosengaertner 2017, 141.

significant amounts of their core funding to migration-related activities. The only reliable sources of disaggregated project-level data on all earmarked funding by donor are IOM financial reports. As such, we have pragmatically chosen IOM as a case study because of both its relevance to migration governance and the availability of financial data.

Historically, IOM was an overlooked and understudied IO with most of the research focusing on UNHCR, but this has begun to change as the literature on migration governance expanded.[41] One common criticism of IOM is its reliance on earmarked funding and its self-touted 'projectization'. For example, Morris questioned whether 'IOM (is) an agency that will do anything as long as there's money with which to do it'.[42] But the literature on IOM has rarely examined the financial structure and funding with only a few recent exceptions.[43] This chapter fills a gap by, first, tracing the role of money in IOM's origins in 1951 to its designation as a UN 'related agency' in 2016. Second, this chapter presents original analysis of IOM finances (2000–2016), including how it spends its money and where the funding comes from based on financial reports.

The Role of Money in IOM's Journey to the UN

Money and state interests were behind the creation of IOM's precursor – the Provisional Intergovernmental Committee for the Movement of Migrants from Europe (PICMME). After World War II, the international community needed institutions to assist more than 10 million displaced persons in Europe. UNHCR was created as a supervisory and normative body to protect the displaced persons, but needed operational support for facilitating their travel and movement. During the 1920s, ILO had filled a similar role collaborating on operations and travel with Fridtjof Nansen, the first High Commissioner for Refugees under the League of Nations. However, at a 1951 intergovernmental conference in Italy, the United States blocked a similar plan for ILO to take up this role.[44] The United States objected to the plan because of Soviet Union membership

---

[41] Andrew and Eden 2011; Brachet 2016; Bradley 2020; Caillault 2012; Collyer 2012; Frowd 2014; 2018a; 2018b; Gabriel and Macdonald 2018; Koch 2014; Nieuwenhuys and Pécoud 2007; Pécoud 2018; Schatral, 2011; Valarezo 2015.
[42] Morris 2005, 43.
[43] Besides McGregor (2019), which examines IOM's revenue (2000–2016), a forthcoming edited collection by Geiger and Pécoud contains a chapter by Patz and Thorvaldsdottir that examines IOM's expenditure patterns from 1999 to 2016.
[44] Perruchoud 1989.

in the ILO. Instead, PICMME was established at the Migration Conference of Brussels on 5 December 1951, and designed to provide operational support by facilitating 'the orderly migration of large numbers of displaced, unemployed or under-employed persons in Western Europe'.[45] The United States used its financial resources to pursue its political interests by influencing the institutional landscape and structure, keeping cooperation on migration largely outside of the UN.

In the subsequent decades, PICMME changed names and structures but continued to reflect the interests of its largest donors, particularly the United States. In 1952, the organization became the Intergovernmental Commission for European Migration (ICEM), becoming a permanent organization responsible for migration. However, the organization's viability and relevance was challenged in the 1960s and 1970s when several key countries left it.[46] The next Director General (DG), James L. Carlin, was tasked with reorganizing the organization, first by removal of the geographical restriction from the organization's name (from 1980 known as the Intergovernmental Committee for Migration [ICM]) to reflect its expansion outside of Europe. Second, DG Carlin oversaw a shift in the type of work: 'in the early years, transport was the priority, but increasingly, more complex and sophisticated migration services (for example, recruitment, selection, labour reinsertion, and integration) took precedence'.[47] In 1989, the organization was renamed a third time to the IOM.

Importantly, another change occurred in the financial structure of IOM which shifted the organization from a small and declining membership to one with a growing budget and membership. The next DG, James N. Purcell Jr., recognized that IOM needed to prove its relevance to its member states. Purcell implemented two major reforms – decentralization and projectization – that have had lasting impact. First, Purcell transferred the 'primary responsibility for initiating and executing IOM service delivery to its Member States' from headquarters to the field.[48] Because IOM is dependent on the finances of richer states for its survival, some scholars have described IOM as a 'quasi-European'[49] and 'quasi-governmental' organization.[50] As IOM is not a norm-setting actor, it

---

[45] Carlin 1989, 35.
[46] Canada (1962), France (1962), New Zealand (1967), United Kingdom (1968), Australia (1973), Spain (1977), and Brazil (1980).
[47] Perruchoud 1989, 507.
[48] IOM 2003b, 2.
[49] Caillault 2012, 134.
[50] Geiger 2010, 151.

raises questions about the organization's ability to criticize the policies of its donor countries. Second, the organization embraced a policy of 'projectization' defined as 'the practice of allocating staff and office costs to the operational activities/projects to which they relate'.[51] This means that IOM includes overhead fees for its projects, which fund both the staff and infrastructure required to deliver a project and other administrative costs like the salary of the Chief of Mission. However, projectization has resulted in internal fragmentation and competition, where regional offices charged with overseeing field offices are themselves in competition for funding.[52] Nevertheless, projectization allowed IOM to have relatively low mandatory contributions and to grow its overall budget. For example, the assessed contributions from the United States to ILO (83.3 million CHF) were nearly double the assessed contributions to IOM from all member states combined (45.5 million CHF). Projectization is attractive for member states because IOM is able to keep its costs very low. In 2003, states cited cost-efficiency as one reason for IOM to remain outside of the UN system, fearing that IOM would become more bureaucratic and costly.[53]

Why then did IOM join the UN system as a related agency in 2016? Since 2003, migration has risen on the global agenda and, by 2015, was cemented as an issue of relevance to the UN through its inclusion in the Sustainable Development Goals (SDGs). Furthermore, the 2016 New York Declaration for Refugees and Migrants called for greater cooperation on migration, which led to the endorsement of the 2018 Global Compact for Safe, Orderly and Regular Migration. In this context, IOM's entry to the UN can be viewed as an act of self-preservation.[54] IOM was a ready-made solution, avoiding the necessity of creating a new international body, and accordingly it was able to join the UN without any amendments to its constitution. The United States, still IOM's largest donor, arguably wanted to maintain influence over migration governance. Money and influence continue to drive the structure of migration governance.

The Role of Money in IOM's Practices

IOM's financial structure – particularly, the projectization and resulting cost-efficiencies – impacts the organization's relationship with states and

---

[51] IOM 2002, vi.
[52] IOM 2003b.
[53] IOM 2003a.
[54] Lebon-McGregor, forthcoming.

its operational practices in the field. IOM's unique financial structure facilitated the rapid growth in membership, which resulted in shifts in IOM's priorities and fragmented operations across the field. The international community has used IOM's flexible finances to expand responses in the Global South for migrants in vulnerable situations who fall outside UNHCR's mandate, while at the same time expanding returns of irregular migrants from the Global North. These findings are based on our analysis of IOM's annual financial reports from 2000 to 2016.[55]

First, voluntary earmarked contributions are the most important source of revenue for IOM, accounting for between 91 and 97 per cent of total revenue each year. Voluntary contributions have generally increased over time, but are subject to large fluctuations. For example, voluntary revenue decreased by 27% (over 250 million USD) from 2005 to 2006 and then increased by 34% (334 million USD) from 2009 to 2010. Mandatory contributions more than doubled from 2000 to 2016, primarily because membership grew from 79 states in 2000 to 166 in 2016. Other non-earmarked voluntary contributions represented less than 1 per cent of voluntary contributions, primarily from the United States, Austria, Belgium, and, until 2006, Switzerland.

Second, almost four fifths (77.9%) of the earmarked contributions to IOM came from high-income countries with several notable outliers. The top ten member states for annual earmarked contributions were the United States (259.3 million), Peru (74.7 million), Australia (46.8 million), Colombia (45.7 million), the United Kingdom (UK) (37.4 million), Japan (28.5 million), Canada (28.0 million), the Netherlands (20.4 million), Germany (18.8 million), and Sweden (16.3 million).[56] In addition, a low-income country like Bangladesh contributed 36.9 million USD in 2011 for the repatriation and reintegration of Bangladeshi returnees from Libya. Although not a member state, the European Union is an important contributor of earmarked funds with an average of 72.8 million USD per year between 2000 and 2016, making it, after the United States and Peru, one of the largest contributors to IOM. Combined, the EU and the top 10 member states contributed 68.3 per cent of all IOM's voluntary contributions, and 86.6 per cent of voluntary contributions from member states (plus the EU). However, there is variation of earmarked contributions over time, which, as discussed above, leads to fragmentation and incoherent project portfolios.

---

[55] For details on the construction of the dataset, see McGregor (2019).
[56] Based on the average annual voluntary earmarked contribution 2000–16.

The contributions of Peru, Colombia, Japan, and Germany are concentrated in specific time periods whereas the United States and Canada follow a general upward trend. Other countries have more erratic contribution patterns. These patterns reflect the unpredictability of voluntary contributions that creates fragmented implementation, patchy service delivery, and job insecurity.

Third, IOM received significant funding outside of member state contributions, including other IOs (the EU and UN), refugee loan repayments, specific funds, and interest income. For example, contributions from the EU tripled from 26.9 million USD in 2003 to 83.0 million USD in 2005, because of an expansion of EU Electoral Observation Missions organized through IOM. Between 2001 and 2008, IOM received 661 million USD from the Foundation 'Remembrance, Responsibility and Future', which financed a compensation programme for former slaves and forced labourers and others affected by the Nazi regime. IOM was one of seven organizations responsible for processing compensation claims from non-Jewish victims around the world (excluding the Czech Republic, Poland, and the Republics of the former Soviet Union) (IOM 2005). IOM's work has also extended beyond traditional migration work. Between 2009 and 2010, almost half of the increase in earmarked revenue can be attributed to major community and economic development projects in Peru (USD 158 million) and Argentina (USD 11 million) and considerable support for disaster response in Haiti (USD 60 million) and Pakistan (USD 14 million).

Fourth, earmarked funding impacts the priorities of IOM's work, particularly related to refugee resettlement and returns. From 2000 to 2016, the United States (41.1%) and Canada (32.3%) earmarked a far larger proportions of their contributions towards refugee-related projects, primarily resettlement. Approximately 40 per cent of all European earmarked funding was allocated to return (primarily through different forms of assisted voluntary return programmes targeted at rejected asylum seekers), compared to just 8 per cent for all other member states. Australia's earmarking is more diverse but with a clear preference for using IOM's services in the area of irregular migration, return, and refugee resettlement. It is not surprising that a large part of IOM's earmarked contributions were for refugee resettlement or return because IOM was created as an operations and logistics organization to help implement the 1951 convention. In South America, Peru earmarked 85% of its voluntary contributions for capacity building and 27.4% for infrastructure,[57] while Colombia earmarked 51.5% for youth and education and 28.3% on IDPs.

Importantly, states utilized IOM's flexible finances in order to expand programmes for vulnerable migrants, IDPs, climate-related migrants, and other displaced people who fall through the gaps of the 1951 refugee convention and thus outside of the mandate of UNHCR. These priorities are reflected in the earmarked contributions of IOM's donors, notably the United States, Columbia, Canada, Japan, Sweden, and to a lesser extent Australia and the UK. Hall argues that IOM's functional mandate, as opposed to UNHCR's normative mandate, made it much easier for states to fund IOM to help these groups.[58] In some ways, IOM's exponential growth – made possible by its flexible funding and non-normative mandate – has compensated for the limitations of the refugee regime.

While IOM has been dismissed as puppet of state interests or controlled by the United States, this chapter shows that IOM's portfolio is shaped by many other states, albeit mostly high-income countries. Surprisingly, Peru and Colombia, both upper-middle-income countries, represented the second and fourth largest contributors for projects only tangentially related to migration. For example, Colombia contributed 400 million USD to IOM for youth and education projects and 127.8 million USD for IDP projects in 2007 and 2008. These priorities reflect the context in Colombia in which one third of displaced people are children. In Peru, the government contracted IOM to renovate the Lima town hall and convention centre and build the headquarters of the Peruvian Central Bank, totalling more than 500 million USD. These infrastructure projects are an outlier in IOM's work and it is unclear why the Peruvian government selected IOM to implement such large-scale construction projects. One explanation is that IOM was subcontracted these projects because it was flexible and cost effective; another explanation is that IOM funding model requires projects no matter how far removed from migration to support the secretariat, and seeks to grow by increasing its profile as a development actor. In addition, it is likely that IOM's funding will become more diverse as more countries transition to upper-middle- and high-incomes, although it is not likely that this will reflect both the interests of countries of origin and destination. As more places become countries of immigration, they will likely become

---

[57] The total exceeds 100 per cent owing to the fact that some projects are coded to both categories. See McGregor (2019) for more information on how the categories were constructed and measured.
[58] Hall 2015.

larger donors in need of IOM's services for irregular migrants, resettlement, or return – in part because of IOM's reputation as more cost effective than even national agencies.

IOM has become one of the largest international organizations active within humanitarian, development, and migration sectors. The organization's history and relationship to its donors have influenced how it implements projects and what projects it prioritizes. The United States was crucial in establishing IOM outside of the UN system and free from the influence of the Soviet Union, and remains the largest donor. IOM's growing membership has dictated how the organization has evolved in the last fifty years, including expansive humanitarian responses for vulnerable migrants who are not protected by UNHCR and an increased prominence of returns. This has made IOM a flexible and innovative actor, as well as one that is easily influenced by new projects and priorities.

Conclusion

The structure of multilateral financing – by excluding IOM from the UN system and through earmarked contributions – has contributed to the informality of international cooperation on migration. Because migration touches on the issue of state sovereignty, states in the Global North resisted efforts to institutionalize migration within the UN system. IOM is a case in point: the organization was created outside of the UN system because the United States did not want to support or cooperate on migration with the Soviet Union. Using its financial power, the United States steered cooperation on migration to intergovernmental – but not international – cooperation. Money also played a role in IOM's relationship with the UN, because IOM's projectization provided states with a cost-effective and non-normative way to cooperate on migration. However, this exacerbated the influence of specific donors to steer cooperation on migration into areas that reflect their interests.

The empirical evidence in this chapter shows that earmarked contributions, particularly from high-income countries, continue to be the most important source of revenue for IOM, in addition to funding from other IOs and specific projects. The United States continues to exert influence on IOM's priorities, particularly on refugee resettlement; however, the EU and its member states have made returns another priority. We also find evidence that IOM's flexible funding coupled with its non-normative mandate allowed states to expand operations to support vulnerable migrants, IDPs, and other displaced populations that are left out of the refugee convention. While some of IOM's exponential growth could be considered opportunist, it also represents an expansion of alternative forms of protection.

The way that migration is governed reflects the interests of powerful countries, and without concrete changes in how migration is financed it will remain fragmented. In 2017, Peter Sutherland called for a 'Financing Facility for Migration' to help implement commitments related to migration in the SDGs, leading to the establishment of the Migration Multi-Partner Trust Fund in 2019.[59] Early indications suggest that the fund will still allow earmarked contributions and this does not change earmarked contributions to IOM.[60] However, voluntary unearmarked contribution to IOM jumped threefold from 7.5 million to 20.8 million, perhaps an unintended side effect of joining the UN.[61] Nevertheless, this chapter shows that global migration governance continues to be characterized by earmarked contributions, informality, and non-binding agreements that reflect the interests of the most powerful states.

References

Aleinikoff, T. A. (2007). International legal norms on migration: Substance without architecture. In R. Cholewinski, R. Perruchoud, & E. Macdonald, eds., *International Migration Law: Developing Paradigms and Key Challenges*, Cambridge: Cambridge University Press, pp. 467–479.

Andrew, J. & Eden, D. (2011). Offshoring and outsourcing the 'unauthorised': The annual reports of an anxious state. *Policy and Society*, **30**(3), 221–234.

Andrijasevic, R. & Walters, W. (2010). The International Organization for Migration and the international government of borders. *Environment and Planning D: Society and Space*, **28**(6), 977–999.

Bayram, A. B. & Graham, E. R. (2017). Financing the United Nations: Explaining variation in how donors provide funding to the UN. *The Review of International Organizations*, **12**(3), 421–459.

Betts, A. (2011). Introduction: Global migration governance. In A. Betts, ed., *Global Migration Governance*, Oxford: Oxford University Press, pp. 2–34.

Bourdieu, P. (1991). *Language and Symbolic Power*, Cambridge: Polity Press.

Brachet, J. (2016). Policing the desert: The IOM in Libya beyond war and peace. *Antipode*, **48**(2), 272–292.

---

[59] United Nations 2017, 25.
[60] MADE Network 2019.
[61] IOM 2018.

Bradley, M. (2020). *The International Organization for Migration: Challenges, Commitments, Complexities*, New York: Routledge.

Broome, A. & Seabrooke, L. (2012). Seeing like an international organisation. *New Political Economy*, **17**(1), 1–16.

Browne, S. (2017). Vertical funds: New forms of multilateralism. *Global Policy*, **8**, 36–45.

Caillault, C. (2012). The implementation of coherent migration management through IOM programs in Morocco, in M. Geiger, & A. Pécoud (eds.), *The New Politics of International Mobility. Migration Management and Its Discontents*, pp. 133–156. Osnabrück: Institut für Migrationsforschung und Interkulturelle Studien (IMIS)

Carlin, J. A. (1989). *Refugee Connection: Lifetime of Running a Lifeline*, Basingstoke: Macmillan Press.

Chamie, J. & B. Mirkin. (2013). Dodging international migration at the United Nations. *PassBlue*. Retrieved from www.passblue.com/2013/01/29/dodging-international-migration-at-the-united-nations.

Chief Executives Board for Coordination (CEB). (2018). Agency Revenue by Revenue Type | United Nations System Chief Executives Board for Coordination. Retrieved from www.unsystem.org/content/FS-A00-01.

Collyer, M. (2012). Deportation and the micropolitics of exclusion: The rise of removals from the UK to Sri Lanka. *Geopolitics*, **17**(2), 276–292.

Dingwerth, K. & Pattberg, P. (2009). Actors, arenas, and issues in global governance. In Whitman, J. (ed.), *Palgrave Advances in Global Governance*, Basingstoke: Palgrave Macmillan, pp. 41–65.

Ege, J. & Bauer, M. W. (2017). How financial resources affect the autonomy of international public administrations. *Global Policy*, **8**, 75–84.

Elie, J. (2010). The historical roots of cooperation between the UN High Commissioner for Refugees and the International Organization for Migration. *Global Governance: A Review of Multilateralism and International Organizations*, **16**(3), 345–360.

Frowd, P. M. (2014). The field of border control in Mauritania. *Security Dialogue*, **45**(3), 226–241.

Frowd, P. M. (2018a). Developmental borderwork and the International Organization for Migration. *Journal of Ethnic and Migration Studies*, **44**(10), 1656–1672.

Frowd, P. M. (2018b). *Security at the Borders: Transnational Practices and Technologies in West Africa*, Cambridge: Cambridge University Press. DOI: 10.1017/9781108556095.

Gabriel, C. & Macdonald, L. (2018). After the International Organization for Migration: Recruitment of Guatemalan temporary agricultural workers to Canada. *Journal of Ethnic and Migration Studies*, **44**(10), 1706–1724.

Geiger, M. (2010). Mobility, development, protection, EU-integration! The IOM's national migration strategy for Albania. In M. Geiger & A. Pécoud (eds.), *The Politics of International Migration Management*, Basingstoke: Palgrave Macmillan, pp. 141–159.

Goetz, K. H. & Patz, R. (2017). Resourcing international organizations: Resource diversification, organizational differentiation, and administrative governance. *Global Policy*, **8**, 5–14.

Graham, E. R. (2015). Money and multilateralism: How funding rules constitute IO governance. *International Theory*, 7(1), 162–194.

Graham, E. R. (2017a). Follow the money: How trends in financing are changing governance at international organizations. *Global Policy*, **8**, 15–25.

Graham, E. R. (2017b). The institutional design of funding rules at international organizations: Explaining the transformation in financing the United Nations. *European Journal of International Relations*, 23(2), 365–390.

Gray, J. (2014). Donor Funding and Institutional Expansions in International Organizations: Failures of Legitimacy and Efficiency. Unpublished Manuscript, University of Pennsylvania. https://scholar.google.com/scholar_lookup?hl=en&publication_year=2014&author=J+Gray&title=Donor+funding+and+institutional+expansions+in+international+organizations%3A+Failures+of+legitimacy+and+efficiency

Hall, N. (2015). Money or mandate? Why international organizations engage with the climate change regime. *Global Environmental Politics*, **15**(2), 79–97.

Heldt, E. & Schmidtke, H. (2017). Measuring the empowerment of international organizations: The evolution of financial and staff capabilities. *Global Policy*, **8**, 51–61.

Hüfner, K. (2017). The financial crisis of UNESCO after 2011: Political reactions and organizational consequences. *Global Policy*, **8**, 96–101.

IOM. (2002). Programme and Budget for 2003, MC/2083.

IOM. (2003a). IOM – UN Relationship: Summary Report of the Working Group on Institutional Arrangements, MC/INF/263.

IOM. (2003b). Review of the Organizational Structure of the International Organization for Migration, MC/2287.

IOM. (2005) Financial Report for the Year Ended 31 December 2005, MC/2196

IOM. (2018). Financial Report for the Year Ended 31 December 2017, C/109/3.

Kahler, M. (1992). Multilateralism with small and large numbers. *International Organization*, **46**(3), 681–708.

Keohane, R. O. (1990). Multilateralism: An agenda for research. *International Journal*, **45**(4), 731.

Koch, A. (2014). The politics and discourse of migrant return: The role of UNHCR and IOM in the governance of return. *Journal of Ethnic and Migration Studies*, **40**(6), 905–923.

Koser, K. (2010). Introduction: International migration and global governance. *Global Governance: A Review of Multilateralism and International Organizations*, **16**(3), 301–315.

Lebon-McGregor, E. (forthcoming) Bringing about the "perfect storm" in migration governance: A History of the IOM. In A. Pécoud & H. Thiollet, eds., *The Institutions of Global Migration Governance*, Cheltenham: Edward Elgar.

MADE Network. (2019). Open Civil Society Briefing on UN Network on Migration and IMRF Modalities. Retrieved from www.youtube.com/watch?v=sElfj66u0dU&feature=youtu.be.

McGregor, E. (2019) Money Matters: The Role of Funding in Migration Governance. *International Migration Institute Working Paper 149*.

McGregor, E. (2020). Migration, the MDGs and the SDGs: Context and complexity. In T. Bastia & R. Skeldon, eds., *Routledge Handbook of Migration and Development*, New York: Routledge, 284–297

Michaelowa, K. (2017). Resourcing international organisations: So what? *Global Policy*, **8**, 113–123.

Morris, T. (2005). IOM: Trespassing on others' humanitarian space. *Forced Migration Review*, **22**, 43.

Naím, M. (29 June 2009). Minilateralism. Retrieved 11 October 2020, from https://foreignpolicy.com/2009/06/21/minilateralism.

Nieuwenhuys, C. & Pécoud, A. (2007). Human trafficking, information campaigns, and strategies of migration control. *American Behavioral Scientist*, **50**(12), 1674–1695.

Pécoud, A. (2018). What do we know about the international organization for migration? *Journal of Ethnic and Migration Studies*, **44**(10), 1621–1638.

Perruchoud, R. (1989). From the intergovernmental committee for European migration to the international organization for migration. *International Journal of Refugee Law*, **1**(4), 501–517.

Rosengaertner, S. (2017). Who will pay for safe, orderly and regular migration? In B. Jenks & J. Topping, *Financing the UN Development System: Pathways to Reposition for Agenda 2030*, New York: Dag Hammarskjöld Foundation and the United Nations Multi-Partner Trust Fund Office (UN MPTFO), 141–146.

Ruggie, J. G. (1992). Multilateralism: The anatomy of an institution. *International Organization*, **46**(3), 561–598.

Schatral, S. (2011). Categorisation and instruction: The IOM's role in preventing human trafficking in the Russian Federation. In T. Bhambry, C. Griffin, J. T. O. Hjelm, C. Nicholson & O. G. Voronina (eds.), *Perpetual Motion? Transformation and Transition in Central and Eastern Europe & Russia*. London: School of Slavonic and East European Studies, UCL, 2-15.

Seitz, K. & Martens, J. (2017). Philanthrolateralism: Private funding and corporate influence in the United Nations. *Global Policy*, **8**, 46–50.

Siegel, M., McGregor, E.W., van der Vorst, V., & Frouws, B. (2013). Independent Evaluation of the ILO's Work on International Labour Migration. Retrieved from http://ilo.org/wcmsp5/groups/public/-ed_mas/-eval/documents/publication/wcms_421232.pdf.

Sridhar, D. & Woods, N. (2013). Trojan multilateralism: Global cooperation in health. *Global Policy*, **4**(4), 325–335.

Thorvaldsdottir, S. (2016). How to Win Friends and Influence the UN: Donor Influence on the United Nations' Bureaucracy, Presented at the Political Economy of International Organizations PEIO, University of Utah. Retrieved from www.svanhildur.com/uploads/3/0/2/2/30227211/howtowinfriends.pdf.

Thouez, C. (2019). Strengthening migration governance: The UN as 'wingman'. *Journal of Ethnic and Migration Studies*, **45**(8), 1242–1257.

United Nations. (2017). Report of the Special Representative of the Secretary – General on Migration, A/71/728, United Nations General Assembly. Retrieved from www.un.org/en/development/desa/population/migration/events/coordination/15/documents/Report%20of%20SRSG%20on%20Migration%20-%20A.71.728_ADVANCE.pdf.

United Nations. (22 January 2018). UN Chief Outlines Reforms that 'Put Member States in Driver's Seat' on Road to Sustainable Development. Retrieved 11 October 2020, from https://news.un.org/en/story/2018/01/1000931.

Valarezo, G. (2015). Offloading migration management: The institutionalized authority of non-state agencies over the Guatemalan Temporary Agricultural Worker to Canada project. *Journal of International Migration and Integration*, **16**(3), 661–677.

Wunderlich, D. (2012). Europeanization through the grapevine: Communication gaps and the role of international organizations in implementation networks of EU external migration policy. *Journal of European Integration*, **34**(5), 485–503.

3

Digging a Moat around Fortress Europe: EU Funding as an Instrument of Exclusion

CATERINA MOLINARI

Introduction

EU funding decisions in the area of migration matters are building blocks in the 'bordering process', namely the process of 'creat[ing] differences',[1] of distinguishing between the included and the excluded, between us and the other. In this chapter, I will examine such EU funding decisions in the area of migration and build on an understanding of borders as multidimensional concepts.[2] Borders can be drawn through different tools, such as regulatory measures,[3] language,[4] or even citizens' 'fears' and their subsequent course of action.[5] I consider money, more precisely public funds, as yet another tool in the multifaceted, multidimensional bordering process characterizing contemporary societies. This 'bordering process' can respond to a predominantly exclusive or predominantly inclusive dynamic: aimed primarily at keeping migrants outside the host society or, conversely, at facilitating their inclusion.[6]

The outbreak of the migration crisis,[7] in 2015, marked a turning point in the use of EU funds for migration management purposes. In response

---

[1] Newman 2003, 15.
[2] See Bauder 2011; Ferdoush 2018; Scott 2006.
[3] Paul 2015, 19–42.
[4] Polanco and Zell 2017, 267–68.
[5] Rumford 2008, 6–7.
[6] Horga and Brie 2010, 3–11.
[7] The use of the expression 'migration crisis' in the context of the present chapter requires some clarifications. Several authors have rightly noticed that the crisis narrative adopted since 2015 was triggered more by reception difficulties created by the Dublin Regulation (European Parliament and Council, Regulation (EU) No 604/2013 Establishing the Criteria and Mechanisms for Determining the Member State Responsible for Examining an Application for International Protection Lodged in One of the Member States by a Third-Country National or a Stateless Person, OJ L 180, 29 June 2013, 31–59) and by

to the migration crisis, the EU has adopted a series of budgetary amendments and created new funds.[8] As noticed by Den Hertog, the EU budgetary response has complemented the legal and political responses and has by no means been less significant, especially if we consider that funding decisions in the EU are often used to compensate for the lack of competences or for lengthy legislative and political processes.[9] I will assess whether these changes in the EU funding landscape responded mainly to an inclusive or exclusive border drawing dynamic. In doing so, I aim to uncover the pivotal role of funding decisions in defining migration policies. I will show that funding choices made at the EU level after 2015 have constituted essential bordering tools, contributing to an exclusive border drawing dynamic and thus illustrating a preference for a migration policy focused on the exclusion of migrants rather than their integration.

To develop this thesis, I will first identify the various areas of the EU migration policy that funding decisions can be intended to support, and classify them as areas with a mainly inclusive or exclusive purpose. The classification will be based on the main objective of the measures adopted in a certain area, leaving aside the indirect consequences of such measures, as this chapter aims at analysing the allocation of public money as a *choice* manifesting certain political priorities. In other words, the chapter checks whether, when confronted with the alternative between investing in the inclusion of migrants or in their exclusion, the EU has expressed a political preference for one or the other through the allocation of its funds (par. 2). In the second part of the chapter, I will illustrate the budgetary response that the migration crisis triggered. The long list of

---

a lack of solidarity amongst EU Member States than by the actual number of migrants reaching the European borders. However, 2015 marked a turning point in the political discourse surrounding migration management in the EU, engendering a series of responses (see, inter alia, Triandafyllidou 2018, 200). The expression 'migration crisis' is used in the present chapter to indicate such a turning point, without implying that the urgency invoked by policy-makers was justified by objective circumstances.

[8] The migration crisis can be identified as the trigger for several budgetary amendments and for the mobilization, during the budgetary exercises that followed its outbreak, of various flexibility instruments (i.e. the Emergency Aid Reserve; the European Union Solidarity Fund; the Flexibility Instrument; the European Globalisation Adjustment Fund; and the Contingency Margin. They can be resorted to using the procedure set out in a 2013 Interinstitutional Agreement. European Parliament, Council and Commission, Interinstitutional Agreement on Budgetary Discipline, on Cooperation in Budgetary Matters and on Sound Financial Management, OJ C 373, 20 December 2013, 1–11). See den Hertog 2016a; 2016b.

[9] den Hertog 2016a, 2–3 and 10.

budgetary interventions explicitly labelled as a reaction to the migration crisis shows that the EU has consciously and extensively used money as a privileged tool to manage migration. I will explain why these changes can be read as an explicit political choice of the EU to use funds as instruments of exclusion (par. 3). Shedding light on the adoption by EU policy makers of a predominantly exclusive migration policy constitutes the premise of any debate on the sustainability of such a choice, as well as on the costs and benefits of alternative approaches.

Exclusive and Inclusive Domains within the EU Migration Policy

The 2015 European Agenda on Migration[10] has identified four pillars of the EU migration management strategy, namely (i) irregular migration management; (ii) border control; (iii) asylum; (iv) legal migration and integration. I will briefly examine the measures taken in each area to reach a conclusion on the mainly inclusive or mainly exclusive purpose of each of the pillars. The exercise will allow us to evaluate whether, since 2015, funds have been mobilized mainly in support of exclusive or inclusive areas.

The EU has shared competences over the management of external borders (art. 77 TFEU); asylum; irregular migration; and legal migration except for the 'volumes of admission of third-country nationals coming from third countries to the[...] territory [of Member States (MSs)] in order to seek work' (art. 79 TFEU). With respect to integration of third-country nationals (TCN), instead, the EU can promote MSs' action in the field, without harmonizing national laws (art. 79(4) TFEU). This allocation of competences[11] allows the EU to intervene with budgetary support in all the four identified policy areas, either to complement its own action or to encourage and promote the action of MSs. Hence, the decision of granting stronger funding support to one area or the other is not dependent on competence matters, but rather on political preferences.

Irregular Migration Management

The EU policy on irregular migration encompasses both the EU return policy and EU action directed at dismantling smuggling networks. The

---

[10] Commission, Communication COM(2015) 240, A European Agenda on Migration, 13 May 2015.
[11] On which see Neframi 2011.

EU return policy is the area of migration policy dealing with the expulsion of irregular migrants from the EU and their return to third countries. From a border drawing lens, the EU return policy has a decidedly exclusive purpose, as it focuses on the quick removal of irregular migrants from the EU territory. The main legislative instrument in the field of return[12] and, even more so, its proposed recast[13] explicitly aim at increasing the number and speed of returns. Other initiatives undertaken by the EU in the field of return pursue similar objectives. Such initiatives include the negotiation of cooperation arrangements aimed at achieving 'fast and operational returns', and the improvement of data storing and sharing with a view to swiftly identifying irregular migrants and returning them.[14] They also encompass the adoption of a European travel document to return irregular migrants[15] and the enhancement of the return competences of the European Border and Coast Guard (Frontex).[16] Funding decisions supporting return arrangements with third countries, increasing the return capabilities of Frontex, or improving the systems of data storing and sharing aimed at facilitating returns can be labelled as border drawing instruments of exclusion.

The fight against smuggling networks is listed among the EU's priorities in both the European Agenda on Migration[17] and the European Agenda on Security.[18] From a border drawing point of view, dismantling smuggling networks can be considered as a neutral activity. It acquires a mainly exclusive or mainly inclusive purpose, depending on the

---

[12] European Parliament and Council, Directive 2008/115/EC on Common Standards and Procedures in Member States for Returning Illegally Staying Third-Country Nationals OJ L 348, 24 December 2008, 98–107.

[13] Commission, Communication COM(2018) 634, Proposal for a Directive of the European Parliament and of the Council on Common Standards and Procedures in Member States for Returning Illegally Staying Third-Country Nationals (Recast), 12 September 2018.

[14] Commission, Communication COM(2015) 453 EU Action Plan on Return, 9 September 2015, Commission, Communication COM (2017) 200, A More Effective Return Policy in the European Union – A Renewed Action Plan, 2 March 2017; Commission, Recommendation C(2017) 1600, Making Returns More Effective When Implementing the Directive 2008/115/EC of the European Parliament and of the Council, 7 March 2017.

[15] European Parliament and Council, Regulation (EU) 2016/1953 on the Establishment of a European Travel Document for the Return of Illegally Staying Third-Country Nationals, OJ L 311, 17 November 2016.

[16] European Parliament and Council, Regulation (EU) 2019/1896 on the European Border and Coast Guard, OJ L 295, 14 November 2019, 1–131.

[17] Commission, European Agenda on Migration.

[18] Commission, Communication COM(2015) 185, The European Agenda on Security, 28 April 2015.

programmatic, legislative, and operational context in which it is developed. EU institutional documents constantly associate the fight against smuggling with return operations and border control, rather than emphasizing the link between the fight against smuggling and the provision of legal migration avenues.[19] The EU's focus on anti-smuggling overlooks the impact of the lack of legal migration avenues on the proliferation of smuggling activities and does not distinguish between exploitative smuggling networks and other forms of facilitation of irregular migration.[20] This approach gives pre-eminence to the exclusive objectives of this policy area. It should be added that a fundamental role in countering migrants' smuggling has been assigned to CSFP operations EUNAVFOR MED Sophia[21] and, more recently, EUNAVFOR MED Irini.[22] Both have been given the task of training the Libyan coastguard and navy, which clearly associates the fight against smuggling and migration prevention.

In light of the explicit linkage between the fight against smuggling, migration prevention, and return, most of the EU funds destined to the fight against migrant smuggling acquire an exclusive connotation.

Border Control

Border management measures are essential elements of States' sovereignty over their territory. In this sense, they are not only migration management tools. However, the Commission has chosen to indicate border control as the second pillar of its migration management strategy and to consistently associate border control funding with migration containment. In addition, the EU has established a close connection between border control and return operations. This connection emerges from the return aspects embedded in Frontex's border control

---

[19] Commission, Communication COM(2015) 285, EU Action Plan Against Migrant Smuggling, 27 May 2015.
[20] Perkowski and Squire 2018, 10–12; see also, De Genova 2013, 1190–91.
[21] Council, Decision (CFSP) 2015/778 on a European Union military operation in the Southern Central Mediterranean (EUNAVFOR MED), OJ L 122, 19 May 2015, 31–35; Council, Decision (CFSP) 2015/972 Launching the European Union Military Operation in the Southern Central Mediterranean (EUNAVFOR MED), OJ L 157, 23 June 2015, 51; Council, Decision (CFSP) 2016/993 Amending Decision (CFSP) 2015/778 on a European Union Military Operation in the Southern Central Mediterranean (EUNAVFOR MED Operation SOPHIA), OJ L 162, 21 June 2016, 18–20.
[22] Council, Decision (CFSP) 2020/472 on a European Union Military Operation in the Mediterranean (EUNAVFOR MED IRINI), OJ L 101, 1 April 2020, 4–10.

operations;[23] from the enhancement of both border control and return competences within the mandate of Frontex;[24] as well as from the mixed border control and return functions that this agency performs in hotspots.[25]

In light of the above, fund allocations directed at strengthening border surveillance and explicitly associated to migration management can be considered as instruments of exclusion.

Asylum

The third pillar of the European Agenda on Migration is the Common European Asylum System (CEAS), launched in 1999 to establish minimum procedural standards for the treatment of asylum applications in the EU.

From a border drawing perspective, the main aim of the CEAS is that of including persons in need of international protection in the host society as swiftly as possible, through the establishment of common procedures for granting and withdrawing international protection;[26] common standards for the reception of applicants for international protection;[27] common grounds for granting international protection;[28]

---

[23] Jones 2017.
[24] European Parliament and Council, Regulation (EU) 2016/1624 on the European Border and Coast Guard, OJ L 251, 16 September 2016, 1–76; European Parliament and Council, Regulation (EU) 2019/1896 (see *supra* fn. 17), 1–131.
[25] Neville, Sy, and Rigon 2016, 17.
[26] European Parliament and Council, Directive 2013/32/EU on Common Procedures for Granting and Withdrawing International Protection, OJ L 180, 29 June 2013, 60–95; Commission, COM(2016) 467 Proposal for a Regulation of the European Parliament and of the Council Establishing a Common Procedure for International Protection in the Union, 13 July 2016.
[27] European Parliament and Council, Directive 2013/33/EU Laying down Standards for the Reception of Applicants for International Protection, OJ L 180, 29 June 2013, 96–116; Commission, COM(2016) 465, Proposal for a Directive of the European Parliament and of the Council Laying down Standards for the Reception of Applicants for International Protection (Recast), 13 July 2016.
[28] European Parliament and Council, Directive 2011/95/EU on Standards for the Qualification of Third-Country Nationals or Stateless Persons as Beneficiaries of International Protection, for a Uniform Status for Refugees or for Persons Eligible for Subsidiary Protection, and for the Content of the Protection Granted, OJ L 337, 20 December 2011, 9–26; Commission, COM(2016) 466, Proposal for a Regulation of the European Parliament and of the Council on Standards for the Qualification of Third-Country Nationals or Stateless Persons as Beneficiaries of International Protection, for a Uniform Status for Refugees or for Persons Eligible for Subsidiary Protection and for the Content of the Protection Granted, 13 July 2016.

and clear rules to allocate responsibility for asylum applications amongst MSs.[29]

MSs are supported in the processing of asylum applications by the European Asylum Support Office (EASO), established in 2010. Funding decisions directed at reinforcing the asylum systems of the MSs and EASO's mandate can be considered primarily as instruments of inclusion.

Legal Migration and Integration

The EU's initiatives in the area of legal migration aim at including TCN in the European society and labour market, temporarily or permanently. They include measures aimed at family reunification,[30] migration for the purpose of study[31] or work,[32] as well as long-term residence.[33] From a border drawing perspective, funding initiatives on legal migration can be classified as inclusive measures. The management of legal migration is left to the MSs; there are no EU agencies or authorities installed to facilitate this type of migration.

The European Agenda on Migration also lists integration objectives in its legal migration pillar and has a specific action plan in the field,[34] even though EU measures concerning integration are bound to be of a limited

---

[29] European Parliament and Council, Dublin Regulation; Commission, COM(2016) 270, Proposal for a Regulation of the European Parliament and of the Council Establishing the Criteria and Mechanisms for Determining the Member State Responsible for Examining an Application for International Protection Lodged in One of the Member States by a Third-Country National or a Stateless Person (Recast), 5 April 2016.

[30] Council, Directive 2003/86/EC on the Right to Family Reunification, OJ L 251, 3 October 2003, 12–18.

[31] European Parliament and Council, Directive (EU) 2016/801 on the Conditions of Entry and Residence of Third-Country Nationals for the Purposes of Research, Studies, Training, Voluntary Service, Pupil Exchange Schemes or Educational Projects and Au Pairing, OJ L 132, 21 May 2016, 21–57.

[32] Council, Directive 2009/50/EC on the Conditions of Entry and Residence of Third-Country Nationals for the Purposes of Highly Qualified Employment, OJ L 155, 18 June 2009, 17–29; European Parliament and Council, Directive 2014/36/EU on the Conditions of Entry and Stay of Third-Country Nationals for the Purpose of Employment as Seasonal Workers, OJ L 94, 28 March 2014, 375–90; European Parliament and Council, Directive 2014/66/EU on the Conditions of Entry and Residence of Third-Country Nationals in the Framework of an Intra-Corporate Transfer, OJ L 157, 27 May 2014, 1–22.

[33] Council, Directive 2003/109/EC Concerning the Status of Third-Country Nationals Who Are Long-Term Residents, OJ L 16, 23 January 2004, 44–53.

[34] Commission, Communication COM(2016) 377, Action Plan on the Integration of Third Country Nationals, 7 June 2016.

nature. Integration remains a national competence, and the EU's only role is one of support and coordination of MSs' individual integration policies (Articles 79(4) TFEU). This does not prevent the use of EU funds in the area: since the EU cannot intervene by harmonizing national laws in the field, funding decisions can end up compensating for the lack of competences,[35] as shown by the frequent reference to funds in the EU's action plan on integration[36] and by the establishment of consultative bodies in the area of migrants' inclusion, such as the European Migrant Advisory Board.[37] The use of EU funds for integration purposes corresponds to an inclusive dynamic and will be treated as such in the context of our analysis.

In sum, the EU migration policy comprises exclusive and inclusive objectives. Irregular migration and border control policies have a mainly exclusive connotation, while policies related to asylum and legal migration generally respond to an inclusive dynamic.

Exclusive Nature of Governance through Funding in the Field of Migration Post-2015

Under the 2007–13 Multiannual Financial Framework (MFF), migration objectives were pursued through funds dedicated to each of the areas identified above. In this context, funds allocated for that period to the return priority[38] were comparable to those allocated to the asylum priority,[39] but inferior to those destined to fulfil integration purposes.[40]

---

[35] den Hertog 2016a, 7.
[36] For example, the Commission undertakes to '*[p]romote the use of EU funds for reception, education, housing, health and social infrastructures for third country nationals and social housing*'; and '*[l]aunch projects under different EU funds promoting* [inter alia] *participation in political, social and cultural life and sports; social inclusion through education, training and youth; preventing and combating discrimination*'. Commission, Action Plan on the Integration of Third Country Nationals.
[37] Created in 2018 as part of the Action Plan of the Partnership on Inclusion of migrants and refugees https://ec.europa.eu/futurium/en/inclusion-of-migrants-and-refugees.
[38] EUR 676 million of the EU return fund (European Parliament and Council, Decision 575/2007/EC Establishing the European Return Fund for the Period 2008 to 2013 as Part of the General Programme 'Solidarity and Management of Migration Flows', OJ L 144, 6 June 2007, 45–65).
[39] EUR 630 million of the EU refugee fund (European Parliament and Council, Decision No 573/2007/EC Establishing the European Refugee Fund for the Period 2008 to 2013 as Part of the General Programme Solidarity and Management of Migration Flows, OJ L 144, 6 June 2007, 1–21).
[40] EUR 825 million of the EU Integration fund for the period 2007–13; Council, Decision Establishing the European Fund for the Integration of Third-Country Nationals for the

One cannot deduce from this a preference of decision makers for inclusive funding allocations, as we have to consider Frontex's yearly budget of EUR 97 million in 2014 and compare it, for example, to that of EASO for the same year, amounting to less than EUR 15 million. However, it is clear that the 2008–13 MFF did not give priority to exclusive purposes either, when distributing budgetary capabilities between the various migration funds. This situation changed with the migration crisis, which brought about a significant increase in the funds dedicated to migration management.

The biggest shift occurred between 2015 and 2016, when the funds dedicated to migration in the EU budget[41] doubled,[42] but the tendency has been ongoing throughout the migration crisis and beyond. As noted by Den Hertog, even though the peak of the migration crisis is over, the overall amount of funds destined to the area has not reverted to levels comparable to the 2015 ones.[43]

In this section, we will identify the main lines along which the new budgetary and extra budgetary resources made available for migration management from 2015 on have been allocated.

First, the amount of funds available to EU agencies in general has constantly increased during the migration crisis, in both absolute and relative terms. Various EU agencies are active in fields related to migration. The mandate of the European Labour Authority, for example, covers the implementation of legislation related to the mobility of workers in the EU, be they EU citizens or TCNs.[44] However, in budgetary terms, one of these agencies stands out: Frontex.[45] Looking closer at the evolution of Frontex's

---

Period 2007 to 2013 as Part of the General Programme Solidarity and Management of Migration Flows, OJ L 168, 28 June 2007, 18–36.

[41] The EU annual budget for 2015 was EUR 145 billion and it slightly increased every year since, with the greatest increase (EUR 10 billion) between 2015 and 2016.

[42] In 2015, the budget allocated to the heading 'Security and Citizenship' was around EUR 2 billion. Around three fourths of the funds could be deployed for migration-related issues. In particular, EUR 416.74 million was dedicated to the Asylum Migration and Integration Fund; EUR 394.76 million to the Internal Security Fund, which finances the management of external borders by MSs; and EUR 534.29 million to decentralized EU agencies, including Frontex. The migration crisis strongly influenced the development of this heading in the transition between the 2015 and 2016 budget. In fact, the amount of funds destined to Security and Citizenship doubled in just a year (from 2 to 4 billion).

[43] den Hertog 2016a, 14.

[44] See Art. 1(4) Regulation (EU) 2019/1149 of the European Parliament and of the Council of 20 June 2019 establishing a European Labour Authority, amending Regulations (EC) No 883/2004, (EU) No 492/2011, and (EU) 2016/589 and repealing Decision (EU) 2016/344, OJ L 186, 11 July 2019, 21–56.

[45] Frontex became the EU agency with by far the largest budget, with 302 million out of the 863 million allocated to all EU agencies in 2017.

funds, we can see that the budget originally planned for 2015 should have consisted of around EUR 140 million, but that this initial estimate was subject to continuous increases, reaching EUR 302 million in 2017[46] and EUR 460 million in 2020.[47] Frontex can support MSs in managing migrants in transit. It assists in the identification of returnees and in the preparation of their departure. It can organize joint return flights or support return operations by plane. It is present in the EU hotspots, has an important operational role in data collection, and can intervene to intercept migrant boats approaching the EU.[48] The increase in the funding allocated to Frontex clearly corresponds to an exclusive dynamic, directed to boost the return rate, enhance external border control, and proceed to naval anti-smuggling operations.

Second, the funds available under the Internal Security Fund (ISF) have also increased as a result of the migration crisis.[49] The resources of this budgetary fund can be spent on border management (around 2.8 billion, according to the 2014–20 MFF) and security-related actions (around 1 billion). As a consequence, their increase responds to a mainly exclusive purpose, although it also encompasses a visa-processing aspect that may be seen as incidentally facilitating legal migration by expediting visa delivery.

Third, the CFSP budget has been partially used for migration management purposes, with the funds allocated to CFSP Operations Sophia and Irini, in order to train the Libyan coastguard in preventing migrants from reaching the EU's borders. Albeit small, this budgetary contribution fulfils exclusive purposes, and supports the efforts in this sense of the participating MSs.

Fourth, most of the EU funds destined to migration management between 2015 and 2016 were allocated to be spent 'outside the EU' (6.2 billion, against 3.9 billion to be spent inside the EU).[50] These funds were directed mostly to Northern and Central Africa (e.g. EU Emergency Trust Fund for Africa,[51] covering North Africa, the Horn of Africa, and

---

[46] Gkliati 2018; Trauner and Angelescu 2018, 2.
[47] EBCG, 'Budget 2020', accessed 8 September 2020, https://frontex.europa.eu/assets/Key_Documents/Budget/Budget_2020.pdf.
[48] See Regulation (EU) 2019/1896 of the European Parliament and of the Council of 13 November 2019 on the European Border and Coast Guard and repealing Regulations (EU) No 1052/2013 and (EU) 2016/1624, OJ L 295, 14 November 2019, 1–131.
[49] The ISF amounted to EUR 394.76 million in the 2015 budget; 647 million in the 2016 one; and 738 in the 2017 one.
[50] Kamarás, Saunier, and Todaro 2016, 17.
[51] Commission, Decision C(2014) 5019 on the Establishment of the European Union Trust Fund for Central African Republic 'Bêkou EU Trust Fund', 11 July 2014. This

the Sahel and Lake Chad region) and the Middle-East (e.g. Madad Fund, supporting displaced Syrian communities in Syria, Turkey, Lebanon, Iraq, Egypt, and Jordan, but also Armenia and the Western Balkans). The tendency to manage migration through funds spent outside the EU is best exemplified by the creation of the Facility for Refugees in Turkey, established in connection with the EU-Turkey Statement. The Facility (i.e. a *sui generis* mechanism to coordinate EU and MS funds) is set up as the EU's counterpart to the migration management effort imposed on Turkey by the Statement, and has mobilized EUR 3 billion in the years 2016-17 and the same amount in the years 2018-19. The 2016-17 tranche of EUR 3 billion was composed of 1 billion coming from the EU budget and 2 billion in MSs contributions. The 2018-19 tranche, instead, consisted of MSs' contributions of 1 billion, with the remaining 2 billion from the EU budget.[52]

A similar use of funding decisions in order to shift the responsibility for migration management on third countries drives the dynamics of the EU Trust Fund for Africa. Although its stated focus consists in addressing the root causes of migration, the Fund has been criticized for its use as a tool to obtain return cooperation from African countries.[53]

Finally, the new Migration Partnership Framework[54] broadly defines the orientation that the EU intends to follow when dealing with third countries in the field of migration. This document introduces a generalized and explicit link between third countries' cooperation in the field of migration and development aid (financed through the EU's budget and the European Development Fund).[55] More generally, it proposes a mainstreaming of the migration priority into all the fields of the EU external action. This implies that even funds mainly intended to pursue other objectives, such as humanitarian or development aid, are incidentally but deliberately used as instruments to pursue migration management targets.[56]

---

extra-budgetary instrument was set up at the 2015 Valletta Summit to foster stability and address root causes of migration. However, its disbursements became progressively subject to readmission conditionality as used as negotiating tools to obtain third countries' cooperation in the EU's migration management effort (see Carrera et al. 2018, 33).

[52] Council, 'Facility for Refugees in Turkey: Member States Agree Details of Additional Funding', Press Release 248/18, 29 June 2018.
[53] Castillejo 2017a.
[54] Commission, Communication COM(2016) 385, Establishing a New Partnership Framework with Third Countries under the European Agenda on Migration, 7 June 2016.
[55] Castillejo 2017b, 13-15; Funk et al. 2017, 3.
[56] Latek 2017, 5-6.

The above considerations do not want to suggest that no funding decisions have been taken to favour legal migration and the inclusion of migrants in the host society between 2015 and today. The asylum system of certain MSs has been supported through the Asylum, Migration and Integration Fund's (AMIF) contributions to national programmes and, when it comes to Greece in particular, through the Emergency Support Instrument. Moreover, the budget of EASO has been increased, although it remains much less significant than the budget of Frontex.[57] Finally, the EU budget funds projects in the field of integration: according to the Commission, for the 2014–20 MFF and in the context of the AMIF national programmes, MSs have committed EUR 765 million (60 million less that in the previous MFF cycle) to integration measures directed specifically at migrants.[58]

Nonetheless, funding decisions in the area of asylum, legal migration, and integration seem to have been less numerous and less ambitious than those in the areas of return and border control. Moreover, at times, the difficulty in implementing certain policies related to asylum has led to a reallocation of the relevant budget, from inclusive purposes to exclusive purposes. An example is the redeployment of funds initially destined to the relocation of 54,000 persons from Greece and Turkey in favour of the resettlement programme envisaged in the EU-Turkey Statement.[59]

Conclusion

In conclusion, although EU funding objectives in the area of migration remain diversified, the migration crisis has boosted the use of funds as border drawing tools of exclusion, as budget amendments and new funds seem to have consistently given priority to the objectives of return and border control. The analysis of funding decisions taken since 2015 has shown the prevalence of exclusive objectives, especially related to the return of migrants to third countries, enhanced border control, and the fight against smuggling as a tool to reduce the migratory pressure at the EU borders. Notwithstanding the decrease in the number of arrivals in the EU, migration remains a priority area for funding decisions at EU level. In 2018, the Commission proposed to triple the funds dedicated to this priority in the

---

[57] EUR 87 million in 2017, EUR 97.7 million in 2018, and EUR 114 million in 2020.
[58] Commission, Action Plan on the Integration of Third Country Nationals.
[59] Council, Decision (EU) 2016/1754 Amending Decision (EU) 2015/1601 Establishing Provisional Measures in the Area of International Protection for the Benefit of Italy and Greece, OJ L 268, 1 October 2016, 82–84.

2021–27 MFF (from the 12 billion of the 2014–20 MFF to 33 billion).[60] According to the latest press material made available by the Commission, COVID-19 led to a scaling back of this initial plan, but migration and border management funds are still likely to double, when compared to the previous MFF.[61]

Considering that the peak of the migration crisis seems to be over for the moment, we might wonder whether the exclusive dynamic expressed by the EU's funding choices is destined to come to an end. The signals in this sense are mixed. On the one hand, the Commission has set forth comprehensive proposals, further amended in the context of the new migration pact launched in September 2020,[62] to reform both the asylum and the legal migration legislation. In the field of asylum, more particularly, the Commission has proposed to transform EASO into an agency with increased competences and budget.[63] On the other hand, the Commission's draft MFF for the years 2021–27 indicates a strong willingness to further invest on border control and return operations. A new Integrated Border Management Fund has been created to sit alongside the AMIF as one of the two funds within the new heading of the budget on migration and border management.[64] Moreover, return cooperation has been streamlined in negotiations concerning different areas of the EU relations with third countries. In particular, the standard approach of the Commission under the new Migration Partnership Framework entails the use of development or humanitarian aid funds to obtain third countries' cooperation on migration prevention and return, so that even funds that are not directly linked to migration objective end up being used as leverage to

---

[60] See European Commission Factsheets of 12 June 2018: 'Migration: Supporting a Robust, Realistic and Fair EU Policy' and 'Securing the EU's External Borders'. For the details, see Commission, COM(2018) 471, Proposal for a Regulation of the European Parliament and of the Council establishing the Asylum and Migration Fund, 12 June 2018 and COM (2018) 473, Proposal for a Regulation of the European Parliament and of the Council establishing, as part of the Integrated Border Management Fund, the instrument for financial support for border management and visa, 12 June 2018.
[61] Commission Factsheet 'EU' s Next Long Term Budget & Next Generation EU: Key Facts and Figures', 11 November 2020.
[62] Communication, COM(2020) 609, a New Pact on Migration and Asylum, 23 September 2020.
[63] Commission, COM(2018) 633, Amended Proposal for a Regulation of the European Parliament and of the Council on the European Union Agency for Asylum, 12 September 2018.
[64] Parry and Sapala 2018, 7.

pursue an exclusive migration policy.[65] Such an approach is reaffirmed in the new migration pact.[66]

The objectives of EU funding decisions will remain diversified and pursue exclusive and inclusive purposes at the same time. However, the effects of the migration crisis on the funding priorities of the EU are here to stay, as confirmed by the emphasis on migration, and especially on funds for border control and return measures, in the draft 2021-27 MFF. This observation is particularly relevant when considering the long-term sustainability of the EU's migration management strategy. As recognized in the recent Global Compact for Safe, Orderly and Regular Migration,[67] migration has always been present in human experience. This will continue to be the case, arguably more than ever in the future, due to global phenomena such as climate change.[68] Several authors have shown that the lack of legal migration avenues creates irregularity and contributes to smuggling.[69] In this context, a migration policy that overwhelmingly focuses on excluding migrants will likely fail to achieve its purpose.[70] The EU should move away from *deliberately* investing in exclusive migration policy and foster more inclusive policies by expanding legal migration avenues.

References

Ackrill, Robert and Adrian Kay. 2006. 'Historical-Institutionalist Perspectives on the Development of the EU Budget System'. *Journal of European Public Policy* 13, no. 1: 113-33

Bauder, Harald. 2011. 'Toward a Critical Geography of the Border: Engaging the Dialectic of Practice and Meaning'. *Annals of the Association of American Geographers* 101, no. 5: 1126-39

Carrera, Sergio. 2016. *Implementation of EU Readmission Agreements: Identity Determination Dilemmas and the Blurring of Rights*. London: Springer International

---

[65] Commission, New Partnership Framework with Third Countries; Concord and CINI 2018, 6; Conte and Cortinovis 2018, 8-10.
[66] Commission, a New Pact on Migration and Asylum, section 6.5.
[67] UN General Assembly, Global Compact for Safe, Orderly and Regular Migration, A/RES/73/195, 19 December 2018, point 8.
[68] Ibid., point 18.
[69] Duvell 2011, 293; Perkowski and Squire 2018, 4 and 9.
[70] See comments on the ineffectiveness that already characterizes the EU return policy. Inter alia, Carrera 2016; Carrera and Allsopp 2018, 70-82 and FRA 2015, 'Legal Entry Channels to the EU for Persons in Need of International Protection: A Toolbox'.

Carrera, Sergio and Jennifer Allsopp. 2018. 'The Irregular Immigration Policy Conundrum'. In Ariadna Ripoll Servent and Florian Trauner (eds), *The Routledge Handbook of Justice and Home Affairs Research*, London: Routledge, pp. 70–82.

Carrera, Sergio, Leonhard Den Hertogh, Jorge Núñez Ferrer, Roberto Musmeci, Lina Vosyliūtė, and Marta Pilati. 2018. 'Oversight and Management of the EU Trust Funds: Democratic Accountability Challenges and Promising Practices'. European Parliament's Committee on Budgetary Control

Castillejo, Clare. 2017a. 'The European Union Trust Fund for Africa: What Implications for Future EU Development Policy?'. Briefing Paper. Bonn: German Development Institute

Castillejo, Clare. 2017b. 'The EU Migration Partnership Framework: Time for a Rethink?'. Discussion Paper 28/2017. Bonn: German Development Institute

Concord and CINI. 2018. 'Partnership or Conditionality? Monitoring the Migration Compacts and EU Trust Fund for Africa'. Brussels: Concord Europe

Conte, Carmine and Roberto Cortinovis. 2018. 'Migration-Related Conditionality in EU External Funding'. Discussion Brief, Brussels: ReSOMA

Crowe, Richard. 2017. 'The European Budgetary Galaxy'. *European Constitutional Law Review* 13, no. 3: 428–52

Csuros, Gabriella. 2013. 'Characteristics, Functions and Changes (?) Of the EU Budget'. *Curentul Juridic*, 59, no. 4: 92–107

Dabrowski, Marek. 2010. 'The Global Financial Crisis: Lessons for European Integration'. *Economic Systems* 34, no. 1: 38–54

De Genova, Nicholas. 2013. 'Spectacles of Migrant "Illegality": The Scene of Exclusion, the Obscene of Inclusion'. *Ethnic and Racial Studies* 36, no. 7: 1180–98

Duvell, Franck. 2011. 'Paths into Irregularity: The Legal and Political Construction of Irregular Migration The Pathways in and out of Irregular Migration'. *European Journal of Migration and Law* 13: 275–96

Ferdoush, Md Azmeary. 2018. 'Seeing Borders through the Lens of Structuration: A Theoretical Framework'. *Geopolitics* 23, no. 1: 180–200

Funk, Marco, Frank Mc Namara, Romain Pardo, and Norma Rose. 2017. 'Tackling Irregular Migration through Development – a Flawed Approach?'. Discussion Paper. European Policy Center, 12

Gkliati, Mariana. 2018. 'The Next Phase of the European Border and Coast Guard: Towards Operational Effectiveness'. EU Law Analysis (blog)

Heinemann, Friedrich, Philipp Mohl, and Steffen Osterloh. 2010. 'Reforming the EU Budget: Reconciling Needs with Political- Economic Constraints'. *Journal of European Integration* 32, no. 1: 59–76

den Hertog, Leonhard. 2016a. 'EU Budgetary Responses to the "Refugee Crisis": Reconfiguring the Funding Landscape'. CEPS Paper in Liberty & Security in Europe No. 93

den Hertog, Leonhard. 2016b. 'Money Talks: Mapping the Funding for EU External Migration Policy'. CEPS Paper in Liberty & Security in Europe No. 95

Horga, Ioan and Mircea Brie. 2010. 'Europe between Exclusive Borders and Inclusive Frontiers'. MPRA Paper No. 44309

Jones, Chris. 2017. 'Frontex: Cooperation with Non-EU States'. Briefing. Statewatch

Kamarás, Éva, Mathieu Saunier, and Laura Todaro. 2016. 'Overview on the Use of EU Funds for Migration Policies'. European Parliament's Committee on Budgets

Latek, Marta. 2017. 'Growing Impact of EU Migration Policy on Development Cooperation'. European Parliament Members' Research Service

Montani, Guido. 2009. 'Which European Response to the Financial Crisis?'. *Perspectives on Federalism* 1: 40–67

Neframi, Eleftheria. 2011. 'Division of Competences between the European Union and Its Member States Concerning Immigration'. European Parliament's Committee on Civil Liberties, Justice and Home Affairs

Neville, Darren, Sarah Sy, and Amalia Rigon. 2016. 'On the Frontline: The Hotspot Approach to Managing Migration'. European Parliament's LIBE Committee

Newman, David. 2003. 'On Borders and Power: A Theoretical Framework'. *Journal of Borderlands Studies* 18, no. 1: 13–25

Parry, Matthew and Magdalena Sapala. 2018. '2021–2027 Multiannual Financial Framework and New Own Resources: Analysis of the Commission's Proposal'. In Depth Analysis. European Parliamentary Research Service

Paul, Regine. 2015. *The Political Economy of Border Drawing Arranging Legality in European Labor Migration Policies*. New York: Berghahn Books

Perkowski, Nina and Vicki Squire. 2018. 'The Anti-Policy of European Anti-Smuggling as a Site of Contestation in the Mediterranean Migration "Crisis"'. *Journal of Ethnic and Migration Studies* 45: 1–18

Polanco, Geraldina and Sarah Zell. 2017. 'English as a Border-Drawing Matter: Language and the Regulation of Migrant Service Worker Mobility in International Labor Markets'. *Journal of International Migration and Integration* 18, no. 1: 267–89

Rumford, Chris. 2008. 'Introduction: Citizens and Borderwork in Europe'. *Space and Polity* 12, no. 1: 1–12

Scott, James Wesley. 2006. 'Wider Europe as a Backdrop'. In J. W. Scott, ed., *EU Enlargement, Region Building and Shifting Borders of Inclusion and Exclusion*. Burlington: Ashgate, pp. 3–14

Trauner, Florian and Irina Angelescu. 2018. '10,000 Border Guards for Frontex: Why the EU Risks Conflated Expectations'. Policy Brief. European Policy Center

Triandafyllidou, Anna. 2018. 'A "Refugee Crisis" Unfolding: "Real" Events and Their Interpretation in Media and Political Debates'. *Journal of Immigrant & Refugee Studies* 16, no. 1–2: 198–216

UNHCR and ECRE (European Council on Refugees and Exiles). 2018. 'Follow the Money: A Critical Analysis of the Implementation of the EU Asylum, Migration & Integration Fund | ALNAP'.

4

The "Refugee Hospital". Aid Money, Migration Politics, and Uncertain Care in Neoliberal Morocco

LORENA GAZZOTTI[1]

Introduction

One day during my fieldwork, Darius, a Malian refugee living in Rabat, told me that he had been robbed while he was heading to the "hôpital des réfugiés" (refugee hospital). But what Darius referred to as a "refugee hospital" was not a public hospital, but a Moroccan medical NGO based in a low-income neighborhood of the capital. This NGO was receiving funding from the UNHCR to help refugees access health care by subsidizing hospital treatment and pharmaceuticals as well as providing complimentary specialist examinations when hospital waiting lists were prohibitively long. The UNHCR, in turn, received financial support for this partnership from several donors, foremost among them Switzerland and Monaco. On the ground in Rabat, however, Darius referred to the NGO simply as "the refugee hospital."

The toponym through which Darius identified the donor-funded drop-in center is symptomatic of the crucial role played by aid money in the assistance to migrant and refugee people in Morocco. Since the mid-2000s, local and international NGOs and international organizations (IOs), mostly funded by European donors, have emerged and expanded in the main urban centers (Rabat and Casablanca) and in border cities (Tangier, Tétouan, Nador, Oujda). The emergence of an aid-funded network of migrant support mirrored the tightening and militarization of the Euro-Moroccan border. Despite the small number of foreigners living in the country and the modest estimations about the

---

[1] This chapter is an edited version of the chapter "Excluding through Care," which features in my book *Immigration Nation: Aid, Control and Border Politics in Morocco*, forthcoming with Cambridge University Press.

number of presumed "irregular migrants," since the late 1990s immigration has become increasingly politicized in Morocco.[2] The global fight against migration justified the implementation of legal, diplomatic, and military measures aiming at containing undocumented mobility across the Strait of Gibraltar. Development aid has constituted a backbone of migration control cooperation between Europe and Morocco. Since the early 2000s, Morocco has received funding for border security, migration dialogues, and migrant assistance from a panoply of European donors, the most prominent certainly being the European Union. This process reflects a broader regional phenomenon, as European donors have allocated funding to development and humanitarian initiatives assisting migrant people in North, Western, and Central Africa as well as in the Middle East, targeting the same people endangered by mechanisms of border control initiated and often directly supported by the EU and European countries.[3]

Building on literature on development securitization and state formation in North Africa, this chapter unravels how this migration industry – and its funders – contributes to the control of securitized populations through practices of care and compassion. By "migration industry" (Gammeltoft-Hansen and Sørensen, 2013), I refer here to the aid-funded network of donors, IOs, and international and local non-governmental organizations (NGOs) involved in migration in Morocco.[4] Aid money defines the shifting boundaries of the industry: organizations like the IOM are steady recipients of aid funding, while others, like advocacy groups, enter and exit the industry, juggling between funding needs and the quest for independence. In this chapter, I explore the institutional conditions that have determined the encroachment of aid money in the provision of basic services to "sub-Saharan" migrants and refugees in the country and the conflicting logics of assistance, exclusion, and deresponsibilization emerging in this space of blurred governance.

The chapter makes three points. First, it shows that the rise of a nonstate apparatus of migrant care is the product of two different exclusionary logics – the European policy of border externalization and Moroccan neoliberal social policy. Border politics provides the aid world both with a population of precarized and marginalized people and with the financial resources to grant them with (partial) assistance. The politics of

[2] Natter, 2018.
[3] El Qadim, 2015.
[4] See also Molinari (Chapter 3); Lebon-McGregor and Micinski (Chapter 2), both this volume.

neoliberal care in Morocco makes it impossible for vulnerable foreigners to access public care provision, providing a space of action for NGOs and IOs. Second, the formation of a system of non-state care does not emerge in the absence of the state, but is actively fostered by Moroccan authorities. The state adopts formal and informal strategies to delegate migrant care to NGOs and IOs operating with donors' financial support. The evolution of the dismissal of care for the poor from state to non-state actors transcends clear neoliberal labels, and is rather symptomatic of a specific relation of the state to government, to "civil society," to the international community – and its aid money.[5] Third, the establishment of a system of non-state, securitized care transforms migrants and refugees into recipients of fleeting, evanescent assistance, thus furthering the exclusionary power of the border regime. On the one hand, outsourcing care for vulnerable foreigners to NGOs and IOs means displacing welfare from the domain of rights to that of voluntariness and possibilities.[6] On the other hand, the multiplication of agents implementing migration governance functions jeopardizes feelings of responsibility over migrants' suffering, depriving migrants of a political referent against which they can channel their dissent for their lack of access to basic rights.[7]

The remainder of the chapter has four sections. I first provide an overview of the theoretical debates informing the article. I then turn to analyze the emergence and stabilization of a system of non-state care provision to migrants and refugees. The next section explores the role of donors and their politically charged funding in the development and stabilization of the migration industry. The last empirical section highlights how the externalization of care to NGOs and IOs lays the basis for the bureaucratic production of exclusion and, at the same time, confuses both migrants and NGOs/IOs about where the responsibility for migrant suffering lies.

Security and Neoliberalization in Migration Politics

In the past two decades, the scope and target of development and humanitarian action have undergone a substantial transformation. After the end of the Cold War, and in particular after the outbreak of

---

[5] Hibou, 2004.
[6] Jiménez Álvarez, 2015.
[7] Andersson, 2014.

the War on Terror, aid disbursement and implementation have assumed a security-oriented approach, becoming explicitly instrumental to maintaining the security of the Global North. Deemed to be the "root causes" of conflicts, poverty and marginalization in aid-recipient countries have become objects of development and humanitarian governance because of their presumed danger for donors' constituencies.[8]

By using aid money to secure their borders, rich countries utilize development politically against the threat of "migrant invasion."[9] Broadly speaking, development aid fulfills six main functions in migration control cooperation. First, aid provides operational support to the functioning of certain sectors of border control cooperation. In the past two decades, development agencies have funded the training of border guards and the establishment of mechanisms of data sharing between the security apparatus of different countries along migration routes.[10] Second, aid serves diplomatic purposes, as it eases the cooperation between countries of origin, "transit," and destination over migration control. As many scholars have underlined, European countries and the EU use funding as an incentive for non-European states to collaborate on migration control. This has, in turn, led host countries in the South to utilize the presence of migrant and refugee populations as a bargaining chip in their foreign policy strategy. "Refugee rentier states" would therefore use the presence of foreigners politically in order to obtain financial or diplomatic benefits from their counterparts in the Global North.[11] Third, aid fulfills a preventive function. Aid agencies tend to perceive it as an instrument to combat irregular migration by spurring the development of sending countries. Building on a sedentary and colonial approach to human development and well-being, developmental policy approaches to migration prevention aspire to forcefully settle "potential" migrants in their origin or "transit" countries by providing them with an economic alternative to migration.[12] Fourth, the investment of development funding in migration control fulfills a strong symbolic and performative function. It allows governments to claim they are "doing something to control their borders whilst still maintaining a humanitarian image."[13] Fifth, development funding determines relations of accountability that are central to the

[8] Duffield, 2013.
[9] De Haas, 2008.
[10] Casas-Cortes, Cobarrubias, and Pickles, 2014.
[11] Tsourapas, 2019, 1.
[12] Tazzioli, 2014.
[13] Oeppen, 2016, 64.

stabilization of the development and humanitarian industry. The shrinking and earmarking of funding sources limit the independence of NGOs and IOs, creating issues of aid politicization, operational fragmentation, and legitimacy.[14] The aid market therefore ensures these organizations will be involved in executing donors' political agenda not only by orienting their action in precise policy areas and approaches, but also by making IOs and NGOs more prone to silencing criticism.[15] Lastly, aid plays a humanitarian function, as it palliates the dire living conditions for migrants and refugees created by border control itself.[16]

That security – in the form of migration control, conflict prevention, or anti-terrorism – has become so cemented in development politics is not at all negligible for dynamics of state formation in aid recipient countries. The encroachment of security within the public policy landscape transforms certain sectors of the population ("unemployed males," "foreign poor people") into beneficiaries of assistance through their potential danger as "potential migrants" or "potential terrorists."[17] In these aid recipient contexts, sovereignty exceeds the limits of the state and is exerted by a range of alternative governing actors, from NGOs to militias, from multinational corporations to faith-based organizations.[18] In places like Morocco, aid-actors largely provide for what – in a strictly Keynesian understanding of the state – are assumed to be "state functions," ranging from schooling and care provision to professional training to make unemployed people more marketable.[19] The plurality of actors involved in governance does not necessarily mean that the state is less central or less in control of the government process. In fact, these alternative governing bodies do not exist despite the state. To different extents, state bureaucracies acknowledge, tolerate, or even encourage the presence of non-state actors in the regulation of the social, the political, and the economy,[20] either by abandoning certain portions of their territory or by directly outsourcing governing duties to private actors.[21] The tendency to outsource what are conventionally defined as "state functions" to non-state actors can be theorized as a mode of governance by

---

[14] McGregor, 2018.
[15] Bloodgood and Tremblay-Boire, 2017.
[16] Bartels, 2017.
[17] Gazzotti, 2019.
[18] Ferguson and Gupta, 2002.
[19] Hibou and Tozy, 2015.
[20] Hansen and Stepputat, 2006.
[21] Hibou, 2004.

"discharge." Hibou refuses to understand discharge as symptomatic of a weakness or loss of state sovereignty, but she conceptualizes it as a (cheaper) mode of government itself. In a context where governance is characterized by a high degree of delegation, the state can still maintain its primacy by being the one dictating the limits for the action of other actors, through which it indirectly controls certain portions of its territory or social groups.[22] The rise of neoliberal social care allowed the Moroccan state to incorporate more firmly non-state actors within the "redeployment"[23] of state power, strengthening the link between Morocco and international actors, integrating the funding, know-how, and support of the latter into the working and legitimation of a social and political strategy formulated by the state.[24]

Migration Policy and the Outsourcing of Care to Non-State Actors

Since migration rose to the top of the Moroccan political agenda in the early 2000s, the state has disengaged from directly providing basic services to migrants and refugees. The way this disengagement has been framed and publicly portrayed, however, has changed over time. From the approval of law 02–03, a repressive migration act criminalizing irregular immigration and emigration, in 2003[25] until 2013, the refusal of the state to ensure social services to migrants was part of a broader security-oriented attitude to migration control, aiming at deterring migrants from both crossing into Europe and settling in Morocco. This strategy of migration prevention included direct forms of violence against migrants, like arbitrary arrests and unlawful deportations at the border with Algeria,[26] as well as more subtle tactics of exclusion and deprivation, like the pervasiveness of obstacles to accessing basic services. Migrants were left completely on their own to find solutions to their daily problems, relying on migrant networks of mutual assistance and on the support of local and international NGOs.[27]

In September 2013, King Mohammed VI caught the national and international community by surprise and announced a "radically new"

---

[22] Hibou, 2004.
[23] Hibou, 1998.
[24] Hibou and Tozy, 2015.
[25] Belguendouz, 2009.
[26] GADEM, 2013.
[27] Alioua, 2011.

human rights–based migration policy. In a break with a past of marked and purposeful disinterest toward migrant integration, the state committed to a major engagement in the field of migrant and refugee integration, promising to reform law 02–03, create two laws on human trafficking and asylum, and launch a regularization campaign.[28] This policy U-turn was formalized with the launch of the National Strategy of Migration and Asylum, adopted by the government in December 2014. The strategy mentions "facilitating the integration of regular migrants" as its first objective. This includes easing access to education and culture, programs for youth and leisure, healthcare, accommodation, social and humanitarian assistance, professional training courses, and employment.[29]

The shift, however, has been more rhetorical than practical. Official discourses about migrant access to state-supported services are largely inconsistent both with the practical implementation of the integration strategy and with the lived reality of bureaucratic obstacles and economic constraints that characterize this field of social assistance. In fact, though the state claims to be extremely open to including migrants in welfare provision, it simultaneously reinforces the financial exclusion of migrants from social assistance and lays the basis for delegating care responsibilities to non-state actors.[30] Healthcare provides a case in point. In principle, migrants have access to medical care in Morocco. In order to limit the spread of transmissible diseases, a circular distributed in 2003 by the Ministry of Health allowed medical institutions to provide health services to irregular migrants.[31] The Hospital Internal Regulation issued in 2011 reiterates that "foreigners, whatever their status, are admitted and treated in the same way as Moroccan citizens."[32] Although access to medical assistance is allowed in theory, access to healthcare is, in practice, *financially* more problematic. Although basic medical assistance is provided free of charge to anyone in Morocco, secondary and tertiary medical care comes at a charge. Costs for consultations, hospitalizations, and medicines can be prohibitive for those migrants who do not have a stable financial situation or private health insurance.

The option to make migrants eligible for state-provided social insurance is a contested subject of debate. Moroccan authorities have given contradictory signals concerning their intention to make migrants

[28] Cherti and Collyer, 2015.
[29] MCMREAM, 2016.
[30] Norman, 2018.
[31] MSF, 2013.
[32] MCMREAM, n.d., 32.

eligible for applying to the Regime of Medical Assistance (RAMED), the system subsidizing healthcare for low-income citizens. In October 2015, the Ministry of Economy and Finance, the Ministry of the Interior, the Ministry of Foreign Affairs, and the Ministry of Migration signed a convention allowing regularized migrants to benefit from the RAMED. In March 2017, the Medical Agency for National Insurance (ANAM) and the Ministry of Migration signed another convention to deliver RAMED cards to migrants.[33] Despite these highly publicized and performative events, however, the two conventions are de facto not operative, and vulnerable migrants are not able to systematically claim, let alone access, free healthcare. If a migrant cannot pay his/her medical bills, healthcare structures can deny the provision of medical treatment. If not on the basis of racial discrimination, vulnerable foreigners risk being excluded from healthcare services because of their precarious economic situation.[34]

In this framework NGOs and IOs – and the donors supporting them – are therefore at the forefront in providing care, de facto substituting healthcare coverage for vulnerable foreigners. The number of migrants claiming support from NGOs to pay for healthcare services can be considerable. In their study of "sub-Saharan" migrants in Morocco, Mourji et al. state 24 percent of respondents declared to have been hospitalized had managed to pay for their medical treatment thanks to the support of an association.[35] Contrary to how it may appear, the rise of non-state actors in providing assistance to migrants and refugees was not a smooth process. The state barely tolerated the action of organizations engaged in assisting and defending migrants' rights, obliging them to operate with great discretion and, at times, denying them legal recognition.[36] In 2013, the state shifted from ostracizing the activity of non-state actors' to actively incorporating them into its own integration strategy. Moroccan authorities, in fact, have adopted formal and informal methods to outsource the costs of welfare provision to NGOs and IOs.[37] One of the most direct and comprehensive measures is its support of state–civil society partnerships in the implementation of the new migration policy. Since 2013, Moroccan authorities have engaged directly with associations working with migrants, inviting an even more active

---

[33] LesEco.ma, 2017a.
[34] Plateforme Nationale de Protections Migrants, 2017.
[35] Mourji et al., 2016.
[36] Natter, 2018.
[37] Plateforme Nationale de Protections Migrants, 2017.

participation of civil society in the governance of migrants' welfare. The importance of involving NGOs in elaborating and implementing the new migration policy is constantly emphasized by politicians,[38] members of human rights institutions, and the promotional texts produced by the Ministry of Migration.[39] During the conference for the third anniversary of the National Strategy of Immigration and Asylum in 2016, the ministry also distributed a newly published guide on civil society associations operating in the context of migrant integration.[40] In their everyday work, NGOs record more informal attempts to outsource the welfare costs of migrants. A report compiled by the National Platform for Migrants' Protection (PNPM) argues that public hospitals try to convince civil society organizations to negotiate "conventions" to cover medical costs incurred by their beneficiaries rather than granting migrants free medical assistance. Similarly, NGOs regularly receive patients referred by hospitals, a process that "seem[s] to integrate the action of NGOs as an insurance covering the medical expenses incurred by foreign patients."[41] This suggests that externalizing the provision of care to vulnerable migrants in Morocco is not a transitory arrangement but is being progressively incorporated into the official system of migration governance in Morocco.

Donors' Money between Care and Security

Reproducing this system of non-state assistance is ensured, by and large, by the presence of international donors willing to fund projects related to migration in Morocco. The European Union, together with Switzerland, has undoubtedly been one of the most prominent donors in the field of migrant assistance in Morocco. The EU already had a long history of economic and technical cooperation with Morocco, starting in the 1970s as part of a broader Mediterranean policy aiming at establishing a dialogue between the North and the South of the Mediterranean in the postcolonial period. Since the Barcelona Declaration in 1995, security has become increasingly relevant in articulating the strategic priorities for the EU–Mediterranean partnership, as development cooperation has become increasingly perceived as a way to protect EU citizens from the "risks" emerging south of the Mediterranean, including by political

---

[38] MCMREAM and CNDH, 2016.
[39] MCMREAM, 2015, 2016.
[40] MCMREAM, 2015.
[41] Plateforme Nationale de Protections Migrants, 2017, 16.

unrest, drug trafficking, terrorism, and, of course, irregular migration.[42] Development cooperation funding constitutes the backbone of the implementation of the EU "external dimension" approach to migration control. Soon after the 1999 Tampere Council, DG Justice and Home Affairs negotiators realized that implementing an external action directed at third countries in the field of migration would have proven very difficult without any specific thematic instrument available, and that an approach focused solely on the security aspects of migration control would have been ineffective to secure the collaboration of third countries. For this purpose, in 2001 the EU created the budget allocation B7-667 for migration control cooperation with third countries, which ran from 2001 to 2003 with a budget of 42.5 million €. In 2004, the B7-667 was substituted by the Aeneas regulation,[43] which ran until 2006 with an overall budget of 250 million €. In 2005 the European Council adopted the Global Approach on Migration (GAM) – renamed Global Approach on Migration and Mobility in 2011.[44] The GAM set out the need to frame actions in the field of preventing irregular migration within broader cooperation initiatives, tackling also the development of sending and "transit" countries and legal migration of the latter's nationals within broader migration debates.[45]

In turn, Switzerland decided to engage in migration in Morocco in the aftermath of the Ceuta and Melilla events in 2005,[46] after starting working in the country in 2004 in the field of disaster-management. Switzerland and Morocco, in fact, already have a bilateral dialogue over the question of return of irregular migrants. Not being an EU member, Switzerland was not bound by the strategic priorities of the EU in terms of migration control cooperation. This has allowed Switzerland more flexibility to operate in the field of migrant protection, including granting funding organizations advocating for the defense of migrant rights and humanitarian actors operating in the borderlands.[47]

---

[42] Afailal, 2016.
[43] Coleman, 2009.
[44] Collyer, 2012.
[45] Collett, 2007. In 2007, the Commission created the Thematic Program on migration and asylum, which lasted until 2013 with an overall 384 million € budget (García Andrade and Martìn, 2015). Since 2016, projects on migration governance in Morocco started being funded also through the EU Trust Fund for Africa, the financial instrument created by the EU to spur migration control cooperation with African countries in the wake of the so-called migration crisis (Gabrielli, 2016).
[46] Interview, Officer of the Swiss Development Agency, Rabat, July 2016.
[47] Interview, Officer of the Swiss Development Agency, WhatsApp, September 2017.

The rise of donors' interest in the field of migration in the mid-2000s coincided with the emergence of civil society activism. Acknowledging the refusal of the state to support any sort of long-term integration of migrants in the country, the EU and the Swiss Development Agency started channeling funding for migrant assistance exclusively through NGOs and IOs. In this way, donors expanded the capacity of non-state actors to function as service providers,[48] allowing NGOs and IOs to fill in the interstices of state disengagement. Over the years, and in particular after 2013, the integration of donors into the bureaucracy of non-state assistance has become so strong that they *de facto* constitute the main funders of Moroccan integration policy.[49] The normalization of donor-funded migrant assistance is not, however, unconditionally accepted by donors. Donors' decisions, in fact, are affected by concerns made at the transnational level, as they are primarily informed by the migration control cooperation that the EU and each European country pursue vis-à-vis Morocco. Donors therefore design their funding policies based on their own expectations of Morocco's role within broader architectures of border control, building on normative considerations and expectations of state–civil society arrangements.[50] Donors convey a clear message about their aspirations for Moroccan migration policy not only through funding allocation, but also by shaping its implementation, i.e., by steering aid toward the implementation of certain activities over others and giving implementing agencies guidelines about public–private partnerships.

In 2013, the announcement of the new migration policy pushed donors to reconsider the way they channeled their support toward migrant assistance. Data from interviews show that donors interpreted the launch of the National Strategy on Immigration and Asylum as an official commitment of the state to reappropriate most of the functions fulfilled by NGOs. In light of these changes, donors expected a substantial readjustment and separation of duties between the state and civil society. This would also mean a retreat from service provision on the part of civil society, whose role would be to focus mostly on monitoring and mediating the implementation of the new migration policy.[51] The decision undertaken by the donor community was charged with symbolic

---

[48] Interview, Two Officers of the Swiss Development Agency, Rabat, July 2016.
[49] GADEM, 2018, 54.
[50] den Hertog, 2016.
[51] Interview, Two Officers of the Swiss Development Agency, Rabat, July 2016; Interview, Officer of the EU Delegation in Morocco.

meaning to encourage Morocco to continue taking on its share of responsibilities in migration governance. To support the new state commitment, donors reviewed the requirements for projects funded through civil society organizations in the field of migration. Both the EU and Switzerland expressed a desire to stop funding civil society projects supporting direct service provision and to privilege initiatives involving state–civil society partnerships. The underlying assumption that emerges from donors' declarations is that the current governance arrangement over migrant welfare provision – rooted in the intertwining of uneven state benevolence, migrants' improvisation, grassroots engagement, and donors' financial support – should be transitory, and that donors' money will not be needed long-term to sustain the provision of social assistance to migrants in Morocco. As the same EU officer commented during the interview, "It is important for Morocco to be manifestly supported with substantial [funding] support and budget support by the EU." The officer also added, with a certain impatience, "but now they [Moroccan authorities] should be able to do this without us [the EU]!"

Aid-Funded Care, Bureaucratic Exclusion, and the Dilution of Responsibility

Although the development and humanitarian industry has become the de facto implementer of the social and humanitarian policy of assistance to migrants in Morocco, NGOs and IOs do not have the capacity or the mandate to provide assistance to the entire migrant population. NGOs and IOs operate with budgets preemptively defined together with donors, setting benchmarks for the number of beneficiaries they aim to reach. Leaflets and operational documents state that donor-funded projects aimed at ensuring, for example, that a specific program "benefitted over 800 women and 400 kids."[52] The number of foreigners living in a state of poverty, however, is undeniably much higher than the benchmarks identified by aid-funded organizations, as testified by the fact that NGOs and IOs often have to reject assistance requests (see Plateforme Nationale de Protections Migrants, 2017). As a former member of the social team of a Moroccan NGO concisely put it, "I mean, we tried to do what we could, but if you do not fit the criteria we had to say no ... at the end of the day, the organization was not a bank."[53] Outsourcing medical

[52] Terre des Hommes – Espagne, 2014, 5.
[53] Interview, former NGO intern, phone, October 2018.

coverage from state to non-state actors therefore does not just mean delegating the duty to help, but also the responsibility to *deny* help. Rejections of assistance requests are not arbitrary, but are the result of a complex bureaucratic process. Bureaucracy frames the denial of care not as a result of a political act of marginalization, but as the unavoidable consequence of a technical process.[54]

In order to cope with the large number of requests that they receive, NGOs and IOs filter their beneficiaries in two ways. First, projects often do not address the entire migrant population, but identify a well-defined category of beneficiaries.[55] The group of beneficiaries is defined according to the mandate of the implementing organization, donors' political agendas, and the limits established by state authorities. In order to receive assistance, migrants therefore have to fulfill the eligibility criteria characterizing the target group. If the person requesting assistance does not fall into one of the categories of beneficiaries, NGOs and IOs normally have to decline help because they are not able to justify the expense to the donor funding the project. When I asked a senior officer of a Moroccan NGO why the organization focused only on refugees, he answered, "Well we do not make distinctions, but the donors do. If someone comes and he is not a refugee, there is nothing we can do for him."[56] It can therefore happen that an NGO already running a community-based program for vulnerable people starts differentiating its beneficiaries into different programs to appease the request of a new donor. In the case of the Moroccan medical NGO working with the UNHCR, the NGO stated that it had a program for refugees and a volunteer-run program for "everybody else." That "everybody else" included all vulnerable members of the local community: Moroccans, foreigners, regular migrants, irregular migrants, asylum seekers, and so on. "Everybody else," however, could not access the program funded by the UNHCR: that was just for the refugees.[57]

Even if migrants fall within the project target, NGOs, the IOM, and the UNHCR generally do not have the financial and organizational capacity to address all the assistance requests that they receive. To further screen their beneficiaries, development and humanitarian actors apply certain criteria of deservedness, the most widespread being "vulnerability."[58]

[54] Hibou, 2012.
[55] Capelli, 2016.
[56] Interview, NGO officer, Rabat, July 2016.
[57] Interview, NGO officer, Rabat, September 2017.
[58] Bartels, 2017.

The IOM also uses the vulnerability framework during its screening interviews to identify which migrants are eligible for the voluntary return program.[59] Vulnerability is an uncertain category. Most often, it is used to refer to "women and children"[60] as a vulnerable population. Other organizations try to leave room for social workers to carry out more individualized assessments of people's vulnerability, in some cases building on the social workers' own experience, for many social workers are migrants themselves.[61] In any case, anyone who does not fall within the categories of beneficiaries targeted by donor-funded projects or who is not considered as vulnerable will likely see his/her assistance request denied.

The overlapping logics of border externalization and neoliberal bureaucracy dilute the responsibility of migration control to a point at which nobody can be held accountable for the marginalization of migrants. The dispersed nature of the border regime hampers the ability to attribute responsibility to anyone over border deaths, migrant suffering, and the production of inequality supported by restrictive migration control policies.[62] The multiplication of intermediaries in the long chain of border externalization and social exclusion pushes migrants to protest in front of interlocutors that do not consider themselves accountable for migrants' suffering. During an interview in September 2017, an NGO officer evoked a quarrel that occurred during the recent launch of a project assisting both immigrants and returning Moroccan migrants in different areas of the country:

> During the launch of the project, one migrant in the public raised his hand and asked "so what have you done so far to help migrants?" We said we had done nothing yet because the project was being launched on that day. Then he kept on asking "why do you just help migrants, and not for example refugees?" But again, our project is about migrants and not refugees and we are not obliged to do everything for everybody... I understand he was frustrated, but he was placing his frustration on the wrong people.[63]

The intervention of NGOs and IOs in the field of migrant assistance is therefore the most visible expression of a long chain of care externalization. Displacing the duty to help and to deny help to non-state actors is

---

[59] IOM, 2010.
[60] Turner, 2018, 119.
[61] Interview, NGO officer, Rabat, August 2016.
[62] Andersson, 2014.
[63] Interview, NGO officer, Rabat, September 2017.

particularly significant, as it deprives migrants of a visible "perpetrator"[64] to blame for their failed access to basic rights.

Conclusion

This chapter has explored the role of European aid money in providing social assistance to migrants and refugees in neoliberal Morocco. Drawing on literature on development securitization, (neoliberal) state formation, and bureaucratic indifference, I have disentangled the functioning and evolution of an aid-funded system of care for migrants and refugees in Morocco, in relation both to the evolution of border control in the Western Mediterranean and to the broader historical trajectory of care for the poor in Morocco. Finally, I have looked at the conflicting practices of care, marginalization, and deresponsibilization that characterize this form of assistance.

Aid money stabilizes a system of non-state care for vulnerable foreigners where logics of neoliberal assistance and migration containment merge and produce contrasting effects of care, exclusion, tension, and indifference. Border control provides the need (precarious migrants) and the funding (aid money) for this system to exist, while neoliberal patterns of state formation ensure the centrality of non-state actors in providing care for the (foreign) poor. The pervasiveness of aid actors in this sphere of social governance should not be understood as a symptom of the passivity of the state vis-à-vis the aid community and the presence of migrants on its territory. On the contrary, the government actively fosters dumping this social group onto aid agencies as part of its migration governance strategy.

The delegation of migrant care to aid-funded charities redraws the boundaries through which inclusion, exclusion, and accountability are conceptualized in the age of border control. First, the non-state system of social assistance *de facto* excludes many poor foreigners from care provision. The final act of rejecting migrants from the care of NGOs and IOs is framed as a bureaucratic process, rather than a political gesture, as it comes as the result of the practical incapacity of NGOs and IOs to meet all the assistance requests that they receive with the resources that they have available. Second, the existence of an extremely broad group of actors involved in providing assistance to migrants and refugees dilutes the sense of responsibility of the duty to care. The obfuscation of the

[64] Andersson, 2014.

responsibility for the marginalization of migrants obliges migrants to express their grievances to the visible front edge of this chain of exclusion – NGOs and IOs, who do not identify themselves as responsible actors for this marginalization. The capacity of people on the move to make their complaints heard, and the ability of aid workers to recognize themselves as the legitimate addressees of those complaints, are extremely low. The dispersion of aid-funded migrant assistance fragments responsibilities and systems of accountability vis-à-vis migrants' marginalization: assistance is given to them, but is not something on which they can count, that they can complain about, or call for.

References

Afailal, Hafsa. 2016. "Las Migraciones Inesperadas: Marruecos y Turquía Entre Diversidad y Seguridad." PhD Thesis, Universitat Rovira i Virgili, Unpublished.

Alioua, Mehdi. 2011. "L'étape Marocaine Des Transmigrants Subsahariens En Route Vers l'Europe: L'épreuve de La Construction Des Réseaux et de Leurs Territoires." PhD Thesis, Université Toulouse II Le Mirail.

Andersson, Ruben. 2014. *Illegality, Inc.: Clandestine Migration and the Business of Bordering Europe*. 1 ed. Oakland, CA: University of California Press.

Bartels, Inken. 2017. "'We Must Do It Gently.' The Contested Implementation of the IOM's Migration Management in Morocco." *Migration Studies* 5 (3): 315–36. https://doi.org/10.1093/migration/mnx054.

Belguendouz, Abdelkrim. 2009. "Le Maroc et La Migration Irrégulière: Une Analyse Sociopolitique." CARIM AS, 2009/07, Robert Schuman Centre for Advanced Studies, San Domenico di Fiesole (FI): Institut universitaire européen.

Bloodgood, Elizabeth and Joannie Tremblay-Boire. 2017. "Does Government Funding Depoliticize Non-Governmental Organizations? Examining Evidence from Europe." *European Political Science Review* 9 (3): 401–24. https://doi.org/10.1017/S1755773915000430.

Capelli, Irene. 2016. "Cibler Les Mères Célibataires: La Production Bureaucratique et Morale d'un Impensable Social." In Hibou Béatrice and Bono Irene eds., *Le Gouvernement Du Social Au Maroc*, 199–232. Paris: Karthala.

Casas-Cortes, Maribel, Sebastian Cobarrubias, and John Pickles. 2014. "'Good Neighbours Make Good Fences': Seahorse Operations, Border Externalization and Extra-Territoriality." *European Urban and Regional Studies* 23 (3): 231–251. http://eur.sagepub.com/content/early/2014/08/12/0969776414541136.abstract.

Cherti, Myriam and Michael Collyer. 2015. "Immigration and Pensée d'Etat: Moroccan Migration Policy Changes as Transformation of 'Geopolitical

Culture'." *The Journal of North African Studies* 20 (4): 590–604. https://doi.org/10.1080/13629387.2015.1065043.

Coleman, Nils. 2009. *European Readmission Policy: Third Country Interests and Refugee Rights*. Leiden and Boston: Martinus Jinhoff Publishers.

Collett, Elizabeth. 2007. "The 'Global Approach to Migration': Rhetoric or Reality?" European Policy Centre.

Collyer, Michael. 2012. "Migrants as Strategic Actors in the European Union's Global Approach to Migration and Mobility." *Global Networks* 12 (4): 505–24. https://doi.org/10.1111/j.1471-0374.2012.00370.x.

Duffield, Mark. 2013. *Development, Security and Unending War: Governing the World of Peoples*. Cambridge: Polity.

El Qadim, Nora. 2015. *Le gouvernement asymétrique des migrations. Maroc/Union européenne*. Paris: Dalloz.

Ferguson, James and Akhil Gupta. 2002. "Spatializing States: Toward an Ethnography of Neoliberal Governmentality." *American Ethnologist* 29 (4): 981–1002.

Gabrielli, Lorenzo. 2016. "Multilevel Inter-Regional Governance of Mobility between Africa and Europe. Towards a Deeper and Broader Externalisation." GRITIM Working Paper Series – Universitat Pompeu Fabra 30.

GADEM. 2013. "Rapport Sur l'application Par Le Maroc de La Convention Internationale Sur La Protection Des Droits de Tous Les Travailleurs Migrants et Des Membres de Leur Famille. Résumé Exécutif."

2018. "Coûts et Blessures. Rapport Sur Les Opérations Des Forces de l'ordre Menées Dans Le Nord Du Maroc Entre Juillet et Septembre 2018 – Éléments Factuels et Analyse."

Gammeltoft-Hansen, Thomas and Ninna Nyberg Sørensen, eds. 2013. "The Migration Industry and the Commercialization of International Migration," Routledge Global Institutions Series, xviii, 278.

García Andrade, Paula and Ivàn Martìn. 2015. "EU Cooperation with Third Countries in the Field of Migration." *Study for the LIBE Committee, European Parliament*, www.europarl.europa.eu/RegData/etudes/STUD/2015/536469/IPOL_STU%282015%29536469_EN.pdf

Gazzotti, Lorena. 2019. "From Irregular Migration to Radicalisation? Fragile Borders, Securitised Development and the Government of Moroccan Youth." *Journal of Ethnic and Migration Studies* 45 (15): 2888–909, DOI: 10.1080/1369183X.2018.1493914

Haas, Hein de. 2008. "The Myth of Invasion: The Inconvenient Realities of African Migration to Europe." *Third World Quarterly* 29 (7): 1305–22. https://doi.org/10.1080/01436590802386435.

Hansen, T. B. and Stepputat, F. (2006). "Sovereignty Revisited." *Annu. Rev. Anthropol*. 35: 295–315.

Hertog, Leonhard den. 2016. "Funding the Eu-Morocco 'Mobility Partnership': Of Implementation and Competences." *European Journal of Migration and Law* 18 (3): 275–301. https://doi.org/10.1163/15718166-12342103.

Hibou, Béatrice. 1998. "Retrait Ou Redéploiement de l'Etat?" *Critique Internationale* 4 (4): 151–68. https://doi.org/10.3917/crii.p1998.1n1.0151
ed. 2004. *Privatising the State / Béatrice Hibou, Editor; Translated from the French by Jonathan Derrick.* London: Hurst.
2012. *La Bureaucratisation Du Monde à l'ère Néolibérale / Béatrice Hibou.* Paris: La Découverte.

Hibou, Béatrice and Mohamed Tozy. 2015. "Gouvernement Personnel et Gouvernment Institutionnalisé de La Charité: L'INDH Au Maroc." In Irene Bono, Béatrice Hibou, Hamza Meddeb, and Mohamed Tozy, eds., *L'Etat d'injustice Au Maghreb. Maroc et Tunisie,* 379–428. Paris: Karthala.

IOM. 2010. "Regional Assisted Voluntary Return and Reintegration (AVRR) Programme for Stranded Migrants in Libya and Morocco. External Evaluation."

Jiménez Álvarez, Mercedes. 2015. "Externalización Fronteriza En El Mediterráneo Occidental: Movilidades, Violencias y Políticas de Compasión." *Revista de Dialectología y Tradiciones Populares* 70 (2): 307–14.

LesEco.ma, 2017. ANAM: les migrants recevront bientot leurs cartes RAMED, www.leseco.ma/maroc/56028-anam-les-migrants-recevront-bientot-leurs-cartes-ramed.html

McGregor, Elaine. 2018. "Money Matters: The Role of Funding in Migration Governance." Paper presented at the workshop "Show me the Money," June 14–15, 2018, University of Amsterdam.

MCMREAM. 2015. Guide pratique pour faciliter votre intégration au Maroc. 1ère édition, http://docplayer.fr/8057025-Guide-pratique-pour-faciliter-votre-integration-au-maroc.html

MCMREAM. 2016. Politique Nationale d'Immigration et d'Asile 2013–2016.

MCMREAM and CNDH. 2016. "3ème Édition Forum Annuel de l'Immigration. Politiques Migratoires: Quel Role Pour La Société Civile? Actes Du Forum". http://marocainsdumonde.gov.ma/ewhatisi/2018/02/acte-forum-immigration-2016.pdf

Mourji, Fouzi, Jean-Noel Ferrié, Saadia Radi, and Mehdi Alioua. 2016. "Les Migrants Sub-Sahariens Au Maroc. Enjeux d'une Migration de Résidence". Rabat, Konrad Adenauer Stiftung.

MSF. 2013. Violences, Vulnérabilité et Migration : Bloqués aux Portes de l'Europe, www.msf.fr/sites/default/files/informemarruecos2013_fr_0.pdf

Natter, Katharina. 2018. "Rethinking Immigration Policy Theory beyond 'Western Liberal Democracies'." *Comparative Migration Studies* 6 (March): 4. https://doi.org/10.1186/s40878-018-0071-9.

Norman, Kelsey P. 2018. "Inclusion, Exclusion or Indifference? Redefining Migrant and Refugee Host State Engagement Options in Mediterranean 'Transit' Countries." *Journal of Ethnic and Migration Studies* 45 (1): 42–60, DOI: 10.1080/1369183X.2018.1482201.

Oeppen, Ceri. 2016. "'Leaving Afghanistan! Are You Sure?' European Efforts to Deter Potential Migrants through Information Campaigns." *Human Geography* 9 (2): 57–68.

Plateforme Nationale de Protections Migrants. 2017. "Etat Des Lieux de l'accès Aux Services Pour Les Personnes Migrantes Au Maroc: Bilan, Perspectives et Action de La Société Civile."

Tazzioli, Martina. 2014. *Spaces of Governmentality: Autonomous Migration and the Arab Uprisings.* London: Rowman & Littlefield International.

Terre des Hommes – Espagne. 2014. "Femmes Migrantes Au Maroc: Une Approche Médicosociale. Rapport de Capitalisation Sur Le Volet Médicosocial Du Projet « Tamkine-Migrants » 2011 – 2014 d'appui à La Prise En Charge de Femmes Migrantes Enceintes et de Leurs Enfants."

Tsourapas, Gerasimos. 2019. "The Syrian Refugee Crisis and Foreign Policy Decision-Making in Jordan, Lebanon, and Turkey." *Journal of Global Security Studies*, 4 (4): 464–481, https://doi.org/10.1093/jogss/ogz016.

Turner, Lewis. 2018. "Challenging Refugee Men: Humanitarianism and Masculinities in Za'tari Refugee Camp." PhD Thesis, School of Oriental and African Studies, Unpublished.

5

Cash Rules Everything: Money and Migration in the Colombian-Venezuelan Borderlands

CHARLES LARRATT-SMITH

Between 2015 and December 2020 more than 16 percent of Venezuela's total population, or an estimated 5.2 million people, migrated abroad to escape food shortages, hyperinflation, and the collapse of the country's healthcare system. A majority of these migrants relocated to other countries in Latin America and the Caribbean due to their limited economic resources. Neighboring Colombia accepted over 1.8 million Venezuelan nationals during this period.[1] Between the disintegration of the value of Venezuela's national currency and the reduction of international air travel to and from Venezuela, most migrants have subsequently been forced to leave their country by land through the volatile Colombian–Venezuelan borderlands, a vast binational region extending 2,219 kilometers from the Caribbean to the Amazon. Along this expansive border, Colombian and Venezuela state authorities both compete and collaborate with armed nonstate actors and organized criminal groups to control and regulate people, territory, and resources.[2] Those migrants who possess both foreign currency and an official passport can minimize their exposure to risks in the borderlands by entering and exiting through one of the limited formal border crossings and then traveling to their intended destination by plane or bus. However, those who lack such money and documentation are forced to traverse one of the hundreds of illegal border crossings, called *trochas*, and then to either continue their journey by foot or, in many cases, stay and attempt to earn money in the sprawling informal border economy.[3]

The challenges facing those Venezuelan migrants who enter, transit through, or settle in the borderlands are enormous. Even though the

[1] Bahar et al. 2020.
[2] Idler 2019.
[3] Ibañez 2018.

Colombian government has offered temporary visas to Venezuelans,[4] less than 40 percent of all migrants have taken advantage of this policy, leaving a majority of Venezuelan nationals in Colombia undocumented and beyond the reach of the state.[5] Of those migrants who remain in the borderlands, most gravitate toward urban centers in search of employment. Yet, these cities are already saturated with too many people seeking too few jobs, as close to half of all working Colombians in cities already toil in the informal economy.[6] Of equal importance, most of these towns and cities host substantial populations of internally displaced persons from the numerous rural war zones found along the border, individuals who similarly compete for housing, employment, and basic services in marginalized neighborhoods.[7] In these spaces, Venezuelan migrants have precarious access to public services such as healthcare and education and are also victims of widespread xenophobia, economic exclusion, and disproportionate levels of selective and indiscriminate violence.[8]

This chapter examines the underexplored topic of how money affects migration in contested spaces. Of particular interest, it explores how a lack of money severely impacts how and where migrants transit and settle in foreign countries, and by extension their ability to make it there. Additionally, this text analyzes how state authorities and armed non-state actors monetize migrants and profit from their entry, settlement, and incorporation into informal economies, before finally assessing how armed actors regulate these processes. While considerable scholarship focuses on transnational refugee flows originating in war-torn countries, little comparable research has examined massive migratory waves coming from countries not at war. Refugees fleeing from armed conflicts experience more traumatic events than other migrants, yet there is evidence to suggest that the international community's response to these crises better facilitate their transit and repatriation in other receiving countries.[9] Migrants who are forcibly displaced by economic collapse on the other hand are generally left to their own devices to relocate, and upon arriving in new countries frequently depend on the informal

---

[4] The complex motivations of successive Colombian governments for adopting this progressive humanitarian policy can be traced to the country's historically weak border enforcement coupled with the demand for an official state response to the migrant crisis inside of Colombia.
[5] Migración Colombia 2020.
[6] DANE 2019.
[7] Ibáñez and Vélez 2008.
[8] Bonilla-Tinoco et al. 2020; Holland et al. 2020; Knight and Tribin 2020.
[9] UNHCR 2016.

economy and charity to survive.[10] Additionally, migrants who transit through and settle in countries afflicted by armed conflict are invariably forced to interact with armed non-state actors who regulate their entry and incorporation into peripheral spaces.[11]

Perhaps no other case study is better suited to examine this phenomenon than the Colombian–Venezuelan borderlands. Despite the magnitude of the Venezuelan migrant crisis, the international response has been underwhelming compared to other humanitarian crises found in the Middle East, sub-Saharan Africa, or South Asia, reflecting the normative and practical limitations of the existing regime on migration governance. Venezuela is poised to overtake Syria as the world's largest net exporter of people, even though the country's humanitarian crisis is the product of severe economic mismanagement rather than armed conflict.[12] Conversely, after more than five decades of armed conflict and political instability, the Colombian state remains unable to protect many of its own citizens, let alone attend to the needs of millions of Venezuelans fleeing their own country.[13] Even though millions of Venezuelans are simultaneously fleeing economic scarcity, the world's highest rates of violent crime, and political repression, only a small minority of those who have left Venezuela over the past five years are formally recognized by migration authorities as asylum seekers or refugees in their receiving countries.[14] Already hindered by a lack of the basic resources needed to properly relocate to another country, the widely applied status of Venezuelans as migrants instead of refugees or asylum seekers further complicates their successful repatriation abroad, leaving many in a legal and diplomatic limbo that only serves to worsen their exposure and vulnerability to "bad faith" actors in contested spaces.[15]

The rest of this chapter is organized as follows. First, I offer a brief review of the Colombian–Venezuelan borderlands and the various actors that operate there. Second, I develop a profile of the *caminantes*, or those migrants who lack the money and documentation required to migrate using formal mechanisms, a demographic that arguably represents a majority of Venezuelans leaving their country in recent years. Third, I examine the political economy of migrants in transit and the impact of

[10] Chauvin and Garcés-Mascareñas 2014.
[11] Lacroix et al. 2011.
[12] Bahar and Dooley 2019.
[13] Delgado 2015.
[14] Amnesty International 2019.
[15] Van Praag 2019.

fees that have to be paid at informal border crossings. Fourth, I analyze the often selective incorporation of Venezuelans into the border economy. Finally, I briefly assess the implications of this phenomenon for Colombia and the broader region. This chapter draws on several semi-structured interviews conducted by the author with Venezuelan migrants, community leaders, humanitarian workers, and government officials conducted in the borderlands between January 2016 and December 2019. Additionally, it includes an expansive array of information from primary and secondary sources including government reports, academic publications, and media articles. All translations are my own.

The Colombian–Venezuelan Borderlands

The Colombian–Venezuelan borderlands represent the longest shared space that links Colombia with any of its neighbors. In regard to administrative units, the borderlands are composed of four Venezuelan states (Zulia, Táchira, Apure, Amazonas), and seven Colombian departments (La Guajira, Cesar, Norte de Santander, Boyacá, Arauca, Vichada, Guainía). Despite the considerable length, there are only seven formal pedestrian crossings located on the border in Paraguachón (La Guajira-Zulia), Puerto Santander (Norte de Santander-Táchira), Cúcuta (Norte de Santander-Táchira),[16] Arauca City (Arauca-Apure), Puerto Carreño (Vichada-Apure), and Puerto Ayacucho (Vichada-Amazonas). Yet, these legal crossings are supplemented by hundreds of informal *trochas* that accommodate a substantial amount of the total binational travel between the two countries.

In the past, many neglected border communities in Colombia were more closely integrated into neighboring Venezuela than with the Colombian interior.[17] This long history of state neglect allowed Colombian insurgent groups to consolidate control of large swaths of the border region over the course of the 1970s and 1980s. These groups were able to further expand their presence into neighboring Venezuelan states with considerable ease when Hugo Chávez Frías assumed office in 1999. A religious leader in the Araucan piedmont describes this dynamic: "With Chávez everything changed. From the beginning he welcomed the guerrillas."[18] The lack of bilateral cooperation between the Colombian

---

[16] There are two pedestrian crossings located in Cúcuta as it is by far the largest entry-exit point between the two countries.
[17] Interview with Former Mayor, Arauquita, January 2016.
[18] Interview with Religious Leader, Arauquita, July 2016.

and Venezuelan authorities over the past two decades has led to a rise in impunity for armed actors who advantageously flout the laws in both countries.[19] Prior to the Venezuelan migrant crisis, armed groups participated in a variety of illegal cross-border activities apart from drug trafficking such as *el bachaqueo*, the contraband of heavily subsidized food staples and medicines in Venezuela to Colombia, and *el pimpineo*, the trafficking of heavily subsidized Venezuelan gasoline to Colombian border zones. At the height of each racket, an estimated sixteen tons of food and 1,125,000 gallons of gasoline were being smuggled across the border every day.[20]

The social composition of civilian communities along the borderlands varies enormously, as do the constellation of state and non-state actors that operate in these distinct spaces. Certain spaces can be characterized as "hegemonic zones" where one armed group or a coalition of actors maintains dominant social, political, economic, and territorial control, such as Arauca and the Venezuelan side of the borderlands.[21] All other spaces can be aptly described as "contested zones" where disparate actors engage in violent competition for supremacy with one another, including Alta Guajira, Serranía del Perijá, Catatumbo, and the Metropolitan Area of Cúcuta.[22] The official state forces that are found to varying degrees in the borderlands are the Bolivarian Armed Forces of Venezuela (FANB) and the Bolivarian National Police on the Venezuelan side, and the Armed Forces of Colombia (FMC) and the Colombian National Police (PONAL) on the Colombian side.[23] Colombia's most powerful Marxist insurgent groups, most notably the Revolutionary Armed Forces of Colombia (FARC), the Army of National Liberation (ELN), and the Popular Liberation Army (EPL), have long enjoyed a strong presence in the borderlands, particularly in the Catatumbo (Norte de Santander) and Piedmont (Arauca) regions, and more recently in neighboring Venezuelan states such as Apure, Táchira, Zulia, and Amazonas.[24]

Apart from state forces and insurgent groups, there is an assortment of other Colombian armed actors known as *bandas criminales* (BACRIM), which maintain a substantive presence in the borderlands such as Los Rastrojos and the Gaitanista Self-Defence Forces of Colombia (AGC),

---

[19] Zulver and Idler 2020.
[20] El País 2017.
[21] Defensoría del Pueblo 2019a.
[22] Defensoría del Pueblo 2020b.
[23] Defensoría del Pueblo 2020a.
[24] Defensoría del Pueblo 2019b.

which are most dominant in Norte de Santander and Táchira. In recent years, smaller binational criminal gangs have emerged such as La Linea, La Frontera, Los Venecos, Los Diablos, Los Canelones, Los Carteludos, and Los Cebolleros in Norte de Santander and Táchira, and Los de la Zona and Los Mercenarios in La Guajira and Zulia.[25] Additionally, Venezuelan prison gangs known as *megabandas* have expanded their operations to the borderlands, most notably El Tren de Aragua in Táchira and Norte de Santander and Los Pranes in Zulia and La Guajira.[26] Recently, a slew of *colectivos armados*, or Venezuelan paramilitary organizations composed of radical partisan activists, criminals, and prisoners, have moved to Táchira over the past three years to shore up the Venezuelan state's presence in geo-strategically important spaces along the border.[27] Finally, there have been increased reports of members of the Sinaloa Cartel and the Jalisco New Generation Cartel, rival Mexican drug cartels, in the Catatumbo region and the Venezuelan states of Zulia, Táchira, and Apure, where they handle the purchasing, processing, and trafficking of cocaine toward Central America and the Caribbean.[28]

Economic Scarcity and the Rise of *Los Caminantes*

Over the past five years, the overwhelming push factor driving Venezuelans from their country has been economic scarcity. Due to hyperinflation, foreign currencies such as the American dollar became widely used from 2018 onward and those Venezuelans with a lack of access to foreign currency were severely affected by the near complete implosion in their purchasing power.[29] This financial predicament fueled the mass exodus from 2015 onward as millions of Venezuelans struggled to feed themselves and their families.[30] According to one *caminante* from a rural town in eastern Venezuela, "You practically had to fight to line up to buy a kilo of flour. People resorted to looting homes and businesses because they didn't have money, work, or food."[31] The widespread economic desperation compounded what were already the world's highest levels of violent crime. One young migrant from Valencia recalls how

---

[25] La Opinión 2018.
[26] Defensoría del Pueblo 2020c; Defensoría del Pueblo 2019d.
[27] Hernández 2019.
[28] InSight Crime 2020.
[29] Interview with Venezuelan migrant 4, Chinácota, Norte de Santander, May 2019.
[30] Interview with Caminante 10, Don Juana, Norte de Santander, May 2019.
[31] Interview with Caminante 3, Don Juana, Norte de Santander, May 2019.

this affected him personally: "Some guys killed my brother when they were robbing him so they could eat. They didn't have anything and neither did he."[32] The collapse of the Venezuelan economy greatly affected all Venezuelans at home, while also directly shaping their prospects for migrating abroad in regard to their ultimate destination, their mode of travel, and, upon arriving, their living conditions and their employment opportunities as well. In Venezuela, a lack of financial resources translates into a lack of identification and documents that are only issued by the government and only for fees beyond the reach of most citizens. This ultimately limits migrants to using illegal border crossings to enter Colombia and to either travel to their intended destination on foot, or, if they are fortunate enough, to hitchhike part of the way.[33]

Whereas Venezuelans could once boast that they hailed from the most affluent country in Latin America, they now have the unfortunate distinction of being a transnational underclass in the world's most unequal region. Besides once being the wealthiest nation in Latin America, Venezuela also received millions of refugees and immigrants following the Second World War, a trend that lasted until the new millennium.[34] During this period, over a million Colombians who were either displaced by the armed conflict or who were merely pursuing better economic prospects resettled in Venezuela.[35] However, this trend saw a reversal beginning in the late 2000s as the entrepreneurial class – largely Venezuelans from the upper and middle classes – began migrating in greater numbers to geographically close countries with similar linguistic and cultural characteristics such as Colombia in an attempt to repatriate their capital when faced with growing expropriations and an increasingly devalued currency at home.[36] In 2015, the culmination of hyperinflation, food insecurity, high levels of violent crime, political repression, and the collapse of the public health system sparked the mass exodus of Colombians residing in Venezuela (*retornados*), and millions of Venezuelans from the middle and working classes to nearby countries to escape the mounting economic scarcity in their country, with Colombia being "the closest and most accessible immigration option for Venezuelans in search of opportunities."[37]

---

[32] Interview with Caminante 4, Don Juana, Norte de Santander, May 2019.
[33] Taraciuk Broner 2018.
[34] Straka 2020.
[35] Guataquí et al. 2017.
[36] De León Vargas 2018.
[37] Pineda and Ávila 2019.

By 2017, the humanitarian crisis in Venezuela had worsened to the extent that hundreds of thousands of poorer Venezuelans with minimal economic resources began migrating to Colombia and other countries in the region on foot, in some cases due to their lack of passports and other documentation that impeded formal modes of transportation, but in most cases because they lacked the necessary funds to pay for a bus or a plane ticket.[38] It is difficult to make generalizations given the diversity found among the *caminantes*, but some research has highlighted certain trends found among this demographic. Whereas earlier there were substantially more male migrants entering and traversing Colombia on foot, this has changed over recent years as a higher number of women, many with young children, have begun making the journey, leveling out a near-equal gender parity between male and female migrants. A majority of *caminantes* are between fifteen and thirty-five years of age and possess some level of high school education.[39] Unsurprisingly, they are more likely than Colombians to be unemployed and living below the poverty line.[40] While the effects of those who do obtain their temporary work visa and enter the formal labor market are negligible, informal trade and commerce in those municipalities with the highest percentages of Venezuelans per capita in border departments like Norte de Santander, La Guajira, and Arauca have been adversely affected by the influx of foreign nationals.[41] Outside of the capital city, Bogotá, the highest concentration of *caminantes* is found in the Colombian–Venezuelan borderlands, as many of them settle in communities near their point of entry because they lack the economic and physical capacity to migrate any further in the Colombian interior and beyond.[42]

The Political Economy of Migrants in Transit

Thousands of *caminantes*, circular migrants, and binational indigenous groups enter Colombia through informal border crossings every day, generating substantial revenues for state authorities and armed non-state actors alike. There is a long tradition of contraband and drug smuggling across clandestine *trochas* in Colombia, and these networks of hundreds of informal crossings are continually being refitted for different purposes

---

[38] Ibañez 2018.
[39] Guategui et al. 2017.
[40] Ibañez, 2018, 59.
[41] Bahar et al. 2020; Palacios 2019.
[42] Defensoría del Pueblo 2020c.

depending on micro- and macro-level economic forces in both countries.[43] The *trocha* economy thrives in large part due to the lack of meaningful state presence on either side of the border, the scarcity of formal border crossings, the prevalence of illicit economies in the borderlands, and the constant border closures mandated by either the Colombian or the Venezuelan government.[44] Over the past five years, there has been a substantial growth in *trochas* due the convergence of three crises: the reconfiguration of the Colombian armed conflict following the 2016 FARC peace treaty, the ever-worsening Venezuelan humanitarian crisis, and the recent outbreak of COVID-19.[45] During this time, the border has been officially closed on numerous occasions for extended periods due to security concerns, diplomatic spats, and more recently for public health reasons. These official border closures have only served to increase the binational traffic of people, goods, drugs, and contraband through the *trochas*, while also allowing armed actors to increase revenues via their control of these informal border crossings.[46] In the words of an indigenous moto-taxi driver in La Guajira, "It doesn't affect me at all if they close the border. For that there are the *trochas*."[47] Even when the official authorities attempt to shut down prominent informal crossings, these are merely moved elsewhere, or reappear once authorities scale back their presence.

Trochas themselves vary enormously throughout the borderlands. Much of the Colombian–Venezuelan border is demarcated by rivers and informal border crossings in these places consist of either boat crossings, as is the case in Arauca, or improvised structures or ropes strung along shallower waters which are then crossed by migrants, which is most common in Norte de Santander.[48] In zones where the border is found on dry land, *trochas* are often footpaths or unpaved access roads that link the two countries together such as those found throughout La Guajira. Ironically, there is a substantial number of these informal border crossings located in the immediate vicinity of formal border crossings, often directly within eyesight of the official authorities, as some of the most heavily traversed *trochas* are located directly adjacent to formal crossings. Each informal crossing is controlled and operated by an armed

---

[43] Defensoría del Pueblo 2019d.
[44] Defensoría del Pueblo 2019a; Defensoría del Pueblo 2019c.
[45] Idler and Hochmüller 2020.
[46] García and Mantilla 2020.
[47] El Heraldo 2015.
[48] FundaRedes 2019, 23.

non-state actor, most often with some degree of collaboration with state authorities on both sides. Members of these groups openly carry firearms and can generally be found on both sides of the crossing where they oversee all traffic between the two countries. Depending on the group, the *trocha*, and the purpose for crossing the border, civilians attempting to cross the border informally are charged a fee. During periods when the border is open, these fares range from $2,000 Colombian pesos (COP) in Arauca ($0.75 USD), to $4,000 COP in Norte de Santander ($1.50 USD), to $5,000 COP in La Guajira ($1.88 USD).[49] During border closures, the price increases dramatically as various *caminantes* interviewed during the border closure in mid-2019 cited paying crossing fees ranging from $10,000 to $20,000 COP ($3.75–$7.50 USD) in highly transited *trochas* in Norte de Santander.[50] With the outbreak of COVID-19, the prices charged by armed groups to use their informal border crossings have skyrocketed, as there are reports of some groups charging up to $300,000 COP ($83 USD) to facilitate illegal border crossings.[51]

In the past, there was violent competition between armed non-state actors for control of illicit economic activities that utilized *trochas* located in the Colombian–Venezuelan borderlands. The 2016 demobilization of the FARC (and the subsequent remobilization of several dissident guerrilla structures), coupled with the Venezuelan humanitarian crisis, has only served to exacerbate the conflict over control of these rackets, leaving Venezuelan migrants extremely vulnerable to the excesses and abuses of disparate armed groups when they are transiting the border region.[52] Armed confrontations and shootouts are common between state authorities and warring groups at heavily transited crossings.[53] Additionally, armed actors frequently kill members of rival groups and leave their bodies on *trochas* to both serve as a warning to others and also because of the inability of state authorities to investigate, let alone prosecute crimes committed on international borders.[54] *Caminantes* and other circular migrants who moved to the borderlands from elsewhere in Venezuela to earn a living in the informal economy are similarly

---

[49] Barráez 2020; Millano 2018.
[50] Interview with Caminante 12, Don Juana, Norte de Santander, May 2019; Interview with Caminante 15, Don Juana, Norte de Santander, May 2019; Interview with Caminante 17, Don Juana, Norte de Santander, May 2019; Interview with Caminante 18, Don Juana, Norte de Santander, May 2019.
[51] Rodríguez 2020.
[52] Defensoría del Pueblo 2019d; FundaRedes, 2019, 14–15.
[53] Defensoría del Pueblo 2020a.
[54] Extra Boyacá 2019.

victimized by armed actors while transiting the *trochas*, as they are frequently robbed of all their money, documents, and other valuable possessions by predatory actors. One *caminante* from Cojedes traveling with multiple small children and a disabled sibling describes such an experience crossing a *trocha* in Norte de Santander: "They searched everything and robbed us of $100 USD which we had. They told us that they were going to help us finance our trip and now we are forced to sleep in the street."[55] There have also been numerous cases of migrants being killed and left on the informal crossings, as many others have been forcibly disappeared, sometimes for as little as not having enough money to pay the crossing fee.[56]

Apart from robbery, extortion, and homicide, there are significant reports of sexual exploitation by armed groups in the borderlands. While in transit, women and children have been sexually abused by members of these groups when crossing *trochas* in La Guajira and Norte de Santander.[57] Additionally, several sex trafficking schemes are known to exist despite the considerable difficulties in uncovering and exposing these illicit rackets.[58] One criminal group operating in Táchira and Norte de Santander, Los Venecos, has recruited young female migrants in Venezuelan border towns with false promises of employment in Colombia and then transported them hundreds of kilometers away to the south of Bolívar department, where they are then sold to other armed non-state actors to work in brothels under their control.[59] In a similar case, the Venezuelan *megabanda* El Tren de Aragua has partnered with the Colombian criminal group Los Rastrojos, where the former recruit and traffic young women in Venezuela under false pretenses of employment in Colombia, where upon arriving they are forced into sex work by the latter group against their will.[60] In another disturbing incident of sexual exploitation of migrants in the borderlands, a local gang in La Guajira abducted and drugged underage male Venezuelan migrants, dressed them as women, and then proceeded to sell them to clients for $60,000 COP ($18 USD) throughout the department.[61]

[55] Interview with Caminante 12, Don Juana, Norte de Santander, May 2019.
[56] FundaRedes, 2019, 15.
[57] Defensoría del Pueblo 2019d.
[58] Zulver and Idler 2020.
[59] Defensoría del Pueblo, "Alerta Temprana N° 035–2020," August 5, 2020.
[60] Defensoría del Pueblo 2019c.
[61] InSight Crime 2019.

The Incorporation of Venezuelan Migrants into the Border Economy

The plight of Venezuelan migrants who settle in the borderlands is wrought with challenges similar to those encountered by *caminantes* who merely transit the zone. A majority of these lack both official status and advanced job skills, deficiencies which drive them to the sprawling informal economy, which is frequently regulated by armed non-state actors which often decide where migrants can settle, what type of work they are permitted to engage in, and ultimately how they behave in these spaces. The manner in which Venezuelan migrants are incorporated into the informal border economy can be broken down into three separate categories: independent workers, employees, and racketeers. Independent workers are those migrants who are either self-employed or hired by another civilian to partake in the informal economy such as selling coffee on the street or working as a freelance day laborer. Employees describe migrants who work in some capacity for armed non-state actors whether engaging in prostitution or harvesting coca. Racketeers are migrants who are members of an armed group, whether they are recruited upon their arrival in the borderlands, or if they are a member of an organization that is attempting to expand its operations to the borderlands by allying or competing with established armed non-state actors there.

While exact information is hard to come by given the nature of the informal economy, it is reasonable to assume that a majority of Venezuelan migrants in the Colombian–Venezuelan borderlands are independent workers. However, these migrants are still regulated by armed non-state actors in a variety of ways in both contested and hegemonic spaces. For example, insurgent groups in Catatumbo require that Venezuelan migrants have the recommendation of someone already living in the zone in order to work or settle there. This formality serves as a regulatory mechanism that bestows responsibility for a migrant's actions on their sponsor, hence minimizing the entry of potentially disruptive individuals into the contested zone.[62] Those migrants who do not have insurgent approval are forced to leave the zone or face lethal consequences. In the ELN-dominated piedmont sub-region of Arauca, all incoming migration into the zone has historically been regulated by the insurgent group, a dynamic that has not changed with the

---

[62] Human Rights Watch 2019, 25.

unprecedented arrival of thousands of foreign nationals to the department.[63] In both Arauca and Catatumbo, insurgent groups wield considerable influence over local communal councils, which have been deployed to monitor and regulate Venezuelan migrants in rural communities, as only those who obtain paid employment are allowed to remain in order prevent any potential resort to criminality by unemployed new arrivals.[64]

The surge of Venezuelan migrants working in the informal economy has put an enormous strain on the informal labor market, and quite simply many are driven by necessity to work in industries controlled by armed non-state actors such as the sex and drug trades. Over the past five years, the number of Venezuelan migrants working in the sex industry has exploded, causing enormous friction with their Colombian counterparts, in some cases even leading to lethal disputes over territory.[65] The proliferation of Venezuelan sex workers has driven prices down, although the manner in which prostitution is regulated varies between spaces according to which actors are in control.[66] Venezuelan criminal groups in contested spaces have proven to be particularly predatory toward their compatriots, as they operate prostitution rings in places like Maicao, where sex workers charge as little as $5,000 COP ($1.88 USD) for their services.[67] In Cúcuta, where Venezuelan prostitutes now constitute 80 percent of all sex workers, a binational criminal group, Los Venecos, has established control of the infamous red light district, El Callejón, with the support of the Gaitanista Self-Defence Forces of Colombia.[68] In these zones, some brothels even offer two Venezuelan women for $5,000 COP ($1.88 USD) and it is not unusual for sex workers to attend to dozens of clients over the course of a weekend.[69] Insurgent groups vary in their regulation of the sex trade, as is evidenced by the ELN, EPL, and the FARC dissident structures in Catatumbo.[70] In some communities the EPL and the FARC dissidents have prohibited prostitution of any kind, while in other spaces the EPL and the ELN permit and

---

[63] Larratt-Smith 2020.
[64] Ibañez 2018, 88.
[65] La Opinión 2019.
[66] Miranda 2019.
[67] Defensoría del Pueblo 2019d; Human Rights Watch 2019, 43.
[68] La Opinión 2016.
[69] Miranda 2019.
[70] Zulver and Idler 2020.

regulate the sex trade by threatening foreign sex workers with violent reprisals if they spread sexually transmitted diseases to anyone else.[71]

In recent years, large numbers of Venezuelan migrants have also migrated to Catatumbo, Colombia's largest coca-growing zone, to work as *raspachines*, or coca harvesters, alongside local peasants. Virtually all facets of this industry are closely controlled by the ELN, the EPL, and the FARC dissidents in this contested zone. Coca harvesters are paid $5,000 COP ($1.88 USD) for every twelve and a half kilos of leaves yielded, representing one of the most lucrative opportunities in the informal border economy. Other Venezuelan migrants have moved to the insurgent zone to benefit from the coca economy, as Venezuelan sex workers who operate in Catatumbo's coca zones can charge as much as $30,000 COP ($9.50 USD) to $50,000 COP ($15.60 USD) per client.[72] Over recent years, Venezuelan migrants have overwhelmed the coca labor market to such an extent that they have driven down wages, as many migrants are willing to work for half the rate that Colombian *raspachines* expect.[73] In a trend similar to other coca producing zones in Colombia, substantial numbers of underage migrants have stopped attending school due to the appeal and dominance of the coca economy in Catatumbo.[74]

Those migrants who can be categorized as racketeers are those recruited by armed groups in the borderlands, or those who migrated to the binational zone already belonging to such an organization. Virtually all armed non-state actors have attempted to recruit Venezuelan migrants in the Colombian–Venezuelan borderlands, often using their precarious socioeconomic and legal status as a means to compel them to join as armed combatants or informants, or to partake in their illegal economic activities.[75] In recent years, the ELN has consolidated control of the Venezuelan side of the border in direct collusion with the Venezuelan authorities and has recruited Venezuelan migrants, many of them underage, into its expanding structure with financial incentives.[76] In Arauca, both the ELN and FARC dissident structures have reportedly attempted to recruit underage Venezuelan migrants, in particular young women, by dispatching militia members to local schools to seduce them into the insurgent ranks.[77] Various

---

[71] Defensoría del Pueblo 2018.
[72] Judex and Herrera 2015.
[73] La Opinión 2017.
[74] Judex and Herrera 2015.
[75] Defensoría del Pueblo 2019a; Ibañez 2018, 88–89.
[76] Defensoría del Pueblo 2019d; Defensoría del Pueblo 2019e.
[77] Mesa 2019.

military deserters from the FANB who have settled in Cúcuta have been approached by criminal groups to join their organizations for $300,000 COP ($100 USD) a day.[78] Numerous Venezuelan armed groups have established a notable presence in the borderlands during this period. These groups either align themselves with established armed non-state actors, or violently compete with them to varying degrees of success for control of illicit economic activities such as drug trafficking, arms trafficking, extortion, contraband, prostitution, and murder for hire.[79] However, both Venezuelan and binational groups that have been able to consolidate a meaningful presence in the Metropolitan Area of Cúcuta and La Guajira have been unable to penetrate those spaces where Colombian insurgent groups maintain a strong presence such as Catatumbo or Arauca. In these zones, armed non-state actors have committed selective assassinations and massacres against Venezuelan migrants who fall afoul of their social code, or who engage in theft, armed robbery, cattle rustling, drug dealing, rape, or murder.[80]

Cash Rules Everything

At the time of writing, the Venezuelan migrant crisis continues unabated. While an estimated 200,000 Venezuelan migrants returned to their country as a result of the global pandemic, most of these and many more will continue to migrate abroad due to the worsening levels of economic scarcity in their country and the clear determination of Nicolás Maduro and his government to not relinquish power under any circumstances. Most of these migrants lack money, a reality that will greatly shape their trajectory and will force them to transit, and in many cases settle, in the Colombian–Venezuelan borderlands. Meanwhile, successive Colombian administrations have attempted to adopt a humanitarian policy response to the millions of Venezuelan migrants transiting and settling in Colombia. Yet, recent policy decisions by Iván Duque's government have both failed to unseat his Venezuelan adversary from office while perpetuating violent competition in the various conflict zones found along the Colombian–Venezuelan border. With no end in sight to either the armed conflict or the humanitarian crisis, Venezuelan

---

[78] Interview with Military Deserter 1, Cúcuta, Norte de Santander, May 2019.
[79] Defensoría del Pueblo 2019d.
[80] Human Rights Watch 2020.

migrants in the borderlands will continue to do whatever they have to do to make money and survive.

References

Amnesty International. 2019. "Welcome Venezuela: People fleeing massive human Rights Violations in Venezuela." May 8. At www.amnesty.org/en/documents/amr53/0244/2019/en/

Bahar, Dany and Meagan Dooley. 2019. "Venezuela refugee crisis to become the largest and most underfunded in modern history." December 9. At www.brookings.edu/blog/up-front/2019/12/09/venezuela-refugee-crisis-to-become-the-largest-and-most-underfunded-in-modern-history/

Bahar, Dany, Meagan Dooley, and Andrew Selee. 2020. "Venezuelan migration, crime, and misperceptions: A review of data from Colombia, Peru, and Chile." September 14. At www.brookings.edu/research/venezuelan-migration-crime-and-misperceptions-a-review-of-data-from-colombia-peru-and-chile/

Bahar, Dany, Ana María Ibañez, and Sandra Rozo. 2020. "Give Me Your Tired and Your Poor: Impact of a Large-Scale Amnesty Program for Undocumented Refugees." *CESifo Working Paper No. 8601.*

Barráez, Sebastiana. 2020. "Un viaje por la frontera de Venezuela hasta Colombia: las extorsiones de los militares y del ELN, más el cobro en pesos y una carita feliz." November 8. At www.infobae.com/america/venezuela/2020/11/08/un-viaje-por-la-frontera-de-venezuela-hasta-colombia-las-extorsiones-de-los-militares-y-del-eln-mas-el-cobro-en-pesos-y-una-carita-feliz/

Bonilla-Tinoco, Laura Juliana, Melissa Aguirre-Lemus, and Julián Alfredo Fernández-Niño. 2020. "Venezuelan migrant population in Colombia: Health indicators in the context of the Sustainable Development Goals." *F1000Research* 9, no. 684: 1–13.

Chauvin, Sébastien and Blanca Garcés-Mascareñas. 2014. "Becoming less illegal: Deservingness frames and undocumented migrant incorporation." *Sociology Compass* 8: 422–432.

De León Vargas, Georgina Isabel. 2018. "Diaspora Venezolana, Cartagena Más Allá de las Cifras." *Revista Jurídica Mario Alario D'Filippo* 10, no. 20: 111–119.

Defensoría del Pueblo. 2018. "Alerta Temprana N° 040–18." April 19.
Defensoría del Pueblo. 2019a. "Alerta Temprana N° 011–19." February 15.
Defensoría del Pueblo. 2019b. "Alerta Temprana N° 029–19." July 11.
Defensoría del Pueblo. 2019c. "Alerta Temprana N° 037–19." September 12.
Defensoría del Pueblo. 2019d. "Alerta Temprana N° 039–19." September 16.
Defensoría del Pueblo. 2019e. "Alerta Temprana N° 024–19." February 15.
Defensoría del Pueblo. 2020a. "Alerta Temprana N° 011–2020." March 13.

Defensoría del Pueblo. 2020b. "Alerta Temprana N° 034–2020." August 4.
Defensoría del Pueblo. 2020c. "Alerta Temprana N° 035–2020." August 5.
Delgado, Jorge. 2015. "Counterinsurgency and the limits of state-building: An analysis of Colombia's policy of territorial consolidation, 2006–2012." *Small Wars & Insurgencies* 26, no. 3: 408–428.
Departamento Administrativo Nacional de Estadística (DANE). 2019. "Boletín Técnico: Medición de empleo informal y seguridad social." December 12. At www.dane.gov.co/files/investigaciones/boletines/ech/ech_informalidad/bol_ech_informalidad_ago19_oct19.pdf
El Heraldo. 2015. "Las fronteras no existen para la Gran Nación Wayuu." September 6. At www.elheraldo.co/nacional/las-fronteras-no-existen-para-la-gran-nacion-wayuu-215788
El País. 2017. "Venezuela, Crimen sin frontera." At www.elpais.com.co/especiales/venezuela-crimen-sin-frontera/
Extra Boyacá. 2019. "Torturados y decapitados en medio de una trocha: con sevicia fueron asesinados." May 25. At https://boyaca.extra.com.co/noticias/judicial/torturados-y-decapitados-en-medio-de-una-trocha-con-sevicia-529979
FundaRedes. 2019. "Informe Anual." At www.fundaredes.org/2020/06/28/informe-anual-fundarede-2019/
García Pinzón, Viviana, and Jorge Mantilla. 2020. "Contested borders: Organized crime, governance, and bordering practices in Colombia-Venezuela borderlands." *Trends in Organized Crime.* https://doi.org/10.1007/s12117-020-09399-3
Guataquí, Juan Carlos, Andrés García-Suaza, Cindy Vanessa Ospina Cartagena, Diana Isabel Londoño Aguirre, Paul Rodríguez Lesmes, and Juan Pablo Baquero. 2017. "Características de los migrantes de Venezuela a Colombia." *Observatorio Laboral de la Universidad del Rosario Informe* 3: 1–9.
Hernández, Rosalinda. 2019. "Frontera: Mientras los colectivos armados buscan la paz, los ciudadanos viven aterrorizados." December 27. At www.fronteraviva.com/frontera-mientras-los-colectivos-armados-buscan-la-paz-los-ciudadanos-viven-aterrorizados/
Holland, Alisha, Margaret Peters, and Yang-Yang Zhou. 2020. "Left Out: How Political Ideology Affects Support for Migrants in Colombia." *Working Paper.* https://papers.ssrn.com/sol3/papers.cfm?abstract_id=3803052
Human Rights Watch. 2019. "The War in Catatumbo: Abuses by Armed Groups Against Civilians Including Venezuelan Exiles in Northeastern Colombia." August 8. At www.hrw.org/report/2019/08/08/war-catatumbo/abuses-armed-groups-against-civilians-including-venezuelan-exiles
Human Rights Watch. 2020. "'The Guerrillas Are the Police': Social Control and Abuses by Armed Groups in Colombia's Arauca Province and Venezuela's Apure State." January 22. At www.hrw.org/report/2020/01/22/guerrillas-are-police/social-control-and-abuses-armed-groups-colombias-arauca

Ibañez, Ana María. 2018. *Migración desde Venezuela a Colombia*. Washington, DC: World Bank.
Ibáñez, Ana María and Carlos Eduardo Vélez. 2008. "Civil conflict and forced migration: The micro determinants and welfare losses of displacement in Colombia." *World Development* 36, no. 4: 659–676.
Idler, Annette. 2019. *Borderland Battles Violence, Crime, and Governance at the Edges of Colombia's War*. Oxford, UK: Oxford University Press.
Idler, Annette and Markus Hochmüller. 2020. "Covid-19 in Colombia's borderlands and the western hemisphere: Adding instability to a double crisis." *Journal of Latin American Geography* 19, no. 3: 280–288.
InSight Crime. 2019. "Migración aumenta casos de explotación sexual infantil en Colombia." October 16. At https://es.insightcrime.org/noticias/noticias-del-dia/migracion-aumenta-casos-de-explotacion-sexual-infantil-en-colombia/#:~:text=Migraci%C3%B3n%20aumenta%20casos%20de%20explotaci%C3%B3n%20sexual%20infantil%20en%20Colombia,-Noticias%20del%20d%C3%ADa&text=Autoridades%20en%20Colombia%20desmantelaron%20una,los%20que%20hab%C3%ADa%20ni%C3%B1os%20venezolanos.&text=Sin%20embargo%2C%20en%20Colombia%2C%20la,estos%20casos%20ha%20sido%20m%C3%ADnima.
InSight Crime. 2020. "Mexican Cartels – Venezuela's Uninvited Guests Here to Stay." April 3. At www.insightcrime.org/news/analysis/mexico-cartels-uninvited-guest-venezuela/.
Judex, Karina and Cristian Herrera. 2015. "Venezolanos y menores, tras la coca del Catatumbo (III parte)." September 13. At www.laopinion.com.co/region/venezolanos-y-menores-tras-la-coca-del-catatumbo-iii-parte-98258
Knight, Brian and Ana Tribin. 2020. "Immigration and Violent Crime: Evidence from the Colombia-Venezuela Border." *NBER Working Paper No. w27620*.
La Opinión. 2016. "El Callejón de la muerte, la droga y la prostitución." December 4. At www.laopinion.com.co/cucuta/el-callejon-de-la-muerte-la-droga-y-la-prostitucion-123852
La Opinión. 2017. "Crece la llegada de venezolanos al Catatumbo para raspar coca." November 21. At www.laopinion.com.co/region/crece-la-llegada-de-venezolanos-al-catatumbo-para-raspar-coca-144106
La Opinión. 2018. "La frontera, una zona codiciada por las bandas criminals." January 15. At www.laopinion.com.co/frontera/la-frontera-una-zona-codiciada-por-las-bandas-criminales-147264
La Opinión. 2019. "Pelea entre trabajadoras sexuales dejó una muerta en Ocaña." July 12. At www.laopinion.com.co/judicial/pelea-entre-trabajadoras-sexuales-dejo-una-muerta-en-ocana-158106
Lacroix, Pauline, Pascal Bongard, and Chris Rush. 2011. "Engaging armed non-state actors in mechanisms for protection." *Forced Migration Review* 37: 10–12.

Larratt-Smith, Charles. 2020. "Navigating formal and informal processes: Civic organizations, armed nonstate actors, and nested governance in Colombia." *Latin American Politics and Society* 62, no. 2: 75–98.

Mesa Rivera, Maria. 2019. "Arauca: El Río que impone los límites en la frontera." At https://especiales.semana.com/migracion-venezolana-a-colombia-historias-al-borde-de-la-frontera/arauca-reclutamiento-de-ninos-venezolanos.html

Migración Colombia. 2020. "Más de 1 Millón 825 Mil Venezolanos Estarían Radicados en Colombia." April 3. At www.migracioncolombia.gov.co/noticias/mas-de-1-millon-825-mil-venezolanos-estarian-radicados-en-colombia

Millano, Jesika. 2018. "La riesgosa travesía de Maicao a Maracaibo." October 7. At www.elheraldo.co/barranquilla/la-riesgosa-travesia-de-maicao-maracaibo-550660

Miranda, Boris. 2019. "Crisis en Venezuela: cómo las mafias y grupos armados de Colombia se aprovechan de los migrantes venezolanos." September 19. At www.bbc.com/mundo/noticias-america-latina-49486230

Palacios, Estefania. 2019. "Maicao: El eterno retorno de los wayuu." At https://especiales.semana.com/migracion-venezolana-a-colombia-historias-al-borde-de-la-frontera/retorno-de-los-indigenas-wayuu-a-venezuela.html

Pineda, Esther, and Keymer Ávila. 2019. "Aproximaciones a la migración colombo-venezolana: Desigualdad, Prejuicio y Vulnerabilidad." *Clivatge* 7: 46–97.

Rodríguez Suárez, Aldair José. 2020. "Migrantes venezolanos regresan a Colombia por trochas de La Guajira." September 28. At www.alertacaribe.com/noticias/migrantes-venezolanos-regresan-colombia-por-trochas-de-la-guajira

Straka, Tomás. 2020. "When Caracas was a safe haven from tyranny." April 20. At www.americasquarterly.org/article/when-caracas-was-a-safe-haven-from-tyranny/.

Taraciuk Broner, Tamara. 2018. "Los caminantes venezolanos – Huir a pie de un país en ruinas." September 5. At www.hrw.org/es/news/2018/09/05/los-caminantes-venezolanos

United Nations High Commissioner for Refugees (UNHCR). 2016. "UNHCR viewpoint: 'refugee' or 'migrant' – Which is right?." July 11. At www.unhcr.org/news/latest/2016/7/55df0e556/unhcr-viewpoint-refugee-migrant-right.html

Van Praag, Oriana. 2019. "Understanding the Venezuelan refugee crisis." September 13. At www.wilsoncenter.org/article/understanding-the-venezuelan-refugee-crisis

Zulver, Julia and Annette Idler. 2020. "Gendering the border effect: The double impact of Colombian insecurity and the Venezuelan refugee crisis." *Third World Quarterly* 41, no. 7: 1122–1140.

6

Recruitment Fees, Indebtedness, and the Impairment of Asian Migrant Workers' Rights

PEDRO DE SENA

Introduction

The intermediation services of recruitment agents are crucial for international labour mobility. They enable workers to have access to jobs otherwise unreachable while supplying employers with the workforce needed. Moreover, they assist both parties in navigating the intricate web of migration procedures, helping them overcome the geographical, linguistic, bureaucratic, and cultural obstacles international migration presents. Who shall pay for these services?

The 2018 United Nations *Global Compact for Safe, Orderly and Regular Migration* (GCM) reveals a clear commitment to 'prohibit recruiters and employers from charging or shifting recruitment fees or related costs to migrant workers' [§22(c)]. This pledge follows ILO's *General principles and operational guidelines for fair recruitment* (2016), and mirrors similar prohibitions enshrined in several ILO conventions. However, whereas international law advocates allocating recruitment fees and related costs to employers for all their workers regardless of skill level, a business model commonly adopted in Asia allocates those fees and costs to migrants who are recruited for low-skill jobs. This practice represents a financial burden for the most vulnerable workers and a direct source of recruitment-induced indebtedness, often associated with unethical recruitment mechanisms.

This chapter examines the impact of recruitment fees and debt in Asian labour migration. It analyses the connection, often overlooked, between the financial features of the recruitment process, how they act as a selection mechanism in labour migration, and the legal protection of migrants. The purpose is to better understand the prevalent recruitment models in Asia and to gather information needed to tackle abuse. First, this chapter reviews empirical research on intra-Asian labour mobility, demonstrating the existence of different approaches to recruitment fees (section 2). The next section departs from the ILO's definition of recruitment fees to examine the nature of costs allocated to migrant workers during the recruitment process and the consequences of specific financing methods in creating a cycle of debt. It also reflects on how migration-related debt is shaped, identifying the economic and political forces contributing to its endurance (section 3). Section 4 analyses the principle of free employment in international law, comparing the wording of the GCM with ILO's more flexible framework. It questions whether recruitment-induced debt must be associated with extreme cases of rights abuses, namely debt bondage. The chapter concludes by stressing the importance of tackling the legal *and* economic features of the recruitment process in order to reinforce the protection of migrants and enhance their migratory projects' chances of success. The absolute prohibition on allocating recruitment fees and related costs to workers might have to be challenged and weighed against a more pragmatic model bringing together prohibition and regulation, two approaches that do not necessarily have to be mutually exclusive.

Heterogeneity of Approaches to Recruitment Fees

Literature on recruitment fees reveals a diversity of approaches depending on the way migrants are perceived within the migration process, but also on different conceptualizations associated with specific social sciences.

Mainstream writings reveal a *negative* and *legalistic* approach to fees and debt, in which migrant workers are seen through the lens of vulnerability and perceived mostly as victims of abuse and exploitation. This approach establishes a link between the abusive practices of the recruitment industry and serious cases of human rights abuses, such as smuggling, human trafficking, forced labour, debt bondage, or modern slavery. This literature conceptualizes migrants' experiences within specific legal frameworks, either as a labour rights issue evoking the long-established international law instruments on forced labour,[1] or as a human rights issue evoking the legal framework on trafficking in persons and slavery.[2] In both cases, recruitment fees and indebtedness are considered risk

---

[1] Lee & Petersen 2006; Cambier 2012; Amnesty International 2017.
[2] Jureidini & Moukarbel 2004; Davidson 2013; Jägers & Rijken 2014; Jureidini 2014; Andrees, Nasri, & Swiniarski 2015; Kara 2017.

factors for migrants' rights: debt might curtail migrants' freedom of choice, increase their vulnerability, and drive them to accept exploitative working conditions.[3]

Whether framing recruitment fees and indebtedness within labour law or human rights law, three additional features surface from the literature. First, a certain terminological ambiguity[4] or 'conceptional confusion' surrounding terms like 'slavery', 'forced labour', 'debt bondage', and 'human trafficking'.[5] Second, the apparent divide between the legal dimension of the above-mentioned acts, particularly slavery, and the 'stereotypical images' of their victims.[6] The general perception of who is a victim of such illegal acts is commonly reserved for the most extreme cases and does not necessarily match the legal technicalities of the 'broad and blurred'[7] legal definitions enshrined in international law instruments. Third, an over-emphasis on the 'systemic misconduct within the recruitment industry',[8] which might contribute to ostracize recruitment agents and cast a shadow on their pivotal role within the migration process.[9]

Besides this 'legal' standpoint, literature also shows the emergence of *neutral sociological* views of fees and debt. This stance shifts the focus from victimization of migrant workers to their personal migration strategies. Workers might be aware of the precariousness migration entails, yet willingly accept periods of sacrifice in order to achieve their goals. Hence, fees are perceived as an investment on future opportunities, while debt is seen as 'not necessarily a force for ill – access to credit can allow people to effectively pursue their chosen ends, and does not automatically lead to their oppression'.[10] This approach does not ignore the vulnerable conditions under which indebted migrants live and work, but stresses the exercise of some degree of agency by migrants willingly choosing to endure such harsh conditions.[11] If based on informed decisions, migrants exercise a 'right to be exploited'.[12] In this sense, debt could be an instrument serving individual life projects and a promoter of migrants' social

[3] UNODC 2015, 14.
[4] Rijken 2015, 2018.
[5] Jordan 2011.
[6] Jureidini 2014, 4.
[7] Rijken 2015, 433.
[8] Farbenblum 2017, 156.
[9] Garcés-Mascareñas 2012, 69–71.
[10] Davidson 2013,190.
[11] Bastia & McGrath 2011.
[12] Szulecka 2012.

mobility: they can only hope that, in the end, their migratory experience provides the benefits that compensate all the adversities.

Recruitment Fees and Financing Methods: The Asian Experience

Recruitment Fees

ILO defines 'recruitment fees and related costs' as 'any fees or costs incurred in the recruitment process in order for workers to secure employment or placement, regardless of the manner, timing or location of their imposition or collection'.[13] This definition is guided by international labour standards and should be read together with the *General principles and operational guidelines for fair recruitment*.

According to the ILO,[14] recruitment fees include payments for recruitment services offered by labour recruiters, whether public or private, in matching offers of and applications for employment; payments made in the case of recruitment of workers with a view to employing them to perform work for a third party; payments made in the case of direct recruitment by the employer; or payments required to recover recruitment fees from workers. On the other hand, related costs, which are expenses integral to recruitment and placement within or across national borders, include medical costs; insurance costs; costs for skills and qualification tests; costs for training and orientation; equipment costs; travel and lodging costs; and administrative costs.

These costs weigh differently on the final bill charged to Asian migrant workers. Regionally, the most relevant component is agency commissions,[15] followed by transportation. However, in some countries such as Pakistan the cost of obtaining a work visa gains prominence due to 'visa market' specificities, which is based on the resale of work permits from the original holder to intermediaries and subsequently to migrants.[16]

Not all Asian migrants pay the same to get an employment opportunity. There are usually significant differences, namely:

i. *Level of skills*: The hiring of highly skilled and skilled workers usually follows an employer-paid model, while the recruitment of semi- and

---

[13] ILO 2019, §9.
[14] ILO 2019, §§9–12.
[15] According to a KNOMAD/ILO survey (Martin 2017), agency commissions account for nearly half of all recruitment fees paid by Indian migrants returning from Qatar and almost 75 per cent for those returning to Nepal.
[16] ILO 2016a.

low-skilled workers follows a worker-paid model. This difference disproportionately impacts workers who earn the lowest wages. Despite the typical distinction between high-skilled and low-skilled workers, there are also reported cases of skilled Asian migrant workers, namely Filipino health professionals migrating to Europe, being charged exorbitant recruitment fees and experiencing recruitment-induced indebtedness.[17]

ii. *Migration corridor*: Recruitment fees differ for workers from the same country migrating to different destinations, as well as for workers of different nationalities migrating to the same destination. The differences can be explained by: the distance between countries of origin and destination and the cost of airfare; the existence of regulatory caps on recruitment fees; the 'market value' of a working visa; the attractiveness of a destination country due to the wage levels, cost of living, or job opportunities; and the connection between agency commission and the salary earned, to mention a few. Furthermore, education, experience, and gender affect worker-paid costs within corridors: 'workers with more education or previous experience working abroad and women pay less than first-time male migrants who are not linked to migration networks'.[18] The reason is that experienced migrants are familiar with the required procedure and thus in a relatively better position to avoid paying inflated visa and agent's fees.[19]

iii. *Type of work/gender*: The recruitment fees charged for jobs usually earmarked for women (typically low-skilled and low-paid work) are lower than the fees charged for other types of work requiring higher skills (mostly performed by men). Female domestic work is paradigmatic: agency commissions are variable (rates are determined in terms of months of salary), which makes them necessarily lower than those for better-paid jobs performed by men; and fees are paid through salary deductions. The fact that female migrants do not pay recruitment fees upfront – the agent or the employer 'finances' recruitment fees by way of advancement loans, repayable through salary deductions[20] – means they can access migration relatively free from debt, while their male counterparts usually start their migration process with heavy financial burdens. Female migrants enter then into what has been described as 'relatively "silently" incurred forms of debt'.[21]

[17] Encinas-Franco 2016, 70.
[18] Martin 2017, 2.
[19] ILO 2016a, 24.
[20] Jureidimi 2014, 35.
[21] Platt et al. 2017, 120.

iv. *Migration channel*: The option between professional agents or informal mechanisms for migration also impacts recruitment fees. The latter encompasses intermediation services provided by networks of relatives, friends, or acquaintances acting as agents, sometimes returnees with knowledge of job opportunities abroad. Studies on the topic reveal conflicting findings. Research on Pakistani labour migrants[22] concludes that recruitment through informal channels is more expensive than through professional agents, which could be explained by the competition among recruitment agents, as well as by governmental monitoring efforts. However, studies on Indonesian migrants in Malaysia[23] and on migrants from Cambodia and Laos to Thailand[24] indicate that documented migrants (formal migration channel) tend to pay higher costs than undocumented ones. This can be explained by the substantial agency commissions both at origin and at destination, working visas, passports, and other required documentation. These higher costs in formal migration channels can 'give migrants an incentive to break the law and migrate informally to avoid fees associated with documentation and to avoid losing wages while waiting for migration paperwork to be processed'.[25] Nevertheless, considering that documented migrants tend to earn higher wages and benefit from better protection at destination, the net benefits from regular migration are still higher than from migrating through unofficial channels.[26]

Financing Methods

Asian migrants show a preference for financing migration within the household, through individual savings, liquidating personal or household assets (selling land, gold, jewellery, livestock), and borrowing money from household members. Despite this preference, migration is often financed through a combination of sources, including borrowing from friends, villagers, or relatives, from informal moneylenders, and from formal financial institutions.[27] Among the various sources of loans, the most prevalent is non-professional lenders, namely relatives and friends.[28]

---

[22] Ghayur 2016; ILO 2016a.
[23] World Bank 2017a, 40–42.
[24] Testaverde et al. 2017, 166.
[25] Testaverde et al. 2017, 165–166.
[26] World Bank 2017a.
[27] Varona 2013, 25.
[28] Sijapati et al. 2017, 14.

There are significant differences in loans obtained within the household and those obtained elsewhere. The former are often interest free or with low interest, easier to obtain and involving a 'relatively higher level of trust'.[29] Borrowing from professional lenders might be a viable solution, although it usually involves paying 'usurious interest rates'[30] to compensate the risk involved in collateral-free loans.[31] In contrast, using the formal financial system might be less expensive, as banks charge lower interest rates, but is not viable for the majority of migrant workers because they cannot satisfy the criteria for a secured loan.

The financing methods Asian migrant workers adopt show that recruitment fees are an economic selection mechanism. They exclude from migration those who do not have the necessary assets to finance it or have kinship relationships from which they can obtain funds. Owning property or belongings is therefore important to limit the financial impact of recruitment fees, whether to directly obtain part of the required funds or to be used as collateral for loans with lower interest rates. Without such assets, potential migrants pay high interest rates from moneylenders. Emigration becomes an economically viable solution mostly for the middle class that owns property that can be sold, pawned, or mortgaged. As recognized by the Work Bank,[32]

> [t]he poorest households may not be able to migrate because of the costliness on international migration. Indeed, there is evidence of an inverse 'U-shaped' relationship between migration and wealth, with the least wealthy households unable to finance migration and the wealthiest households unwilling to migrate because of the high opportunity costs of doing so.

The Cycle of Debt

In the context of temporary labour mobility, indebtedness is a product of contradictory economic and political factors going beyond the economistic view of 'push and pull' factors based on labour surplus and shortages,[33] which are noticeable both at origin and at destination.

---

[29] ILO 2016a, 23.
[30] Farbenblum & Nolan 2017.
[31] In Nepal, for instance, there were reported annual rates up to 50 per cent (Amnesty International 2017:27).
[32] Work Bank 2017b, 92.
[33] Pellerin 2015, 145.

Recruitment fees are determined by a system based on the interplay *of supply and demand*. In countries of origin, economic, social, and demographic conditions – unemployment and low salary levels, the concept of filial piety and the financial responsibilities it entails, the extended notion of family prevalent in Asian societies,[34] to name a few – create a high demand for jobs abroad with a significant and constant supply of undifferentiated workers. In this scenario, the competition to get a job placement in a country with a big wage differential raises the value of job brokers, reducing the bargaining power of workers. Those who are not willing or cannot afford to pay recruitment fees are easily replaceable by other workers who can pay them. Market forces also govern recruitment fees in destination countries. The supply of jobs, even in booming economies where workers are in high demand due to demographic imbalances and labour force idiosyncrasies, is easily matched with an even higher supply of workers. This prevents better working conditions for workers,[35] not only in terms of the total amount of recruitment fees but particularly in terms of access to working visas, a commodity with a market price.

The *economic interests of the recruitment industry* also shape debt. This industry involves a multitude of actors, from multinational companies to informal sub-agents acting at village level, all of whom want to be remunerated for their services. Unsurprisingly, they have been reluctant to accept tighter regulation attempting to curb recruitment fees. For instance, the adoption of Nepal's 'Free visa, free ticket' policy (2015) was received with distrust by the country's recruitment industry, with agents claiming that the policy was impractical for businesses, capped recruitment fees were too low, and fees should be determined by the market, not the government.[36] The industry's resistance to this policy reveals the relative strength of private economic interests in search of their businesses' profitability vis-à-vis the governments' political will to protect migrant workers. Moreover, the profits of moneylenders and 'loan sharks', even when considered illegal, are a forceful incentive to maintain the *status quo*. The same economic interests exist in countries of destination, as illustrated by the visa market operating in the shadows of sponsorship systems. A survey in Kuwait 'showed that large amounts were paid by workers for their visas, with the money going to Kuwaiti

---

[34] Afsar 2009.
[35] Surak 2013.
[36] Amnesty International 2017, 48.

citizens who have permission to recruit foreign workers, not the Kuwaiti government. Kuwaiti citizens sell permissions to recruiters in migrant-sending countries, and they in turn pass the cost on to workers.'[37] Individuals and companies thus have a vested interest to continue this profitable system, though highly detrimental to migrant workers' interests. Employers also want to recoup the expenses ('investment') incurred during the recruitment process,[38] which justifies maintaining restrictions on workers' labour mobility and their diminished bargaining power to negotiate recruitment fees and working conditions.[39]

The scope of *admission policies* has a significant impact on the financials of temporary labour migrants' recruitment: 'migrant indebtedness is in large part produced by the immigration policies pursued by states, and the systems of labour import and export they foster'.[40] Tightening access to a national labour market increases the value of such access, which entails higher recruitment fees. Similarly, when countries of destination implement tighter border controls, intensify deportation of irregular migrants, or apply stricter sanctions to employers hiring them, the outcome might be an increase, rather than decrease, in the flow of irregular migrants and might sometimes promote debt-financed migration.[41] Similar conclusions have been seen in different contexts: Gustafsson highlights the interdependence between legal and financial constraints to labour mobility and debt-bounded sexual exploitation and trafficking, as the trafficking organizations act as creditors in debt-financed irregular migration;[42] Czaika and Hobolth conclude that the deterrence effect of restrictive asylum policies is counterbalanced by an increase of irregular migrants, what is then called a 'deflection into irregularity'.[43]

The impact of migration policies on recruitment fees can also be witnessed in countries that worked to reduce the role of intermediaries. The South Korean experience seems to demonstrate that recruitment fees and debt can be curbed through state intervention. In this particular case, migration policies were designed towards a state-controlled system with a smaller role for intermediaries, resulting in worker-paid costs as a share

---

[37] Abella & Martin 2014, 10.
[38] Garcés-Mascareñas 2012, 75.
[39] Vlieger 2011.
[40] Davidson 2013, 188.
[41] Friebel & Guriev 2006.
[42] Gustafsson 2005, 58.
[43] Czaika and Hobolth 2014.

of earnings being lowest for migrants in South Korea when compared with other Asian destinations.[44] Similarly, capping recruitment fees or adopting 'no fees' policies in Nepal and the Philippines might prevent recruitment fees being fixed solely by capitalist labour markets, although with questionable practical results. Also questionable are the effects of specific policies aimed at protecting migrants, like age and gender bans or proscriptions on certain sectors or countries deemed not to respect migrant workers' rights or unsafe due to civil conflicts.[45] These well-intended measures might force people into informal migration channels where charges and vulnerability are higher.[46]

Lastly, the level of *legal protection* afforded to migrant workers impacts the risk of indebtedness they endure. A feeble legal protection leads to a submissive and malleable workforce,[47] unable to negotiate recruitment fees, and without the means to escape from recruitment-induced debt:

> The existence of the debt – and workers' urgent need to repay it – means that workers can more easily be manipulated by employers to accept lower wages than were promised by recruiters, poor working conditions, excessive work hours, or similar abusive practices. Debt-burdened migrant workers are also much more vulnerable to threats of deportation – and consequent loss of their earning potential – than workers with no debt obligations.[48]

Indebted migrant workers lose the ability to exercise the most basic right to leave an abusive or simply undesired working relationship. In this case, 'if quitting means being forced to return to the country of origin, the right to quit is meaningless to those who have heavily indebted themselves in order to migrate'.[49] In any case, recruitment-induced indebtedness curtails migrants' ability to strive, either individually or collectively, for better working conditions, particularly in jurisdictions where migrant workers are excluded from the full protection of labour law or prevented from forming and/or joining trade unions. The enhancement of legal protection afforded to migrant workers, whether at origin or at destination, can have a destabilizing effect – which is not necessarily undesirable – for international labour markets. However, it might increase the risk of 'supply-market shopping', inducing employers' search for cheaper

---

[44] Martin 2016.
[45] Oh 2016, 200.
[46] Ruhs 2013; Sijapati 2015.
[47] Surak 2013.
[48] UNODC 2015, 9.
[49] Davidson 2013, 183.

options among regional competitors, or jeopardizing the destination country's economic advantages if its economic and developmental models are grounded on low salaries and feeble labour rights for its (migrant) workforce.

The Principle of Free Employment: Divergences in International Law?

The principle of free employment is well established in international law, dating back to 1919 and the ILO's Unemployment Convention (No. 2) and the Unemployment Recommendation (No. 1). The prohibition on charging recruitment fees and related costs to migrant workers is best exemplified by ILO Convention No. 181 (Private Employment Agencies Convention, 1997), considered the most up-to-date instrument in this area[50] but without a significant number of ratifications among Asian countries, with the notable exceptions of Israel, Japan, and Mongolia. Pursuant to article 7(1), 'private employment agencies shall not charge directly or indirectly, in whole or in part, any fees or costs to works'. This prohibition applies to both domestic and international recruitment. A similar principle can be found in ILO standards on forced labour, namely the Protocol of 2014 to the Forced Labour Convention 1930 (ratified by only five Asian countries: Israel, Sri Lanka, Tajikistan, Thailand, and Uzbekistan), and the Forced Labour Supplementary Measures Recommendation, 2014 (No. 203). The Recruitment and Placement of Seafarers Convention, 1996 (No. 179) and the Maritime Labour Convention, 2006, also prohibit charging recruitment fees and related costs to workers, including migrants. In turn, the Domestic Workers Convention, 2011 (No. 189), which has been ratified in Asia by only the Philippines, bans deducting fees charged by private employment agencies from the remuneration of (migrant) domestic workers [article 15(1)]. In this respect, one can but wonder if the Convention No. 189 legitimizes charging recruitment fees to workers, as long as they are not deducted from wages, contrary to other instruments of international law. Most recently, the principle of free employment was consolidated in the document that approved ILO's definition of recruitment fees and related costs,[51] according to which

> [r]ecruitment fees or related costs should not be collected from workers by an employer, their subsidiaries, labour recruiters or other third parties

[50] ILO 2018, 8.
[51] ILO 2019.

providing related services. Fees or related costs should not be collected directly or indirectly, such as through deductions from wages and benefits [Appendix, II(6)].

Despite being a paramount principle, it is not without derogations. Article 7(2) of Convention No. 181 allows some exceptions, which shall be established, upon consultations, in the interest of the workers concerned and only in respect of certain categories of workers (such as artists, professional sportspersons, high-level professionals and executives), as well as specified types of services provided by private employment agencies (such as access to computer databases containing information about vacancies, specialized training services, or special employment-related services).[52] The same admissibility of exceptions is envisaged in the definition of recruitment fees and related costs. Whereas allocating recruitment fees to workers is prohibited, it is recognized that national legislation has the flexibility to allow workers to be charged costs related to the recruitment process. This possibility is subject to some conditions, including compliance with relevant international labour standards and tripartite consultations, as long as they are in the interest of the workers concerned; limited to certain categories of workers and specified types of services; and the corresponding related costs are disclosed to the worker before the job is accepted.[53]

The GCM followed the path towards prohibition. The signatory States commit to 'prohibit recruiters and employers from charging or shifting recruitment fees or related costs to migrant workers in order to prevent debt bondage, exploitation and forced labour' [§22(c)]. Though partially aligned with other international law instruments, the GCM has important consequences from what is (or not) written in its text. First, it seems to adopt an absolute prohibition, as it does not acknowledge the possibility of legitimate exceptions. Second, it establishes a direct link between the violation of the free employment principle and serious cases of labour and human rights abuses, namely debt bondage, exploitation, and forced labour.

The GCM, being 'the softest of soft law',[54] represents an authoritative, albeit non-binding, stance of the international community on the most compelling issues arising from migration. That is why the inflexibility shown in terms of exceptions to prohibiting charging recruitment fees to

---

[52] ILO 2018.
[53] Annex, II B (11).
[54] Newland 2019.

migrants, although ranking high in terms of principles, might be unrealistic since it does not accommodate the interests of the industry. Therefore, ILO's approach seems preferable as it provides some degree of flexibility in allocating to migrants the price of goods or services directly provided to them. One has to recognize that the legal provision for such exceptions entails a significant risk since national regulation might not comply with the narrow sense those exceptions have in international law. However, the flexibility provided by ILO standards, which appears absent in the GCM, could act in favour of migrant workers' interests if it induces the recruitment industry's compliance with the general principle of free employment. Recruitment agents would not charge migrants for agency commissions, but could immediately recoup the costs of some of the services provided. The above-mentioned negative reaction of the Nepalese recruitment industry to the 'free visa, free ticket' policy is an example of the importance of not antagonizing the economic interests of long-standing business models. One should consider the compromise of regulating the allocation of recruitment fees and related costs, prohibiting the former, and allowing some of the latter.

The link between recruitment fees and migrant workers' vulnerability should not, on the other hand, be broadened to the point of perceiving (indebted) migrants as *necessarily* victims of extreme cases of exploitation, in particular of debt bondage. Such linkage appears in the GCM and is frequently suggested in literature (see above). The concept of debt bondage helps explain serious cases where migrant workers 'become trapped in situations of bondage by borrowing money at exorbitant interest rates to pay recruitment fees or by taking an advance payment from intermediaries to secure work in the country of destination'.[55] However, the framing of a situation as debt bondage should be a matter of degree. It seems excessive and even counterproductive, due to the risk of stigmatization of workers and the reduction of opportunities for legal migration channels,[56] to suggest that all indebted migrant workers are performing bonded labour, i.e. are in a situation similar to slavery. These concepts should be reserved for the worst forms of exploitation, where the typical element of perpetual collateralization of labour is present. Cases where work is performed as repayment of a loan *and* the situation entails an endless cycle of servitude; where the value of work is not

[55] Bhoola 2016, 12.
[56] Jureidini 2014.

applied towards the liquidation of an artificial debt (manipulation of debt) and the length and nature of the service are not defined or such length is not reasonable.[57] Without diminishing the plight of migrant workers and the economic coercion they often endure, recruitment-induced indebtedness does not automatically turn them all into contractual or modern slaves. The GCM rightly calls the world's attention to some of the worst cases of abuses and the importance of fair recruitment to avoid them. However, it does it in a way that might end up 'victimizing people who should not be victimized'.[58]

Conclusion

Analysing the interrelation between recruitment fees, indebtedness, and the rights of migrant workers confirms that 'unchecked misconduct within the recruitment industry at home contributes to migrant worker vulnerability and exploitation abroad'.[59] Any attempt to address this issue should start with incorporating the employer-pay model in accordance with international standards. This requires a strong political will of governments and their constituencies, and its effectiveness greatly depends on the support of the recruitment industry and on a change of the perception of the benefits of labour migration. As addressed in the GCM, and before it in the UN General Assembly's New York Declaration for Refugees and Migrants (2016), it is important to internalize the idea that labour migration brings socioeconomic contributions in both countries of origin and destination. Eventually, this would even require a transformation of mentalities, not only in destination countries where migrant workers still represent a 'commodity' to be imported or re-exported, but also at origin where they are often seen as exploitable citizens whose main purpose is to support financially their families and national communities.

Besides political will and change of mentalities, the economic determinants of the current worker-pay model must also be addressed, particularly the interests of the myriad agents and subagents in being remunerated. This chapter has shown how recruitment fees and related costs are structured and has suggested that they should not be banned altogether. Questions remain regarding the scope of admissible

---

[57] Jordan 2011.
[58] Rijken 2018, 204.
[59] Farbenblum 2017, 158.

exceptions to the principle of free employment and the feasibility of reducing those exceptions through promoting ethical recruitment practices. Further research is needed on the role of commercial and economic incentives, such as certification programs of compliance or recruitment industry codes of practice, as well as on the ways of reducing the number of intermediaries in the recruitment process. Despite the push for implementing the employer-pay model coming from the GCM, Asian jurisdictions might use the ILO's framework and regulate a clear recruitment fee structure and determine which costs can be charged to migrant workers. In any case, any meaningful initiative addressing recruitment fees and indebtedness has to involve stakeholders at both ends of the migration process and adopt a rights-based approach capable of breaking the shackles of debt.

References

Abella, M. and Martin, P. (2014), *Migration Costs of Low-skilled Labor Migrants: Key Findings from Pilot Surveys in Korea, Kuwait and Spain* (draft), Global Knowledge Partnership on Migration and Development (KNOMAD), www.knomad.org/sites/default/files/2017-05/KNOMAD_TWG3_Report%20on%20Migration%20Cost%20Pilot%20Surveys%20May%2011_final%20%28002%29_1.pdf.

Afsar, R. (2009), *Unravelling the Vicious Cycle of Recruitment: Labour Migration from Bangladesh to the Gulf States*, Working Paper No. 63, International Labour Office.

Amnesty International (2017), *Turning People Into Profits: Abusive Recruitment, Trafficking and Forced Labour of Nepali Migrant Workers*, London: Amnesty International. www.amnesty.org/download/Documents/ASA3162062017ENGLISH.PDF

Andrees, B., Nasri, A. and Swiniarski, P. (2015), *Regulating Labour Recruitment to Prevent Human Trafficking and to Foster Fair Migration: Models, Challenges and Opportunities*, Geneva: ILO.

Arif, G. M. (2009), *Recruitment of Pakistani Workers for Overseas Employment: Mechanisms, Exploitation and Vulnerabilities*, Working Paper No. 64, International Labour Office.

Bastia, T. and McGrath, S. (2011), *Temporality, Migration and Unfree Labour: Migrant Garment Workers*, Manchester Papers in Political Economy, Working Paper No. 6.

Bélanger, D. (2014), 'Labor Migration and Trafficking among Vietnamese Migrants in Asia', *The Annals of the American Society of Political and Social Science*, 653(1): 87–106.

Bhoola, U. (2016), *Report of the Special Rapporteur on Contemporary Forms of Slavery, Including its Causes and Consequences*, Geneva: Human Rights Council, United Nations, Doc. A/HRC/33/46.

Cambier, G. (2012), *The Relation between Forced Labour and Trafficking in Human Beings*, Tilburg: Tilburg University, http://arno.uvt.nl/show.cgi?fid=128387.

Chee, Liberty L. (2015), *Power as Practice in Global Governance: Recruitment Agencies and Domestic Worker Migration in Southeast Asia*, Thesis submitted for the degree of Doctor of Philosophy, Department of Political Science, National University of Singapore.

Czaika, M. and Hobolth, M. (2014), *Deflection into Irregularity? The (Un)Intended Effects of Restrictive Asylum and Visa Policies*, International Migration Institute Working Paper No. 84, University of Oxford.

Davidson, J. O. (2013), 'Troubling Freedom: Migration, Debt, and Modern Slavery', *Migration Studies*, 1(2): 176–195.

Encinas-Franco, J. (2016), 'Promising Practices Emerging from the Recruitment Industry in the Philippines', in D. Calenda (ed.), *Case Studies in the International Recruitment of Nurses: Promising Practices among Agencies in the United Kingdom, India, and the Philippines*, Geneva: International Labour Organization, 63–89.

Farbenblum, B. (2017), 'Governance of Migrant Worker Recruitment: A Rights-Based Framework for Countries of Origin', *Asian Journal of International Law*, 7(1): 152–184.

Farbenblum, B. and Nolan, J. (2017), 'The Business of Migrant Worker Recruitment: Who Has the Responsibility and Leverage to Protect Rights?', *Texas International Law Journal*, 52(1): 477–496.

Frantz, E. (2013), 'Jordan's Unfree Workforce: State-Sponsored Bonded Labour in the Arab Region', *The Journal of Development Studies*, 49(8): 1072–1087.

Friebel, G. and Guriev, S. (2006), 'Smuggling Humans: A Theory of Debt-Financed Migration', *Journal of the European Economic Association*, 4(6): 1085–1111.

Garcés-Mascareñas, B. (2012), *Labour Migration in Malaysia and Spain: Markets, Citizenship and Rights*, Amsterdam: Amsterdam University Press.

Gardner, A., Pessoa, S., Diop, A., Al-Ghanim, K., Trung, K. L., and Harkness, L. (2013), 'A Portrait of Low-Income Migrants in Contemporary Qatar', *Journal of Arabian Studies* 3.1:1–17.

Ghayur, S. (2016), *From Pakistan to the Gulf Region: an Analysis of Links between Labour Markets, Skills and the Migration Cycle*, Islamabad: Deutsche Gesellschaft für Internationale Zusammenarbeit (GIZ) GmbH and International Labour Organization.

Goh, C., Wee, K. and Yeoh, B. S. (2016), 'Who's Holding the Bomb? Debt-financing Migration in Singapore's Domestic Work Industry', *Migrating Out of Poverty – Research Programme Consortium*, Working Paper 38.

Gustafsson, D. (2005), *Debt-financed Migration and Debt-bounded Sexual Exploitation: A Study from an Economic Perspective*, Master thesis, Department of Economics, University of Lund.

ILO (2015a), Fair recruitment in international labour migration between Asia and the Gulf Cooperation Council: realizing a fair migration agenda – labour flows between Asia and the Arab States, ILO Regional Office for Asia and the Pacific; ILO Regional Office for Arab States.

(2016a), *The cost of migration: what low-skilled migrant workers from Pakistan pay to work in Saudi Arabia and the United Arab Emirates*.

(2016b), *General principles & operational guidelines for fair recruitment*, International Labour Office, Fundamental Principles and Rights at Work Branch (FUNDAMENTALS); Labour Migration Branch (MIGRANT).

(2018), *Findings from the global comparative study on the definition of recruitment fees and related costs*, Background paper for discussion at the Tripartite Meeting of Experts on Defining Recruitment Fees and Related Costs (Geneva, 14–16 November 2018), International Labour Office, Conditions of Work and Equality Department.

(2019), *Report of the Meeting of Experts on Defining Recruitment Fees and Related Costs (Geneva, 14–16 November 2018)*, Governing Body, 335th Session, Geneva, 14–28 March 2019, (GB.335/INS/14/2).

IOM (2003), *Labour Migration in Asia: Trends, Challenges and Policy Responses in Countries of Origin*, Geneva: IOM.

Jägers, N. and Rijken, C. (2014), 'Prevention of Human Trafficking for Labor Exploitation: The Role of Corporations', *Northwestern Journal of International Human Rights*, 12(1): 47–73.

Jones, K. (2015), *For a Fee: The Business of Recruiting Bangladeshi Women for Domestic Work in Jordan and Lebanon*, Working Paper No. 2/2015, International Labour Office.

Jordan, A. (2011), *Slavery, Forced Labor, Debt Bondage, and Human Trafficking: From Conceptional Confusion to Targeted Solutions*, Center for Human Rights & Humanitarian Law Issue Paper 2, Washington College of Law, American University.

Jureidini, R. (2014), *Migrant Labour Recruitment to Qatar*, Report for Qatar Foundation Migrant Worker Welfare Initiative, Bloomsbury/Qatar Foundation Publishing.

(2016), *Ways Forward in Recruitment of 'Low-skilled' Migrant Workers in the Asia-Arab States Corridor*, ILO white paper, ILO Regional Office for the Arab States.

Jureidini, R. and Moukarbel, N. (2004), 'Female Sri Lankan Domestic Workers in Lebanon: A Case of 'Contract Slavery'?, *Journal of Ethnic and Migration Studies*, 30(4): 581–607.

Kara, S. (2017), *Modern Slavery: A Global Perspective*, Columbia University Press.
LeBaron, G. (2014), 'Reconceptualizing Debt Bondage: Debt as a Class-Based Form of Labor Discipline', *Critical Sociology*, 40(5): 763–780.
Lee, P. W. Y. and Petersen, C. J. (2006), *Forced Labour and Debt Bondage in Hong Kong: A Study of Indonesian and Filipina Migrant Domestic Workers*, Centre for Comparative and Public Law, Faculty of Law, The University of Hong Kong, Occasional Paper No. 16.
Lindquist, J. (2010), 'Labour Recruitment, Circuits of Capital and Gendered Mobility: Reconceptualizing the Indonesian Migration Industry', *Pacific Affairs* 83(1): 115–132.
Martin, P. (2016), 'Reducing Worker-Paid Migration Costs', in J. Howe and R. Owens (eds.), *Temporary Labour Migration in the Global Era: The Regulatory Challenges*, Hart Publishing: 377–392.
    (2017), *Merchants of Labor: Recruiters and International Labor Migration*, Oxford University Press.
Mantouvalou, V. (2016), 'Temporary Labour Migration and Modern Slavery', in J. Howe and R. Owens (eds.), *Temporary Labour Migration in the Global Era: The Regulatory Challenges*, Hart Publishing: 223–240.
Newland, K. (2019), 'The Global Compact for Safe, Orderly and Regular Migration: An Unlike Achievement', *International Journal of Refugee Law*, 20(20): 1–4.
Oh, Y. A. (2016), 'Oligarchic Rule and Best Practice Migration Management: The Political Economy Origins of Labour Migration Regime of the Philippines', *Contemporary Politics*, 22 (2): 197–214.
Pellerin, H. (2015), 'Global Foreign Workers' Supply and Demand and the Political Economy of International Labour Migration', in L. S. Talani and S. McMahon (eds.), *Handbook of the International Political Economy of Migration*, Cheltenham & Northampton: Edward Elgar Publishing, 145–166.
Platt, M., Baey, G., Yeoh, B. S., Choon, Y. K. and Lam, T. (2017), 'Debt, Precarity and Gender: Male and Female Temporary Labour Migrants in Singapore', *Journal of Ethnic and Migration Studies*, 43(1): 119–136.
Rahman, M. M. (2011a) *Recruitment of Labour Migrants for the Gulf States: The Bangladeshi Case*, ISAS Working Paper No. 132, National University of Singapore.
    (2011b), *Does Labour Migration Bring about Economic Advantage? A Case of Bangladeshi Migrants in Saudi Arabia*, ISAS Working Paper No. 135, National University of Singapore.
Rijken, C. (2015), 'Legal Approaches to Combating the Exploitation of Third-Country National Seasonal Workers', *The International Journal of Comparative Labour Law and Industrial Relations*, 31 (4): 431–452.
    (2018), 'When Bad Labour Conditions Become Exploitation: Lessons Learnt from the Chowdury Case', in C. Rijken and T. de Lange (eds.), *Towards*

a Decent Labour Market for Low-Waged Migrant Workers, Amsterdam: Amsterdam University Press, 189–206.

Ruhs, M. (2013), *The Price of Rights: Regulating International Labor Migration*, Princeton University Press.

Sijapati, B. (2015), *Women's Labour Migration from Asia and the Pacific: Opportunities and Challenges*, Issue in Brief No. 12, IOM Regional Office for Asia and the Pacific and the Migration Policy Institute.

Sijapati, B., Lama, A., Baniya, J., Rinck, J., Jha, K., and Gurung, A. (2017), *Labour Migration and the Remittance Economy: The Social-Political Impact*, Centre for the Study of Labour and Mobility (CESLAM).

Sobieszczyk, T. (2002), *Risky Business: Debt Bondage International Labour Migration from Northern Thailand*, Paper presented at the IUSSP Regional Population Conference on Southeast Asia's Changing Population in a Changing Asian Context, Bangkok.

Surak, K. (2013), 'Guestworkers: A Taxonomy', *New Left Review* 84:84–102.

Szulecka, M. (2012), 'The Right to be Exploited: Vietnamese Workers in Poland', in C. V. D. Anker and I. V. Liempt (eds.), *Human Rights and Migration: Trafficking for Forced Labour*, Basingstoke: Palgrave Macmillan, 161–192.

Testaverde, M., Moroz, H., Hollweg, C. H., and Schmillen, A. (2017), *Migrating to Opportunity: Overcoming Barriers to Labor Mobility in Southeast Asia*, Washington: World Bank Group.

UNODC (2015), *The Role of Recruitment Fees and Abusive and Fraudulent Recruitment Practices of Recruitment Agencies in Trafficking in Persons*, www.unodc.org/documents/human-trafficking/2015/Recruitment_Fees_Report-Final-22_June_2015_AG_Final.pdf.

Varona, R. (2013), *License to Exploit: A Report on the Recruitment Practices and Problems Experienced by Filipino Domestic Workers in Hong Kong*, Alliance of Progressive Labor (APL-SENTRO).

Verité (2012), *An Ethical Framework for Cross-Border Labor Recruitment: An Industry/Stakeholder Collaboration to Reduce the Risks of Forced Labor and Human Trafficking*, www.verite.org/wp-content/uploads/2016/12/ethical_framework_paper.pdf.

Vlieger, A. (2011), *Domestic Workers in Saudi Arabia and the Emirates: A Socio-Legal Study on Conflicts*, New Orleans: Quid Pro Books.

World Bank (2017a), *Indonesia's Global Workers: Juggling Opportunities and Risks*, The World Bank Office Jakarta, The World Bank Group.

(2017b), *Sustaining Resilience: East Asia and Pacific Economic Update (April)*, Washington, DC: The World Bank.

7

Pushing Out the Poor: Unstable Income and Termination of Residence

ANNETTE SCHRAUWEN

Introduction

The formal EU discourse presents free movement within the European Union as allowing EU citizens to improve their living and working conditions, promote their social advancement while participating in an efficient and flexible European labour market, and contribute to social cohesion within the EU.[1] The discourse on entitlements of EU citizens is almost the opposite of the discourse on migration from outside the EU.[2] Rights for migrants from outside the EU are granted or restricted according to the interests of the receiving Member States who control first access.[3] The receiving state may weigh the costs and benefits of immigrants based on their contribution to the economy, their impact on welfare distribution, on national identity and social cohesion.[4] Labour immigration from outside the EU is considered a potential threat to the nation-state that should be controlled, mainly by requiring specific skills or income.[5] Until recently, the European discourse on labour migration from outside the EU emphasized the need to attract high-skilled migrants to the EU.[6] The 2020 New Pact on Migration and Asylum presents a more comprehensive approach to labour migration by introducing Talent Partnerships as instruments to select and match labour

---

[1] Preamble recital 4 of Regulation 492/2011 on free movement of workers, OJEU L141/1 of 27.5.2011; preamble recital 17 of Directive 2004/38 on citizens' movement and residence rights, OJEC L158/77 of 30.4.2004.
[2] Boswell and Geddes 2011, 180.
[3] Ruhs 2013, 23.
[4] Ruhs 2013, 26.
[5] Boswell and Geddes 2011, 78–79 and 180.
[6] A European Agenda on Migration, COM(2015) 240 final of 13 May 2015, III.4 A new policy on legal migration.

immigration to skills needs in the EU, as part of the global race for talent, next to attracting high-skilled immigrants.[7] In contrast, the formal labour mobility framework for EU citizens does not include selection as a means to match labour migration to skills or as a means to control migration in order to protect national identity.

The distinction between 'beneficial' mobility by EU citizens and 'threatening' migration by TCNs increasingly gets blurred in high-level income Member States. Existing populations in receiving communities make few distinctions as to the nationality of new immigrants, especially when a rapid influx of migrant workers creates tensions in towns and cities because of pressure on public services (school places, hospital beds) and housing.[8] A 2017 study on relations between employers and employees within EU labour movement from eastern Member States in Austria, Sweden, and the Netherlands showed that employers in the field of low-paid work prefer workers having less knowledge about their rights, duties, and labour market position. Employers limit resources of information to be able to pay wages lower than those paid to national workers.[9] Where different services are combined in a labour contract, such as transport and housing, EU workers may become homeless when they lose their job. It makes EU workers vulnerable, while the receiving population perceives them as just another category of 'immigrants' who can be subject to exclusion.[10]

In the context of the economic crisis that started in 2008, concerns about intra-EU mobility became more prominent, in line with the general reflection that the benefits of immigration for employers and the labour market of the receiving society become more difficult to sustain in times of rising unemployment.[11] In receiving Member States, the economic crisis led to a cost–benefit framing of intra-EU mobility similar to the framing of immigration from outside the EU. This chapter explores how these concerns and blurring of the different frames have led to adaptations in national practices falling under the scope of the legal framework on intra-EU mobility. In particular, it looks at how claims for welfare benefits from EU citizens were connected with decisions on termination of lawful residence. The paradigm underlying immigration

---

[7] The New Pact on Migration and Asylum, COM(2020) 609 final of 23 September 2020, point 6.6 and 7.
[8] Collett 2013, 6; van Ostaijen 2017.
[9] van Ostaijen, Reeger, and Zelano 2017, 13.
[10] Barbulescu and Favell 2020, 151.
[11] Anderson 2010, 301.

law (at both national and EU levels) towards selecting non-EU migrants based on income and employment now permeates the framework of intra-EU mobility.[12]

Several authors have used the term 'earned citizenship' to describe the recent practices of linking EU citizens' welfare claims to termination of residence.[13] The term signals that EU citizenship, instead of an automatic right to membership based on residence, is transformed into a status to be earned as a result of fulfilling certain criteria, such as money and income, imposed on newcomers.[14] Others see the concerns on intra-EU mobility as a 'nativist' turn where a growing number of voters think that nationals should have priority in terms of jobs and welfare and conclude that a rethink of solidarity between EU citizens is necessary.[15] This chapter offers a third perspective: instead of focusing on the subjects of concern (the citizens that are not 'deserving') or the systematic failures (the lack of an underlying solidarity), it takes up the point that European states' immigration policies still 'hover undecidedly between perfecting the strategies for keeping out the huddled masses while laying out red carpets for the (...) skilled'[16] – irrespective of whether the masses and skilled are EU citizens or not.[17]

This chapter is structured as follows. First, it will address policy practices responding to concerns on EU free movement expressed during the economic crisis in the UK, Germany, and the Netherlands – the most vocal Member States in contesting free movement of persons in the EU.[18] It selects its sources mainly from existing research and case law on those practices. Though the UK has left the EU as of this writing, its policy towards intra-EU mobility is included here because it fits a wider trend in north-western Europe.[19] Examples from other Member States as reported in literature are included where relevant. These practices send out the message that low-income workers are not welcomed to stay on a more permanent basis. Subsequently, the chapter compares the policy

---

[12] See also Mantu, Chapter 11.
[13] Kramer 2016; Kramer 2020; Spaventa 2017.
[14] Kramer 2020, 52.
[15] Ferrera 2016; Sankari and Frerichs 2016; Schiek 2017.
[16] Joppke 2011.
[17] O'Brien 2016.
[18] In April 2013, the Ministers of the Interior of those three Member States plus Austria sent a letter to the Irish Council presidency asking for an urgent discussion of access to social benefit rights for recently arrived EU citizens, Council Document 10313/13; Ruhs 2017, 22; Heindlmaier and Blauberger 2017; Verschueren 2014, 148.
[19] Barbulescu and Favell 2020

practices to the EU regime for legal labour immigration from outside the EU. The chapter concludes with several remarks on the appropriateness of the notion of citizenship.

Tightening EU Citizens' Right to Work and Reside – the Selective Role of Earnings

In several (high-income) Member States, the key change in discourse about intra-EU free movement started 'somewhere between the onset of the economic downturn in 2008 and the end of the transitional restrictions on the employment of Romanians and Bulgarians in January 2014'.[20] The key change in national practices included the creation of precarious residence via a restrictive interpretation of a residence condition of 'sufficient resources' for economically inactive citizens and a higher income and/or working hours condition to qualify for residence rights as a 'worker'.[21] The concept of precariousness combines factors of instability, insecurity, lack of protection, and social or economic vulnerability.[22] The discourse accompanying the creation of precarious residence contests intra-EU mobility and includes portrayal of EU workers as 'abusers', 'welfare tourists', or 'poverty migrants'.[23] The debate took on a new dimension when politicians openly started to contest free movement within the EU, as noted by Mantu and Minderhoud.[24] Similar to what happens often in political and popular debates about migration, the wealthy are not imagined to be 'migrants',[25] and they are not considered to be 'abusers' of free movement either. The discussion seems to be about a 'conflated group' of mobile poor,[26] who are looking for work, engage in poorly paid work, are from poorer Member States, or are working under increasingly 'flexible' contracts that are on-call, zero-hours, short-time, temporary, or substitute.[27] Such contracts make it difficult to provide evidence of being a worker according to the CJEU definition, performing 'genuine and effective work that is not merely marginal and ancillary'.[28] The application

---

[20] Ruhs 2017, 24.
[21] Eggebø and Staver 2021 Chapter 8 in this volume; O'Brien, Spaventa, and De Coninck 2016, 63–65.
[22] Anderson 2010, 303.
[23] Mantu and Minderhoud 2016, 5–6.
[24] Mantu and Minderhoud 2016, 6.
[25] Anderson 2013, 73–74.
[26] Mantu 2017, 225–226.
[27] Gutiérrez-Barbarrusa 2016.
[28] Case C-66/85 *Lawrie -Blum* ECLI:EU:C:1986:284.

of increasingly higher financial thresholds for the qualification of 'EU worker' and the increased practice of non-standard employment relations result in precarious residence status, even for young, university-educated migrants.[29] What is more, nuisance and abuse arguments are used to terminate residence of EU citizens who do not meet the financial thresholds.

In the UK, where discontent on free movement was a prominent theme in the Brexit discussion, access to welfare benefits as well as the definition of who qualifies as a 'worker' under EU law is 'actively deployed as a mechanism for controlling the mobility of EEA nationals'.[30] In 2014, new rules were introduced that EU workers would be considered 'genuine workers' only if for the last three months prior to claiming supplementary benefits they have been earning at the level at which employees start paying National Insurance, equivalent to working 24 hours a week at minimum wage. A broader range of criteria would be taken into account in case they have some income, but not the minimum threshold. Furthermore, in order to qualify for a right to reside as jobseeker and being entitled to income-based jobseekers' allowance, they must live in the UK for three months and satisfy the Habitual Residence Test. They will be ineligible for housing benefits. Those who are economically inactive are not entitled to claim benefits at all.[31] The rules are drafted in such a way that compatibility with EU law is questionable.[32]

The rules in place since February 2017 and applicable until 1 January 2021 included the provision that EEA nationals or their family members had no initial right to reside for three months in the UK if they were 'an unreasonable burden on the social assistance system of the

---

[29] Simola 2020.
[30] Anderson 2015, 189. She signals that harsher conditions on access to welfare and the discourse accompanying it resulted in public excoriation of those who claim benefits 'that parallels the excoriation of migrants'.
[31] O'Brien 2016, 940 ff. For 2020 the income threshold is at £183 a week (£681 per month) for a continuous period of three months immediately before the date from which the benefit has been claimed, www.citizensadvice.org.uk/benefits/claiming-benefits-if-youre-from-the-EU/before-you-apply/check-if-you-have-the-right-to-reside-for-benefits/ (last visited 28 November 2020). Below the threshold, other elements can be taken into consideration, notably regularity of work, periods of work, whether work was intended to be short term or long term, number of hours worked, and income. However, O'Brien, Spaventa, and De Coninck 2016, 64–65, note that in several Member States citizens working below the thresholds in practice are quasi-irrefutably presumed not to qualify as workers.
[32] O'Brien, Spaventa, and De Coninck 2016, 75–76.

United Kingdom', so it seems they were effectively excluded from all benefits.[33] Furthermore, they might be removed from the United Kingdom.[34] If they attempted to enter the United Kingdom within twelve months after removal without being able to provide evidence that they do meet the conditions for a right to reside longer than three months, it was considered 'misuse of rights'.[35] An application that material circumstances have changed could be made to the Secretary of State, but only from outside the United Kingdom.[36] There was an increasing reliance on deportation and even detention of EU citizens for misuse of rights, as well as systematic removal of rough-sleepers, including EU citizens working in precarious jobs in the construction or hospitality sector where they might have been paid in cash.[37] Rough-sleepers were subject to re-entry restrictions for twelve months following their removal. In December 2017, the High Court ruled that consideration of rough sleeping, 'even accompanied by low level of offending such as begging, drinking in a public place and other street nuisances', does not lead to the conclusion that a person who otherwise satisfies the conditions for residence undermines the purposes of EU law and therefore abuses free movement rights. According to the Court, the UK policy 'appeared to circumvent the protections afforded to EU citizens by Article 27 [of Directive 2004/38], and to do so (in part) to serve economic ends.'[38] With Evans one could conclude that the UK policy emptied the content of both EU citizenship and free movement rights, and confined an entire category of EU citizens in a system of immigration control that should not be applicable to them before Brexit.[39]

In Germany EU citizens do not have to show they are workers or have sufficient resources in order to stay longer than three months. They only have to report their presence at the municipal registration office (Bürgerambt),[40] following which a registration certificate will be issued. According to the administrative guidelines of February 2016,[41] if EU

---

[33] The Immigration (European Economic Area) Regulations 2016, Regulation 13(3).
[34] Idem, Regulation 23(6) under a.
[35] Idem, Regulation 26(2).
[36] Idem, Regulation 26(5).
[37] Evans 2020.
[38] R(Gureckis) a.o. v. Secretary of State for the Home Department, [2017] EWHC 3298, para 96.
[39] Evans 2020, 320-321.
[40] Heindlmaier and Blauberger 2017, 1210.
[41] *Allgemeine Verwaltungsvorschrift zum Freizügigkeitsgesetz/EU*, GMBI 2016 nr. 5 of 18 February 2018, 86. These were still in use in 2020.

citizens claim a social benefit, the authorities may examine whether they have a right to reside, and the immigration authorities can decide, after examination of the individual circumstances of the persons concerned, that they no longer have a right to reside and must leave Germany. Accordingly, local welfare authorities assess the right of residence if social benefits are claimed, following which local immigration authorities may declare that there is no longer a right of residence – but that rarely happen in practice.[42] The amended Freedom of Movement Act/EU of 2014, however, provides that an exclusion order (entry ban) shall be issued against an EU citizen in very serious cases, in particular if the person repeatedly pretends that she fulfils the entry or residence requirements.[43] The legislator motivated this change by stating that such behaviour constitutes 'abuse of rights' under Article 35 of Directive 2004/38.[44] Furthermore, the 2014 amendments included a provision that jobseekers' right to reside is limited to six months, unless they can prove that they have a genuine chance to be employed. The 2016 administrative guidelines provide that a residence right can be lost before the period of six months has ended in case a person is not actively looking for a job, and that a 'genuine chance' of being engaged depends on qualifications of the person concerned and the situation on the German labour market. Neither the Freedom of Movement Act/EU nor the 2016 administrative guidelines provide a fixed amount that count as 'sufficient resources' or a fixed amount of weekly or monthly working hours that would qualify a person as 'worker'. In principle, EU citizens are supposed to have sufficient resources as long as they do not claim social benefits. If they do, the authorities may start examining their resources (excluding jobseeker's allowances). The amount of 'sufficiency' also depends on the regional levels of eligibility for social assistance. For the definition of worker the guidelines refer to the criteria the CJEU has given in its case law, notably in its 2010 judgment in Genc.[45]

The German Social Code (§ 7 SGB II and §23 SGB XII) simply denies jobseekers and economically inactive citizens access to social benefits. The EU Court of Justice has accepted this policy as compatible with EU

---

[42] Heindlmaier and Blauberger 2017, 1211
[43] §7 (2) third sentence of the Freedom of Movement Act/EU.
[44] Idem, 31; Bundestagsdrucksache 18/2581, 17.
[45] Case C-14/09, Genc EU:C:2010:57, mentioning the number of working hours, the level of remuneration, the right to days of paid leave, the continued payment of wages in the event of sickness, and a contract of employment which is subject to the relevant collective agreement.

law in its judgments in *Dano, Alimanovic,* and *García-Nieto.*[46] The combination of no access to social assistance and not withdrawing residence rights leads to EU citizens whose presence is tolerated with no access to minimum subsistence benefits. Arguably, persons working under flexible contracts in poorly paid jobs may find themselves in such precarious situations. A judgment of the German Federal Social Court in December 2015 triggered a debate on social benefits for EU citizens.[47] It ruled that the German policy to tolerate the presence in Germany of EU citizens who have no right to reside while denying them access to social benefits is not compatible with German law. The Federal Social Court found that the provision of the Social Code denying minimum subsistence benefits to foreigners who entered Germany in order to obtain social assistance or whose residence right arises solely out of the search for employment[48] could not be applied to those who, due to a lack of enforcement of the immigration authorities, stayed longer than six months in Germany. The Court ruled that the state then becomes responsible to ensure they can lead a life in human dignity.[49]

In October 2016, the German legislator adopted a bill to 'clarify' access to social benefits of EU citizens: those who are not lawfully resident in Germany can receive temporary benefits for the period until they leave the country – for a maximum of one month. They also can get a loan for a return ticket to their home country.[50] According to then Federal Labour Law Minister Nahles, the bill 'restores legal certainty' and is 'boosting confidence in the European ideal and one of its greatest achievements: the free movement of workers'. And it is 'protecting our municipalities from financial overstretch, as they have to shoulder the cost of social assistance benefits'.[51] These clarifications do not seem to help those in precarious, flexible, and poorly paid jobs. However, the underlying message is clear.

---

[46] Case C-333/13, *Dano* EU:C:2014:2358; Case C-67/14, *Alimanovic,* EU:C:2015:597; Case C-299/14, *García-Nieto,* EU:C:2016:114. See also Mantu 2021 Chapter 11 in this book.
[47] Bundessozialgericht, judgment of 3 December 2015, B 4 AS 44/15 R.
[48] SGB XII §23 Abs.1 S.1, S. 3.
[49] Bundessocialgericht, n. 55, para 56–57.
[50] SGB XII § 23, Abs. 1, S.1, S.3 and S.3a, amended by Article 2 – Gesetz zur Regelung von Ansprüchen ausländischer Personen in der Grundsicherung für Arbeitsuchende nach dem Zweiten Buch Sozialgesetzbuch und in der Sozialhilfe nach dem Zwölften Buch Sozialgesetzbuch of 22 December 2016, BGBl I 2016 S. 3155. The bill entered into force on 29 December 2016.
[51] See www.bmas.de/EN/Services/Press?recent-publications/2016/clarification-of-access-to-social-benefits.html

In the Netherlands,[52] the administrative guidelines indicate that the status of 'worker' in any case covers those who work at least 40 per cent of the usual full working time a month or earn more than 50 per cent of the usual social assistance level.[53] Individual circumstances need to be taken into consideration for those who do not meet the thresholds. Access to social assistance is linked to lawful residence based on EU law,[54] and is since 2004 regulated according to a 'sliding scale' – on the basis of periods of lawful residence, and periods, frequency, and amount of the claims for assistance. Over time, the sliding scale was subject to increasingly restrictive access to social assistance.[55]

The restrictions started with a 'narrative change' that turned 'migrant labourers' into 'labour migrants' taking place in the years before 2011.[56] In 2011, the new centre right government coalition presented an 'action package' that targeted migration from central and eastern Europe and focused on workers, jobseekers, the economically inactive, and students.[57] The tone in the package is that of 'increasing numbers', 'problems', 'exploitation', and 'fraud'. Subsequently it turned out that fewer EU workers from central and eastern Europe registered than previously presumed, and that there was not much 'welfare tourism'. The Minister stated that it was not a guarantee that it would not happen in the future, that 'bottlenecks caused by free movement of workers are certainly visible in society', and that although this is about 'a relatively small amount of people, it does not mean that the Cabinet will not put efforts to prevent a "honeypot effect" on the Dutch system'.[58]

Meanwhile, municipalities regularly denied social benefits to EU citizens because they saw the application of social assistance as 'proof' of their unlawful residence. On 18 March 2013, however, the Central Appeals Tribunal (the highest court in social security matters) ruled that municipalities, when deciding on allowances, may not refuse these allowances with the argument that recourse to social assistance is proof of the absence of the right to stay in the

---

[52] The author owes many thanks to Merel Huizer for her invaluable assistance in collecting case law and tracking the arguments used by policymakers and in administrative guidelines supporting the restrictive turn on residence rights for EU citizens at the lower end of the labour market.
[53] Aliens circular B.10/2.2.
[54] Articles 10 and 11 of the Aliens Law 2000.
[55] Kramer 2016, 285.
[56] van Ostaijen 2017, 127.
[57] Parliamentary Documents, TK 2011-2012, 29 407, Nr. 132.
[58] van Ostaijen 2017, 129-130.

Netherlands.[59] The Tribunal stressed that recourse to social assistance cannot automatically result in removal: the immigration authorities (IND) decide on the residence status and the municipalities decide on allowances. After the Tribunal's ruling the policy practice changed. Municipalities now signal to the IND those applicants for social benefits who have difficulty in providing evidence of their worker status or do not meet the sufficient resources requirement. The IND investigates the evidence and may terminate residence. Working instructions determine that non-contributory benefits of a Dutch partner are not considered for the sufficient resources requirement, which might put mixed-status families in a difficult position.[60] Residence terminations after notification from municipalities increased from 20 in 2012 to 620 in 2016.[61] In 2019 the Council of State, the highest administrative court in the Netherlands, ruled in three cases involving (family members of) EU citizens that never applied for social assistance but nevertheless were considered to lack lawful residence because they did not meet the sufficient resources or the sufficient income condition. The court in these cases concluded that the IND attached too much value to the reference criteria at the cost of considering individual circumstances.[62]

In the context of the 2011 action package a pilot on active removal policy started whereby EU citizens' recourse to homeless facilities was connected to a removal measure based on a sliding scale that links periods of residence to a maximum number of nights in a homeless shelter.[63] Next to that, the authorities focused on removal of rough sleeping EU citizens in a pilot named 'nuisance causing citizens'. Instances of rough sleeping, eating from a bin, public drunkenness, or shop thefts are compiled in a single file. An extensive file gives rise to a police hearing, with the possibility of the IND verifying whether there would be circumstances preventing a removal decision.[64] If not, a removal decision for lack of lawful residence follows where expulsion on public policy grounds under EU law conditions would not have been possible. In August 2019 the Council of State confirmed the policy practice of compiling a file followed by verification of financial means.

---

[59] Centrale Raad van Beroep, 18 March 2013, ECLI:NL:CRVB:2013:BZ3853, BZ3854, BZ3855, and 19 March 2013, ECLI:NL:CRVB:2013:BZ3857.
[60] Working instructions Union citizens WI2020/10, point 2.3.2; de Jong and de Hart 2021
[61] Kramer 2020, 214.
[62] ABRvS ECLI:NL:RVS:2019:2502, 2503 and 2504.
[63] Kramer 2017, 22–23; Parliamentary Documents TK 2011-2012 29 407 no. 118.
[64] Kramer 2017, 24.

However, in deciding on lawful residence, other individual circumstances should be considered next to the reference criteria.[65]

In contrast to Germany and the UK, the Netherlands does not refer to 'misuse' or 'abuse of rights' where EU citizens re-enter after removal on grounds of lack of legal residence. However, the Council of State has referred a preliminary question to the CJEU on whether Article 15 CRD allows a period of entry denial for EU citizens removed on grounds other than public policy, public security, or public health despite its explicit prohibition to impose a ban on entry.[66]

The short illustration above shows restrictive policies towards EU workers with a low or unstable income in the UK, Germany, and the Netherlands by way of raising thresholds on income and average working hours in national implementing law. As national practice does not always take into consideration individual circumstances, the raised thresholds have a disproportionate impact on atypical workers including already disadvantaged groups such as disabled workers, carers, and lone parents. A 2020 study on EU migrant atypical workers' rights in the UK shows the shortfalls in the EU definition of work and how it allows Member States to exclude atypical workers and simply ignore their economic contribution to the receiving society.[67] Raising thresholds for access to benefits and stricter enforcement of the link between residence rights and financial conditions for residence were found in all three Member States. They all signal a transformation of domestic policies and illustrate how Member States, in the absence of formal possibilities to limit EU citizens' access to their labour market, use 'strategic compliance'[68] or 'strategic non-compliance'[69] with, or 'manipulation'[70] of the free movement regime and 'containment' of Court rulings[71] on free movement to protect the national welfare system.

The European Commission is aware of non-compliant national practices, but noted as early as 2013 that it is difficult to tackle administrative practices via infringement procedures, especially where rules formally comply with EU law.[72] Not all affected persons will file individual

---

[65] ABRvS ECLI:NL:RVS:2019:2873.
[66] Case C-719/19, ECLI:EU:C:2021:506.
[67] Welsh 2020
[68] Kramer 2020, 277.
[69] Valcke 2020, 166.
[70] O'Brien 2016.
[71] Heindlmaier and Blauberger 2017.
[72] European Commission, *Impact assessment accompanying the document directive of the European Parliament and of the Council on measures facilitating the exercise of rights*

complaints or know that the practice is not compliant with EU law. The Commission's infringement priority criteria of systemic and serious breaches make it unlikely that individual complaints are followed up in a formal way. The rise of more informal problem-solving mechanisms at EU level, such as SOLVIT, aims at fast and pragmatic solutions for individual citizens on the basis of complaints. However, the informal and more individual nature of the mechanism is less appropriate to tackle structural practices of non-compliance. EU measures taken since 2010 to strengthen enforcement of free movement rules focus on information, contact points, and provision of legal remedies.[73] The willingness of certain Member States to go beyond a minimalist approach to implement can be questioned, as the Dutch authorities illustrate with their opinion that Directive 2014/54 did not require major adaptions in Dutch law and practice because the Netherlands already was doing a good job.[74] In the summer of 2019, the EU issued a Directive addressing flexible and atypical work by laying down minimum rights for transparent and predictable employment that apply to 'every worker in the Union who has an employment relationship in which pre-determined and actual working time is more than an average of three hours per week in a reference period of four consecutive weeks'.[75] The preamble of the Directive makes clear that atypical workers, including persons declared self-employed while fulfilling the conditions of an employment relationship, fall within the scope of the Directive as long as they fulfil the criteria of 'worker' as developed in the Court's case law. The directive does not concern access to social benefits. It remains to be seen whether the three-hour threshold will eventually influence national practices of assessment whether a person has the status of EU worker and the ensuing residence rights.

That said, the current deployment of the national legal definitions and financial conditions implementing free movement law as instruments to control and expel the poor resembles closely the system regulating labour immigration from outside the EU.

conferred on workers in the context of freedom of movement of workers SWD(2013) 149 final

[73] Directive 2014/54/EU of the European Parliament and the Council of 16 April 2014 on measures facilitating the exercise of free movement of workers in the context of freedom of movement for workers, *OJEU* 2014 L128/8.

[74] Minderhoud 2017, 63.

[75] Directive 2019/1152 of the European Parliament and of the Council of 20 June 2019 on transparent and predictable working conditions in the European Union, *OJEU* 2019 L 186/105, Article 1 (3).

Comparing Restrictions: Fewer Rights for 'Poor' EU and Non-EU Migrants

Where EU citizens *have the right* to work and reside in a Member State other than that of their nationality, TCNs are *granted permission* to enter the labour market of Member States. Legal labour migration from outside the EU is still a bastion of state sovereignty in the EU. Member States retain control over first admissions and are not forced in any way to issue work and entry permits. At the turn of the century, individual Member States started their attempts to attract high-skilled migrants, and the European Commission's Blue Card proposal of 2007 offering the possibility of accessing twenty-seven labour markets helped them in doing so.[76] The Blue Card Directive was supposed to be the EU's asset in the 'global race for talent'.[77] Persons granted permission to enter a Member State under this scheme can lose their residence permit if they become unemployed for more than three months, but if they continue to work for a period of five years they may acquire a long-term resident status.[78] On the other hand, Member States' need for temporary labour in seasonal activities is regulated by the seasonal workers directive. It allows Member States to admit workers from outside the EU without having to be concerned about a cost–benefit analysis. Indeed, the Directive[79] aims to 'regulate the admission of seasonal workers with a view to enhancing the EU's economic competitiveness, optimizing the link between migration and development, while guaranteeing decent working and living conditions for the workers, alongside incentives and safeguards to prevent overstaying or permanent stay'.[80] These workers cannot acquire a long-term resident status. The two Directives can be seen as a sign that the EU is heading towards a labour market where the underlying mechanism is selecting winners who can earn a permanent stay, while allowing low-paid workers only as long as there is a need for them.

The practices of the UK, Germany, and the Netherlands towards EU workers with a low or unstable income described above show a similar mechanism. The CJEU, in a very nuanced way, seemed to allow the

---

[76] Joppke 2008, Joppke 2011, 232.
[77] Directive 2009/50/EC on the conditions of entry and residence of third-country nationals for the purposes of highly qualified employment OJEU L155/17 of 18 June 2009.
[78] Directive 2003/109/EC concerning the status of third-country nationals who are long-term residents OJEU L16/44 of 23 January 2004.
[79] Directive 2014/36/EU on the conditions of entry and stay of third-country nationals for the purpose of employment as seasonal workers OJEU L94/375 of 28 March 2014.
[80] Peers 2015.

restrictive turn. First, in *Dano* the Court implied that the examination of an individual situation concentrates on the question whether a person fulfils the financial *residence* conditions of the Directive and not on the question whether a person is an unreasonable burden for the public finance of the host Member State.[81] Furthermore, the Court explicitly accepted the 'welfare magnet' or Dutch 'honeypot' argument in its ruling in *Alimanovic*.[82] One could see this as what Sassen indicates as 'microtransformation in the institution of citizenship'.[83] In the judicial construction of EU citizenship entitlements and free movement of workers, a turn is taken towards excluding those who are in low-paid temporary part-time jobs as beneficiaries of free movement – in contrast to initial case law on the concept of EU workers.[84] The economic arguments that underlie public debates on immigration and state power to send migrants back to where they came from, and distinctions made between high-level income and low-level income migrants, affect both intra-EU mobility and labour migration from outside the EU. A cost–benefit narrative erases the distinction between movement of EU citizens and migration from outside the EU.

Concluding Remarks

This chapter noted that the distinction in rights between economically stronger and high-income persons on the one hand and economically weaker and low-income workers that is present in the framework for EU labour migration from outside the EU can equally be found in national practices towards EU citizens, at least in those Member States that openly started to contest intra-EU labour mobility in 2013–14. The mechanism underlying national practices, denying low-paid or poor migrants residence and sending them back to their home state, makes the distinction between high-income and/or wealthy persons on the one hand and low-income and/or poor persons on the other significantly more relevant. That distinction might offer a better starting point to look at the complexities of movement of workers in *and* to the EU than the distinction between intra-EU mobility and labour migration from outside the EU.[85] EU citizenship has little or no relevance for EU citizens finding themselves in poverty or

---

[81] *Dano* para 69. For a more extensive analysis of this point Schrauwen 2016, 48.
[82] *Alimanovic* para 62.
[83] Sassen 2003.
[84] Case 139/85, *Kempf* EU:C:1986:223 para 15.
[85] Maas 2007, § 5.3.

in precarious jobs.[86] For them, it does not add much to what Brubaker describes as the 'embryonic institution' of national citizenship, notably to divide up between states the responsibility for the migrating poor, so that one state would not dump its poor on the territory of others.[87] The notion of earned citizenship is not adequate where it presumes the entitlements of EU citizenship are attainable for all. The restrictive practices towards EU workers ignore those who find themselves stuck in low-paid part-time jobs, are simply poor, or work in the informal economy. They are pushed out – out of the host State and de facto out of EU citizenship.

References

Anderson, Bridget. 2010. 'Migration Immigration Controls and the Fashioning of Precarious Workers'. *Work, Employment and Society* 24(2): 300–317.
  2013. *Us & Them. The Dangerous Politics of Immigration Control.* Oxford: Oxford University Press.
  2015. 'Heads I Win, Tails You Lose'. *Current Legal Problems* 68: 179–96.
Barbulescu, Roxanna and Adrian Favell. 2020. 'Commentary: A Citizenship without Social Rights? EU Freedom of Movement and Changing Access to Welfare Rights'. *International Migration* 58(1): 151–65.
Boswell, Christina and Andrew Geddes. 2011. *Migration and Mobility in the European Union.* The European Union Series. Basingstoke: Palgrave Macmillan.
Brubaker, Rogers. 1992. *Citizenship and Nationhood in France and Germany.* Cambridge, MA: Harvard University Press. eBook Academic Collection (EBSCOhost). At https://search.ebscohost.com/login.aspx?direct=true&db=e000xww&AN=282615&site=ehost-live&scope=site.
Collett, Elizabeth. 2013. 'The Integration Needs of EU Mobile Citizens. Impediments and Opportunities'. Migration Policy Institute Europe. At https://emnbelgium.be/sites/default/files/publications/mpieurope_-_integration_mobile_eu_citizens.pdf, accessed September 25, 2020.
de Jong, Judith and Betty de Hart. 2021. 'Divided Families and Devalued Citizens. Money Matters in Mixed-Status Families in the Netherlands'. In Tesseltje de Lange, Willem Maas, and Annette Schrauwen, eds. *Money Matters in Migration. Policy, Participation, and Citizenship,* Cambridge: Cambridge University Press.
Eggebø, Helga and Anne Staver. 2021. 'Follow the Money: Income Requirements in Norwegian Immigration Regulations'. In Tesseltje de Lange, Willem Maas,

---

[86] van Ostaijen 2017.
[87] Brubaker 1992, 69; Maas 2009; Maas 2021.

and Annette Schrauwen, eds. *Money Matters in Migration. Policy, Participation, and Citizenship*, Cambridge: Cambridge University Press.

Evans, Matthew. 2020. 'Abusing or Misusing the Right of Free Movement? The UK's Policy towards EU Nationals Sleeping Rough'. In Sandra Mantu, Paul Minderhoud, and Elspeth Guild, eds. *EU Citizenship and Free Movement Rights. Taking Supranational Citizenship Seriously* Immigration and Asylum Law and Policy in Europe, Volume 47 Leiden/Boston: Brill Nijhoff, 302–322.

Ferrera, Maurizio. 2016. 'The Contentious Policies of Hospitality: Intra-EU Mobility and Social Rights'. *European Law Journal* 22: 791–805.

Gutiérrez-Barbarrusa, T. 2016. 'The Growth of Precarious Employment in Europe: Concepts, Indicators and the Effects of the Global Economic Crisis'. *International Labour Review* 4: 478–508.

Heindlmaier, Anita and Michael Blauberger. 2017. 'Enter at Your Own Risk: Free Movement of EU Citizens in Practice'. *West European Politics* 40, no. 6 Routledge: 1198–1217.

Joppke, Christian. 2008. 'Comparative Citizenship: A Restrictive Turn in Europe?' *Law & Ethics of Human Rights* 2, no. 1 bepress, Walter de Gruyter GmbH: 6–41.

 2011. 'European Immigration Policies: Between Stemming and Soliciting Still'. In Erik Jones, Paul Heywood, Martin Rhodes, and Ulrich Sedelmeier, eds., *Developments in European Politics*, 2nd ed. Basingstoke/ New York: Palgrave Macmillan, 220–240.

Kramer, Dion. 2016. 'Earning Social Citizenship in the European Union: Free Movement and Access to Social Assistance Benefits Reconstructed'. *Cambridge Yearbook of European Legal Studies* 18: 270–301.

 2017. '"In Search of the Law": Governing Homeless EU Citizens in a State of Legal Ambiguity'. *SSRN Electronic Journal.* https://papers.ssrn.com/sol3/papers.cfm?abstract_id=3091539

 2020. *Earning Social Citizenship. Free Movement, National Welfare and the European Court of Justice.* PhD Thesis Vrije Universiteit Amsterdam.

Maas, Willem. 2007. *Creating European Citizens.* New York: Rowman & Littlefield.

 2009. 'Unrespected, Unequal, Hollow – Contingent Citizenship and Reversible Rights in the European Union'. *Columbia Journal of European Law* 15: 265–80.

 2021. 'Money in Internal Migration: Financial Resources and Unequal Citizenship'. In Tesseltje de Lange, Willem Maas, and Annette Schrauwen, eds., *Money Matters in Migration. Policy, Participation, and Citizenship.* Cambridge University Press.

Mantu, Sandra. 2017. 'Alternative Views on EU Citizenship'. In Carolus Grüters, Sandra Mantu and Paul Minderhoud, eds., *Migration on the Move. Essays on the Dynamics of Migration.* Leiden; Boston: Brill Nijhoff, 225–246.

2021. 'Women as EU Citizens: Caught between Work, Sufficient Resources, and the Market'. In Tesseltje de Lange, Willem Maas, and Annette Schrauwen, eds., *Money Matters in Migration. Policy, Participation, and Citizenship*. Cambridge University Press.

Mantu, Sandra and Paul Minderhoud. 2016. 'Exploring the Limits of Social Solidarity: Welfare Tourism and EU-Citizenship'. *UNIO-EU Law Journal* 2: 4–19.

Minderhoud, Paul. 2017. 'Free Movement of Workers: Some Reflections'. In Carolus Grütters, Sandra Mantu, and Paul Minderhoud eds., *Migration on the Move: Essays on the Dynamics of Migration Immigration and Asylum Law and Policy in Europe 42*, Leiden; Boston: Brill Nijhoff, 54–75.

O'Brien, Charlotte. 2016. 'Civis Capitalist Sum: Class and the New Guiding Principle of EU Free Movement Rights'. *Common Market Law Review* 53: 937–78.

O'Brien, Charlotte, Eleanor Spaventa, and Joyce De Coninck. 2016. 'Comparative Report 2015. The Concept of Worker under Article 45 TFEU and Certain Non-Standard Forms of Employment'. FresSco, European Union. Available via https://ec.europa.eu/social/main.jsp?pager.offset=10&catId=1098&langId=en&moreDocuments=yes

Peers, Steve. 2015. 'Ending the Exploitation of Seasonal Workers: EU Law Picks the Low-Hanging Fruit'. *EU Law Analysis Blog*. At http://eulawanalysis.blogspot.nl/2015/02/ending-exploitation-of-seasonal-workers.html, accessed 5 December 2020.

Ruhs, Martin. 2013. *The Price of Rights: Regulating International Labor Migration*. Princeton: Princeton University Press.

2017. 'Free Movement in the European Union: National Institutions vs Common Policies?' *International Migration* 55 Wiley-Blackwell: 22–38. Academic Search Alumni Edition.

Sankari, Suvi and Sabine Frerichs. 2016. 'From Resource to Burden: Rescaling Solidarity with Strangers in the Single Market'. *European Law Journal* 22, no. 6 Wiley-Blackwell: 806–821.

Sassen, Saskia. 2003. 'Citizenship Destabilized'. *Liberal Education* 89, no. 2 Association of American Colleges & Universities: 14–21. Academic Search Premier.

Schiek, Dagmar. 2017. 'Perspectives on Social Citizenship in the EU: From Status Positivus to Status Socialis Activus via Two Forms of Transnational Solidarity'. In Dimitry Kochenov, ed. *EU Citizenship and Federalism: The Role of Rights*. Cambridge: Cambridge University Press. At www.cambridge.org/core/books/eu-citizenship-and-federalism/perspectives-on-social-citizenship-in-the-eu-from-status-positivus-to-status-socialis-activus-via-two-forms-of-transnational-solidarity/A0E8612A8FEFA468F8EA8A472E970685, accessed 16 November 2020.

Schrauwen, Annette. 2016. 'Citizenship: A Balancing Exercise?' In Annette Schrauwen, Christina Eckes, and Maria Weimer, eds. At https://papers.ssrn.com/sol3/papers.cfm?abstractid=2835345, accessed 5 December 2020.

Simola, Anna. 2020. 'EU Citizenship as Precarious Status for Precarious Workers: Implications of National Policies Restricting EU Citizens' Rights for Young University-Educated EU Migrants in Brussels'. In Sandra Mantu, Paul Minderhoud and Elspeth Guild, eds., *EU Citizenship and Free Movement Rights. Taking Supranational Citizenship Seriously*, Leiden; Boston: Brill Nijhoff, 190–214.

Spaventa, Eleanor. 2017. 'Earned Citizenship – Understanding Union Citizenship through Its Scope'. In Dimitry Kochenov, ed. *EU Citizenship and Federalism: The Role of Rights*, Cambridge: Cambridge University Press, 204–225.

Valcke, Anthony. 2020. 'Expulsion from the "Heart of Europe": The Belgian Law and Practice Relating to Termination of EU Residence Rights'. In Sandra Mantu, Paul Minderhoud, and Elspeth Guild, eds., *EU Citizenship and Free Movement Rights. Taking Supranational Citizenship Seriously* Immigration and Asylum Law and Policy in Europe, Volume 47, Leiden/Boston: Brill Nijhoff, 155–189.

van Ostaijen, Mark. 2017. *Worlds between Words. The Politics of Intra-European Movement Discourses (Phd Thesis)*. Rotterdam.

van Ostaijen, Mark, Ursula Reeger, and Karin Zelano. 2017. 'The Commodification of Mobile Workers in Europe – a Comparative Perspective on Capital and Labour in Austria, the Netherlands and Sweden'. *Comparative Migration Studies* 5, no. 6: 1–22.

Verschueren, Herwig. 2014. 'Free Movement or Benefit Tourism: The Unreasonable Burden of Brey'. *European Journal of Migration and Law* 16, no. 2 Brill Nijhoff, sec. European Journal of Migration and Law: 147–179.

Welsh, Alice. 2020. *Vanishing Safety Nets, the Citizenship Illusion, and the Worker That Isn't: A Case Study of EU Migrant Atypical Workers' Rights in the UK*. York: University of York.

8

Follow the Money: Income Requirements in Norwegian Immigration Regulations

HELGA EGGEBØ AND ANNE BALKE STAVER

Introduction

In 2015, more than one million asylum seekers crossed into Europe, fleeing conflict in countries including Syria, Iraq, and Afghanistan. This unprecedented number of arrivals sparked a situation often referred to as 'the refugee crisis', as many European countries struggled to politically and administratively handle high numbers of asylum seekers. In the wake of the refugee crisis, many European countries introduced restrictive immigration policy measures in the areas of border control, asylum legislation, and procedures.[1] Moreover, the refugee crisis sparked restrictions in the regulation of immigration more broadly, particularly family migration.[2] Finally, the crisis led to changes in integration policies, some of which were also intended as indirect immigration control measures.[3]

The Norwegian government took the opportunity presented by this crisis to overhaul immigration and integration policies. In this chapter, we investigate two income requirements included in the crisis reform package: (1) The proposed extension of the general family migration income requirement to refugee sponsors, who were previously exempted. (2) The introduction of a new income requirement for permanent residence applicable to all refugees and migrants.[4]

We show how making money increasingly determines entry and long-term stay. Money is a tool of social stratification which stands in for ethnic, class, and gender inequalities – however, this is not immediately visible given its neutral veneer. When these underlying categorizations

---

[1] E.g. Brekke and Staver 2018; Gammeltoft-Hansen 2017.
[2] E.g. Bech, Borevi, and Mouritsen 2017.
[3] Hernes 2018.
[4] See also Eggebø and Staver 2020.

were laid bare by NGOs and government agencies participating in the public consultation process, the income requirement for refugee family reunification was discarded by a parliamentary majority. They found common cause because it had recently been raised to exceed entry-level pay in low-paid professions. With regard to the income requirement for permanent residence, however, the inherent inequalities in implementing such a 'price of membership' were not problematized to the same extent. When Parliament voted on the proposal, this measure was passed into law.

Norway has been at the forefront of the introduction of monetary instruments for regulating family migration. Thus, the Norwegian case provides a rich illustration of the role of money in migration, demonstrating the extent to which income requirements are complex and versatile tools to regulate migration. This chapter is based on discourse analyses of policy documents, more specifically the consultations, legislative proposals, law, and regulations introduced in Norway in the wake of the refugee crisis under the name 'Restrictions II'. We argue that these restrictions must be understood in a broader debate on the sustainability of the welfare state. In the following, we first present some previous research on migration regulations. Next, we present our methodological approach. This is followed by an analysis of the income requirement for family migration and the income requirement for permanent residence permits. Finally, we present conclusions and discuss findings.

Immigration and the Welfare State

The refugee crisis in 2015 reinforced disquiet about immigration in Europe along several dimensions, one of which taps into debates about the future of the welfare state. Public expenditure is expected to increase due to an ageing population, higher unemployment, and high expectations for services. For decades it has been argued that the welfare state in the current moment is in a form of crisis.[5]

In Norway, a particular focus of this debate on welfare state sustainability has concerned the labour market participation of immigrants, since the Nordic generous welfare model relies on near-full employment.[6] Since the end of the 1960–70s period of labour migration, non-Western immigrants have primarily come through the refugee and family immigration

---

[5] Kuhnle 1999.
[6] Brochmann and Hagelund 2011.

streams.[7] As opposed to the selected, highly skilled labour migrants that states sometimes even compete to attract,[8] these categories of migrants are more often viewed as a potential threat to the sustainability of the welfare state.[9] First, concerns arise about higher welfare dependency of refugees and family migrants, as compared to labour migrants and native-born workers. Second, concerns about the cultural integration of family migrants and refugees into host countries have been prominent. Poor integration, resulting in segregated societies, is assumed to undermine the solidarity and normative foundation underpinning modern welfare states.[10] Family migrants and refugees are more often portrayed as an economic and social problem placing unmanageable burdens on welfare budgets and services. Refugees have perhaps received the most attention among politicians and scholars, alongside labour migration, but since the beginning of the 2000s, there has been an increased interest in understanding the regulation of family migration.[11]

In the face of macro-level economic concerns about welfare state sustainability, micro-level incentives are a possible policy lever to encourage universal labour market participation which have also made their way into immigration regulation. For example, income requirements for sponsoring family migrants have been introduced in many European countries, and concerns about integration and welfare dependency have served as justifications for such financial measures.[12] Norway has the highest income requirement in Europe, followed by the UK, after sharp increases introduced in 2010 and 2012 respectively.[13] In Norway, improving integration, ensuring self-sufficiency, and preventing forced marriages were key arguments in favour of this requirement.[14]

Existing research documents that such income requirements may have indirectly discriminatory effects. Women, migrants from low-income

---

[7] Brochmann and Hagelund 2011.
[8] See Shachar 2006.
[9] See Bonjour and Duyvendak 2018.
[10] See discussion in Koopmans 2010.
[11] Eggebø and Brekke 2018.
[12] Eggebø and Brekke 2018; Staver 2015; Sirriyeh 2015.
[13] In 2017, the Norwegian requirement was an annual income of 26,500 euros, while in the UK it is 21,000 euros. In the UK, however, the requirement is raised by 4,300 euros for the first child and 2,700 for additional children. Thus, the UK requirement would be higher than the Norwegian one for sponsoring a partner and two children. Moreover, the UK requirement is probably the highest relative to income levels. These income levels are higher than what would be permitted under the EU Family Reunification Directive, but Norway and the UK are not bound by it.
[14] Eggebø 2010.

countries, ethnic minorities, and young people are most heavily affected due to their more marginal position in the labour market.[15] For example, recent analysis from the United Kingdom suggests that 'British working women are 30 percentage points less likely to earn enough to sponsor a non-EEA partner compared to males, while working British ethnic minorities are 7 percentage points less likely to earn enough compared to the British White group'.[16] As such, these regulations lead to a direct reduction in immigration by family migrants which fit the profile of low labour market participation.[17]

In the literature about restrictions on family migration there has been relatively limited focus on refugees, as they have been largely spared these restrictions. There is a small precedent in Norway, where there has been a widely held assumption that liberal family migration rules act as a pull factor for asylum seekers.[18] When Norway introduced an income requirement for family reunification for persons with permits on humanitarian grounds in 2003, it was intended to reduce the number of asylum arrivals as well as promoting labour market participation for sponsors.[19] In the intervening years the income requirement has – in addition to promoting integration, ensuring self-sufficiency, and preventing forced marriages – been seen as a tool to reduce asylum inflows.[20]

Based on similar assumptions, Sweden and Germany limited access to family reunification as a response to the refugee crisis in 2015, reverting to the minimum rules allowed under the EU Family Reunification Directive. Sweden introduced temporary permits with no right to family migration for persons granted subsidiary protection status as opposed to Convention Refugee status.[21] This represented a reversal of past Swedish policies.[22] Denmark also imposed a three-year restriction on access to family reunification for persons granted temporary protection status.[23] Since access to family migration is perceived as both a possible pull factor and an accelerant of existing asylum flows, the regulation of these two migration flows is intertwined.

---

[15] Kofman 2018; Sumption and Vargas-Silva 2018.
[16] Sumption and Vargas-Silva 2018, 64.
[17] Bratsberg and Raaum 2010.
[18] Staver 2014.
[19] Bratsberg and Raaum 2010.
[20] Staver 2014.
[21] Bech, Borevi, and Mouritsen 2017, 16.
[22] Barker 2017.
[23] Gammeltoft-Hansen 2017, 105.

Methods

In this chapter we investigate the role of money in immigration regulations. More specifically, we examine the proposal for new immigration regulations in the wake of the refugee crisis. We 'follow the money' and focus on two important financial requirements: (1) The income requirement for family migration and (2) the income requirement for permanent residence permits. We focus on the 2015–16 changes, but discuss them in relation to the historical development and previous changes to these financial measures.

We adopt an approach to public policy analysis developed by Carol Lee Bacchi,[24] which is often referred to by its key analytical question: 'what is the problem represented to be?' Asking this question leads one to investigate the implicit or explicit diagnosis of the problem that a given policy is designed to address. This diagnosis is contained in the legislation and in underlying documents leading up to it (consultations, policy papers, and other preparatory material). This is a form of discourse analysis in which we investigate dominant public discourses and arguments in favour of given policy solutions. These texts – in particular those by key stakeholders in the public consultation process, which is an important part of the Norwegian policymaking process – also reveal contestation and competing representations of the 'problem', which Bacchi encourages researchers to attend to. In line with this approach, we focus on how income requirements are developed in order to 'solve' the problems identified.

'Restrictions II': The 2015–16 Norwegian Immigration Reform

In December 2015, the Norwegian Parliament reached a political settlement about restrictions on migration. The arrival of more than 30,000 asylum seekers – a record number – had caused extensive political debate and a general political consensus that amendments to the immigration rules were necessary.

Shortly after, during the Christmas holidays, the populist right/conservative government presented a comprehensive proposal for changes to the Immigration Act.[25] The 150-page document was submitted for public consultations with a deadline of only six weeks – significantly shorter than the three-month norm – because the situation was perceived as an

---

[24] Bacchi 2009.
[25] Ministry of Justice and Public Security 2015.

unprecedented crisis that required immediate action. The proposal included restrictions on the regulation of asylum, family migration, permanent residence permits, unaccompanied minors, and changes in assessment procedures. It caused extensive public debate, and civil society mobilized broadly against it. In spite of the short deadline, 229 institutions, organizations, and individuals submitted responses, most highly critical of the proposed changes.

Following the consultation, the Ministry of Justice and Public Security published its formal law proposal in April[26] – with relatively minor amendments compared to the original document. This document was followed by the parliamentary committee's recommendations in early June 2016,[27] based on which Parliament passed changes to the Immigration Act. Many of the initial proposals, including one of the financial measures we analyse here, were ultimately defeated in Parliament.

The Income Requirement for Family Reunification for Refugees

Norwegian immigration legislation has contained an income requirement for family reunification since 1988. While it was initially applicable only for certain labour migrant sponsors, it has since 2003 successively been expanded to cover almost all sponsors, including Norwegian citizens. Refugees have, however, been exempted. Since 2010, the requirement has been fixed at approximately 26,500 EUR – which the sponsor must demonstrate to be earning both in the year of application and in the preceding year. The income requirement regulations also specify that those who have received means-tested welfare benefits the preceding year are disqualified regardless of their income. There has been some controversy over this requirement, and in particular its possible discriminatory effects, since decision-making statistics have revealed that rejection rates are higher for applications with a sponsor who is female, of minority background, or both.[28]

Throughout the period of expansion of the income requirement, from 2003 onwards, Convention Refugees were consistently exempted, as long as the application for family reunification was submitted within the first year (reduced to six months in April 2015). Their admission is

---

[26] Ministry of Justice and Public Security 2016.
[27] Innst. 391 L 2016.
[28] Eggebø 2013, 20–22.

based on protection needs and it has been widely understood that Norwegian obligations under the European Convention on Human Rights Article 8 would limit the restrictions placed on refugee family reunification. The assumption that refugees merit particular protections was almost entirely missing from the December 2015 consultation letter, and it was proposed that refugees should have to fulfil it just like everyone else. The income requirement was intended to 'ensure that the family is self-sufficient'; it was argued that these rules should apply generally, for a range of reasons: equal treatment, efficiency, that it would make the rules simpler, and that it would encourage integration.[29]

Through this application of the income requirement to *refugees*, the proposal departed sharply from previous decades of refugee and family reunification policies, and introduced a new logic of economic selection to an otherwise humanitarian and rights-based entry category. In the legislative proposal, the Ministry expressed deep concerns about the sustainability of the welfare state, since this new situation was characterized by high inflows of persons who were expected to have low labour market participation. The text was also inscribed into the general sense of crisis, where policymakers worried about the unprecedented inflows continuing over time. Thus, low labour market participation among refugees and high inflows are the two main 'problems' policymakers sought to address. Extending the income requirement to refugee sponsors was presented as a solution to both these problems: it would promote self-sufficiency through labour market participation and thus prevent welfare dependency, but also contribute to a lower inflow of asylum seekers in the first place through deterrence. Once refugees became cast as a macro-economic problem, they became subject to economic considerations also at the micro level.

There was strong mobilization against these proposed measures, with critical voices coming from governmental agencies, international organizations, and national stakeholders. Several agencies – including the Equality and Anti-discrimination Ombud, the Directorate of Integration and Diversity (IMDi), and the Directorate of Children, Youth and Family Affairs (Bufdir) – emphasized the particular challenges of immigrant women in the labour market. Many respondents questioned the assumption that the measure would improve integration, highlighting the damaging effects of family separation. They also questioned the legitimacy of

---

[29] Ministry of Justice and Public Security 2015, 73 [All translations are ours].

applying an economic logic to refugees, since their admission is based on protection needs.

In the April law proposal the Ministry conceded some terrain to these opposing voices, noting that 'family reunification is of significant importance for the wellbeing of refugees'.[30] In this way, it indirectly acknowledged competing representations of the problem which have to do with family separation. They continued, however, by noting that 'the significant inflow' of asylum seekers made it necessary to consider 'whether the current regulations are too generous', and argued that 'to require integration and self-sufficiency is very important in order to *ensure that immigration remains sustainable*'.[31] This was followed by a calculation of possible secondary migration of family members of asylum seekers, in order to quantify the scale of the 'problem'. As a concession to the many critics, they proposed shortening the requirement for four years of work or education in Norway to three years, while maintaining the proposed income requirement. They also proposed a three-year sunset clause for the new restrictions for refugees, that is the three-year rule and income requirement, 'in light of the present unpredictable situation'.[32] This was an oblique acknowledgement of the fact that the 'problem' which the entire proposal was responding to – the 2015 crisis – had been replaced by the lowest asylum inflow since 1997 by spring 2016.[33]

Unlike in the December 2015 consultation letter, the law proposal contained a fuller discussion of the international legal framework and the compatibility of the proposal with ECHR art. 8. Noting that the assessment relies on a weighing of the interests of the individual and society at large – through a proportionality assessment – the law proposal argued that the situation of high inflows of asylum seekers shifts the balance of this assessment as compared to earlier times. According to this logic, high inflows change Norway's international obligations with regard to family reunification, by shifting the result of the proportionality assessment.[34] The Ministry argued that introducing an income requirement for refugees was necessary in order to 'ensure that the Norwegian welfare and reception systems are not burdened beyond what is sustainable', specifying that the objective of the income requirement was 'partly to reduce the flow of asylum seekers to Norway and partly to ensure that

[30] Ministry of Justice and Public Security 2016, 86.
[31] Ministry of Justice and Public Security 2016, 86 [our emphasis].
[32] Ministry of Justice and Public Security 2016, 77.
[33] Tjelle 2016.
[34] Ministry of Justice and Public Security 2016, 89.

refugees and their family members are self-sufficient and integrated, and thereby do not become an economic burden on the Norwegian welfare system'.[35]

Around the same time as the publication of the proposal, the Ministry took a separate initiative to raise the income requirement from approximately 26,500 EUR to 32,000 EUR.[36] Since the actual income level is only specified in secondary legislation, this change was announced in a circular which did not mention refugees. By the time the proposal reached parliamentary committee, in June 2016, this separate change had an unexpected effect. All the opposition parties, that is Labour, the Socialist Left Party, the Liberals, and the Christian Democrats, suddenly found common cause in opposing these changes – centred specifically around the question of money. The newly increased income requirement of 32,000 EUR meant that one could now work full-time in the public sector and still not qualify for family reunification. This was unacceptable to Labour on the grounds of solidarity with workers, as the class dimensions of the proposal became obvious.

Furthermore, calculations carried out for the parliamentary committee concluded that only two out of ten refugees would make enough money after four years, and only half would make enough money after sixteen years in Norway. The opposition also highlighted the negative consequences for women, noting that 'spouses and children cannot come to Europe through family reunification, and will likely choose to undertake a long and dangerous journey'.[37] This assumption about the gendered impact of the proposal was shared by academic and civil society respondents. The Socialist Left Party noted that women might have particular difficulty meeting the requirement, referring to evidence that the new level was near the median income for women in Norway, and thus that nearly half of women earn less. It was therefore clear that such a requirement would have highly selective effects along lines of immigration category, class, and gender, and exclude many – if not most – refugees from family reunification.

In the end, a united opposition forced the government to not only shelve the income requirement for refugees, but also to reduce the general requirement back to its previous level. This unexpected

---

[35] Ministry of Justice and Public Security 2016, 89.
[36] In Norway, wages are negotiated between employers and employees, and there is no general minimum wage. In a few sectors, however, there are legally defined minimum wage levels; see the Norwegian Labour Inspection Authority 2019.
[37] Innst. 391 L 2016, 72.

parliamentary majority concluded that the income requirement should not exceed entry-level pay in low-paid professions, since this would encompass most immigrants and thus make it difficult for most to comply with – even if they succeeded in entering employment, which was ostensibly the problem intended to be solved. The failure of the proposed introduction of an income requirement for refugees was therefore ensured not due to the principle of refugees' right to family reunification – as had been the case in the past – but due to the actual *amount* of income required, which was deemed to be too steep. It was, thus, presented as a money matter more than a rights matter.

The Income Requirement for Permanent Residence

The law proposal included three new requirements for permanent residence: (1) a five-year waiting period, (2) passing a final test following the mandatory language and social studies course, and (3) a requirement for self-sufficiency, that is an income requirement. Increasing the waiting period from three years to five years had been previously proposed and debated,[38] and mandatory language tests to qualify for citizenship were introduced in 2015. The introduction of an income requirement for permanent residence, however, was an entirely new proposal that had never been expounded or debated earlier.[39] This requirement would apply regardless of the type of first residence permit, meaning it would apply to refugees as well.

The Ministry deemed it necessary to 'place further demands on the alien before such a [permanent residence] permit is granted', stressing that immigrants are expected to learn Norwegian, gain knowledge about Norwegian society, and be self-sufficient.[40] They argued, 'It is of utmost importance that immigration regulations encourage people to take up education and apply for work rather than passively receiving welfare benefits.'[41] Creating incentives and promoting integration served as the two main arguments for the new restrictions in access to permanent residence. The argument that immigration regulations serve to promote integration is widespread in European immigration policy.[42]

---

[38] NOU 2004:20 2004.
[39] See also Eggebø and Staver 2020.
[40] Ministry of Justice and Public Security 2015, 80.
[41] Ministry of Justice and Public Security 2015, 80–82.
[42] E.g. Charsley et al. 2020; Eggebø and Brekke 2018.

The proposal contained little detail about the income requirement for prospective permanent residents. It was only suggested that this new income requirement served the same purpose as the existing ones for family migration and labour migration, that is to ensure economic self-sufficiency as opposed to welfare dependency.[43] Rhetorically, this entirely new income requirement was presented as a logical extension of existing ones, thus understating the novelty of the proposal. As with the income requirement for family migration, it is laid down in general terms and only specified in secondary legislation. Thus, the actual level of income required was not up for debate, as it was only specified in a consultation letter the following year,[44] when the requirement had already been passed into law. With the exception of being marginally lower, it largely mirrors the income requirement for family reunification.

In the 2016 consultation, the income requirement for permanent residence was broadly criticized. Several organizations questioned the idea that the regulation would promote integration, noting that many migrants struggle to find a job, and may suffer from discrimination in the labour market. Thus, an income requirement for permanent residence would leave many people with temporary permits and insecurity for a long time and this would prevent integration rather than promoting it.

In Parliament, the income requirement for permanent residence did not face the same level of opposition as the income requirement for family migration for refugees. Most representatives stated that they supported the proposal's intentions of promoting integration, labour market participation, and self-sufficiency.[45] The Christian Democrats, the Liberal Party, and the Socialist Left party worried that the income requirement would lead to a situation of permanent temporary status for some refugees, and argued that such insecurity may lead to segregation and undercut a sense of belonging.[46] Nevertheless, the parliamentary opposition did not unite to oppose the income requirement for permanent residency as they had with the income requirement for family migration, not even for refugees.

This lack of opposition to the income requirement for permanent residence may be because another requirement for permanent residence permits, extending the three-year waiting period to five years, received far more attention. The three-year waiting period had been heavily

---

[43] Ministry of Justice and Public Security 2016, 136.
[44] Ministry of Justice and Public Security 2017.
[45] Innst. 391 L 2016, 96.
[46] Innst. 391 L 2016, 97.

criticized by the women's movement for decades. During the waiting period, marriage migrants lose their residence permit in case of divorce. This dependency leaves marriage migrants – who are predominantly women – in a subordinated position vis-à-vis the sponsor and makes them vulnerable to domestic violence. Thus, when the government proposed a five-year waiting period, a range of organizations mobilized to oppose the proposal. Their arguments were primarily related to the prolonged dependency of female marriage migrants.[47] On the basis of this massive opposition from organizations and institutions the parliamentary majority voted against the proposal.[48] The main argument was that such a proposal 'would pressure women who suffer from domestic violence to stay in the relationship because they fear losing the residence permit'.[49]

Notably, these arguments related to gender discrimination and domestic violence were not considered by the parliamentary committee when they discussed the income requirement for permanent residency.[50] This is somewhat puzzling since such a requirement would probably cause a much longer period of insecurity and temporary residency than a fixed five-year waiting period: calculations show that many refugees and family migrants will not obtain the necessary level of income after ten years of residence.[51] However, these numbers were not presented in the proposal, in the consultation process, or the Parliament. Contrary to the debate about the income requirement for family migration, the actual amount was not debated and no calculations were done in order to expose the possible consequences.

There are several possible explanations for why the income requirement for permanent residence was not opposed to the same extent as the extension of the income requirement for family migration and the five-year waiting period. First, this income requirement was a previously unknown measure presented as a part of a comprehensive 150-page document. Given the extent, magnitude, and novelty of proposals and the limited six-week consultation period, organizations and institutions probably had a hard time to consider every single proposal. The numerous NGOs opposing the proposal also had to pick their battles. The proposal for a five-year waiting period was an obvious one given its long-standing

---

[47] See summary in Ministry of Justice and Public Security 2016.
[48] Innst. 391 L 2016, 91.
[49] Innst. 391 L 2016, 91–92.
[50] Innst. 391 L 2016, 96–97.
[51] Eggebø and Staver 2020.

history of criticism from the women's movement. A second possible explanation may be the pervasiveness and versatility of financial requirement: it seems difficult to challenge the self-evident arguments that people who settle permanently in Norway must be self-sufficient in order for the welfare state to be sustainable.

Discussion

In this chapter, we have investigated how money matters in migration regulation by examining a policy proposal introduced in Norway in the wake of the 2015 refugee crisis. A dominant problem representation, put forward by the government, establishes the arrival of an unprecedented number of asylum seekers first and foremost as a challenge for Norwegian society. This narrative focuses on the macro-economic situation of the welfare state, its future sustainability, and the importance of labour market participation. These are issues relating to money in the broadest sense – namely public finances. This macro-economic problem, according to policymakers, could be solved through the introduction of one income requirement for sponsoring family members, and another one for permanent residence. These micro-level economic requirements function both as selection mechanisms and as incentives. The family migration income requirement both incentivizes the resident spouse to work in order to realize his or her right to family life, and indirectly screens out migrant spouses who may have 'poor prospects' in the labour market. The income requirement for permanent residence significantly raises the bar for permanent stay, insisting that new members fulfil the social contract of full employment and do not depend on welfare.

An alternative problem representation, brought forward by NGOs and some public institutions and members of Parliament, recasts the problem at the individual level, bringing attention to the concrete effects of such requirements on specific groups of migrants and refugees, for example women. In this way, they demonstrate the dimensions of difference which are obscured by the foregrounding of money. While these actors also focus on the importance of integration and labour market participation, they question the efficacy and legitimacy of these incentives. They highlight the fact that such regulations would effectively bar many migrants from access to family reunification and permanent residence, and emphasize the negative consequences that family separation and lack of secure legal status will have for individuals and families. They also highlight the existence of discrimination in the labour market that prevents people from working despite incentives and individual willingness to participate.

Of the two monetary migration regulation measures we have examined in this chapter, one proposal was adopted and the other was not. We believe that an explanation for these different outcomes can be identified by 'following the money'. The discussion related to the income requirement for permanent residence largely stayed in the domain of macroeconomics, emphasizing the concerns over the welfare state and budgets. The income requirement for family reunification started out as an argument at this level of analysis, but NGOs and public institutions in the hearing process, as well as some members of Parliament, foregrounded the individual rights and concerns of these migrants through a focus on gender, victimization, and vulnerability.

The debate highlighted the fact that the income requirement exceeded minimum wages for full-time employment in certain sectors, as were concrete projections of how many refugees would be denied family reunification. This led the opposition to conclude that the literal 'cost of admission' was too high. This same calculation and reflections on the actual consequences of the measure were not brought to the fore in discussions regarding the income requirement for permanent residence. Politicians – and to a certain extent stakeholders – accepted the principled argument that future permanent members of Norwegian society should have to contribute fully to it. By placing a price on becoming a permanent resident of Norwegian society, the income requirement for permanent residence thus mirrors the discussions around citizenship for sale (see Chapters 13–15). Indeed, only permanent residents can obtain citizenship in Norway. Thus, the income requirement effectively bars low-income refugees and immigrants from full membership even in the longer term.

As we have noted, the Norwegian income requirements are inscribed in a broader trend in European immigration policies where income requirements have become an increasingly important tool to regulate immigration. We have suggested that this trend should be understood in the context of a broader and longer debate about the sustainability of the welfare state. In the face of high immigration, even migrants who came for humanitarian reasons are required to demonstrate that they contribute to the overall macroeconomic performance of the state.[52]

---

[52] See also Bonjour and Duyvendak 2018.

Previous literature on family migration has pointed out the centrality of gender and ethnicity in family migration regulation, while more recent research has brought back an attention to class.[53] Our analysis suggests the importance of an intersectional perspective which is attentive to both, and reveals some of the plasticity of immigration regulation through financial requirements: at first blush, it is a neutral and objective way to distinguish between those who should enter (and stay) and those who should not, albeit one with clear class dimensions. It avoids explicit nationality, gender, or race-based categorization, which have been largely discredited or even prohibited in the modern era as unlawful forms of discrimination. However, it does not take much effort to uncover that income requirements may have ordering effects that are differentiated according to precisely those characteristics. In the case of the income requirement for entry, that process of uncovering – of following the money to see what it could do – took place, and there was attention to the consequences, e.g. for women. In the case of the income requirement for permanent stay, this did not happen, and there was no discussion about possible indirect discrimination or negative consequences. The economic arguments were taken at face value. This suggests the importance of careful analyses of such policy instruments and their effects, in line with, e.g., quantitative studies in the United Kingdom,[54] to understand mechanisms of inclusion and exclusion through financial tools, which are now firmly entrenched in Europe migration regulation.

References

Bacchi, Carol Lee. 2009. *Analysing Policy: What's the Problem Represented To Be?* Frenchs Forest, N.S.W.: Pearson Education.
Barker, Vanessa. 2017. *Nordic Nationalism and Penal Order: Walling the Welfare State*. Abingdon, Oxon.: Routledge.
Bech, Emily Cochran, Karin Borevi, and Per Mouritsen. 2017. 'A "Civic Turn" in Scandinavian Family Migration Policies? Comparing Denmark, Norway and Sweden'. *Comparative Migration Studies* 5, no. 1: 7.
Bonjour, Saskia and Jan Willem Duyvendak. 2018. 'The "Migrant with Poor Prospects": Racialized Intersections of Class and Culture in Dutch Civic Integration Debates'. *Ethnic and Racial Studies* 41, no. 5: 882–900.
Bratsberg, Bernt and Oddbjørn Raaum. 2010. 'Effekter Av Krav Om Forsørgelsesevne Ved Familiegjenforening'. 4/2010 Oslo: Ragnar Frisch

---

[53] Kofman 2018.
[54] Sumption and Vargas-Silva 2018.

Centre for Economic Research. www.frisch.uio.no/publikasjoner/pdf/rapp10_04.pdf
Brekke, Jan-Paul and Anne Staver. 2018. 'The Renationalisation of Migration Policies in Times of Crisis: The Case of Norway'. *Journal of Ethnic and Migration Studies* 44, no. 13: 2163–2181.
Brochmann, Grete and Anniken Hagelund. 2011. 'Migrants in the Scandinavian Welfare State'. *Nordic Journal of Migration Research* 1, no. 1: 13–24.
Charsley, Katharine, Marta Bolognani, Evelyn Ersanilli, and Sarah Spencer. 2020. *Marriage Migration and Integration*. Cham: Palgrave Macmillan Studies in Family and Intimate Life Palgrave Macmillan.
Eggebø, Helga. 2010. 'The Problem of Dependency: Immigration, Gender, and the Welfare State'. *Social Politics: International Studies in Gender, State & Society* 17, no. 3: 295–322.
    2013. 'The Regulation of Marriage Migration to Norway'. PhD dissertation, The University of Bergen. At https://bora.uib.no/handle/1956/6421, accessed 22 November 2016.
Eggebø, Helga and Jan-Paul Brekke. 2018. 'Family Migration and Integration: A Literature Review'. 4 NF-Report Bodø: Nordland Research Institute. At www.nordlandsforskning.no/getfile.php/1322503-1526993549/Dokumenter/Rapporter/1018/NF-report%204_2018.pdf.
Eggebø, Helga and Anne Staver. 2020. 'Mer Midlertidighet – Innvandringspolitikken Etter Asylforliket'. *Nytt Norsk Tidsskrift* 37, no. 2: 125–136.
Gammeltoft-Hansen, Thomas. 2017. 'Refugee Policy as "Negative Nation Branding": The Case of Denmark and the Nordics'. Fischer, K. and Mouritzen, H. (eds.), *Danish Foreign Policy Yearbook 2017*. Copenhagen: Danish Institute for International Studies, pp. 99–125.
Hernes, Vilde. 2018. 'Cross-National Convergence in Times of Crisis? Integration Policies before, during and after the Refugee Crisis'. *West European Politics* 41, no. 6: 1305–1329.
Innst. 391 L. 2016. 'Innst. 391 L (2015–2016) Innstilling fra kommunal- og forvaltningskomiteen om Endringer i utlendingsloven mv. (innstramninger II) [Recommendation from the Municipal and Management Committee concerning changes to the Immigration Act etc (Restrictions II)]'. At www.stortinget.no/no/Saker-og-publikasjoner/Publikasjoner/Innstillinger/Stortinget/2015-2016/inns-201516-391/, accessed 19 May 2018.
Kofman, Eleonore. 2018. 'Family Migration as a Class Matter'. *International Migration* 56, no. 4: 33–46.
Koopmans, Ruud. 2010. 'Trade-Offs between Equality and Difference: Immigrant Integration, Multiculturalism and the Welfare State in Cross-National Perspective'. *Journal of Ethnic and Migration Studies* 36, no. 1: 1–26.
Kuhnle, Stein. 1999. 'Survival of the European Welfare State'. *ARENA Working Papers Number 99/19*.

Ministry of Justice and Public Security. 2015. 'Høringsnotat – endringer i utlendingslovgivningen (innstramninger II) [Consultation brief – changes to the Immigration Act (Restrictions II)]'. At www.regjeringen.no/no/doku menter/horing-endringer-i-utlendingslovgivningen-innstramninger-ii /id2469054/, accessed 19 May 2018.

    2016. 'Prop. 90 L (2015–2016) Endringer i utlendingsloven mv. (innstramninger II) [Immigration Bill Restrictions II]'. At www.regjeringen.no/no/doku menter/prop.-90-l-20152016/id2481758/, accessed 27 August 2017.

    2017. 'Høringsbrev – endringer i utlendingsforskriften – krav om selvforsørgelse for rett til permanent oppholdstillatelse [Consultation memorandum – changes to the Immigration Regulations – requirement of self-reliance for a right to permanent residence]'. At www.regjeringen.no/no/dokumenter/ horing-endringer-i-utlendingsforskriften–krav-om-selvforsorgelse-for-rett- til-permanent-opphold stillatelse/id2545453/, accessed 19 May 2018.

Norwegian Labour Inspection Authority. 2019. 'Minimum Wage'. At www .arbeidstilsynet.no/en/working-conditions/pay-and-minimum-rates-of-pay /minimum-wage/, accessed 26 April 2019.

NOU 2004:20. 2004. 'Ny Utlendingslov [New Immigration Act]'. Norwegian Official Report 2004:20 Arbeidsdepartementet.

Shachar, Ayelet. 2006. 'Race for Talent: Highly Skilled Migrants and Competitive Immigration Regimes'. *NYUL Rev.* 81: 148.

Sirriyeh, Ala. 2015. '"All You Need Is Love And\pounds 18,600": Class and the New UK Family Migration Rules'. *Critical Social Policy* 35, no. 2: 228–247.

Staver, Anne. 2014. 'From Right to Earned Privilege? The Development of Stricter Family Reunification Rules in Denmark, Norway and the United Kingdom'. PhD thesis, University of Toronto.

    2015. 'Hard Work for Love – The Economic Drift in Norwegian Family Immigration and Integration Policies'. *Journal of Family Issues* 36, no. 11: 1453–1471.

Sumption, Madeleine and Carlos Vargas-Silva. 2018. 'Love Is Not All You Need: Income Requirement for Visa Sponsorship of Foreign Family Members'. *Journal of Economics, Race, and Policy* 2, no. 1: 62–76.

Tjelle, Irina. 2016. 'UDI: Laveste asylankomster til Norge på 19 år'. *NRK.no*, July 5, Online edition. At www.nrk.no/norge/udi-laveste-asylankomster-til-norge- pa-19-ar-1.13027939, accessed 22 August 2018.

PART II

Participation

9

"This Is Affordable!" The Role of Money Matters in the Use of Live-In Migrant Care Arrangements

ANITA BÖCKER, MARÍA BRUQUETAS-CALLEJO, VINCENT HORN, AND CORNELIA SCHWEPPE

Introduction

Care arrangements in which migrants care for elderly people on a live-in basis are a growing phenomenon in various European countries. Such live-in migrant carer (LIMC) arrangements were first observed and are still most widespread in southern Europe, where long-term care (LTC) for the elderly has remained largely a family responsibility and families sought ways to reduce their burden. Countries with more extensive public LTC provision have only recently seen the emergence of LIMC arrangements. The development of these transnational care arrangements thus seems to be related to the specific national LTC regime.[1]

LIMC arrangements in southern Europe tend to be in breach of labour and social law regulations and often also of immigration rules. This irregularity makes the arrangement affordable for a broader group of families and is therefore tacitly accepted by policymakers.[2] However, both the quality of the working conditions and the quality of the care may be endangered, in particular where the care worker does not have the right to stay in the country.[3]

This chapter explores how money and financial considerations translate into the emergence and use of LIMC arrangements in two western European countries with different LTC regimes: Germany and the

---

[1] Bettio, Simonazzi, and Villa, 2006; Da Roit, 2010; Da Roit and Weicht, 2013; Österle and Bauer, 2012; Theobald, 2011; Van Hooren, 2012.
[2] Ambrosini and Triandafyllidou, 2011.
[3] Anderson, 2012.

Netherlands. It combines a governance approach and a coping-strategies approach to explore, on the one hand, how the two countries' LTC regimes – in particular policies aimed at ensuring the fiscal sustainability of the LTC system – have provided incentives for, and shaped the modes of employment of LIMCs and, on the other hand, how families in both countries decide on entering into an LIMC arrangement and choosing a specific – less or more law-compliant – employment mode against the backdrop of the respective LTC regimes. We are particularly interested in how family carers cope with having to balance cost considerations against the need to ensure fair working conditions for the LIMC and good-quality care for their dependent relative.

The chapter is based on interviews with key informants (including managers of LIMC placement agencies) and users of LIMC arrangements in the two countries. The interviews were conducted as part of a research project on the emergence and significance of transnational care arrangements in Germany and the Netherlands.[4] These two countries were chosen for their different LTC regimes. One of the aims of the project was to study the relation between national LTC regimes and the occurrence and characteristics of LIMC arrangements.

The chapter is structured as follows. The two sections that follow use a governance approach to describe the LIMC arrangements in Germany and the Netherlands. Section 2 briefly discusses relevant notions from the existing literature on LTC regimes and the demand for migrant care workers. Section 3 describes and compares the prevalence and characteristics of LIMC arrangements in Germany and the Netherlands and how these have been influenced by the national LTC regimes. Section 4 uses a coping-strategies approach and is based on our interviews with family carers in both countries. It analyses how their decisions and choices are influenced by money matters. The conclusion combines the results of the governance approach and the coping-strategies approach and evaluates and compares the relative role of financial considerations in the emergence and use of LIMC arrangements in Germany and the Netherlands.

---

[4] The ESTRANCA (Emergence and Significance of Transnational Care Arrangements) project was financed by the German Research Foundation and the Netherlands Organisation for Scientific Research in the framework of the Open Research Area (ORA) programme.

Long-Term Care Regimes, the 'Baumol Effect', and the Demand for Migrant Carers

LTC involves a variety of services which support the needs of people with chronic illnesses or disabilities that affect their ability to perform activities of daily living on their own. LTC systems in European countries are typically a mix of state, family, and market services.[5] However, the division of costs and responsibilities differs from country to country. National LTC systems can be placed on a spectrum with informal care–led regimes at one end and service-led regimes at the opposite end. Informal care–led regimes are characterized by a heavy reliance on family carers and limited state responsibility for LTC. The family is responsible for providing care or buying private professional care services; the state may then subsidise some of the financial cost. Public care services are accessible for people in need only if their family cannot provide care or pay for private care services. In countries with service-led regimes, by contrast, the LTC mix is dominated by public or publicly funded services. The responsibility of the family has been reduced through the implementation of universal rights to public in-kind care services for people in need regardless of their family circumstances. Most LTC systems fall somewhere in between these extremes and the trend, moreover, appears to be towards convergence.[6] Another nuance is that service-led systems differ in the way care services are provided. Services may be provided directly by the state (social-democratic welfare systems) or the state may outsource them to private providers (liberal welfare systems). The Dutch LTC regime can be described as a (predominantly) service-led system in which care services are increasingly outsourced to private providers; the German LTC regime can be characterized as a (predominantly) informal care-led system.

Both informal care-led and service-led LTC systems are facing strains due to population ageing, changing family structures, and the increased labour market participation of women, who traditionally provide the bulk of informal care. The provision of LTC depends on high labour inputs. In the formal LTC sector, labour productivity gains are practically impossible because technological innovations can only partly replace human care workers. The sector can be seen as suffering from 'Baumol's cost disease': wages in the sector tend to rise in line with wages in sectors with higher productivity gains – because if they don't,

[5] Bettio and Verashchagina, 2012.
[6] Anderson, 2012; Pavolini and Ranci, 2008.

the jobs in this sector will be avoided by anybody who has alternatives – leading to increasing labour costs per unit of output.[7]

As has been argued by Sciortino and Finotelli, it is almost impossible to escape Baumol's cost disease in a closed system, and that is where labour immigration comes in.[8] Hiring migrant care workers who are willing to accept wages that are not acceptable to native workers is a way to escape the Baumol effect. Migrants may be willing to accept lower wages because the pay is still better than for jobs in their country of origin and/or because they are barred from other, better-paid jobs in the host country due to discrimination or because of their immigration status.[9] According to Sciortino and Finotelli, there are signs of a growing demand for migrant care workers even in countries with social-democratic systems. They conclude that 'the demand for foreign care workers is not an occasional pathology but rather a structural feature of contemporary welfare states, a resource to be taken into account in any debate about its future'.[10]

The Baumol effect explains why many countries have a demand for migrant care workers, but it does not provide insight in what happens at the micro level. How do families with elderly members with increasing care needs decide on employing an LIMC and on how to employ her? What role do financial considerations and concerns play in these decisions and in the day-to-day management of the care arrangement? How are financial considerations reconciled with other concerns, particularly the migrant carers' working conditions and the quality of the care? Our chapter thus contributes to the literature by focusing on families as employers of migrant care workers.

Financial Incentives and Barriers in the German and Dutch LTC Regimes

LIMC arrangements have become widely used in Germany. A recent estimate is that between 100,000 and 300,000 elderly Germans are cared for in their own home by LIMCs.[11] Nearly all the LIMCs are women from Poland and other Central and Eastern European (CEE) EU member states. It is estimated that more than half, perhaps even 90 per cent of

---

[7] Baumol and Bowen, 1966; Baumol, 2012; Mosca et al., 2017; Sciortino and Finotelli, 2015.
[8] Sciortino and Finotelli, 2015
[9] Cf. Van Hooren, 2012.
[10] Sciortino and Finotelli, 2015, 202–203.
[11] Arend and Klie, 2017.

them are employed directly by families – nearly always on an informal basis.[12] A minority are hired through private LIMC placement agencies. These agencies have partner companies in CEE countries which may either act as employers and send the care workers to Germany under the EU Posted Workers Directive[13] or just recruit the care workers and send them to Germany as self-employed workers.

In the Netherlands, LIMC arrangements are a recent and still very small-scale phenomenon. Our estimate is that less than a thousand elderly Dutch are cared for by LIMCs, nearly all of whom are women from CEE EU member states.[14] Unlike in Germany, the LIMC market in the Netherlands is based to a large extent on the activity of private placement agencies. Similarly to their counterparts in Germany, most agencies have partner companies in CEE EU member states, and the LIMCs are often employed as posted workers. Direct recruitment and employment by families are rare and we have not found cases of employment on a purely informal basis in the Netherlands.[15]

The differences in the use of LIMC arrangements in Germany and the Netherlands cannot be explained by different labour immigration policies and programmes. In the years before the 2004 and 2007 EU enlargements, Germany implemented a recruitment programme for *Haushaltshilfen* (home helps) from CEE countries to ease the burden on families with members in need of care, while the Netherlands experimented with a bilateral agreement to recruit Polish nurses to work in care homes. However, neither programme was successful.[16]

The different size and characteristics of the LIMC markets in Germany and the Netherlands can be explained to a large extent by the national LTC regimes.

The German LTC regime is characterized by a relatively high level of family responsibility for LTC, a strong preference for home-based care, a relatively low level of public LTC expenditure, and the availability of relatively unregulated cash-for-care benefits. These characteristics have favoured a growing reliance on LIMCs.[17] The German LTC insurance

---

[12] Krawietz, 2014; Emunds, 2016; Stiftung Warentest, 2017.
[13] Directive 96/71/EC of the European Parliament and of the Council of 16 December 1996 concerning the posting of workers in the framework of the provision of services, OJL 18, 21 January 1997.
[14] Cf. Van Grafhorst, 2014; Da Roit and Van Bochove, 2017.
[15] Cf. Da Roit and Van Bochove, 2017.
[16] De Lange and Pool, 2004; De Lange, 2007; Lutz, 2009; Lutz and Palenga-Möllenbeck, 2010; Theobald, 2012.
[17] Böcker, Horn and Schweppe, 2017; Da Roit and Le Bihan, 2010; Theobald, 2011.

scheme has from its beginning promoted the use of cash-for-care benefits (*Pflegegeld*). Although these cash benefits are relatively low (max. 901 euros per month) as compared to the costs of in-kind benefits, 80 per cent of the LTC insurance beneficiaries opt for cash benefits.[18] The cash benefits are paid directly to the dependent person and their use is left to the recipient's discretion. They are often used to pay family members or other informal carers. The strong preference for (relatively low) cash benefits has helped to maintain the fiscal sustainability of the German LTC insurance scheme.[19] However, the cash benefit scheme has also been criticized for reinforcing traditional gender roles and for creating a grey or black market for irregularly employed (migrant) care workers.[20] German politicians and public authorities have tacitly accepted the semi-legal nature of many LIMC arrangements. The role of the German state has been characterized as one of complicity: 'knowing and pretending ignorance at the same time; acting officially in a restrictive way, while tacitly accepting the violation of self-made rules.'[21]

Compared to the German regime, the Dutch LTC regime is characterized by a high level of public expenditure and a lower level of family responsibility for LTC, high use of in-kind benefits and other publicly funded care services, and a stronger preference for formal care services.[22] Cash-for-care benefits ('personal care budgets') were a late addition to the Dutch LTC insurance scheme. They were introduced primarily to give more freedom of choice to LTC insurance beneficiaries. The Dutch personal care budgets are much more generous (on average amounting to 3,400 euros per month) than the German cash benefits, but their use is tightly regulated and controlled. Beneficiaries have to draw up a budget plan stating what care services they intend to buy from which care provider(s) and they must sign a contract with each care provider. The Social Insurance Bank then pays the care providers out of the beneficiary's budget. Unlike the German cash benefits, the Dutch personal care budgets have not resulted in cost containment. A recent study found that they have rather increased the total cost of LTC as they 'appeal to a group of people who would not have applied for care (in-kind) if they had not had the option of having their own budget'.[23] However, most LTC

---

[18] BMG, 2017.
[19] Nadash et al., 2012.
[20] Da Roit and Le Bihan, 2010; Nadash et al., 2012; Österle and Hammer, 2007.
[21] Lutz and Palenga Möllenback, 2010, 426.
[22] Böcker, Horn, and Schweppe, 2017; Mot, 2010.
[23] Mosca et al., 2017, 201.

insurance beneficiaries still opt for in-kind benefits. In 2018, only 6 per cent of LTC recipients aged 65 and over had a personal care budget.[24]

In conclusion, the development of a large, and to a large extent grey, LIMC market in Germany can be seen as an effect of the strong preference for home-based care, the relatively low level of public LTC expenditure, the availability of relatively unregulated cash benefits, and the toleration of the often irregular nature of LIMC arrangements by politicians and public authorities. In the Netherlands, the emergence of a still very small LIMC market can be seen as an unintended side effect of policies aimed at ensuring the financial sustainability of the LTC system. Over the last decades, Dutch policymakers have pursued policies to reduce the use of residential care (for example by raising user charges) and promote home-based care arrangements.[25] These reforms have moved the Dutch system in the direction of the German system and have been perceived as opportunities by entrepreneurs who saw a market for LIMC arrangements. Placement agencies in the Netherlands advertise that the costs of an LIMC arrangement can be paid from the client's personal care budget. However, the Dutch cash benefits remain tightly regulated and the trend is towards more, not less, controls. This explains why a grey LIMC market is less likely to develop in the Netherlands.

Money Matters in Families' Decision-Making Processes

Cash benefits can be used by governments to contain the costs of LTC. Although Germany is more clearly a case in point than the Netherlands, both countries have set the level of LTC cash benefits below the cost of in-kind LTC services. Families are thus compelled to develop their own strategies to contain the costs of dependent family members' care packages. In this section, we turn to the decision-making processes of families that make use of LIMC arrangements. As we will see, using an LIMC arrangement may in itself be a cost-containment strategy. We successively analyse the role of money and financial considerations in the decision to enter into an LIMC arrangement, the choice of a specific employment mode, and decisions that may have to be made

[24] CBS Statline, Monitor langdurige zorg, Personen met gebruik Wlz-zorg; leveringsvorm, zorgzwaartepakket, https://mlzopendata.cbs.nl/#/MLZ/nl/dataset/40065NED/table?dl=4339D (accessed 18 June 2020), own computations.

[25] The term 'residential care' refers to long-term care given to elderly people who do not stay in their own home or family home, but in a care home or nursing home.

subsequently, for example, when the care needs of the care recipient increase. In all these decisions, cost considerations may have to be balanced against considerations about the quality of the care and the LIMC's working conditions.

This section is based on our interviews with family carers in Germany and the Netherlands. The interviews were conducted between May 2016 and March 2018. We interviewed 27 family carers who had arranged an LIMC arrangement for an elderly relative, 14 in Germany and 13 in the Netherlands. In most cases, the family carer was a son or daughter of the elderly care recipient. While the socio-economic profiles of the German respondents varied considerably, the majority of the Dutch respondents were highly educated and employed full-time. Recruiting respondents was difficult in both countries, although for different reasons. In the Netherlands, the main obstacle was that LIMC arrangements are still rare, so that snowballing was of little use. Most respondents were recruited via LIMC placement agencies. In Germany, the main obstacle was the respondents' reluctance to participate because their LIMCs were working undeclared. In both countries, all LIMCs came from CEE EU member states. In Germany, the majority came from Poland. In the Netherlands, the majority came from Slovakia. Most of the care recipients were men or (more often) women in their seventies or eighties. Most of them needed continuous supervision and help with activities of daily living.

The Decision to Enter into an LIMC Arrangement

When the care needs of an elderly dependent increase to the point that they need continuous care or supervision, family carers are faced with the challenge of reconciling availability, acceptability, and affordability.

The parents or spouses of our respondents suffered from conditions such as dementia, Parkinson's disease, old-age frailty, or a combination of these. Most family carers responded to their dependent's increasing care needs by organizing a mix of formal home-based care and informal (family) care. Residential care was rejected by them because it was not compatible with their (or their dependent's) preference for a more personalized and holistic model of care. In Germany, the high user charges were another important reason to avoid residential care.

Coming to the point when their parent or spouse needed continuous care or supervision, family carers in both countries were faced with the problem that regular home care services providers cannot provide 24/7 care – at least not at an affordable price. Family carers in the Netherlands were disappointed to discover that the Dutch LTC insurance offers neither 24/7 home care services in kind, nor cash benefits that are high enough to buy 24/7 care services from regular home care providers. Many were advised to move their parent or spouse to a care home. In Germany, family carers who contacted home care services providers discovered that 24/7 home-based care would be even much more expensive than residential care.

As they found regular 24/7 home care services to be 'unaffordable' or 'certainly not sustainable in the longer run', family carers in both countries searched for alternative care arrangements, which had to be affordable as well as compatible with their (dependent's) care preferences. They found that an LIMC arrangement could fulfil both requirements. Family carers in Germany learnt about this possibility through various channels, including neighbours and friends as well as 'trust intermediaries', i.e. family doctors, social service departments in hospitals, regular home care services providers, or other persons or organisations endowed with moral or professional authority.[26] In the Netherlands, LIMC arrangements are much less known. Most of our Dutch respondents discovered this possibility by searching the internet and landing on the websites of LIMC placement agencies. Several Dutch family carers related how relieved they were to find out that an LIMC arrangement would not only meet their dependent's care needs and preferences, but was also affordable.

The Choice of a Specific LIMC Arrangement

In combination with the preference for home-based care, affordability is an important motive in the decision to enter into an LIMC arrangement. However, the costs of LIMC arrangements vary and depend, among other things, on how the migrant carer is employed, whether she (or he) is hired through an agency, and on her (or his) skills and qualifications. For example, an EU worker arrangement costs more than an arrangement with posted or self-employed workers, and care workers who have formal nursing qualifications or who speak the client's language cost more than care workers who do not have such skills or qualifications. Users can thus to a certain extent adapt the costs of the arrangement to what they are able and willing to pay.

---

[26] Cf. Ambrosini, 2015.

Many of our German respondents hired their relative's LIMCs directly and on an informal basis. These respondents often pointed out that hiring through an agency would be much costlier. For some families, employing their LIMCs informally, i.e. undeclared, was the only affordable option. Families who hired their LIMCs through a German placement agency tended to have larger financial resources. They opted for hiring through an agency because it ensured continuity of care (replacement of the case worker in case of illness, during holidays, etc.) and a higher degree of legality. Instead of using an agency in Germany, families may directly use an agency abroad. One family carer reported that she hired her dependent's LIMC through an agency in Slovakia because she did not want to support the 'greedy' business model of German placement agencies. Another family carer reported that she initially hired through an agency in Romania, which sent the LIMC as a 'self-employed' worker to Germany. The respondent was not happy with this employment mode, she was afraid of the family's reputation in the village, and therefore decided to employ the LIMC regularly, as *Haushaltshilfe*. Interestingly, in some cases, the employment mode had been determined by opportunity rather than by the family carer's choice. Recommendations by neighbours, relatives, or friends led to the decision to employ a specific LIMC, with the family carer accepting the mode of employment chosen by this care worker or the agency through which she worked.

In the Netherlands, nearly all respondents hired their relative's LIMCs through a placement agency. Initially, they simply were not aware of other possibilities. Later on several Dutch respondents considered the possibility of hiring the LIMCs directly. They found the margin between what the agency charged them and what the carers earned excessively large and calculated that they could lower their costs as well as offer the carers better pay by circumventing the agency and entering into direct negotiations with the LIMCs. However, most of them decided against it because the agency ensured continuity and because they dreaded the administrative burden. Moreover, they did not want to become employers. As one family carer explained, 'As a family, we are just a buying party, we have a budget with which we buy care [. . .], but we do not employ anybody.' When LIMCs are hired through an agency, the mode of employment is determined by the agency. However, several family carers had consciously looked for an agency that offers its LIMCs good working conditions and/or a Dutch employment contract. They said they preferred to pay a higher fee rather than making use of LIMCs who are employed abroad.

Cost considerations may thus also weigh heavily in the choice of a specific employment mode. Having sufficient financial resources enables care recipients and their families to reconcile affordability with a higher degree of legality. This holds true for families in both countries. However, as the Dutch LTC insurance scheme provides higher levels of benefits than the German one, private resources tend to be a more decisive factor in Germany than in the Netherlands.

The Day-to-Day Management of the LIMC Arrangement

In both countries, LTC insurance cash benefits can be (and are) used to pay at least part of the costs of the LIMC arrangement. However, as the German LTC cash benefits are lower than the Dutch ones, German users are faced with larger gaps between their cash benefits and their care costs.

In the Netherlands, the costs of the LIMC arrangement were in some cases covered completely by the dependent's cash benefit. In Germany, by contrast, all users had to draw upon private resources to cover the costs of the LIMC arrangement. In both countries, the actual amount and proportion paid by the users depended on the choices they made, both with regard to the specific LIMC arrangement (the mode of employment and the skills and qualifications of the migrant carer) and with regard to buying additional care services to relieve the migrant carer or themselves.

Generally, sons and daughters did not have problems with using their parents' savings to pay for the LIMC arrangement and other care services. They tended to say that it was their parents' money and that they found it important that their parents' care needs and preferences were met. Some of them added, however, that they were not prepared to contribute towards their parents' care costs with their own money. Several sons and daughters in the Netherlands noted, moreover, that the LTC insurance scheme should have covered all the costs. Our Dutch respondents tended to hold the state responsible for the provision of LTC for the elderly. Their German counterparts rather seemed to accept their having to draw upon private resources as a fact of life, though a few of them did state that the state should bear a larger part of the costs of LTC for the elderly.

As stated above, family carers have to contain the costs of their relative's care package, and using an LIMC arrangement may in itself be a cost-containment strategy. Additional strategies are developed in the day-to-day management of the care package. Several family carers related in detail how they managed to 'stretch' their relative's cash benefit. For example, one family carer asked her mother's LIMC to take her weekly day off on a weekday, as respite care services would be more expensive on weekend days. Another strategy to keep the care package affordable is to constantly make make-or-buy choices. Our interviews showed that LIMC arrangements are nearly always supplemented by informal care and sometimes also by formal care services. Family carers often replace the LIMC during her weekly day off. This allows them to achieve two goals in one strike: saving costs and fulfilling their personal desire to spend time with their relative. Of course, having sufficient financial resources enables care recipients and their family members to base their make-or-buy decisions not only on cost considerations, but also on quality considerations and personal preferences.

Financial resources may also play a role in maintaining or improving the quality of the LIMC arrangement. Respondents in both countries reported making gifts or extra payments to the migrant carers, for example when they temporarily returned home, to acknowledge their good work and to entice them to come back. In their role as care managers, family carers may also have to deal with requests for pay rises from their relative's LIMC. Care needs tend to increase over time, altering the balance between the LIMC's workload and pay. In such situations, respondents in both countries were inclined to pay more under the motto 'never change a well-functioning care arrangement'. Family carers in Germany tended to accept requests for pay rises from their irregularly employed LIMCs. They felt they were in the weaker position as they depended more on the LIMC than vice versa. In both countries, respondents who hired LIMCs through placement agencies negotiated with the agency about a pay rise for the LIMC. In the Netherlands, there were also respondents who had switched, together with the LIMC, to another agency, or who were considering such a switch in order to ensure the LIMC better pay. Family carers sometimes also negotiated other solutions with the LIMC. For example, one family carer whose mother started to keep the LIMC awake at night first tried to convince the LIMC to catch up on some sleep during the day. When the LIMC objected, the family carer decided to buy a few night shifts per week from a regular home care provider. She was able to pay for these shifts thanks to the fact that her mother's cash benefit had been raised.

In short, money continues to play a role after the decision to enter into an LIMC arrangement. It is a means to manage, maintain, and improve the quality of the arrangement.

Balancing Financial and Other Considerations

The literature on live-in migrant care workers sees the lack of controls as a weakness of LIMC arrangements. It would compromise both the quality of the care and the quality of the working conditions of the carers. Our interviews showed that family carers tend to downplay both dangers.

Respondents in both countries were aware that LIMCs are usually not trained nurses, but they did not think that the quality of the care is less, or less guaranteed, than with residential care or professional home-based care. Several respondents thought that the risk of errors and accidents is higher in care homes, where a patient is cared for by many different care workers. Moreover, most respondents adhered to a care ideal in which social and emotional aspects weigh more heavily than compliance with professional nursing standards.

Respondents in both countries also downplayed the danger of exploitation of LIMCs. They tended to see the LIMC arrangement as a win-win situation: the care recipient could stay in his or her familiar surroundings; the migrant carer earned much more than she could in her home country; and the family had an affordable solution for their relative's care needs. In both countries, only few family carers had moral problems with the LIMC being on call more or less around the clock while being paid on the basis of a 40- to 48-hour working week. Common justifications given were that the LIMCs do not work all the time, that they get free board and lodging, that they earn much more than what they could earn in their country of origin, and, as a Dutch family carer put it: 'That is what makes this arrangement affordable.'[27]

In short, family carers do not see affordability as incompatible with good care and fair working conditions. Nevertheless, in everyday reality, they are sometimes faced with challenges in reconciling these different aspects. Several Dutch respondents did have doubts about whether the agency through which they hired their relative's LIMCs complied with all relevant laws and regulations. They argued, however, that they were only buyers of care services and therefore could not be held responsible for ensuring a law-compliant employment mode. In their view, the

---

[27] See also Horn et al., 2019.

placement agencies have prime responsibility for the working conditions and the state should control the agencies. In Germany, family carers who hired their relative's migrant carers on an informal basis showed little concern about being detected and held responsible for violating labour and social security law regulations.[28] They nonetheless deployed various justifications for their resorting to an irregular arrangement. For one thing, they blamed the country's LTC regime, pointing out that the system would collapse if the authorities started to enforce labour and social security law regulations. For another thing, they diffused their own responsibility by pointing to the 'thousands of others' who were doing the same. In addition, they blamed LIMC placement agencies for being 'greedy'. One family carer explained that the migrant carer herself did not want to be employed on a formal basis, because it would reduce her net income by the income tax and social security contributions. However, the LIMC was present at this conversation and her reaction showed that this was perhaps not an adequate description of her preferences.

Family carers clearly see it as their first priority, and responsibility, to ensure that their dependent gets good and sufficient care. For respondents who hired their relative's carers through an agency, the price was not the most important consideration in choosing an agency and a specific LIMC arrangement. They were willing to pay more – provided, of course, that they had the means – for LIMCs who were experienced and who could communicate with their relative in his or her own language. Moreover, regardless of the mode of employment, family carers in both countries were prepared to accept requests for pay rises because they did not want to risk spoiling a well-functioning care arrangement.

Some family carers were also willing to pay more for fair and law-compliant working conditions. As mentioned, several Dutch respondents consciously looked for a placement agency that offers its LIMCs good working conditions and/or a Dutch employment contract. German respondents who decided against hiring LIMCs on an informal basis did so because they wanted continuity but in some cases also because they did not want to be involved in an irregular arrangement. The latter respondents were not necessarily afraid of legal sanctions; their family's reputation and their own moral standards seemed to play a larger role. As we

---

[28] This could be due to a bias in our sample, though, since those who worry about legal consequences are presumably less likely to consent to being interviewed. On (the risk and functioning of) employer sanctions for hiring non-EU migrants lacking work authorization, see in this volume Chapter 10, Morgan, 2021.

saw above, however, families with limited financial means did not have another option than to resort to irregular arrangements.

Conclusions

In many European welfare states, migrant care workers are recruited as a way to manage strains caused by the growing scarcity of informal and professional carers. This chapter has concentrated on the deployment of live-in migrant carers to provide LTC to elderly people in Germany and the Netherlands.

In the first part of the chapter we used a governance approach to describe and explain the emergence and significance of LIMC arrangements in the two countries. The public LTC schemes of both countries do not provide 24/7 home-based care or supervision. Paying Dutch or German care workers to provide these services comes at a price that is not affordable for all but the most wealthy families. This explains why in both countries a market for LIMC arrangements has developed. However, the scale and structural characteristics differ greatly. Germany has seen the development of a large – and to a large extent grey – market, with many families hiring LIMCs for their elderly relatives on an informal basis. The market in the Netherlands is very small and largely based on the activities of private placement agencies. We have shown that these differences are related to the different national LTC regimes.

In the second part of the chapter we used a coping-strategies approach to analyse the role of financial considerations and resources in the choices and decisions of family carers who hire LIMCs for their elderly relatives. In both countries, the use of an LIMC arrangement is in itself a way to solve what could be called the trilemma of availability, acceptability, and affordability of care services. Affordability on its own does not explain why German and Dutch family carers opt for an LIMC arrangement. It is rather in combination with acceptability: LIMC arrangements offer a form of care close to the users' preferences – a form of care that is otherwise not available, at least not at an affordable price. This being said, the less generous German LTC scheme creates a context in which LTC recipients and their families face sharper affordability issues than their counterparts in the Netherlands.

Cash benefits compel LTC recipients and their families to develop their own strategies to contain the costs of the care arrangement. While this is true in both countries, the lower German cash benefits result in German families more often employing their LIMCs on a purely informal basis. For German users with less private resources, this may be the only affordable option. In the Netherlands, this option is more or less precluded by the tight regulation of LTC cash benefits. However, users can opt, for example, for a cheaper placement agency to adapt the costs of the LIMC arrangement to what they are able and willing to pay. Family carers in both countries develop additional cost-containment strategies in the day-to-day management of the care arrangement. They constantly make make-or-buy decisions; they try to 'stretch' their relative's cash benefit, and they try to limit their use of private resources.

In both countries, full compliance with labour law regulations is almost impossible. Typical for LIMC arrangements is that the migrant carers are being paid on the basis of a 40- to 48-hour working week while being on call more or less around the clock. Our findings indicate that family carers in both countries prefer not to reflect too much on the issue of what should count as working time, as it might make the arrangement unaffordable. In this respect, their reasoning is similar to that of policymakers in countries with large informal LIMC sectors. This does not mean, however, that LIMCs do not have bargaining power vis-à-vis their (involuntary) employers. Most family carers see it as their first priority and responsibility to ensure that their relative gets good care, but this also makes them willing to invest (literally) in good relations with the LIMCs.[29]

Our findings show that at the country level, different levels of (regulation of) cash benefits translate into different employment modes, with different degrees of legality. At the level of individuals and families, different levels of financial resources translate into different abilities to reconcile affordability with other concerns and considerations. More extensive financial resources enable the users of LIMC arrangements to opt for a more law-compliant employment mode, to choose a placement agency that offers its LIMCs better working conditions, to hire better-qualified LIMCs, and to purchase additional LTC services to relieve the LIMCs and/or the family carers themselves. By contrast, having limited financial resources may mean that other considerations have to be subordinated to affordability.

We conclude with a brief look at the future prospects of these transnational care arrangements. In both Germany and the Netherlands, the demand for LTC for the elderly will continue to increase in the coming

---

[29] On LIMCs' 'agency', see Bruquetas-Callejo, 2019; Ignatzi, 2014; Kniejska, 2016.

years, and labour shortages in each country's LTC sector are expected to increase even more. Add to this the desire of more and more elderly people to stay in their own home, and the future for this type of care arrangement looks very bright. However, it is important to also take into account developments at the European level and in the countries of origin of the LIMCs. In both Germany and the Netherlands, the development of an LIMC industry, although at a very different scale, has been facilitated by the EU free movement laws and EU enlargement to central and eastern Europe. The vast majority of the LIMCs in Germany and the Netherlands are EU citizens from CEE member states. However, few of them benefitted from the EU free movement of workers regime. The free provision of services regime has played a more important role. The recent revision of the Posted Workers Directive (application to posted workers of all the mandatory elements of remuneration and, for postings longer than 12 or 18 months, application of free movement of workers rules)[30] might affect the affordability of LIMC arrangements. Another development that is likely to affect the future of the industry is the already emerging shortage of supply of labour in a few countries of origin, especially Poland. A survey conducted among LIMC placement agencies in Germany found that a large majority saw the limited supply of suitable care workers in CEE countries as the main challenge for the future.[31] It remains to be seen what will happen if the labour supply in EU member states dries up. It is conceivable that, on the one hand, it may lead to better bargaining positions and working conditions for EU citizens working as live-in carers, while on the other hand, LIMC placement agencies may seek to set up recruitment structures in non-EU countries.

References

Ambrosini, Maurizio. 2015. 'Employers as "care managers": Contracts, emotions and mutual obligations within Italy's invisible welfare system'. In Anna Triandafyllidou and Sabrina Marchetti, eds., *Employers, agencies and immigration: Paying for care*. Farnham: Ashgate.

Ambrosini, Maurizio and Anna Triandafyllidou. 2011. 'Irregular immigration control in Italy and Greece: Strong fencing and weak gate-keeping serving

---

[30] Directive (EU) 2018/957 of the European Parliament and of the Council of 28 June 2018 amending Directive 96/71/EC concerning the posting of workers in the framework of the provision of services, OJL 173, 9 July 2018.
[31] Petermann et al., 2016.

the labour market'. *European Journal of Migration and Law* 13, 3: 251–273. DOI: 10.1163/157181611X587847.

Anderson, Alice. 2012. 'Europe's care regimes and the role of migrant care workers within them'. *Journal of Population Ageing* 5, 2: 135–146. DOI: 10.1007/s12062-012-9063-y.

Arend, Stefan and Thomas Klie. 2017. *Wer pflegt Deutschland? Transnationale Pflegekräfte – Analysen, Erfahrungen, Konzepte*. Hannover: Vincentz Verlag.

Baumol, William J. and William G. Bowen. 1966. *Performing arts: The economic dilemma*. New York: The Twentieth Century Fund.

Baumol, Willim J. 2012. *The cost disease: Why computers get cheaper and health care doesn't*. New Haven: Yale University Press.

Bettio, Francesca, Annamaria Simonazzi, and Paola Villa. 2006. 'Change in care regimes and female migration: The "care drain" in the Mediterranean'. *Journal of European Social Policy* 16, 3: 271–285. DOI: 10.1177/0958928706065598.

Bettio, Francesca and Alina Verashchagina. 2012. *Long-term care for the elderly: Provisions and providers in 33 European countries*. Luxembourg: Publications Office of the European Union.

BMG. 2017. Zahlen und Fakten zur Pflegeversicherung. Stand 20 October 2017. www.bundesgesundheitsministerium.de/fileadmin/Dateien/3_Downloads/Statistiken/Pflegeversicherung/Zahlen_und_Fakten/Zahlen_und_Fakten.pdf.

Böcker, Anita, Vincent Horn, and Cornelia Schweppe. 2017. 'National old-age care regimes and the emergence of transnational long-term care arrangements for the elderly'. In Luann Good Gingrich and Stefan Köngeter, eds., *Transnational social policy: Social welfare in a world on the move*. London: Routledge.

Bruquetas-Callejo, María. 2019. 'Long-term care crisis in the Netherlands and migration of live-in care workers: Transnational trajectories, coping strategies and motivation mixes'. *International Migration* 58, 1: 105–118. DOI: 10.1111/imig.12628.

Da Roit, Barbara. 2010. *Strategies of care: Changing elderly care in Italy and the Netherlands*. Amsterdam: Amsterdam University Press.

Da Roit, Barbara and Blanche Le Bihan. 2010. 'Similar and yet so different: Cash-for-care in six European countries' long-term care policies'. *Milbank Quarterly* 88, 3: 286–309. DOI: 10.1111/j.1468-0009.2010.00601.x.

Da Roit, Barbara and Marianne Van Bochove. 2017. 'Migrant care work going Dutch? The emergence of a live-in migrant care market and the restructuring of the Dutch long-term care system'. *Social Policy and Administration* 51, 1: 56–75. DOI: 10.1111/spol.12174.

Da Roit, Barbara and Bernhard Weicht. 2013. 'Migrant care work and care, migration and employment regimes: A fuzzy-set analysis'. *Journal of European Social Policy* 23, 5: 469–486. DOI: 10.1177/0958928713499175.
De Lange, Tesseltje. 2007. *Staat, markt en migrant: De regulering van arbeidsmigratie naar Nederland 1945–2006*. Den Haag: Boom Juridische Uitgeverij.
De Lange, Tesseltje and Cathelijne Pool. 2004. 'Vreemde handen aan het bed. De werving van Poolse verpleegkundigen in Nederland'. *Migrantenstudies* 20, 3: 130–144.
Emunds, Bernhard. 2016. *Damit es Oma gutgeht: Pflege-Ausbeutung in den eigenen vier Wänden*. Frankfurt am Main: Westend Verlag.
Horn, Vincent, Cornelia Schweppe, Anita Böcker, and María Bruquetas-Callejo. 2019. 'Live-in migrant care worker arrangements in Germany and the Netherlands: Motivations and justifications in family decision-making'. *International Journal of Ageing and Later Life* 13, 2: 83–113. DOI: 10.3384/ijal.1652-8670.18410.
Ignatzi, Helene. 2014. *Häusliche Altenpflege zwischen Legalität und Illegalität: dargestellt am Beispiel polnischer Arbeitskräfte in deutschen Privathaushalten*. Berlin: Lit-Verlag.
Kniejska, Patrycja. 2016. *Migrant care workers aus Polen in der häuslichen Pflege*. Wiesbaden: Springer Fachmedien.
Krawietz, Johanna. 2014. *Pflege grenzüberschreitend organisieren. Eine Studie zur transnationalen Vermittlung von Care-Arbeit*. Frankfurt am Main: Mabuse.
Lutz, Helma. 2009. 'Who cares?: Migrantinnen in der Pflegearbeit in deutschen Privathaushalten'. In Christa Larsen, Angela Joost, and Sabine Heid, eds., *Illegale Beschäftigung in Europa: Die Situation in Privathaushalten älterer Personen*. Mering: Rainer Hampp.
Lutz, Helma and Ewa Palenga-Möllenbeck. 2010. 'Care work migration in Germany: Semi-compliance and complicity'. *Social Policy and Society* 9, 3: 419–430. DOI: 10.1017/S1474746410000138.
Mosca, Ilaria, Philip J. van der Wees, Esther S. Mot, Joost J. G. Wammes, and Patrick P. T. Jeurissen. 2017. 'Sustainability of long-term care: Puzzling tasks ahead for policy-makers'. *International Journal of Health Policy and Management* 6, 4: 195–205. DOI: 10.15171/ijhpm.2016.109.
Mot, Esther. 2010. *The Dutch system of long-term care*. The Hague: CPB Netherlands Bureau for Economic Policy Analysis.
Nadash, Pamela, Pamela Doty, Kevin J. Mahoney, and Matthias von Schwanenflugel. 2012. 'European long-term care programs: Lessons for community living assistance services and supports?' *Health Services Research* 47, 1: 309–328. DOI: 10.1111/j.1475-6773.2011.01334.x.
Österle, August and Gudrun Bauer. 2012. 'Home care in Austria: The interplay of family orientation, cash-for-care and migrant care: Home care in Austria'.

Health and Social Care in the Community 20, 3: 265–273. DOI: 10.1111/ j.1365-2524.2011.01049.x.

Österle, August and Elisabeth Hammer. 2007. 'Care allowances and the formalization of care arrangements: The Austrian experience'. In Clare Ungerson and S. Yeandle, eds., *Cash for care in developed welfare states*. Basingstoke: Palgrave Macmillan.

Pavolini, Emmanuele and Costanzo Ranci. 2008. 'Restructuring the welfare state: Reforms in long-term care in Western European countries'. *Journal of European Social Policy* 18, 3: 246–259. DOI: 10.1177/0958928708091058.

Petermann, Anne, Annika Ehl, Anne Speicher, Marc Rütters, Michael Paul, Jamila Niegisch, and Dagmar Flade. 2016. *Zukunftsthemen und Herausforderungen für Unternehmen in der Betreuung in häuslicher Gemeinschaft*. Saarbrücken: Institut für Qualität und Management, BAGGS.

Sciortino, Guiseppe and Claudia Finotelli. 2015. 'Closed memberships in a mobile world? Welfare states, welfare regimes and international migration'. In Leila Simona Talani and Simon McMahon, eds., *Handbook of the international political economy of migration*. Cheltenham UK: Edward Elgar.

Stiftung Warentest. 2017. Pflege: Betreuungskraft aus Osteuropa – die besten Vermittler. www.test.de/Pflege-Betreuungskraft-aus-Osteuropa-die-besten-Vermittler-5170957-0/.

Theobald, Hildegard. 2011. 'Migrant carers in elder care provision: Interaction of policy fields'. In Birgit Pfau-Effinger and Tine Rostgaard, eds., *Care between work and welfare in european societies*. London: Palgrave Macmillan.

Theobald, Hildegard. 2012. 'Home-based care provision within the German welfare mix: Home-based care provision'. *Health and Social Care in the Community* 20, 3: 274–282. DOI: 10.1111/j.1365-2524.2012.01057.x.

Van Grafhorst, Arwen. 2014. *Verantwoorde buitenlandse zorg aan huis: Een verkennend onderzoek naar inwonende buitenlandse zorgverleners in Nederland*. Amsterdam: Stichting WEMOS.

Van Hooren, Franca J. 2012. 'Varieties of migrant care work: Comparing patterns of migrant labour in social care'. *Journal of European Social Policy* 22, 2: 133–147. DOI: 10.1177/0958928711433654.

10

De-magnetizing the Market: European Integration, Employer Sanctions, and the Crackdown on Undeclared Work

KIMBERLY J. MORGAN

Immigration control often brings to mind the formal measures taken at borders to block entry of unwanted non-nationals. Yet, in Europe today, most undocumented migrants arrive legally and remain after their visas expire or asylum claims are rejected.[1] Moreover, the free movement of people within the Schengen zone has undercut European states' abilities to physically bar unauthorized visitors from the territory. In response, many countries have adopted employer sanctions and other penalties on unauthorized migrant work that have been reinforced by European-level initiatives. These policies use economic inducements as a form of migration policy, threatening financial punishment of employers and the well-being of unauthorized migrant workers in an effort to influence the behaviour of both.

This chapter examines the development of measures barring undocumented migrants from paid work, which became a growing priority by the 1990s and especially in the 2000s. These developments are, in part, a consequence of the deepening and widening of European integration. The lifting of formal border controls through the Schengen agreement led policymakers in many signatory states to shift some national immigration control to domestic labour markets. The measures levied penalties on employers for hiring migrants lacking work authorization, required them to document the legal status of all workers, often penalized undocumented migrant workers, and built up state enforcement capacities. Extension of the Schengen zone to new member states in the 2000s spurred further measures targeting unauthorized migrant work and diffusion of these policies across the continent – developments actively

[1] Triandafyllidou 2010, 21.

promoted by EU actors. Increasingly these campaigns have targeted fraudulent employment practices of all kinds, including undeclared work by citizens and legal denizens as well as violations of collective agreements or labour laws by companies that bring non-national workers into the country.

These findings have implications for theorizing immigration enforcement in a borderless Europe. Europeanization has reconfigured states into multilevel governing authorities, shifting some of their responsibilities to supranational bodies while moving others down to regional and local governments.[2] Immigration enforcement in Europe also has moved 'up, out, and down'.[3] Yet, that should not obscure the continued vitality of the centre that has directed these efforts, as state officials have pioneered new ways to fight undocumented migration. Globalization and Europeanization, once thought likely to erode the power and autonomy of states, has instead brought about a reconfiguration and even expansion of state responsibilities. In the development of employer sanctions and related measures targeting all forms of undeclared work, governments have turned employers into gatekeepers and tried to incentivize their adherence to the law, but they have backed this up with increased enforcement and expanded oversight of a broad array of economic transactions and relationships.

Employer Sanctions and Immigration Enforcement

Borders are central to state sovereignty, as failure to maintain territorial boundaries is often seen as symptomatic of a weakened or absent state. Moreover, modern states accumulated what Torpey describes as a monopoly over the means of movement, regulating who can enter or re-enter a territory.[4] The rise in global migration, supra-nationalization of immigration policy, and formal demise of borders within much of Europe may therefore seem to seriously impair state sovereignty and autonomy.[5]

Yet, starting in the 1990s, scholars began noting that governments were expending more energy on immigration enforcement, drawing on a diverse array of techniques and actors. In Guiraudon and Lahav's apt characterization, immigration control shifted up to international and

[2] Hooghe and Marks 2001.
[3] Guiraudon and Lahav 2000.
[4] Torpey 1998.
[5] Sassen 1998.

European efforts and institutions, down to local governments, and out to non-state actors, including employers, landlords, charitable associations, and transport companies. Others have charted the deployment of new surveillance technologies, using computerized records, coordinated databases, and biometric information to identify undocumented denizens.[6] Immigration control has not declined, but its particular forms have changed as state officials attempt to compensate for the thinning of formal borders with new modes of migration control.

This chapter examines these processes through one form of internal immigration enforcement – the move to erect and enforce barriers to national labour markets. Labour markets draw and support undocumented migrants[7] and are difficult to monitor in large, decentralized economies. Policymakers therefore have sought to incentivize people to assist them in enforcement – to induce migrants to voluntarily leave the country, for instance, or to convince employers not to hire those without work authorization. Sanctioning employers who hire undocumented migrants tackles demand for this labour rather than the difficult-to-track supply.[8]

Employer sanctions levy financial penalties on employers who hire migrants lacking work authorization, including migrants with or without legal residence rights as well as, in the past, individuals from EU countries who had not yet gained full employment rights. Beyond financial penalties on firms, governments have the authority to threaten jail time, confiscation of material, worksite closure, revocation of licenses, and/or public shaming.[9] In some countries, those engaging in unauthorized work also may face fines and/or prison sentences.[10] Moreover, governments increasingly have widened their focus to the informal economic sector that is rife with labour law violations and other legal infractions.[11] Reflecting this broader concern, firms now often must notify authorities before all hires. Even without these policies, employer sanctions laws generally require firms to scrutinize and maintain copies of workers' employment documents. Employers thus become labour market guardians,[12] but officials back this up with enforcement, such as worksite raids.

---

[6] Bigo 2005; Broeders 2009.
[7] Orrenius and Zavodny 2016.
[8] Ruhs 2006, 16.
[9] European Migration Network 2017, 26–9.
[10] European Migration Network 2017, 33–4.
[11] Samers 2004.
[12] de Lange 2011.

In the two sections that follow, I analyse the development of employer sanctions and other policies aiming to constrict unauthorized migrants' labour market access. The focus is on common trends. Certainly, there are many differences in policy architectures, as well as in the intensity of enforcement. Yet it is also striking how, despite varying migrant labour demand, political traditions, and state bureaucracies, European countries have adopted a similar template of measures. This chapter aims to understand the emergence of that template and logic that underpins it.

To uncover the forces behind these developments, I divide the narrative into two time periods. The first covers the late 1980s and 1990s, a time when, faced with growing asylum claims and prospect of ending formal border controls, a number of northern European states adopted measures to control labour market access. In the second, starting by the 2000s, EU enlargement, asylum pressures, and mobilization of EU actors led to a second wave of reforms further strengthening the control apparatus in northern Europe and diffusing these measures south, east, and towards the UK. A final section considers larger implications of these developments for states, markets, and migrants.

The 1990s: Schengen, Asylum Seekers, and the Build-up of Labour Market Controls

Governments in Europe have not always vigorously protected labour markets against undocumented migrants. Although economic slowdown led many to stop large-scale labour or post-colonial migration by the mid-1970s, policies to target employers or unauthorized migrant workers were non-existent or weakly enforced. In France, enforcement of employer penalties was inconsistent, while in Germany, judges sympathetic to employer appeals often reduced the administrative fines imposed on them.[13] Officials in the Netherlands were even more lax, as the employer sanctions adopted in 1979 were not rigorously enforced through the 1980s,[14] and many undocumented migrants could obtain a social-fiscal number enabling them to legally work.[15] Italy and Spain adopted sanctioning laws in the mid-1980s, but weak enforcement did little to impede unauthorized migrant employment.[16] The UK rejected

---

[13] Miller 1987, 48–9.
[14] Martin 2003, 60.
[15] van der Leun 2006.
[16] Calavita 1994, 316–17; Cornelius 1994, 346–9.

the idea of employer sanctions entirely in the 1970s and 1980s as unnecessary for an island nation.[17]

Given these truncated national efforts, it is not surprising there was little European-level agreement on how to reduce employment of undocumented migrants. The ILO's 1975 convention on migrant workers gave international approval to employer sanctions, and in 1976, the Council of the European Communities called for increased member state coordination against unauthorized migration. The Commission then proposed a directive to harmonize laws on 'illegal migration and illegal employment', but the directive never moved forward, apparently because of British opposition.[18]

By the late 1980s, however, as member states moved towards eliminating formal borders between them, policymakers trained renewed attention on labour markets as sites of immigration enforcement. In 1985, France, Germany, and the Benelux countries signed the Schengen agreement committing them to lifting border checks, and in June 1990 they signed a convention applying the agreement. Several more countries joined the convention over the next several years, heightening concerns about how states would prevent unauthorized migration as the Schengen zone grew.[19] The move towards the formal demise of borders came at a time of increasing asylum requests and other migratory movements owing to the collapse of communism, breakup of Yugoslavia, and humanitarian crises in other regions. Faced with the prospect of lifting formal borders, officials feared that even with strict immigration and asylum laws, looser practices by neighbouring countries would contribute to growing undocumented populations in their own countries.[20]

The confluence of these developments spurred domestic and EU initiatives to augment internal controls, including labour market enforcement. In France, a series of laws, decrees, and labour code reforms in the second half of the 1980s signalled the growing priority of combatting undocumented migrant work.[21] More significant legislative shifts took shape in the 1990s, starting with a 1991 law coordinating dispersed bureaucratic efforts and instituting a requirement that employers file a formal declaration prior to all new hires.[22] In 1994, the government created a new body

---

[17] Ryan 2014, 240.
[18] Ryan 2014, 240.
[19] Maas 2005.
[20] Groenendijk 2011.
[21] Miller 1987.
[22] Marie 1994, 125.

dedicated to uncovering unauthorized employment and effecting deportations, taking 6,000 former border control agents and shifting them towards these new objectives.[23] In 1996, the government created an office attached to the national police to target unauthorized foreign workers, and in March 1997 another law strengthened the fight against illegal work and created an interministerial entity to pursue this objective.

Germany also began mobilizing against undocumented migrant work during the 1990s.[24] Employers were mandated to check a person's wage card, health insurance card, and social security number before hiring, with the subsequent crosschecking by computer systems linked to these cards often uncovering false documents or numbers and triggering the attention of immigration authorities.[25] Other laws augmented enforcement capabilities: in 1992, customs authorities gained the power to inspect employers and worksites, which had previously been done by labour inspectors from local employment offices,[26] and 1,000 former East-West customs officials were redeployed to labour law enforcement.[27] In 1997, these customs agents were enabled to act independently to inspect worksites and take action against violations, rather than having to coordinate these actions with the police.[28] By 2000, according to Martin and Miller, Germany spent 'more to prevent the employment of illegal foreign workers than any other country'.[29]

In the Netherlands, internal migration controls intensified in the early 1990s. Since then, only lawful residents can get the official number enabling legal work, and the 1994 Compulsory Identification Act mandated that employers keep records of their employees' identification documents.[30] Penalties on employers for hiring undocumented workers increased, the number of labour market inspectors rose, and in 2000 a new agency was created to focus on criminal organizations involved in undocumented migrant work.[31] These measures, added to the 1998 Linkage Act that excluded undocumented migrants from accessing social benefits, significantly constrained unauthorized migrants' earning abilities.[32]

---

[23] Inciyan 1994.
[24] Junkert and Kreienbrink 2010, 151.
[25] Vogel 2000, 408.
[26] Tangermann and Grote 2017, 31.
[27] Martin and Miller 2000, 21.
[28] Junkert and Kreienbrink 2008, 52.
[29] Martin and Miller 2000, 21.
[30] Doomernik 2008, 137.
[31] Broeders 2009, 80–1, 85.
[32] Doomernik 2008, 137–8; Van der Leun 2006.

Outside of these northern European countries, the adoption of employer sanctions and other labour market measures was more half-hearted. For example, Italy, Greece, and Spain adopted or expanded measures to combat unauthorized migrant employment in the 1990s but enforcement was limited.[33] In the United Kingdom, a Conservative government adopted a measure in 1996 targeting employers of undocumented migrants, but the law imposed only a criminal sanction. In general, criminal penalties are less often imposed than administrative fines, as employers often persuade judges to limit or overturn the sanctions.

The growing priority given to combatting undocumented migration opened up space for EU action. Fearing the effects of a borderless Europe on domestic immigration control, by the start of the 1990s the European Council asked the Commission to promote cooperation in this area. In the formal recommendations and informal urgings that would follow, the Commission regularly included targeting undeclared work in its list of recommended actions.[34] These recommendations were part of the EU's growing focus on combatting undocumented migration.

In sum, eliminating formal borders at a time of increasing fears over asylum claimants and undocumented migration spurred officials in a number of countries to turn labour markets into sites of migration control. Given the difficulties of overseeing all economic relationships, financial incentives were at the core of these initiatives – putting penalties on employers who violate the law and disincentivizing unauthorized migrants from coming and remaining. Some states went further and required employers to verify workers' documents before hiring them – a practice that would diffuse across the EU in the succeeding decade.

The Europeanization of Employer Sanctions and Campaigns against Undeclared Work

The push of refugees and asylum seekers for entry into Europe continued during the 2000s and, coupled with EU enlargement in 2004 and 2007, spurred further efforts to close off labour markets to undocumented

---

[33] Triandafyllidou and Ambrosini 2011.
[34] For example: *Commission Communication to the Council and the European Parliament on Immigration* sec(91) 1855 final, 23 October 1991; *Council Recommendation on Harmonizing Means of Combating Illegal Immigration and Illegal Employment and Improving the Relevant Means of Control* 96/C5/01 (22 December 1995); *Council Recommendation on Combating the Illegal Employment of Third-Country Nationals* 96/C 304/01 (27 September 1996).

migrants. At the start of the new millennium, a number of EU countries experienced rising asylum requests – often from people fleeing conflict in Asia Minor, sub-Saharan Africa, and the Middle East. Given the now open borders between many EU countries, policymakers feared that people who got across external EU borders would move freely between countries. An additional concern was that EU enlargement to new member states, mostly in Central and Eastern Europe, would induce workers from these countries to look for work in the West. Most EU countries responded by imposing a transitional period before people from the new member states could work, yet because people from these countries could still travel freely across borders, this fostered the growth of undeclared work.[35]

These migrants sought employment not only in the large informal economies of Southern Europe,[36] but also in increasingly flexibilized northern European labour markets. By the 2000s, policymakers in these countries enabled and encouraged new forms of work, including temporary employment, atypical working hours, short-term contracts, and part-time work.[37] Growing demand for care and household services also fuelled the growth of low-end personal service jobs, particularly in cleaning and elder care.[38] And European integration contributed to the growing complexity of work arrangements, with firms now moving across borders and bringing workers with them. Europeanization also encouraged a more profound reorganization of labour markets, particularly in industries such as construction where transnational employment agencies and contractors constitute complex production chains.[39] The flowering of these forms of work created employment niches for unauthorized migrant workers – many coming from the new EU member states – should they find employers willing to pay them off the books.

While Europeanization was contributing to the expansion of unauthorized migrant work, it also became a source of ideas for fighting it. The Treaty of Amsterdam extended the EU's competence to undocumented migration. In the reports, communications, recommendations, and directives that followed, the European Commission highlighted how the 'pull factor' of employment and illegal work contributed to unfair

---

[35] In the 2004 enlargement to ten new member states, only Ireland, Sweden, and the UK did not impose a transitional period on workers from these countries.
[36] Reyneri 2002.
[37] Emmenegger et al. 2012.
[38] Carbonnier and Morel 2015.
[39] Wagner and Berntsen 2016, 196.

competition and social dumping.[40] EU enlargement only heightened the concerns: the December 2006 European Council meeting included both a welcome to Bulgaria and Romania as new members of the EU and a call for intensified cooperation in combating undocumented migration, including through ramped-up external controls and increased efforts against illegal employment.[41]

The culmination of these activities at the EU level was the 2009 directive for minimum standards on sanctions and other penalties against employers who hire undocumented third-country nationals (TCNs).[42] The directive requires states to bar the employment of TCNs lacking residence rights, levy sanctions against employers violating the prohibition, and mandate that employers verify individuals are lawfully able to work and notify authorities when they hire them. The directive also made employers liable for subcontractors' hiring practices. Member-states should conduct worksite inspections to uncover these abuses and report annually to the Commission how many inspections they have done.

The EU directive impelled some strengthening of labour market controls and employers' sanctions, particularly in some new member states.[43] However, prior to the directive, many countries had already increased penalties on employers of undocumented migrants and required them to verify workers' status before hiring them.[44] For instance, France increased penalties on employers hiring unauthorized migrants in 2003, 2006, and 2009, and the 2006 law also required employers check all foreign workers' status with the local prefect before hiring them.[45] A 2004 Dutch measure required employers to register workers on their first day of work and instituted an administrative sanction to replace a rarely employed criminal one.[46] As labour

---

[40] *Communication from the Commission to the Council and European Parliament on a common policy on illegal immigration* COM(2001) 672 final; *Proposal for a Comprehensive Plan to Combat Illegal Immigration and Trafficking of Human Beings in the European Union* 2002/C 142/02.
[41] Council of the European Union, *Brussels European Council* 16879/1/06 REV 1 (12 February 2007).
[42] Directive 2009/52/EC of the European Parliament and of the Council of 18 June 2009 providing for minimum standards on sanctions and measures against employers of illegally staying third-country nationals, OJ L 168, 30 June 2009 . The United Kingdom, Ireland, and Denmark opted out.
[43] European Migration Network 2017.
[44] ILO 2008.
[45] Coste 2008, 72–3.
[46] Diepenhorst 2012, 47.

inspectorates could now directly impose fines on employers, rather than go through the lengthy and uncertain process of referring cases to prosecutors, the administrative sanction produced a sharp uptick in the numbers levied.[47] Germany also adopted a 2004 law that included penalties for hiring unauthorized migrant workers involving prison time and fines as high as € 500,000.[48]

Governments in southern Europe, recognizing that their large informal economies could attract undocumented workers, began adopting similar measures – fines and potential jail time for employers, and requirements that they check the workers' status before hiring. A 2002 Italian law increased employer sanctions and created an administrative fine if employers failed to report a non-national's employment to the local immigration office, while in 2006 the government created an administrative sanction on employers whose workers lacked proper documentation and a civil sanction for not paying social security contributions.[49] The measure also required employers to report new hires to the social insurance funds before starting work.[50] In Spain, the 2009 Aliens Act instituted tough fines, ranging from €10,000 to €100,000, on employers of undocumented migrants, while stepped-up labour market inspections yielded a large number of violators.[51]

Even the UK, long resistant towards these types of labour market measures, strengthened sanctions and their enforcement during the 2000s. One impetus for reform came in 2004, when the horrific deaths of undocumented migrants picking cockles in Morecambe Bay led to the creation of the Gangmasters' Licensing Authority in 2006 to combat the exploitation of foreign workers in agriculture and food processing. But the bigger impetus was rising asylum claims at the turn of the millennium and, after EU enlargement in 2004, the Labour government's decision granting people from new member states immediate access to UK labour markets. The public backlash spurred a turn to internal immigration control. Between 2004 and 2008, the government converted the criminal penalty on employers to an administrative one, expanded the penalty to £10,000 per illegal worker, added the threat of jail time, and worked to improve enforcement.

---

[47] Broeders 2009, 86–7; De Lange 2011, 187–9.
[48] Sinn et al. 2004, 46–7.
[49] ILO 2009, 85.
[50] Ciccarone and Raitano 2007, 8.
[51] ILO 2013, 12.

Since the 2000s, there also has been a growing emphasis on targeting the informal economy as a whole.[52] Fears about the pull of informal employment markets dovetailed with concerns of finance officials and labour inspectorates about a larger array of labour market violations, including employment of those lacking work authorization, underreporting of hours worked, underpayment of social insurance contributions, and/or undeclared work during receipt of unemployment insurance. EU officials have long articulated a similar set of concerns in various reports and communications.[53] In 2016, the Council and European Parliament created a platform on undeclared work to promote cooperative action on this issue and share best practices.

To address this larger phenomenon, governments have beefed up labour market enforcement machinery. In France, governments in the 2000s created various coordinating bodies to connect actors involved in combatting workplace violations – including police, labour inspectors, tax authorities, and social security agencies. Since April 2008, a National Delegation for the Fight against Fraud meets regularly and puts forth two-year plans for how to combat fraudulent economic activities. In Germany, a central agency was created in 2004 to fight illegal work and tax fraud.[54] The agency has vigorously applied employer sanctions laws: in 2005, for instance, 6,200 customs agents were tasked with rooting out undeclared work and tax fraud, and 81,300 criminal procedures were launched in that year against violators.[55] Italy and the Netherlands also reformed their labour inspection systems: the 2012 Dutch reform created a new social inspection agency (SZW) combining different labour market inspection services,[56] while Italy overhauled its labour inspectorate in 2004.[57] Spain in 2012 launched a plan to fight undeclared work and social security fraud that entailed greater coordination between agencies and expanded staff for the labour and social security inspectorate.[58]

---

[52] Samers 2004; Williams 2008.
[53] *Communication from the Commission on Undeclared Work*, COM(1998) 219 (7 April 1998); *Council Resolution on transforming undeclared work into regular employment* OJ C 260, 29 October 2003; Communication from the Commission to the Council, the European Parliament, the European Economic and Social Committee and the Committee of the Regions, *Stepping Up the Fight Against Undeclared Work*, COM (2007) 628 final.
[54] Junkert and Kreienbrink 2010, 157.
[55] Volger-Ludwig 2007, 6.
[56] Renooy 2013, 17–28.
[57] Fasani 2011, 11.
[58] European Commission 2017, 170.

The 2014–16 surge of people seeking asylum in Europe, and populist backlash against migration, did not produce major changes in these labour market measures. Most countries already had sanctions laws and enforcement apparatuses in place, and thus governments largely reaffirmed their commitment to using this machinery against unauthorized migrant work. In Germany, for instance, as politicization of asylum seekers drew attention to the possibility that failed applicants might find a foothold in Germany through undeclared work, a 2017 reform sought to further strengthen the authorities' labour market enforcement capacities.[59] Italy in 2016 created a National Labour Inspectorate to coordinate efforts against undeclared work.[60] In the Netherlands, the labour inspectorate's focus in recent years has been on a wider array of labour violations, rather than unauthorized migrant work per se.[61]

In the UK, by contrast, where labour market oversight has developed more slowly, governments accelerated their efforts between 2014 and 2016 in an effort to soothe the angry, anti-immigrant sentiment fuelling the drive to exit the EU. In 2014, the Liberal-Conservative coalition doubled the maximum fines on employers of unauthorized workers and created an Immigration Enforcement Directorate that raids worksites and businesses to check the immigration status of workers. In 2015, a Conservative government pushed the Home Office to more vigorously pursue sanctions against employers, and 1,200 civil penalties were issued between July and December 2015 (worth £21.5 million).[62] A 2016 Immigration Bill made working without documentation a criminal offence for workers, enabled authorities to seize the wages of those caught engaging in it, and imposed greater penalties on employers and the threat of their businesses being closed. The bill also created a Director of Labour Market Enforcement to coordinate action against labour exploitation, including that involving illegal migrant work. The proposals were accompanied by tough rhetoric, with Immigration Minister James Brokenshire declaring that the 'full force of government machinery' would be deployed against 'rogue employers'.[63]

The European Union has continued to push for further strengthening of sanctions and other labour market enforcement efforts across the

---

[59] European Migration Network 2017, 24–5.
[60] European Commission 2017, 97.
[61] Berntsen and de Lange 2018.
[62] www.ukemploymenthub.com/illegal-working-penalties-for-employers-are-more-than-a-slap-on-the-wrist.
[63] Mason 2015.

continent. In September 2020, the Commission announced a 'New Pact on Migration and Asylum' that sought to improve coordination and burden-sharing among the member states for asylum seekers. The pact also called for intensifying the fight against migrant smuggling, and in that context committed the Commission to evaluating the employer sanctions directive and considering ways to strengthen its implementation.[64]

Implications

What should we make of these initiatives targeting unauthorized migrant labour and other forms of undeclared work? Notable is the amount of EU and national-level policy-making activity on this issue. Undoubtedly, some of this activity is symbolic – highly publicized worksite raids, for instance, may be immigration enforcement performance for public consumption, rather than actions that do much to repress unauthorized migrant work. Yet, alongside these more performative actions, many countries have spent years, even decades, building up and refining the tools they use to try to deter, detect, and punish these violations.

Do these measures reduce the unauthorized employment of migrants? On the one hand, their effectiveness seems limited. In trying to suppress unauthorized migrant work and the informal economy, officials face constantly shifting terrain. Adopting one set of measures – requirements that employers maintain copies of work authorizations, for instance – fuels new practices to evade these requirements, such as a market of falsified documents. Violators work to mask their activities, and decentralized market economies give them room to hide. Moreover, efforts to promote more flexible forms of employment in recent decades have contributed to increasingly variegated labour markets that multiply the sites at which violations occur. Labour market enforcement is therefore often a few steps behind market developments.

Some evidence for this claim may lie in the relatively small numbers of unauthorized migrant workers who are found through worksite enforcement actions. In France, for instance, the total number of penalties issued against illegal work has expanded since the early 2000s, reaching 11,000 in 2017, but only 12.6 per cent of these infractions involved the

---

[64] Communication from the Commission to the European Parliament, the Council, the European Economic and Social Committee and the Committee of the Regions on a New Pact on Migration and Asylum. Brussels, 23 September 2020 COM(2020) 609 final.

employment of undocumented migrants.[65] In the Netherlands, where labour inspectorates have doled out what appears to be a particularly high number of sanctions against employers in 2014 (1,084), their efforts turned up only 332 undocumented migrants – a small fraction of the estimated 35,000 irregular migrants living in the country.[66] Undocumented migrants thus remain a continuing challenge to the capacity of states to 'encompass' their denizens, to use Torpey's terminology.

On the other hand, the low numbers of unauthorized migrant workers detected through these activities may indicate that these policies have some efficacy. Their goal is less to locate large numbers of violators than to incentivize individual agents, both employers and workers, to adhere to the law. For employers, the risk of getting caught may remain relatively low, yet the financial and other costs of being caught have risen significantly over the past few decades. Incentivizing adherence to the law constricts the options for individual migrants, some of whom may then return home or seek work in other countries. Of course, not all people are mobile: those with family and other ties to an adopted country, and/or who face the threat of physical violence in their home country, may find their only option is to retreat into extreme marginality.[67] But migrants appear cognizant of cross-national differences in work availability and the risk of authorities catching them, and may thus choose where to settle accordingly.[68]

This is why the EU has pushed for stricter labour market controls, particularly in southern Europe. The Commission and northern states have not only pressured southern and eastern European governments to augment external immigration controls, they have also promoted the construction of bureaucratic capacities that exist, more or less, in northern countries and that are held up as essential for rooting out and deterring undocumented migrant work. The ideal-typical vision here is of economies that minimize irregularity, in which employment is largely declared, regulated, and taxable, and violators are uncovered by an efficient and well-functioning labour inspectorate and/or police force. Many European states are far from this ideal, but they and the EU have nonetheless pushed this ideal on other countries.

---

[65] Direction Générale du Travail 2019, 22, 27.
[66] Berntsen and de Lange 2018, 216.
[67] Leerkes 2016.
[68] Reyneri 2002, 22; van Meeteren 2014, 121–22.

This policy agenda has implications for the well-being of migrants. One concern about employer sanctions is that they conflate two issues – labour market violations and immigration enforcement. Many would agree that cracking down on unscrupulous and exploitative employers is a valid goal but worry that migrants end up bearing the brunt of these initiatives. The employer sanctions directive requires states to adopt measures to ensure workers can receive back pay and that employers pay taxes and social security contributions due to them, but there is little evidence that unauthorized migrants' rights are protected in this way.[69] A more effective measure could offer to regularize the status of undocumented migrants who reveal to authorities they are employed in an unauthorized fashion or in violation of labour laws. This could disincentivize these practices by employers while offering some protections to undocumented migrant workers who, if they report workplace violations, could lose their jobs, find themselves in jail, face steep fines, and/or be subject to forced removal.

Conclusion

The formal demise of borders in much of Europe, coupled with increased numbers of labour migrants and asylum seekers, has led state officials to seek new modes of migration control. Unable to police every entry or record every exit, states in Europe use economic inducements to prevent the long-term stay of undocumented migrants. The aim is less to find, detain, and deport than to deter by making it difficult for people to sustain themselves economically. By constructing walls around labour markets, governments attempt to make it harder for undocumented migrants to subsist at a reasonable standard of living.

These measures turn employers into gatekeepers of employment markets. They must scrutinize the papers of workers, contact state officials to make sure individuals have the right to work, and maintain copies of this documentation. Failing to do so can result in high monetary and other penalties. To make sure they follow the law, governments have expanded their enforcement machinery, conducted high-profile raids of worksites, and engaged in information campaigns to sensitize employers to the risks of non-compliance. As has occurred in other areas of immigration enforcement, expanding labour market controls has led to growing scrutiny of a wider array of employer hiring practices. Not only are

---

[69] Picum 2015.

migrants scrutinized, but potentially all workers are: firms often must declare every new hire to public authorities, and the drive to build up labour market controls has metamorphosed into a wider focus on the informal economy. With this has come a wider recasting of the relationship between states and economies, with attempts to formalize the informal, regulate the unregulated, and bring into the light economic transactions that had hitherto been conducted in the shadows. The thinning of formal borders has led to an intensification of the state's role in overseeing economic transactions and attempts to monitor the lives of all its denizens.

References

Bernsten, Lisa and Tesseltje de Lange. 2018. 'Employer Sanctions: Instrument of Labour Market Regulation, Migration Control, and Worker Protection'. In Conny Rijken and Tesseltje de Lange, eds., *Towards a Decent Labor Market for Low Waged Migrant Workers?* Amsterdam: Amsterdam University Press, pp. 207–30.

Bigo, Didier. 2005. 'Frontier Controls in the European Union: Who is in Control?' In Didier Bigo and Elspeth Guild, eds., *Controlling Frontiers: Free Movement Into and Within Europe.* Aldershot: Ashgate, pp. 49–99.

Broeders, Dennis. 2009. *Breaking Down Anonymity: Digital Surveillance of Irregular Migrants in Germany and the Netherlands.* Amsterdam: Amsterdam University Press.

Calavita, Kitty. 1994. 'Italy and the New Immigration'. In Wayne Cornelius, Philip Martin, and James Hollifield, eds., *Controlling Illegal Immigration: A Global Perspective.* Palo Alto: Stanford University Press, pp. 303–26.

Carbonnier, Clément and Nathalie Morel, eds. 2015. *The Political Economy of Household Services in Europe.* London: Palgrave.

Ciccarone, Giuseppe and Michele Raitano. 2007. *Article on Undeclared Work from SYSDEM Correspondent.* Brussels: European Employment Observatory.

Coste, Fréréric. 2008. 'Report from France'. In Jeroen Doomernik and Michael Jandl, eds., *Modes of Migration Regulation and Control in Europe.* Amsterdam: Amsterdam University Press, pp. 63–80.

Cornelius, Wayne. 1994. 'Spain: The Uneasy Transition from Labour Exporter to Labour Importer'. In Wayne Cornelius, Philip Martin, and James Hollifield, eds., *Controlling Illegal Immigration: A Global Perspective.* Palo Alto: Stanford University Press, pp. 387–429.

De Lange, Tesseltje. 2011. 'The Privatization of Control over Labour Migration in the Netherlands: In Whose Interest?' *European Journal of Migration and Law* 13, no. 2: 185–200.

Diepenhorst, Denis. 2012. *Practical Measures to Reduce Irregular Immigration: Netherlands*. Rijswijk, The Netherlands: Ministry of the Interior and Kingdom Relations Immigration and Naturalisation Service.
Direction Générale du Travail. 2019. *Analyse de la verbalization du travail illégal en 2017*. https://travail-emploi.gouv.fr/IMG/pdf/rapport_2017_verbalisation_du_travail_illegal.pdf.
Doomernik, Jeroen. 2008. 'Report from the Netherlands'. In Jeroen Doomernik and Michael Jandl, eds., *Modes of Migration Regulation and Control in Europe*. Amsterdam: Amsterdam University Press, pp. 129–45.
Emmenegger, Patrick, Silja Häusermann, Bruno Palier, and Martin Seeleib-Kaiser, eds. 2012. *The Age of Dualization: The Changing Face of Inequality in Deindustrializing Societies*. Oxford: Oxford University Press.
Engbersen, Godfried and Dennis Broeders. 2009. 'The State versus the Alien: Immigration Control and Strategies of Irregular Immigrants'. *West European Politics* 32, no. 5: 867–85.
European Commission. 2014. Communication from the Commission to the European Parliament and the Council on the Application of Directive 2009/52/EC Providing for Minimum Standards on Sanctions and Measures against Employers of Illegally Staying Third Country Nationals. COM(2014) 286 final.
European Commission. 2017. *European Platform Tackling Undeclared Work: Member State Factsheets and Synthesis Report*.
European Migration Network. 2017. *Illegal Employment of Third-Country Nationals in the European Union*. Brussels: European Commission.
Fasani, Mario. 2011. *Labour Inspection in Italy*. Geneva: ILO.
Groenendijk, Kees. 2011. 'Introduction: Migration and Law in Europe'. In Elspeth Guild and Paul Minderhoud, eds., *Immigration and Asylum Law and Policy in Europe: The First Decade of EU Migration and Asylum Law*. Leiden, NL: Brill Nijhoff, pp. 1–22.
Guiraudon, Virginie and Gallya Lahav. 2000. 'A Reappraisal of the State Sovereignty Debate: The Case of Migration Control'. *Comparative Political Studies* 33, no. 2 (March): 164–95.
Hooghe, Liesbet and Gary Marks. 2001. *Multi-Level Governance and European Integration*. Boulder, CO: Rowman & Littlefield.
Inciyan, Erich. 1994. 'Pour appliquer la nouvelle législation sur l'entrée et le séjour des étrangers M. Pasqua met en place une police de l'immigration'. *Le Monde*, 18 January.
ILO. 2008. *Addressing the Irregular Employment of Immigrants in the European Union: Between Sanctions and Rights*.
  2009. *Regularization and Employer Sanctions as Means towards the Effective Governance of Labour Migration Russian Federation and International Experience*.

2013. *Labour Inspection and Undeclared Work in the EU*. Working Document no. 29.

Junkert, Christoph and Axel Kreienbrink. 2008. 'Irregular Employment of Migrant Workers in Germany: Legal Situation and Approaches to Tackling the Phenomenon'. In Marek Kupiszewski and Heikki Mattila, eds., *Addressing the Irregular Employment of Immigrants in the European Union: Between Sanctions and Rights*. Washington, DC: International Organization for Migration, pp. 13–88.

Junkert, Christoph and Axel Kreienbrink. 2010. 'Illegal Employment of Immigrants in Germany: Combating the Phenomenon versus Social Rights?' In Mally Shechory, Sarah Ben David, and Dan Soen, eds., *Who Pays the Price? Foreign Workers, Society, Crime and the Law*. Hauppage, NY: Nova Science, pp. 151–67.

Leerkes, Arjan. 2016. 'Back to the Poorhouse: Social Protection and Social Control of Unauthorized Immigrants in the Shadow of the Welfare State'. *Journal of European Social Policy* 26, no. 2: 140–54.

Maas, Willem. 2005. 'Freedom of Movement Inside "Fortress Europe"'. In Elia Zureik and Mark Salter, eds., *Global Surveillance and Policing: Borders, Security, Identity*. Portland: Willan, pp. 233–45.

Marie, Claude-Valentin. 1994. 'From the Campaign against Illegal Migration to the Campaign against Illegal Work'. *Annals AAPSS* 534 (July): 118–32.

Martin, Philip. 2003. *Bordering on Control: Combating Irregular Migration in North America and Europe*. Washington, DC: International Organization for Migration Research Series, no. 13.

and Mark Miller. 2000. *Employer Sanctions: French, German and US Experiences*. International Migration Papers 36. Geneva: International Labour Office.

Mason, Rowena. 2015. 'Immigration: UK's Rogue Employers to be "Hit from All Angles"'. *The Guardian*, 10 August.

Miller, Mark. 1987. *Employer Sanctions in Western Europe*. Occasional Paper No. 7. New York: Centre for Migration Studies.

OECD. 2003. *Trends in International Migration*. Paris: OECD.

Orrenius, Pia M. and Madeline Zavodny. 2016. 'Irregular Immigration in the European Union'. Working Paper 1603. Federal Reserve Bank of Dallas Research Department. www.dallasfed.org/-/media/documents/research/papers/2016/wp1603.pdf

Picum. 2015. *Employers' Sanctions: Impacts on Undocumented Migrant Workers' Rights in Four EU Countries*. Brussels: Picum.

Renooy, Piet. 2013. *Labor Inspection Strategies for Combating Undeclared Work in Europe: The Netherlands* (Regioplan).

Reyneri, Emilio. 2002. *Migrants Involvement in Irregular Employment in the Mediterranean Countries of the European Union*. Geneva: ILO International Migration Paper.

Ruhs, Marin. 2006. 'The Potential of Temporary Migration Programmes in Future International Migration Policy'. *International Labor Review* 145, no. 1–2: 7–36.

Ryan, Bernard. 2014. 'Employer Checks of Immigration Status and Employment Law'. In Cathryn Costello and Mark Freedland, eds., *Migrants at Work: Immigration and Vulnerability in Labour Law*. Oxford: Oxford University Press, pp. 239–56.

Samers, Michael E. 2004. 'The "Underground Economy," Immigration and Economic Development in the European Union: An Agnostic-Skeptic Perspective'. *International Journal of Economic Development* 6, no. 3: 199–272.

Sassen, Saskia. 1998. 'The *de facto* Transnationalizing of Immigration Policy'. In Christian Joppke, ed., *Challenge to the Nation-State*. Oxford: Oxford University Press, pp. 49–85.

Sinn, Annette, Axel Kreienbrink, and Hans Dietrich von Loeffelholz. 2005. *Illegal Resident Third-Country Nationals in Germany: Policy Approaches, Profile and Social Situation*. Berlin: Federal Office for Migration and Refugees.

Tangermann, Julian and Janne Grote. 2017. *Illegal Employment of Third-Country Nationals in Germany*. Working Paper no. 74. Berlin: Federal Office for Migration and Refugees.

Triandafyllidou, Anna. 2010. 'Irregular Migration in Europe in the Early 21st Century'. In Anna Triandafyllidou, ed., *Irregular Migration in Europe: Myths and Realities*. Surrey, England: Ashgate, pp. 1–21.

Triandafyllidou, Anna and Maurizio Ambrosini. 2011. 'Irregular Immigration Control in Italy and Greece: Strong Fencing and Weak Gate-Keeping Serving the Labour Market'. *European Journal of Migration and Law* 13: 251–73.

Torpey, John. 1998. 'Coming and Going: On the State Monopolization of the Legitimate "Means of Movement"'. *Sociological Theory* 16, no. 3 (November): 239–59.

Van der Leun, Joanne. 2006. 'Excluding Illegal Migrants in the Netherlands: Between National Policies and Local Implementation'. *West European Politics* 29, no. 2: 310–26.

Van Meeteren, Masja. 2014. *Irregular Migrants in Belgium and the Netherlands: Aspirations and Incorporation*. Amsterdam: Amsterdam University Press.

Vogel, Dita. 2000. 'Migration Control in Germany and the United States'. *International Migration Review* 34, no. 2: 390–422.

Vogler-Ludwig, Kurt. 2007. *Germany: Undeclared Work*. Brussels: European Employment Observatory.

Wagner, Ines and Lisa Berntsen. 2016. 'Restricted Rights: Obstacles in Enforcing the Labor Rights of Mobile EU Workers in the German and Dutch Construction Sector'. *Transfer* 22, no. 2: 193–206.

Williams, Colin C. 2008. 'Evaluating Public Sector Management Approaches towards Undeclared Work in the European Union'. *International Journal of Public Sector Management* 21, no. 3: 285–94.

11

Women as EU Citizens: Caught between Work, (Sufficient) Resources, and the Market

SANDRA MANTU

Introduction

EU citizens enjoy different positions within the EU free movement framework, largely dependent on their capacity for financial self-sufficiency, at least for the first five years of their residence in a host Member State. Financial self-sufficiency is attained either through paid work or by having independent financial means to support oneself. While EU scholarship has paid extensive attention to this aspect of EU citizenship under the label of 'market citizenship' due to its exclusionary effects that constrain the mobility of economically less potent EU citizens,[1] the gendered aspects of EU citizenship have received less attention.[2] That is not to say that gender is totally absent from EU law. A host of measures have been adopted at EU level that aim to facilitate women's equal access to employment, regulate working time to make it compatible with caring and family-related responsibilities, and to develop and promote social inclusion measures.[3] These regulatory interventions are underpinned by the presence of a general principle of equality in EU law that has led scholars to conclude that gender mainstreaming is constitutionally embedded.[4] Notwithstanding the existence of a well-developed gender equality law and jurisprudence,[5] the success of EU regulatory interventions is contested. Some authors consider that the EU has developed a comprehensive gender regime,[6] while others highlight that despite the

---

[1] O'Brien 2016; Mantu 2017, 2018.
[2] For exceptions see, Ackers 1996; Shaw 2002; Askola 2012; Guth and Elfving 2018.
[3] Walby 2004.
[4] Shaw 2002; Mushaben and Abels 2015.
[5] Mahon 2006.
[6] Walby 2004.

promotion of an adult worker model, EU policy and law continue to reinforce gendered stereotypes and fall short of achieving equal gender policies.[7]

While one could argue that EU women who move to another Member State will also benefit from that state's implementation of EU laws in the field of gender equality, it still remains the case that gender has not permeated fully EU free movement law. Moreover, it is unclear how gender considerations are incorporated into existing legal rules and in their interpretation by the Court of Justice. Although the starting point seems to be that as EU citizens, men and women encounter a level playing field when exercising their rights, Ackers has addressed the gendered nature of free movement provisions, since they operate under the assumption that EU women migrate mainly as family dependents and in order to join a male breadwinner in the host state.[8] As such, the failure to address gender in analyses of free movement and EU citizenship obscures questions about the role played by law in fostering or constraining women's exercise of mobility rights. The next sections will examine in more detail how the determination to value the mobility of financially self-sufficient citizens affects mobile EU women. I argue that the gulf between law's neutral language and the reality of EU women's mobility needs to be explored from the perspective of the capacity of EU citizenship law to accommodate different life trajectories, interests, choices, and, more broadly, difference. In this context Shaw's call for 'importing gender' into analysis of EU law[9] is still highly relevant since it forces us to critically examine EU mobility rights and their links with 'money matters', in this case the market model that favours the economically active and the financially self-sufficient.

This chapter will take up this analysis by first considering how money matters in EU free movement law for different categories of EU citizens and how this affects women. Earning a certain amount of money is relevant for meeting the conditions of being an 'EU worker', while having 'sufficient resources' will condition EU citizens' access to the welfare system of their host state. This latter aspect is discussed through an analysis of the Court's jurisprudence in relation to EU women claiming social rights, which usually translate into cash benefits, with a view to ensuring a minimum income in the host state. I contrast the Court's

---

[7] Weldon-Johns 2013; Gutiérrez-Rodríguez 2014; Gottfried 2015.
[8] Ackers 1996; 1998.
[9] Shaw 2000.

approach with cases where women manage to retain a close relationship with the market and where claiming benefits remains an option. Finally, I conclude by arguing that the extent to which EU citizenship rules accommodate migrating women and their experiences should be part of a critical discussion on how EU citizenship changes, recalibrates, or reinforces the nexus between paid work and mobility.

Mobile Women as EU Workers

Ackers' criticism of free movement rules as gendered and with implications for how EU women's mobility is institutionalized by the legal provisions on EU citizens' mobility and residence rights is linked to the history of free movement rules. The forerunner of what is now Article 45 TFEU provided for a narrow form of free movement limited to workers employed in the coal and steel industries, which were male-dominated professions. Although free movement was extended to workers in all sectors with exceptions for public service, the exclusivity of the relationship between free movement of persons and economic activity remained in place until the 1990s, when a series of Directives extended further free movement to economically inactive, but financially self-sufficient persons.[10] Directive 2004/38 – which contains the applicable legal rules on the exercise of free movement rights by EU citizens – retains existing distinctions between economically inactive and active EU citizens.

While the applicable legal rules do not link the exercise of EU citizens' mobility with the possession of a certain sum of money, the idea of money informs the legal categories under which EU citizens can exercise their EU citizenship right to free movement and residence for longer than three months in line with the provisions of Article 7 of Directive 2004/38. EU workers are not required to show sufficient resources or comprehensive medical insurance, but, as will be discussed below, the *amount* and *type of remuneration* they receive are relevant for deciding whether they meet the threshold of the definition of EU worker. Economically inactive EU citizens must possess sufficient resources and comprehensive sickness insurance not to become an unreasonable burden on the social assistance system of their host state (Recital 16 Directive 2004/38). This requirement is mirrored by EU citizens' differentiated access to the welfare system of the host state, with EU workers and permanent resident EU citizens enjoying full equal treatment with nationals of the host state.

[10] Maas 2007.

Although legally resident economically inactive EU citizens enjoy equal treatment (Article 24(1) Directive 2004/38), in their case asking for welfare benefits may be interpreted as failure to fulfil the sufficient resource condition.[11] This may lead to termination of their right to reside, exclusion from equal treatment, and even expulsion. Jobseekers are in an intermediate situation: they can reside in a host state to look for a job for longer than three months without having to show sufficient resources or comprehensive medical insurance as long as they can show that they are genuinely looking for a job and have reasonable chances of finding one. Nevertheless, one can speak of an implied assumption that such persons have resources to support themselves since EU law does not entitle them to social assistance benefits paid by the host state prior to acquiring worker status or a right of permanent residence (Article 24(2) Directive 2004/38).

Directive 2004/38 does not offer a clear definition of what 'sufficient resources' are, except that they are needed in order not to become an unreasonable burden on the host state's welfare system. In the case of workers and self-employed EU citizens, resources are generated through performing economic activities in exchange for money (I discuss the position of economically inactive citizens in the following section). Nonetheless, the Court's jurisprudence on the notion of EU worker is fraught with cases where work alone does not generate enough remuneration to ensure a minimum income. While addressing the minimum requirements that a person needs to meet in order to qualify as an EU worker, the Court has clarified that topping off resources generated from work with benefits from the host state's welfare system is allowed and hence not perceived as an *unreasonable burden* as long as the elements of the definition of EU worker are met. In a case dealing with a trainee teacher in Ireland, the Court stated that this definition must be based on objective criteria, while 'the essential feature of an employment relationship is that for a certain period of time a person performs services for and under the direction of another person in return for which he receives remuneration'.[12] Moreover, work implies an economic activity and the services performed must be capable of being regarded as forming part of the normal labour market in the sense that there is demand for and a supply of such services.[13] Remuneration is understood as taking the

---

[11] Mantu and Minderhoud 2017.
[12] Case 66/85 *Lawrie-Blum*, EU:C:1986:284, para 17.
[13] Case C-287/05 *Hendrix*, EU:C:2007:494.

form of money, with only few exceptions in the case law. In *Steymann*, the Court accepted that remuneration can take the form of providing in kind for the needs of the members of a religious community, but insisted on the existence of a link with the normal labour market.[14] In this case, the link existed since the services performed by members such as Mr Steymann were part of the commercial activities of the community and aimed at ensuring its self-sufficiency.

From the perspective of women's incorporation into the definition of EU worker, the requirement that the activity performed must have an economic value, otherwise it is not recognized as work, is problematic. Reinforcing the link between activities that can be considered 'work' and the market will affect women who engage in activities that are not considered part of the 'normal labour market' or activities that are not assigned an economic or monetary value because they belong to the private sphere, such as care work or rearing children. Free movement law fails to reflect calls to acknowledge that 'housework and care, as well as various forms of other work outside the relations of the market ... are not merely residual activities but an integral part of capitalist economies'.[15] It is not so much that EU women cannot or do not move, but that the market dictates the conditions and categories under which mobility gives rise to legal status and rights and makes it more likely that women will move to follow a male breadwinner.[16]

Part-time work and lower remuneration derived from part-time, atypical, or casual work are common characteristics of female employment.[17] The Court's approach towards part-time work and the level of remuneration are examples of mechanisms through which women's specificities in terms of labour market participation can be accommodated within the definition of EU worker. In cases such as *Levin, Raulin, Kempf,* or *Ninni-Orasche,* the Court reasoned that part-time work and even atypical work lead to acquisition of EU worker status, if work is real and genuine to the exclusion of activities that are purely ancillary. Consequently, the type of employment relationship, the duration of employment, the working hours, the size and origin of remuneration, and whether income is supplemented are not criteria in themselves allowing a distinction between who is regarded as worker.[18]

[14] Case C-196/87 *Steymann*, EU:C:1988:475.
[15] McDowell 2014: 827.
[16] Ackers 1996.
[17] Eurostat 2020.
[18] Iben Jensen 2013: 29.

The move towards a more flexible interpretation of the notion of EU worker was driven by structural changes in the labour market itself, and not by gender considerations, although all cases involved female applicants. Equally, the extension of the scope of EU worker came with costs in terms of allowing access to the host state's welfare system. Two cases are illustrative of the gendered consequences of this more flexible interpretation of EU worker status. In *Geven*, a Dutch woman working in Germany but living in Holland asked for a child benefit from Germany as a part-time worker in minor employment.[19] In *Hartmann*, the stay-at-home wife of an EU worker in full-time employment applied for the same benefit.[20] To obtain the benefit, German law had a residence requirement, or, in its absence, a requirement of minimum fifteen hours of work. Ms Hartmann obtained the benefit, but Ms Geven was denied the allowance since she did not meet the residence and minimum employment criteria.

I want to stress that in the above cases gender does not play a role in the Court's analysis, which focused exclusively on indirect discrimination on grounds of nationality stemming from the residence condition attached by German legislation to the grant of the allowance. It accepted as legitimate the reasoning of the German legislature that sought to exclude from the receipt of the allowance persons who did not have a sufficiently close connection with German society, either because they did not reside there, or because they were in minor employment.[21] A gender-sensitive approach may have prompted the Court to consider the link between minor employment and gender, which is well documented by data on employment rates and labour market integration among EU citizens.[22] In my view, these two cases show the limits of a jurisdictional analysis of discrimination that limits itself to nationality, while excluding other possible/intersectional grounds for discrimination. Therefore, gendered assumptions about part-time work or women's role as caretakers remain unchallenged by case law. This sits in contrast with the same Court's approach to gender discrimination in labour law where the Court has shown sensitivity to the gender implications of national laws that allowed part-time workers (predominantly women) to be paid less than full-time workers (predominantly men) and their justifications.[23]

---

[19] Case C-213/05 *Geven*, EU:C:2007:438.
[20] Case C-212/05 *Hartmann*, EU:C:2007:437.
[21] *Geven*, paras 28&29.
[22] Eurostat 2020.
[23] Case 170/84 *Bilka-Kaufhaus*, EU:C:1986:204; Shaw 2002.

EU Citizenship: A Game Changer for Mobile EU Women?

The previous section has discussed the intersection of gender with the notion of EU worker and with money, as an intrinsic element of that notion. In this section, I explore if, and how, the introduction of EU citizenship changes the dynamic between gender, work, and money by allowing women to exercise free movement rights and to claim social rights as EU citizens, independent of them engaging in paid work.

The process of liberalization of the free movement rules is seen as leading to the introduction by the Maastricht Treaty (1992) of EU citizenship as a legal status that entitles its holder to a fundamental, individual, and directly applicable right to move and reside freely in another Member State.[24] Costello describes EU citizenship status as Janus-faced, drawing on existing rights – workers' rights – but promising much more, including an expectation of equality as citizenship's main frame of reference and basis for some financial solidarity between mobile EU citizens and their host state.[25] These expectations were encouraged by the Court's interpretation of EU citizenship as intended to be the fundamental status of nationals of the Member States.[26] Yet, Article 21 TFEU clarifies that the exercise of the right to move and reside is subject to the limitations and conditions laid down in the Treaties and by the measures adopted to give them effect.

Based on Article 7 Directive 2004/38, economically inactive EU citizens can reside in a host state for longer than three months provided that they have sufficient resources and comprehensive medical insurance not to become an unreasonable burden on the welfare system of the host state. If in the context of EU workers (although with exceptions; see *Geven*), sufficient resources could be derived from a combination of paid work and financial benefits paid by the host state, for economically inactive EU citizens the option to supplement their resources with benefits from the host state is problematic. Directive 2004/38 is ambiguous: on one hand, it entitles EU citizens who reside lawfully in a host state to equal treatment and in theory access to benefits, while on the other hand, it makes possession of sufficient resources a condition for lawful residence for longer than three months.[27] Once the EU citizen acquires permanent residence – after five years of lawful and continuous

---

[24] Case C-413/99 *Baumbast*, EU:C:2002:493, para 81.
[25] Costello 2014.
[26] C-184/99 *Grzelczyk*, EU:C:2001:458, para 31.
[27] Minderhoud 2016.

residence – he/she gains unconditional access to the welfare system of the host state. When mobile EU women appear before the Court of Justice in their capacity as EU citizens – not as EU workers – and claim social rights, the analysis of such claims will depend on whether such women reside legally in the host state.

The requirements attached to the exercise of free movement for economically inactive citizens in terms of sufficient resources and health insurance coverage can be seen as encouraging the mobility of rich EU citizens who can afford to move. The jurisprudence shows that equality, in the guise of financial solidarity, remains linked to nationality discrimination, without paying attention to gender, class, or ethnicity as potentially affecting the mobility of EU citizens, despite the fact that mobile women with care and child responsibilities are a constant presence in the Court's jurisprudence. Moreover, gender is absent from the relevant legal provisions, too. Directive 2004/38, which codified and clarified the rights of mobile EU citizens, uses a neutral notion of 'national of the member state' or 'EU citizen' and fails to offer a more comprehensive definition of EU worker. According to its preamble, the Directive should be implemented without any discrimination between beneficiaries on grounds of sex, race, colour, ethnic or social origin, genetic characteristics, language, religion or beliefs, political or other opinion, membership of an ethnic minority, property, birth, disability, or sexual orientation (Recital 31). Beyond this standard of interpretation, there is no other mention of sex or gender as relevant aspects of how EU citizenship rights are constructed and applied.

Women Claiming Social Rights as Economically Inactive EU Citizens

Martinez Sala, one of the first cases in which the Court relied on EU citizenship coupled with the principle of equality to deal with claims for social rights,[28] illustrates the different levels of discrimination that women can face in their enjoyment of EU citizenship status. Ms Martinez Sala had a patchy employment history interrupted by periods of unemployment and child caring. In its examination of the claim for child benefits, the Court dwelt on equality as the underlying basis of EU citizenship but without discussing gender aspects, setting the tone for the failure to engage in an analysis of discrimination beyond nationality

---

[28] Case C-86/96 *Martinez Sala*, EU:C:1998:217.

grounds. Ms Martinez Sala was found to be legally resident in the host state based on an international law convention and therefore entitled to equal treatment. From the perspective of EU citizenship scholarship, this case is seen as opening up a new chapter in the history of the notion since it enlarged the personal scope of EU law to cover economically inactive persons legally resident in a host state in their capacity as EU citizens.[29] Yet, from a gender perspective, the Court's analysis and reliance on Ms Martinez Sala's regular residence have been analysed as eluding some difficult questions about the position of migrant EU women who choose to engage in unpaid care work or to withdraw from paid employment and the security of their residence in the host state.[30] Hence, the Court's approach can be criticized for the fact that while Ms Martinez Sala got the social benefit in question, the failure to engage with the gendered aspects of free movement goes beyond this individual case, and potentially affects all EU women.

Gender blindness continues to characterize the Court's analysis of EU citizenship, and its consequences are amplified in the context of a restrictive turn in interpreting the link between sufficient resources and unreasonable burden. Based on *Dano*,[31] *Alimanovic*,[32] or *Garcia-Nieto*[33] entitlement to benefits depends on meeting the conditions of residence for longer than three months, in which case the applicant can rely on Article 24 of Directive 2004/38 and claim equal treatment with nationals of the host state. However, asking for benefits to meet the sufficient resources condition becomes an indication that the person does not fulfil the criteria of lawful residence, and as posing an unreasonable burden.[34] In *Dano*, the applicant was a Romanian Roma woman who lived with her son in Germany in the apartment of her sister, who was also responsible for their maintenance. The case file showed that Ms Dano had no qualifications, had not worked in either Romania or Germany, and was not looking for a job in Germany. Her claim for benefits was rejected because they were reserved for jobseekers. The Court stated that Member States must have the possibility to refuse to award social benefits to an economically inactive EU citizen, such as Ms Dano, who has exercised her right to free movement with the sole aim of obtaining another state's social assistance. The Court's

---

[29] Maas 2007: 64–65.
[30] Shaw 2000, 2002.
[31] Case C-333/13 *Dano*, EU:C:2014:2358.
[32] Case C-67/14 *Alimanovic*, EU:C:2015:597.
[33] Case C-299/14 *Garcia-Nieto*, EU:C:2016:114.
[34] Verschueren 2015; Mantu and Minderhoud 2017.

decision has been interpreted as stating that by (simply) asking for a social benefit Ms Dano showed that she had no resources and therefore failed to meet the requirements of Article 7 Directive 2004/38, meaning that the only economically inactive EU citizens who can ask for social assistance from their host state are those who have sufficient resources of their own and are not in need of assistance.[35] Moreover, the Court's position in *Dano* suggests that resources mean financial resources, excluding benefits in kind that are exchanged outside the marketplace (e.g. housing or maintenance in exchange for household work), thereby questioning the flexibility advocated by the Commission in judging whether sufficient resources exist.[36]

Similar to *Martinez Sala*, the legal focus was on the residence issue, and not on possible gender or ethnic aspects. An attempt to discuss *Dano* from an intersectionality perspective and not simply as a case of nationality discrimination in the exercise of EU citizenship rights would lead to different questions being raised. Do Roma citizens move as freely as other EU citizens?[37] Under what circumstances can Roma women move? How easily can women make use of their EU citizenship rights when they move as mothers or to be with their family without any engagements with the market? If Ms Dano is being maintained by her sister and she also receives a small amount of money for her child, is she really without any resources and outside the scope of Directive 2004/38? Moreover, how can one quantify the maintenance received by a mobile EU citizen from another family member? At this point it is useful to recall that feminist theorists stress that cleaning your family's house is not an economic activity, while cleaning someone else's house in exchange for money is, and that the different value attached to the same activity relates to economics but also to cultural norms about what constitutes (productive) work.[38] Disappointingly, such issues have not reached the Court's radar when discussing the scope and limits of EU citizenship or what it can offer to those mobile EU citizens who remain outside the normal labour market.

The Magnetic Force of the Labour Market

The Court's case law shows that prior to acquiring a right of permanent residence, mobile EU women with care responsibilities and career breaks

---

[35] Verschueren 2015.
[36] Minderhoud 2016.
[37] Gehring 2013.
[38] Gutiérrez-Rodríguez 2014.

stand the best chance of enjoying social rights if they manage to retain sufficiently strong links with the labour market. EU citizenship rules fail mobile EU women who opt out of employment due to care obligations for longer periods of time since Directive 2004/38 does not take into consideration the scenario where a mobile EU citizen gives up work to care for her child in the host state. The only scenario dealt with by the Directive is the situation where a migrant woman goes back to her state of origin for a maximum of one year due to childbirth or pregnancy; this option will not compromise the acquisition of the right to permanent residence in the host state (see Article 16(3)). The legislator considered that a woman who worked for say three years in a host state and who decides to return to her state of origin for one year will not lose her acquired rights, but a woman who decides to remain in the host state but gives up work to care for the child will no longer be within the scope of EU citizenship rights if she is not self-sufficient during that one year.

This type of legal framing of residence rights reinforces Askola's point that in a system where only the 'economically useful' are valued and allowed to take full advantages of the opportunities of EU citizenship, women will be generally disadvantaged as they are less likely to take up paid work or stay in paid work once they have children, even if they migrated as workers.[39] In *Dias*, the applicant's fragmentary residence and employment histories led the UK authorities to reject her claim for income support on grounds that the gaps in employment meant she did not enjoy an EU law-based right to reside. The Court spent considerable space discussing a period of one year when Ms Dias took time off work to care for her child. It found that during this period of time she had been voluntarily unemployed as her unpaid care work didn't qualify as work under EU law; hence, she did not retain worker status.[40] Moreover, since she was unemployed and not complying with self-sufficiency requirements, the Court argued she could not be seen as legally resident.[41] Eventually, Ms Dias got her allowance because prior to the year in question, she had acquired permanent residence, which entitled her to equal treatment.

Nonetheless, mobile EU women with complicated life stories and trajectories that deviate from the traditional worker-citizen model have difficulties in enjoying full solidarity rights in their host state prior to

---

[39] Askola 2012.
[40] Mantu 2013.
[41] Case C-325/09 *Dias*, EU:C:2011:498, para 55.

acquiring permanent residence. For example, in *Alimanovic*, a Swedish national and mother of three children born in Germany re-entered that state after an absence of a decade.[42] The mother and eldest daughter worked in short-term jobs or under employment promotion measures for less than one year. After the applicant stopped working, the German authorities paid social benefits to the family for six months, after which payment was stopped because under applicable provisions, non-nationals (EU citizens included) whose right of residence arises solely out of their search for employment are excluded from such benefits. The Court argued that Ms Alimanovic retained worker status in line with the provisions of Article 7 (3) of Directive 2004/38 for a maximum of six months, after which she returned to being a first-time jobseeker. In this capacity, she cannot be expelled from the host state as long as she can show she is looking for a job and has a chance of finding one. However, she is not entitled to social benefits – Article 24(2) of Directive 2004/38. This case illustrates how co-existing work and citizenship models intersect with each other in EU law, not always in coherent ways. For Ms Alimanovic, the combination of work and children may yet prove to be her saving in terms of entitlement to social rights. Under EU law (Article 10 Regulation 492/2011), Ms Alimanovic's former employment in Germany entitles her children to receive education in that Member State. As an extension of this right, Ms Alimanovic enjoys a right to reside with them and to claim benefits as she cannot be classed as deriving a right to reside only from her job-seeking activities.[43] The children's right to education trumps the state's desire to limit access to social benefits, and even terminate the residence of unemployed parents who lack resources. While this position is intermediated by the parent's engagement with the labour market, it nonetheless shows that EU free movement law can integrate special markers such as age into its fabric.

Career breaks linked to pregnancy and afterbirth have received a more positive treatment, although not expressly dealt with in legislation. Directive 2004/38 in Article 7(3) lists a number of situations in which worker and self-employment status will be retained, although there is no employment relationship as such. These include illness, accident, involuntary unemployment, and, under specific conditions, embarking upon vocational training. Women giving up their job as a result of pregnancy or childbirth are not expressly dealt with by the Directive, which

---

[42] Case C-67/14 *Alimanovic*, EU:C:2015:597.
[43] Case C-310/08 *Ibrahim*, EU:C:2010:80 and Case C-480/08 *Teixeira*, EU:C:2010:83.

complicates matters further by linking retention of worker status in case of involuntary unemployment to the person being available for work and registered as a jobseeker.[44] In *Saint Prix,* the Court confirmed that pregnancy cannot be equated with illness. Instead, the situation of the applicant had to be legally asserted by interpreting the status of EU worker broadly enough to include a woman who gives up work in the final stages of her pregnancy and the aftermath of childbirth, provided she returns to work or finds another job within a reasonable period of time.[45] The length of time that one can opt out of the market without consequences in terms of residency and social rights depends upon the national rules applicable in the host state. While in the *Dias* case, the Court struggled with the one-year voluntary break from employment taken by the applicant to raise her child, in *Saint Prix* a prompt return to work after childbirth meant that the applicant retained worker status and entitlement to equal treatment in respect of social benefits on a par with nationals of the host state.[46] Although *Saint Prix* is an important case for mobile EU women who have to interrupt their work because of pregnancy, it is also a case that points towards the importance of being and remaining an EU *worker* when it comes to enjoying fully EU citizenship rights, prior to acquiring permanent residence.

Concluding Remarks: What Place for EU Women Citizens without 'Money'?

This chapter has looked at how gender is reflected in EU citizenship case law concerning the social rights of mobile EU women. The position occupied by gender in the fields of free movement of persons and EU citizenship is obscured by the fact that these rights assume that the EU citizen is a neutral legal subject in line with the requirements of the rule of law. Legal notions such as 'work' and 'sufficient resources' structure the exercise of EU mobility rights and condition EU citizens' eligibility for social benefits in a way that makes it difficult to understand how, from a legal perspective, EU citizenship provisions accommodate different life stories or different choices made in relation to children, family life, care obligations, etc. The current legal rules fail to engage with a series of issues that concern women: the value of care work, opting out of

[44] Mantu 2014.
[45] C-507/12 *Saint Prix,* EU:C:2014:200, paras 29 and 47.
[46] This position has been confirmed in relation to self-employed mobile EU women in Case C-544/18 *Dakneviciute,* EU:C:2019:761.

employment for family reasons, concentration in low-paid, short-term, and insecure jobs, working life interruptions, etc. All of the above choices have implications for women's capacity to meet the conditions attached to EU worker status or those that allow economically inactive EU citizens to reside for longer than three months in a host state while claiming financial assistance from the host state. Moreover, a gender dimension is lacking not only in the formulation of legal rules, which echo the market's dominance with requirements of 'sufficient resources', but also from the Court's interpretation of such rules. The Court has yet to apply gender considerations in its interpretation of EU citizenship, despite many cases concerning women as migrant EU citizens and the accelerated feminization of migration in the EU.[47]

A first step towards taking gender seriously when examining EU citizenship requires the articulation of EU citizenship as a gendered category, with consequences flowing from this situation for both women and men. One can equally question whether EU intervention in the fields of equality law is enough to ensure that men and women can exercise EU citizenship equally. Free movement law needs to be opened up to scrutiny from the perspective of gender and move beyond nationality discrimination as the only evil that impairs the exercise of EU citizenship. As Gottfried forcefully puts it, 'gender inequality will persist as long as the basis for equal treatment refers back to the golden age of industrial or company citizenship based on a standard male work biography reflecting continuous and relatively stable employment unburdened by care responsibilities.'[48] For now, EU citizenship remains attached to the 'market model' as work, the performance of economic activities in exchange of money, and financial self-sufficiency dictate its parameters.

By taking the male full-time waged worker as its unit of analysis, the market citizen model is also a gendered citizenship model that is equally exclusionary of those (women and men) who fail to meet its requirements because they fail to engage in paid work or choose a different work–life balance. A paradigm shift whereby work and the market are no longer the main driving forces of EU citizenship legitimacy has yet to materialize. Although the mobility of EU nationals is couched in terms of citizenship with all the normative baggage that entails, including in relation to equality and financial solidarity, the need to show sufficient resources and be financially self-reliant without needing to access the

[47] Saarinen and Calloni 2012.
[48] Gottfried 2015: 159.

host state's welfare system is akin to an inbuilt selection and exclusion mechanism. Viewed from this perspective, EU citizenship is closer to a privileged migration status, where 'money' plays a similar role to that of visa lists or financial thresholds in regulating migration from third countries. The failure to acknowledge the gender implications of this system at both legislative and judicial levels is disappointing, especially in light of the EU institutions' insistence that mobile EU citizens are important driving forces within the European Union, and that the exercise of free movement rights gives meaning to EU citizenship. This chapter argues that it is high time to highlight the exclusionary effects of EU citizenship and depart from the money-oriented EU citizenship model that benefits the traditional (male) breadwinner and move towards a citizenship that grants rights to its citizens for fulfilling the community's needs, whose 'work' represents integration values, which – in the long run – may be more important for the common EU project than just money matters.

References

Ackers, Louise. 1996. 'Citizenship, Gender and Dependence in the European Union: Women and International Migration'. *Social Politics* 5: 316–330.

Ackers, Louise. 1998. *Shifting Spaces. Women, Migration and Citizenship in the European Union*. Bristol: Policy press.

Ackers, Louise and Paul Dweyer. 2002. *Senior Citizenship? Retirement, Migration and Welfare in the European Union*. Bristol: Bristol University Press.

Anderson, Bridget. 2013. *Us and Them: The Dangerous Politics of Immigration Control*. Oxford: Oxford University Press.

Askola, Helli. 2012. 'Tale of Two Citizenships? Citizenship, Migration and Care in the European Union'. *Social & Legal Studies* 21, no. 3: 341–356.

Costello, Cathryn. 2014. 'Reflections on an Anniversary: EU Citizenship at 20'. In Bridget Anderson and Michael Keith, eds., *Migration: A COMPAS Anthology*. Oxford: COMPAS.

Eurostat. 2020. *Women's employment in the EU*. At https://ec.europa.eu/eurostat/web/products-eurostat-news/-/EDN-20200306-1, accessed 1 October 2020.

Gehring, Jacqueline. 2013. 'Roma and the Limits of Free Movement in the European Union'. In Willem Maas, ed., *Democratic Citizenship and the Free Movement of People*. Leiden: Brill Nijhoff: 143–174.

Gottfried, Heidi. 2015. 'Why Workers' Rights are not Women's Rights'. *Laws* 4: 139–163.

Guild, Elspeth, Steve Peers and Jonathan Tomkin. 2014. *The EU Citizenship Directive. A Commentary*. Oxford: Oxford University Press.

Guth, Jessica and Sanna Elfving. 2018. *Gender and the Court of Justice of the European Union*. London: Routledge.

Gutiérrez-Rodríguez, Encarnación. 2014. 'The Precarity of Feminisation: On domestic Work, Heteronormativity and the Coloniality of Labour'. *International Journal of Politics, Culture and Society* 27, no. 2: 191–202.

Iben Jensen, Ulla. 2013. 'Free Movement of Au Pair EU Workers: Obstacles to Temporary and Part-Time EU Workers'. *Online Journal on Free Movement of Workers within the European Union* 5: 27–36.

Maas, Willem. 2007. *Creating European Citizens*. Lanham MD: Rowman & Littlefield.

Mahon, Rianne. 2006. 'Introduction: Gender and the Politics of Scale'. *Social Politics: International Studies in Gender, State and Society* 13, no. 4: 457–461.

Mantu, Sandra. 2013. 'Concepts of Time and European Citizenship'. *European Journal of Migration and Law* 15, no. 4: 447–464.

Mantu, Sandra. 2014. 'Protecting EU Workers in Case of Involuntary Unemployment. Retention of Worker Status'. *Online Journal on Free Movement of Workers in the European Union* 7: 15–24.

Mantu, Sandra and Paul Minderhoud. 2016. 'Exploring the Limits of Social Solidarity: Welfare Tourism and EU Citizenship'. *UNIO – EU Law Journal* 2: 4–19.

Mantu, Sandra. 2017. 'Alternative Views on EU Citizenship'. In Carolus Grutters, Sandra Mantu and Paul Minderhoud, eds., *Migration on the Move – Essays on the Dynamics of Migration*. Leiden: Brill Nijhoff: 225-246.

Mantu, Sandra and Paul Minderhoud. 2017. 'EU Citizenship and Social Solidarity'. *Maastricht Journal of European and Comparative Law* 24, no. 5: 703–720.

Mantu, Sandra. 2018. 'Controlling "Poverty Migration" – Asserting Gradations of EU Citizenship'. In Heidi Mercier, E. Ni Chaoimh, L. Damay and G. Delledone, eds., *La libre circulation sous pression, Régulation et dérégulation des mobilités dans l'Union européenne*. Bruxelles: Bruylant: 170–184.

McDowell, Linda. 2014. 'Gender, Work, Employment and Society: Feminist Reflections on Continuity and Change'. *Work, Employment & Society* 28, no. 5: 825–837.

Minderhoud, Paul. 2016. 'Sufficient Resources and Residence Rights under Directive 2004/38'. In Herwig Verschueren, ed., *Residence, Employment and Social Rights of Mobile Persons. On How EU Law Defines Where They Belong*. Intersentia: 47–73.

Minderhoud, Paul and Sandra Mantu. 2017. 'Back to the Roots? No Access to social Assistance for Union Citizens Who are Economically Inactive'. In Daniel Thym, ed., *Questioning EU citizenship. Judges and the limits of Free Movement and Solidarity in the EU*. Oxford: Hart Publishing: 191–207.

Mushaben, Joyce and Gabriele Abels. 2015. 'The Gender Politics of the EU'. In U. Liebert and J. Wolff eds., Interdisziplinäire Europastudien: *Eine Einführung*. Springer VS: 309–321.

O'Brien, Charlotte. 2016. 'Civis Capitalist Sum: Class as the New Guiding Principle of EU Free Movement Rights'. *Common Market Law Review* 53, no. 4: 937–978.

Saarinen, Aino and Marina Calloni. 2012. *Builders of a New Europe: Women Immigrants from the Eastern Trans-regions*. Helsinki: Kikimora Publications.

Shaw, Jo. 2000. 'Importing Gender: The Challenge of Feminism and the Analysis of the EU Legal Order'. *Journal of European Public Policy* 7, no. 3: 406–431.

Shaw, Jo. 2002. 'The European Union and Gender Mainstreaming: Constitutionally Embedded or Comprehensively Marginalized'. *Feminist Legal Studies* 10, no. 3: 213–226.

Walby, Sylvia. 2004. 'The European Union and Gender Equality: Emergent Varieties of Gender Regime'. *Social Politics: International Studies in Gender, State & Society* 11, no. 1: 4–29.

Verschueren, Herwig. 2015. 'Preventing "Benefit Tourism" in the EU: A Narrow or Broad Interpretation of the Possibilities Offered by the ECJ in Dano?'. *Common Market Law Review* 52: 363–390.

Weldon-Johns, Michelle. 2013. 'EU Work-Family Policies – Challenging Parental Roles or Reinforcing Gendered Stereotypes'. *European Law Journal* 19, no. 5: 662–681.

12

Migrant Financial Inclusion versus the Fight against Money Laundering and Terrorist Financing

TESSELTJE DE LANGE AND ELSPETH GUILD

Introduction

This chapter takes as its point of departure Objective 20 of the Global Compact on Migration to promote faster, safer, and cheaper transfer of remittances and foster financial inclusion of migrants.[1] In order to achieve this objective, signatory states are called upon to facilitate remittance infrastructures and see to it that measures to combat illicit financial flows and money laundering do not impede migrant remittances through undue, excessive, or discriminatory policies. The objective also calls for accessing payment system infrastructure, such as bank accounts. Without access to a bank account, the so-called unbanked are at a disadvantage economically and cannot participate in consumption easily. Especially during the COVID-19 lockdowns, when cash payments were simply refused, the unbanked, often undocumented migrants, faced exclusion from multiple services, ranging from municipal services to grocery stores. For the unbanked and even more so the foreigner, such financial exclusion equates to a certain level of 'expulsion'.[2]

While propagating financial inclusion in the Global Compacts, the UN also has a strong impact on financial exclusion of migrants through its instruments against money laundering and terrorist financing. This dichotomy is echoed by the European Union where the right of access to a payment account, also for migrants, has been acknowledged in Directive 2014/92, while at the same time banks are asked to prevent money laundering in Directive 2015/849. Undue, excessive, or discriminatory policies or practices are at play on the ground in the UK and EU

---

[1] On this topic in the African context see in this volume d'Orsi 2021.
[2] Coined by Sassen (2014) and touched upon by De Hart and de Jong in this volume.

Member States (e.g., the Netherlands), keeping migrants from opening a payment account which then allows for the use of safe money transfers. Financial exclusion creates a kind of 'border': a border embedded in the law or bureaucracy of the receiving society at which private actors such as banks become border guards.[3] This border is created by clashing norms and this bordering is exactly what the UN Global Compact warns against in its objective on remittances, stressing how money matters for migrants. This chapter goes to the heart of the theme of this volume as it unpacks a substantial barrier that migrants face when it comes to money matters: what entitlement to financial inclusion do migrants have in the EU context, and how does the global fight against money laundering and terrorist financing jeopardize this?

The chapter evolves as follows. First, we map the UN instruments against money laundering and terrorist financing (section 2), followed by the EU legal framework on access to bank accounts and its intersection with the fight against money laundering (Section 3). In Sections 4 and 5, on-the-ground access to a bank account is mapped for the UK, where considerable attention is given to the importance of a bank account for migrants especially for the purpose of sending remittances, and for the Netherlands, where the topic has received scant attention. In Section 6 we draw our conclusions.

The UN: Instruments against Money Laundering and Terrorist Financing

The international community, pushed by US security interests after the attacks of 11 September 2001, began adopting an increasing volume of international instruments, mainly in the UN, to combat money laundering and in particular terrorist financing. While this was not the beginning of international efforts against money laundering it was a starting place for the elision of money laundering and terrorism, which includes an increasing focus on foreigners as the objects of suspicion.[4]

The UN convention against the illicit traffic in narcotic drugs and psychotropic substances 1988[5] was the first international convention to

---

[3] Excluding migrants from having a bank account impedes on their obligations in immigration law to, e.g., prove sufficient means, a topic discussed in this volume by Mantu and by Staver and Eggebø.

[4] Cole, 2008; Oliveira, 2014.

[5] UN General Assembly, *Draft Convention against Traffic in Narcotic Drugs and Psychotropic Substances and Related Activities*, 14 December 1984, A/RES/39/141, currently enjoying 191 parties, available at: www.refworld.org/docid/3b00f225c.html [accessed 30 June 2020]

criminalize money laundering. In 1997 the UN Office on Drugs and Crime (UNODC) was established, amalgamating two quite separate UN entities, one on drugs and the other on crime, into one reinforced body. UNODC would be the beneficiary of numerous responsibilities with a vague relationship with crime including money laundering and terrorism, though parts of these competences would be shared with other UN bodies. In 1999, the UN convention for the suppression of the financing of terrorism was opened for signature,[6] coming into force in 2002.[7] Once again UNODC was charged with the supervision.

The 2001 attacks in the United States led to the UN Security Council adopting Resolution 1373(2001), which consolidated and widely extended the commitment of the UN members to countering the financing of terrorism.[8] In terms of linking terrorist financing and migration, the Resolution is written in terms of obligations on states to prevent their nationals or any persons or entities in their territories from carrying out a variety of suspect financial activities. Thus, on the one hand there is a duty on states to prevent their nationals (anywhere in the world, including when their nationals are migrants in other countries) from carrying out a variety of financial activities, but also persons within the territory of their state – these include migrants (or stateless persons) – as nationals have already been covered. But it goes substantially further: at section 2(g) states are required to 'prevent the movement of terrorists or terrorist groups by effective border controls and controls on the issuance of identity papers and travel documents' and at section 3(f) and (g) to ensure, before granting refugee status, that the asylum seeker has not planned, facilitated, or participated in terrorist acts and that refugee status is not abused by perpetrators, organizers, or facilitators of terrorist acts. It is worth bearing in mind that the UN has not agreed on a definition of 'terrorism'.[9] The linking of terrorism, including its financing, migration, and money laundering, was introduced, notwithstanding a weak evidential basis for this convergence.

The push at the UN level to adopt measures against the financing of terrorism (including money laundering), in the 2000s, was accompanied by an expansion of the use of sanctions, including financial sanctions,

---

[6] UN General Assembly, *International Convention for the Suppression of the Financing of Terrorism*, 9 December 1999, No. 38349, available at: www.refworld.org/docid/3dda0b867.html [accessed 30 June 2020]
[7] Bantekas, 2003.
[8] Rosand, 2003.
[9] Saul, 2006; Hodgson and Tadros, 2013.

against named individuals accused or suspected of financing terrorism. While the UN has, since 1966, established thirty sanctions regimes, the early sanctions decisions were adopted as comprehensive economic and trade sanctions to more targeted measures such as arms embargoes, travel bans, and financial or commodity restrictions.[10] The use of financial sanctions against named individuals is more recent – gathering notoriety in particular after the adoption of the Al Qaeda and ISIS Sanctions Resolutions.[11] As of this writing, there are 710 individuals and 305 entities on the UN's consolidated sanctions list globally.[12] The impact of the financial sanction listing on individuals in Europe has given rise to numerous challenges on procedural and human rights grounds. The most famous challenges were those launched by Mr Kadi before the Court of Justice of the European Union, which resulted in the Court finding that the sanctions were contrary to EU procedural rights.[13] Mr Kadi is a Saudi national while his co-applicant Yusuf, who was also put on the sanctions list, is a Somali national. The result of the application of the UN sanctions measures in the EU resulted in the freezing of their funds and, in the case of Mr Yusuf, destitution for him and his family (in Sweden, the country where he was living). In the application of the UN sanctions regimes freezing assets of named individuals, non-EU citizens (i.e., migrants) were most affected.

The second most famous European victim of the UN sanctions listing system was Mr Nada, whose assets were frozen and his movement prohibited by the Swiss authorities (the country where he lived). The measures were found by the European Court of Human Rights to be a violation of Article 8 (the right to private life) and Article 13 (the right to a remedy) of the European Convention on Human Rights.[14] Mr Nada is a dual Egyptian and Italian national, though from his treatment by the Swiss authorities, they clearly considered his dominant citizenship to be Egyptian. It may be accidental that the applicants in the key European cases challenging sanctions were migrants in Europe. However, neither of their cases have been followed up by complaints to either of the courts by own (or EU) nationals. Before the CJEU, there have been many challenges on similar grounds to Mr Kadi – fund freezing because of

---

[10] www.un.org/securitycouncil/sanctions/information [accessed 30 June 2020].
[11] Kokott and Sobotta, 2012.
[12] www.un.org/securitycouncil/content/un-sc-consolidated-list#individuals [accessed 30 June 2020].
[13] C-402/05 P and C-415/05 P *Kadi* ECLI:EU:C:2008:461
[14] *Nada* v. *Switzerland*, no. 10593/08, European Court of Human Rights 12 September 2012.

being on the UN Sanctions List, most recently two challenges, one by a Ukrainian national and the other by a Syrian.[15] Most of the subsequent challenges were by Iranian banks. The ECtHR has not revisited the subject.

Money laundering is not always (or even not frequently) tied to terrorism.[16] While at the UN level, and in particular in the discourse of UNODC, the two are tightly linked in its Global Programme, in the practices of money laundering, the biggest scandals in Europe are unrelated to terrorism. The single biggest money laundering scandal which was revealed and pursued by the authorities in the EU was in respect of the Danske Bank's Estonia branch, which involved the laundering of more than EUR 200 billion mainly on behalf of Russian clients.[17]

The EU: Financial Inclusion vs. Fighting Money Laundering and Terrorism Financing

Two European Union Directives are at the core of the dichotomy at play: Directive 2014/92, on the right of access to a payment account, also for migrants, and Directive 2015/849 on preventing money laundering. The EU Payment Account Directive 2014/92 requires the EU Member States to guarantee consumers the possibility to open a payment account without being discriminated against on the basis of their nationality or place of residence.[18] Preamble 34 introduces the key issue at stake in our contribution: 'While it is important for credit institutions to ensure that their customers are not using the financial system for illegal purposes such as fraud, money laundering or terrorism financing, they should not impose barriers to consumers who want to benefit from the advantages of the internal market by opening and using payment accounts on a cross-border basis.' Article 15 of the Directive is a non-discrimination provision which obliges Member States to ensure that banks do not discriminate against consumers who are legally resident in the Union when applying for or accessing a payment account within the Union, on grounds of nationality, residence, or any other ground referred to in

---

[15] C-530/17 P, Azarov ECLI:EU:C:2018:1031; C-313/17 P Haswani, ECLI:EU:C:2019:57
[16] Yeoh, 2019.
[17] www.theguardian.com/business/2018/sep/20/danske-bank-money-laundering-is-biggest-scandal-in-europe-european-commission [accessed 30 June 2020].
[18] Directive 2014/92/EU of the European Parliament and of the Council of 23 July 2014 on the comparability of fees related to payment accounts, payment account switching, and access to payment accounts with basic features

Article 21 of the Charter. The conditions for maintaining a basic payment account should also be non-discriminatory. Migrants as consumers are entitled to a bank account when 'legally resident' in the Union. The term 'legally resident' is not linked to the EU Migration Law acquis and includes Union citizens and third-country nationals with and without a residence permit. Also, Member States should be able to extend the concept of 'legally resident in the Union' to third-country nationals present on their territory not listed in the Directive (preamble 36), which appears to be the result of negotiations on an ever-increasing list of exceptions to the requirement of legal residence. Indeed, the Directive includes consumers as legally resident in the Union asylum seekers, and foreigners who are not granted a residence permit but whose expulsion is impossible for legal or factual reasons. They also have the right to open and use a payment account with basic features. Following from the debate in the European Parliament, consumers should demonstrate a link with the country in which they wish to open a bank account, for example through work or study. A migrant may be required to show a genuine interest in opening a bank account while Member States shall ensure that the exercise of the right is not made too difficult or burdensome for the consumer.[19] It is doubtful that such a call for a not-too-burdensome process will make banks prioritize the consumer's need for financial inclusion over the pressure – and sanctions if they fail – to fight money laundering and terrorist financing. Indeed, all migrant-consumer rights are without prejudice to the requirements adopted to prevent money laundering.[20]

The EU has been particularly avid in linking money laundering and terrorism financing. Its most recent Directive on the subject is 2015/849, on the prevention of the use of the financial system for the purposes of money laundering or terrorist financing.[21] As the preamble states, the justifications for EU measures are that the soundness, integrity, and stability of credit institutions and financial institutions, and confidence in the financial system as a whole could be seriously jeopardized by the efforts of criminals and their associates to disguise the origin of criminal proceeds or to channel lawful or illicit money for terrorist purposes. Similarly, the preamble suggests that border movement is a relevant

---

[19] Article 16(2) 2014/92.
[20] Article 16(4) Directive 2014/92.
[21] Amending Regulation (EU) No 648/2012 of the European Parliament and of the Council, and repealing Directive 2005/60/EC of the European Parliament and of the Council and Commission Directive 2006/70/EC.

factor in the pursuit of the directive's objectives.[22] For the moment there is little judicial guidance on interpretation of the Directive, though seven cases are pending at the time of writing, most of them referred from Bulgarian and Romanian courts in the context of criminal proceedings.[23]

According to Eurostat data, outflows of personal remittances from the EU-27 have increased since 2013 and amounted to EUR 33.2 billion in 2019.[24] The strong EU support of remittances to families was confirmed on 16 June 2020, international day of family remittances, by the European Commissioner of International Partnerships Jutta Urpilainen, who said, 'Remittances are a lifeline that millions depend on. Falling remittances due to COVID-19 will exacerbate economic hardship and deepen existing vulnerabilities for many. The European Union is determined not to leave the migrants and their families to cope with this crisis alone. We should help those who help – migrants are often key workers in host societies and key providers for their families. We are working to raise awareness, build alliances and promote coordinated efforts to that end.'[25] As remittances from the EU to the rest of the world are very important, facilitating them is an important feature of a bank account.

Another important feature that comes with a bank account is a payment card. Without a payment card, 'unbanked' consumers, including foreigners, are dependent on cash payments. As societies move more towards digital payment, this means that the unbanked are excluded from certain services. On this matter, in the *Hessischer Rundfunk* case, Advocate General Pitruzzella reiterated that when companies reject cash payments this is highly relevant to 'a significant number of vulnerable people who still do not have access to basic financial services digital payment'.[26] Pitruzzella concludes that despite Directive 2014/92/EU,

---

[22] Preamble para 24.
[23] C-544/19 ECOTEX BULGARIA EOOD v Teritorialna direktsia na Natsionalnata agentsia za prihodite; C-790/19 Criminal proceedings against LG, MH; C-811/19 criminal proceedings against FQ, GP, HO, IN, JM; C-859/19 Criminal proceedings against FX, CS and ND; C-926/19 Criminal proceedings against BR, CS, DT, EU, FV, GW; Case C-37/20 WM v Luxembourg Business Registers; Case C-49/20 SF v Teritorialna direktsia na Natsionalna agentsia za prihodite — Plovdiv.
[24] https://ec.europa.eu/eurostat/statistics-explained/index.php/Personal_remittances_statistics#Surge_in_migration_in_2015_re-emphasises_the_importance_of_migrant_transfers, [accessed 1 December 2020].
[25] https://ec.europa.eu/international-partnerships/news/international-day-family-remittances-tackling-covid-19-challenges_en [accessed 22 July 2020].
[26] Conclusion delivered on 29 September 2020, Joined Cases C-422/19, C-423/19.

a significant number of people who are legally residing in the Union are unbanked and vulnerable since cash 'is the only form of accessible money and thus the only means of exercising their fundamental rights linked to the use of money'. She thus calls for a requirement to take into account the 'social inclusion element of cash' when analysing the proportionality of measures 'excluding the use of cash'.[27] At the same time, large cash transactions call for suspicion under Directive 2015/849.[28]

The tensions between the instruments which target money laundering and terrorism financing (where implementation is resulting in action primarily against migrants) and the encouragement of remittances to families, as well as of digital payment instead of cash, in public and private settings, are evident.[29]

The UK

The UK implemented the Payment Account Directive (2016/92) through the Payment Accounts Regulations 2015. The Money Advice Service was designated responsible for ensuring access to basic bank account services. Nine banking institutions in the UK were designated as providers of basic bank services. Fee-free basic banking services are provided to those who can prove their ID and address. However, banks are also are required to carry out immigration status checks on people applying for current accounts, under the Immigration Act 2014, and to keep this information up to date. Under this immigration legislation, banks are under a duty not to provide services to those without specified immigration status and to close the accounts of those who no longer hold the designated immigration status. Thus, while on the one hand the UK implemented the PAD, on the other it did so only for some people in the UK, thus by definition weeding out those migrants whom the Home Office designated as without the necessary immigration status. Not only are these persons to be refused access to open bank accounts, but banks are also required to carry out periodic reviews, and if someone who previously held a permitted immigration status no longer holds one, banks are

---

[27] Ibid., para. 137–138.
[28] Article 11(1)(c) Directive 2015/849/EU requires customer due diligence of cash transactions amounting to EUR 10,000.
[29] The tension, which has resulted in debanking of NGOs, has gained the attention of the European Central Bank: www.eba.europa.eu/calendar/eba-virtual-panel-%E2%80%98risk-management-and-access-financial-services-impact-%E2%80%98de-risking%E2%80%99-not [accessed on 17 January 2021].

required to close their bank accounts (subject to a delay currently in place, see below).

The UK implementation of the PAD, which has the objective of ensuring access to bank accounts for all, does not sit very comfortably with the Global Compact on Migration objective (of promoting faster and cheaper remittances for migrants, in the UK, through access to the official banking sector). The UK has a strong development policy which promotes remittances by migrants in the UK to their families, particularly in the developing world. But the immigration control objective of national policy creates a tension in achieving this aim. Two objectives enter into competition – on the one hand immigration control and the government's objective to exclude from banking (and other) services persons without designated immigration statuses, and on the other hand its development-related objective to ensure access to cheap and fast remittances.

On 22 May 2020 the British International Development Secretary Anne-Marie Trevelyan said:

> The coronavirus pandemic means we are all concerned about how our family and friends here and overseas are coping. That's why we're making it easier for diaspora communities in the UK and other countries to continue to transfer money to their relatives. (...) This will be lifesaving for some families in developing countries where coronavirus is making a lack of food and healthcare, and extreme poverty, even worse. We are helping to prevent fragile economies from facing potential collapse during the pandemic.[30]

This statement follows a long-standing policy of the Department for International Development to assist and encourage migrants in the UK to send remittances to their families overseas. In 2000 the UK government issued a White Paper on Eliminating Work Poverty: Making Globalisation Work for the Poor which recognized remittances as a significant benefit for developing countries.[31] In 2004, the House of Commons International Development Committee published the results of its investigation into migration and development, which recognized remittances as an important contributor to the objective of world poverty reduction.[32] It identified three main ways in which people in the UK send

---

[30] www.gov.uk/government/news/uk-calls-for-global-action-to-protect-vital-money-transfers [accessed 23 July 2020].
[31] Cm 5006, para 133.
[32] International Development Committee: Migration and Development: How to Make Migration work for Poverty Reduction HC 79-I, 8 July 2004.

money abroad: (1) family and friends take cash when going to the destination country; (2) money transfer operators (MTOs) such as Western Union or MoneyGram and banks; (3) informal hawala brokers.

According to a recent research paper,[33] people in the UK send twice as much money abroad as is received by people living in the UK from abroad. There are numerous ways of measuring the number of remittances by country, depending on GDP of the receiving country, population, etc. According to the study, no matter what measurement is used, four countries come out as top destinations of remittances from the UK: Kenya, Nigeria, Zimbabwe, and Lithuania. But the cost of sending money abroad remains stubbornly high in the UK. The costs of remittances from the UK currently stand at 7.12 per cent of the value of the transfer. The SDGs have established a goal of 3 per cent by 2030. It does not look likely that the UK will achieve this without substantial and sustained leadership committed to results. The cost of sending money abroad from the UK varies greatly depending on how and where it is sent.[34] Cash transfers are significantly more expensive than bank transfers, according to the report. The average cost of remitting cash was 9.54 per cent of the value in 2019, whereas the cost of a bank transfer using a debit/credit card was 4.88 per cent. Thus, there is an important saving for those people who can open and retain bank accounts as regards remittances.

However, for non-British citizens, opening and retaining bank accounts became substantially more difficult in 2014 when the government adopted a new policy, formerly known as the hostile environment (renamed the compliant environment), which has been much criticized but remains in place.[35] The policy is designed to reduce the number of migrants who are present in the UK without permission. It was first proposed in 2012, and the objective was to exclude migrants without permission from various aspects of life in the UK, thus, to encourage them to leave the country voluntarily. The measures adopted include limiting and preventing access to work, housing, healthcare, bank accounts, driving licences, and justice. Most of the measures were enacted by the Immigration Act 2014, extended in 2016.[36] The consistency of these provisions with the PAD is highly questionable, not least

---

[33] Silva and Klimaviciute, 2020.
[34] Silva and Klimaviciute, 2020.
[35] www.theguardian.com/uk-news/2018/aug/27/hostile-environment-anatomy-of-a-policy-disaster; https://lordslibrary.parliament.uk/research-briefings/lln-2018-0064/ [both accessed 23 July 2020].
[36] Section 40 UK Immigration Act 2014.

because of its very restrictive interpretation of the 'legally resident' qualification of Article 15.

The 2014 Act simplified procedures to expel persons identified by the Home Office as illegally present. In order to assist in identifying them, checks in various databases are carried out comparing data held by various state authorities on individuals with immigration status in the Home Office database.[37] Among many problems with the measures, one has been that the capacity of the Home Office to identify correctly who is irregularly present in the UK was seriously overestimated. It turned out that the implementation of the policy could not identify properly many migrants whose permission to live in the UK depends on statute rather than the Home Office database per se. This came to light in particular with regard to many nationals of Caribbean states who had come to the UK at young ages, when their states of origin were still colonies of the UK (though later became independent), and whose permission to remain in the UK was based on a legal presumption rather than the UK's database. Because the Home Office database did not reflect their immigration status as 'lawful' the full force of the hostile environment measures was applied to them, including the mandatory closure of their bank accounts. This became known as the Windrush scandal, named after the famous ship *Empire Windrush*, which brought Caribbean British subjects (as they then were) to the UK as workers in 1949.[38] The injustice which the Hostile Environment policy delivered to these migrants was the subject of investigative journalism from 2017 onwards, as well as an investigation by the House of Lords.[39]

Section 40 of Immigration Act 2014 requires banks and other financial institutions to refuse to open an account, to review existing accounts on a quarterly basis, and to notify the Home Office if any account holder appears to be disqualified on immigration status grounds.[40] Further, it gives power to the Home Office to notify banks of accounts which must be closed on account of the immigration status of the holder. The relevant secondary legislation came into force in 2017; the delay not least was the result of sustained criticism by lawyers,[41] banks, and financial institutions

---

[37] Webber, 2019; Goodfellow, 2019.
[38] Mead, 2009.
[39] Gentleman, 2019.
[40] The Immigration Act 2014 (Current Accounts) (Excluded Accounts and Notification Requirements) Regulations 2016
[41] https://ilpa.org.uk/wp-content/uploads/resources/21111/13.10.22ILPA-Briefing-Immigration-Bill-HC-2R.pdf [accessed 24 July 2020].

themselves.[42] A report by the Independent Chief Inspector of Borders and Immigration (ICIBI) on driving licences and bank accounts issued in 2016[43] outlined very clearly the problems both for banks and migrants of the legislation which had been adopted, and the high risk of inaccuracy. Further investigation by the ICIBI[44] indicates that 10 per cent of the cases of bank account closures (information provided by the Home Office itself) inspected by the ICIBI were in respect of persons who had been incorrectly included on the list of the disqualified. The consequence of the new obligations on banks and other financial institutions has been to create a reluctance in the institutions to open or retain bank accounts for migrants.[45]

In 2018, the Home Office paused the application of its legislation which forces banks to refuse services to potential and existing clients on the basis of immigration status in light of the Windrush scandal.[46] However, the duty of banks to close bank accounts and refusal to open them for migrants with uncertain immigration status is still on the Home Office website.[47]

For the purposes of this chapter, the UK legislation limiting migrants' access to formal banking services clearly increases the costs of their remittances. As outlined above, the cheapest way to send remittances is via banks (debit and credit card transfers). If migrants cannot get access to the formal banking system in the UK then they must fall back on other more expensive or uncertain ways of sending money to their families in countries of origin, including via friends or hawala systems. The UK legislation also contributed to migrants' financial and social exclusion or 'expulsion' from UK society as unbanked.

The Netherlands

In 2001, Dutch consumer banks concluded a covenant to regulate access to a basic bank account for anyone who did not have access to one. This

---

[42] Humphries, 2004.
[43] ICIBI report of the hostile environment measures relating to driving licences and bank accounts, October 2016.
[44] House of Commons Home Affairs Committee *Immigration Policy: a Basis for Building Consensus* 15 January 2018 HC 500 Session 2017-2019.
[45] House of Lords, Impact of the Hostile Environment Debate 14 June 2018.
[46] www.theguardian.com/uk-news/2018/may/17/home-office-suspends-immigration-checks -on-uk-bank-accounts [accessed 24 July 2020].
[47] www.gov.uk/government/publications/current-account-closed-or-refused-based-on- immigration-status [accessed 24 July 2020].

was part of their social responsibility policies as a means to provide access to a bank account for the homeless in particular, not specifically migrants. Briefly, in 2006, parliamentary attention was drawn to the costs of remittances for migrants in the Netherlands, but this did not lead to any policy changes.[48] A 2013 report on remittances positioned the Netherlands as a medium costly (8.51 per cent in 2012) country to send remittances from.[49] Access to a bank account was not problematized; remittances were mostly paid through other channels such as MTOs (Western Union, MoneyGram) or informal services (including e-hawala).[50] Access to a bank account for migrants over the age of 18 years who could identify themselves was not an issue.[51] If indeed that was the case, financial inclusion has not necessarily improved since then.

In 2016 the covenant was replaced by the implementation of the PAD in the Dutch Financial Supervision Act (Wft). The brief political debate illustrates how unaware the politicians were of the relevance of a bank account for migrants and the relation with their (lack of a) residence status. The government stipulated that a genuine interest in a basic bank account would naturally exist in case of a clear relationship with the Netherlands. Such a relationship would be assumed in the case of lawful residence but also be present when someone has 'Dutch nationality, family ties, professional practice, work placement or apprenticeship, exploration of employment opportunities or other professional activities, study or vocational training, residence or property in the Netherlands and an asylum or migration application that is still being processed'.[52] Interestingly, the Minister also said, 'The consumer's place of residence, for example, should not be a factor in this; what is important is that the consumer is legally resident in the European Union. Banks may therefore *not require the consumer to be lawfully resident in the Netherlands.*'[53] So, unlike in the UK, unlike Dutch social security law, and unlike the Dutch Linking Act (linking residence status to access to public services), access to a bank account, at least in theory, was not linked to residence status.[54]

In practice, however, barriers to access or to maintain a bank account exist in a wide range of situations, of which we mention three. First,

---

[48] Parliamentary Documents II 2005/06, 26234, nr.56.
[49] Parliamentary Documents II 2014/15, 30573, nr.126.
[50] De Winter et al, 2014.
[51] Parliamentary Documents II 2014/15, 30573, nr.126.
[52] Parliamentary Documents II 2015/16, 34480, nr.3.
[53] Parliamentary Documents II 2015/16, 34480, nr.6. Our italics.
[54] De Lange, 2020.

unauthorized migrants will almost never have all the documents banks require from a consumer under the 'know your client' policies to prevent terrorist financing and money laundering.[55] A citizen service number (BSN) is one of the requirements, pursuant to the Money Laundering and Terrorist Financing Prevention Act, to open a bank account.[56] Unauthorized migrants usually do not have a BSN because of the Linking Act.[57] Thus they remain unbanked and cannot use a bank account to send remittances home or participate in society through digital payment systems. Second, the right to a bank account is not properly implemented for asylum seekers. Only after six months into the asylum procedure may a BSN be obtained.[58] As a result, asylum seekers cannot open a bank account during the first six months of the asylum procedure. The reception centres hand them a prepaid money card from Rabobank, which allows them to withdraw money at ATMs or make payments in shops, but it does not allow for digital banking and transferring of remittances. A money card is not linked to a bank account, so it does not provide a payment account within the meaning of the PAD. Third, in recent years, more (business) customers have seen their bank accounts closed due to stricter anti-money laundering rules. Banks must terminate the business relationship if established facts demonstrate that there is an unacceptable risk of money laundering or terrorist financing.[59] To comply with the money laundering or terrorist financing legislation, banks ask very detailed information of their customers, including details on financial transactions of business partners, customers, and suppliers. In fact, in 2019, the national central bank found that the scrutinizing did not go far enough and that they had to re-evaluate customers involved in payments to Russia, Angola, or Malta.[60] In 2020, MTO Suri-Charge, who was responsible in 2014 for one third of the Dutch MTO-market

---

[55] These policies follow from Section 11 of the Law on the prevention of money laundering and terrorist financing (Wwft), Section 4 of the Wwft Implementation Regulations on the obligation to identify, and Section 47b of the National Taxes Act, which outline the administrative requirements banks have to comply with.
[56] Art. 11 Wwft and art. 47b National Taxes Act.
[57] Linking migration status to entitlements. Entitlement to the BSN is regulated in Decree on the registration of foreign nationals who have not been admitted, *Dutch Official Bulletin* 2017, 315.
[58] Art. 21(1)(f) Decree Basic Registration of Identification data.
[59] Appeals Court Amsterdam 29 October 2019, ECLI:NL:GHAMS:2019:3898.
[60] www.businessinsider.nl/rabobank-krijgt-tik-op-de-vingers-van-dnb-40-000-nederlandse-klanten-moeten-opnieuw-worden-doorgelicht-op-witwassen/ [accessed 6 December 2020]

facilitating remittances to Suriname,[61] saw its account with a Dutch bank closed because of many unexplained cash payments.[62]

Due to these obligations, customers with migrant backgrounds or those performing transactions with foreign accounts, be it for remittances or otherwise, are at risk of being unbanked and financially and socially excluded due to the banks' (interpretation of the) obligations. Media reports and court cases on these terminations do not give evidence (as yet) of banks specifically targeting migrants or people with a migrant background. However, they do illustrate that a foreign name or banking with non-EU nations are triggers for enhanced controls. For example, a Polish entrepreneur operating in the Netherlands (trading second-hand cars and small electronics) could not sufficiently inform the bank of his business model and failed in his challenge against Rabobank closing his business accounts. This was not enough reason, however, to close his personal account, thus 'unbanking his business' but not 'unbanking' the individual.[63] Unfortunately, continuing one's business without a business account is difficult; hence, these decisions contribute to an 'expulsion' of foreigners who are otherwise permitted to remain in the country. The extent to which such scrutiny by Dutch banks, for example 'know-your-client' investigations to prevent money laundering, disproportionately excludes people with a foreign background remains unclear. Cursory evidence does seem to point towards disproportionate targeting based on a foreign name, country of birth,[64] foreign transactions,[65] etc.

Conclusion

Safely storing money, sending money home, and paying digitally, especially when cash is less and less commonly accepted, are money issues

---

[61] Winter, 2014.
[62] Interim measure Court Amsterdam 13 March 2020, ECLI:NL:RBAMS:2020:1722.
[63] Amsterdam District Court 30 April 2019, ECLI:NL:RBAMS:2019:3157; Appeals Court Amsterdam 3 November 2020, ECLI:NL:GHAMS:2020:2937.
[64] https://joop.bnnvara.nl/nieuws/fotograaf-salih-kilic-geen-abn-amro-rekening-vanwege-achternaam, [accessed 6 December 2020]; Media relays the ABNAMRO defence as the obligation to conduct extra, time-consuming, checks on accounts for a Foundation involving non-EU foreigners as board members.
[65] A Russian shareholder and selling flowers to Russia should not have led to closing an account, Amsterdam District Court 22 September 2020, ECLI:NL:RBAMS:2020:4902. A Dutch-Russian couple saw their personal ABNAMRO account frozen after the Russian wife handed ten five hundred euro banknotes to the bank for remitting to her son's account in Russia for medicines; the uncommonly used high banknotes triggered the bank: https://radar.avrotros.nl/uitzendingen/gemist/item/fraudecontrole-van-banken-schiet-door/ [inspections by banks are excessive, accessed 6 December 2020].

that matter to migrants. Such money matters demarcate social and financial inclusion or exclusion. Although not necessarily obliged to leave the country, financial exclusion can result in a form of 'expulsion' from society, from running a business, paying for services, and sending remittances home. Our chapter illustrates how the UN and EU norms on combating money laundering and terrorist financing jeopardize the UN Global Compact goals of financial inclusion. Indeed, EU regulation that aims to facilitate financial inclusion clashes with EU and national laws and practices that aim to contribute to the global fight against money laundering and terrorist financing. The latter goal has the upper hand. The elision of terrorism, money laundering, and migration has proved a fertile ground for the exclusion of various categories of migrants from banking services including for the purpose of remittances. Increasingly, irregular migration and the risk of terrorism or money laundering have been intertwined in public discourse with the effect of rendering irregularly present migrants as a source of potential threat against which very coercive measures are justified. As we have investigated here, while on the one hand the PAD has provided a very strong basis to diminish those who are unbanked, the national legislative use of the term 'legally resident', as a qualifying criterion for access to bank services, has been used by two states in the implementation of the Directive as a way to further immigration control objectives, to diminish access to banking services for some migrants, rather than to pursue the objective of the Directive to enlarge that access.

This policy tension between immigration control objectives and access to basic banking services has resulted in substantial disadvantage for migrants. While both the Netherlands and the UK endorsed the UN Global Compact on Migration and consider remittances by migrant workers on their territory to third countries as an important aspect of development, this has not constituted a brake on the coercive use of access to banking services for migrants on the basis of their immigration status. Rather, the immigration and money laundering control imperative has taken the upper hand over the access to banking services/development objectives.

With the continued occurrence of money laundering scandals in the EU, the European Central Bank has called for EU-wide anti–money laundering rules.[66] Obviously, after Brexit, any rules that the EU may

---

[66] Opinion of the European Banking Authority on the future AML/CFT framework in the EU, 10 September 2020 EBA/OP/2020/14.

design might only indirectly impact the UK. However, all EU member states *and* the UK have committed to the UN Global Compact, under which they have pledged to stimulate financial inclusion for migrants.

References

Ampudia, M., Ehrmann M. 2017. 'Financial inclusion: What's it worth?', ECB Working Paper Series No 1990, www.ecb.europa.eu/pub/pdf/scpwps/ecbwp1990.en.pdf.

Bantekas, Ilias. 2003. 'The international law of terrorist financing'. *The American Journal of International Law* 97.2: 315–333.

Cole, David. 2008. 'Terror financing, guilt by association and the paradigm of prevention in the "war on terror"'. *Counterterrorism: Democracy's Challenge*, Bianchi & Keller, eds., Oxford: Hart Publishing, 233–250.

De Lange, Tesseltje. 2020. 'Het recht op een bankrekening voor vreemdelingen in Nederland' [the right to a bank account for foreigners in the Netherlands], *Asiel & Migrantenrecht* 6–7: 296–301.

De Winter, Daniëlle, Laudra Archangel, Gerd Junne and Jane Martie-Chatlein. 2014. *Remittances Market in the Netherlands!* Amsterdam: The Network University (TNU).

D'Orsi, Cristiano. 2021. "Migrant remittances and money laundering in Africa." In Tesseltje de Lange, Willem Maas, and Annette Schrauwen, eds. *Money Matters in Migration. Policy, Participation and Citizenship*. Cambridge: Cambridge University Press.

Gentleman, Amelia. 2019. *The Windrush Betrayal: Exposing the Hostile Environment*. London: Faber & Faber.

Goodfellow, Maya. 2019. *Hostile Environment: How Immigrants Became Scapegoats*. London: Verso Books.

Hodgson, Jacqueline S. and Victor Tadros. 2013. 'The impossibility of defining terrorism'. *New Criminal Law Review* 16.3: 494–526.

Humphries, Beth. 2004. 'An unacceptable role for social work: Implementing immigration policy'. *British Journal of Social Work* 34.1: 93–107.

Kokott, Juliane and Christoph Sobotta. 2012. 'The Kadi case – constitutional core values and international law – finding the balance?'. *European Journal of International Law* 23.4: 1015–1024.

Mead, Matthew. 2009. 'Empire Windrush: The cultural memory of an imaginary arrival'. *Journal of Postcolonial Writing* 45.2: 137–149.

Oliveira, Inês Sofia. 2014. "Catch me if you can: Or how policy networks help tackle the crime–terror nexus'. *Global Crime* 15.3–4: 219–240.

Rosand, Eric. 2003. 'Security Council Resolution 1373, the counter-terrorism committee, and the fight against terrorism'. *The American Journal of International Law* 97.2: 333–341.

Sassen, Saskia. 2014. *Expulsions. Brutality and Complexity in the Global Economy.* Cambridge: Harvard University Press.

Saul, Ben. 2019 'Defining terrorism: A conceptual minefield'. In Erica Chenoweth, Richard English, Andreas Gofas, and Stathis N. Kalyvas eds., *The Oxford Handbook of Terrorism,* Oxford: Oxford University Press. DOI: 10.1093/oxfordhb/9780198732914.013.2

Silva, Carlos Varga and Luka Klimaviciute. 2020. 'Migrant remittances to and from the UK'. *The Migration Observatory at the University of Oxford* 24, 4th revision. https://migrationobservatory.ox.ac.uk/wp-content/uploads/2016/04/Briefing-Migrant-Remittances-to-and-from-the-UK.pdf

Stewart, David P. 1989. 'Internationalizing the war on drugs: The UN convention against illicit traffic in narcotic drugs and psychotropic substances'. *Denv. J. Int'l L. & Pol'y* 18: 387.

Webber, Frances. 2019. 'On the creation of the UK's "hostile environment"'. *Race & Class* 60.4: 76–87.

Winter, Daniëlle de, Laudra Archangel, Gerd Junne, and Jane Martie Chatlein. 2014. 'Remittances Market in the Netherlands!' TNU.

Yeoh, Peter. 2019. 'Banks' vulnerabilities to money laundering activities'. *Journal of Money Laundering Control.* 23.1: 122–135.

13

Migrant Remittances and Money Laundering in Africa

CRISTIANO D'ORSI

Introduction

Remittances are vital for the existence of many African families and to the survival of many African economies.[1] Yet the African market of remittances persists in its underdevelopment in terms of the regulatory environment as well as financial organization.[2] Remittances represent a resource through which the formal financial system includes also the rural population. Additionally, they have a positive influence on both financial development and poverty in Africa.[3]

The African Migration Project's (AMP) assessment of African households discloses three arrangements. First, domestic and African intra-regional transfers of money are remitted through non-formal networks. Additionally, a huge portion of remittances from other continents are controlled by a handful of international money transfer agencies. They are frequently working in cooperation with African post offices and banks. Finally, the implementation of new banking and mobile money transfer tools is changing the setting for financial services and remittances on the continent.[4]

This tendency has shown the necessity for regulatory frameworks to control the sector under scrutiny as it puts pressures on countries and institutions. For example, the Central Bank of Kenya recognizes that the technology that delivers mobile money services poses threats of, for instance, money laundering and financial fraud.[5] Indeed, Africa has earned

---

[1] Terry 2005, 8–9.
[2] Staff Writer 2016.
[3] Cooray 2012, 937–939.
[4] Staff Writer 2016.
[5] Mwega 2014, 17.

a wicked reputation as a port of call for money laundering. However, things are changing on the continent because banks are facing increasing external influences to conform to anti–money laundering (AML) legislation seriously and local banks realize that they must play their part in fighting money laundering if they want to become credible financial actors in the global market.[6]

Formal regional and international service providers specializing in remittances are increasing their competition. This is evident among banks and mobile telecommunication operators (MTOs), because each of them has a wide offer that includes selling point, account, online, mobile, or a blend of these products.[7] Moreover, banks and telecom companies are financing a technical design. They do so both to facilitate future continental and regional growth and to meet domestic necessities. These developments contribute to migrant financial inclusion and create occasions for persons who had been left out of financial markets in the past.[8]

This chapter investigates the intersection of the regulatory framework and practice of remittances of emigrants in Africa on the one hand and the regulatory frameworks of combating money laundering. The chapter contributes to the nascent scholarly literature on the peculiarities of interaction between the state parties of the African Union (AU) on the issues related to remittances and combating money laundering. The investigation reveals a complex relationship. At the core of this relationship lie a myriad of normative concepts relating to migrants and 'money': the fear of financing terrorism and human trafficking, the need for financial institutions to participate in the international financial configuration, the importance of remittances for the economies back home, and the struggle for migrants' financial inclusion and reduced risk of falling victim to shady financial services, high costs, or even loss of their money. The chapter first discusses the global framework for remittances as designed by the World Bank (WB) and its relationship with the fight against money laundering and then presents three case studies: Somalia, South Africa (SA), and Kenya.

Global and Regional Initiatives on Remittances

Globally, the WB plays an important role in facilitating remittances, which is part of the WB's mission:

---

[6] Lawrence 2017.
[7] Staff Writer 2016.
[8] Lagarde 2014.

[T]o end extreme poverty and promote shared prosperity. Justice and the rule of law are key to achieving these twin goals. A lack of justice is a central dimension of poverty, and increasing evidence points to the importance of accountable and effective justice institutions in creating the enabling environment for a range of development outcomes – from improved basic services to increased private sector investment and reduced corruption.[9]

Through its Global Remittances Working Group (GRWG), a public–private business with the goal to enhance transparency and to shrink the cost of transfers, the WB provides evidence-based policy recommendations on remittances and migration; strengthens international partnerships in leveraging migration for comprehensive development; mobilizes diaspora investments for development and leveraging remittances for financial inclusion; and monitors, and analyses the global flows of remittances and migration.[10] The WB argues that the high cost of transactions is reducing the positive effect remittances can have on poverty considering that around 120 million Africans depend on them.[11]

The Global Compact for Safe, Orderly and Regular Migration (Global Compact)[12] offers another global structure – although not mandatory – stressing the importance of financial inclusion and remittances.[13] In this regard, Objective No. 20 ('Promote faster, safer and cheaper transfer of remittances and foster financial inclusion of migrants') stipulates that signatory states commit to promoting 'faster, safer and cheaper' remittances. States do so through the development of favourable regulatory environments and policy through favouring the economic presence of migrants. Among other actions, this objective will be reached by

> Harmoniz[ing] remittance market regulations and increase[ing] the interoperability of remittance infrastructure along corridors by ensuring that measures to combat illicit financial flows and money-laundering do not impede migrant remittances through undue, excessive or discriminatory policies.

In Africa, the Making Finance Work for Africa (MFW4A) initiative was launched in 2007 to create a common platform to facilitate and harmonize the development of the financial sector and knowledge

---

[9] UN undated.
[10] World Bank Group 2017.
[11] World Bank 2015. For example, for the relation between migration, remittances, and education, see Luo and Treiman 2011.
[12] United Nations General Assembly (UNGA) 2018.
[13] On its relevance in the EU context see De Lange and Guild in this volume.

sharing on the African continent.[14] In this framework, which backs up the work of the WB, initiatives were undertaken in order to tackle financial crime on the continent.[15] Noteworthy also is the work of the 2018 African Institute of Remittances (AIR), a Specialized Technical Office of the African Union Commission.[16] Its objectives include to

> Promote appropriate changes to the legal and regulatory frameworks for remittances, payments and settlements systems as well as use of innovative technology so as to promote greater competition and efficiency, resulting in reduction of transfer costs; and leverage the potential impact of remittances on social and economic development of Member States, as well as promoting financial inclusion.[17]

One of the main goals of the AIR is that both Africans of the diaspora and their families in Africa could take advantage of the low costs of remittance transfers, thus encouraging the social and economic growth of their countries of origin.[18]

On the other hand, combating money laundering remains an international problem hurting diaspora remittance transfers. For example, the phenomenon of bank 'de-risking' (financial institutions terminating the accounts of customers they estimate to be of 'high risk'), as illustrated by De Lange and Guild in this volume, is now widely accepted. De-risking impacts negatively on remittances to Africa, which impact has not yet been comprehensively documented.[19]

Global and Regional Initiatives on Fighting Money Laundering

The 1999 OAU Convention on Prevention and Combating of Terrorism set a range of problems related to money laundering issues, making them clear only in the enacting clause:

---

[14] African Development Bank (AfDB) undated.
[15] AfDB 2016.
[16] Anonymous 2014, 20275A: 'The African Union (AU) Executive Council has accepted Kenya's offer to host the African Institute for Remittances (AIR), which is due to take off in 2014 and become fully operational in 2015 [...] The decision to create AIR was taken by the AUC within the framework of the Africa-EU partnership on Migration, Mobility and Employment, for the purpose of leveraging the untapped development potential of remittance flows to the African continent. The precise volume of the remittances is unknown and presumed underestimated, their transfer cost remains unacceptably high by international standards and their full potential for economic and social development is largely unexploited.'
[17] AIR. Statute 2018.
[18] AIR. Progress Report 2018, 4.
[19] E.g. Broadway 2015.

> The Member States of the Organization of African Unity: [...] Aware of the growing links between terrorism and organized crime, including the illicit traffic of arms, drugs and money laundering.[20]

The subsequent 2002 Action Plan of the high-level intergovernmental meeting of the African Union for the Prevention and Combating of Terrorism in Africa defined a clear set of steps necessary to improve the effectiveness of combating money laundering on the continent.[21] Member States undertake to 'introduce legislation to criminalize the financing of terrorism and money laundering' (Action Plan article 13 (c)); 'train personnel in charge of preventing and combating money laundering, with international technical assistance where necessary' (Action Plan article 13(i)); 'cooperate with International Financial Institutions for the development of a global, comprehensive, Anti-Money Laundering and Combating the Financing of Terrorism' (Action Plan article 13(j)).

The fight against money laundering is still far from won. In this regard, in 2019 the European Commission adopted a new listing of twenty-three countries with deficits in both their counter-terrorist financing and anti–money laundering agendas. Because of the listing, banks complying with European Union anti–money laundering rules apply more detailed checks on financial operations carried out by financial institutions and customers from the list. This is done to better detect any suspicious movement of money. Among the twenty-three countries listed, six are African: Botswana, Ethiopia, Ghana, Libya, Nigeria, and Tunisia.[22] Besides, the 'Objectives, Standards, Criteria and Indicators' for the African Peer Review Mechanism, of the New Partnership for Africa's Development (NEPAD) Heads of State and Government Implementation Committee have been put in place, committed to fighting money laundering on the continent through, for example, the 'enactment and enforcement of effective [...] anti-money laundering laws'.[23]

Despite the efforts of the AU to combat money laundering, regional progress remains insignificant. The main underlying reason for this is the lack of necessary political will, limited opportunities for the implementation of necessary measures, and, ultimately, non-compliance of activities of the member states.[24]

---

[20] OAU 1999.
[21] AU 2002.
[22] European Commission 2019.
[23] NEPAD Secretariat 2002, para 3.4.3 (b) ("Examples of Indicators").
[24] Bokosi, and Chikumbu 2015, 3.

The Cases of Somalia, South Africa, and Kenya

Somalia

Being a Muslim country Somalia follows the Islamic model of finance. The foundations of Islamic finance are gambling, excessive uncertainty, and, above all, risk and profit sharing between financial partners as well as the prohibition of usury or interest ('riba'). Furthermore, assets and investments are made in, and only derive from, activities complying with Shariah, and tangible and identifiable underlying assets must support transactions. A Shariah Supervisory Board (SBD) supervises the institutions offering Islamic financial services.[25]

For more than twenty years, remittances have been at the foundations of the Somali financial system. In 2014, the International Monetary Fund (IMF) organized a mission to Somalia. The missions discovered that $2 billion in money transfers in Somalia are run by money transfer agencies providing shadow banking services given the lack of licensed commercial banks in the country. This is the 'xawilaad' system, the equivalent of the Arabic 'hawala'.[26]

Somali diaspora is experiencing difficulties in sending remittances back home. This is partly because commercial banks in sending countries are de-risking: in response to domestic and international regulations to fight against the financing of terrorism and money laundering, those commercial banks close the bank accounts of Somali MTOs. The involuntary result of these regulations has been that commercial banks have responded to the augmented burdens of the regulatory risks by stopping dealing with Somali MTOs because they are excessively risky.[27]

Since 2011, the United States Agency for International Development (USAID) has provided more than $328 million in development assistance and $1.3 billion in humanitarian assistance to Somalis.[28] According to USAID, its contribution in expanding economic opportunities consists of enabling Somalia's growth potential by reducing or removing economic barriers as well as giving access to finance. Moreover, USAID supports policy and regulation to create openings for economic growth, comprehensive of all the major financial stakeholders of the country.[29]

---

[25] MFW4A undated. For the effectiveness of the SBD: Waemustafa and Abdullah 2015, 458.
[26] Plaza 2014.
[27] Office of the High Commissioner for Human Rights (OHCHR) 2016.
[28] USAID 2017.
[29] USAID Undated, 13.

The establishment of a working group on remittances to Somalia led by the National Security Council proves that the Somali government appreciates the costs of an interruption of the flow of remittances to the country.

The USAID and the US Treasury Department have cooperated with the Central Bank of Somalia to develop the management of its public financial system, including its supervision unit, in order to allow the country to make progress in its banking system and become financially autonomous.[30] In 2014, the Money Remittances Improvement Act entered into force,[31] allowing the Treasury Secretary to use State examinations instead of federal reporting requirements, making it at easy for institutions like money service agencies to make available transfer payments worldwide.

Perhaps most encouraging was the United States Treasury Department's September 2014 assurance to shed light on the opportunities for banks dealing with high-risk MTOs; an assurance reproducing the political engagement to focus on the challenges meeting the remittance pathways problematic to be served. Its Financial Crimes Enforcement Network emphasized that banks are not supposed to know every remitter or to regulate the money services business. For example, in the context of Somalia, the WB advises Somali authorities to establish financial governance systems, which must be credible in the long run while taking prompt steps to diminish the possibility of money laundering. This last action serves to demonstrate reduced risk to money senders and to banks showing interest in transferring money to or doing business in Somalia.[32]

In Somalia, the WB also helped to establish in 2014 the Financial Governance Committee (FGC), to offer an opportunity for advice and dialogue on financial governance matters. The FGC noted that refining the supervision and regulation of Somalia's financing system was precarious in many aspects. Its purpose was to re-establish relations with international banks, hence protecting the remittances to Somalia, which, in 2017, amounted to nearly 25 per cent of GDP.[33] The adoption of the Anti-Money Laundering and Countering the Financing of Terrorism Act in 2016 also represented an important landmark. Its implementation should

---

[30] ADESO, Global Centre on Cooperative Security, and OXFAM 2015, 7.
[31] US Government Publishing Office 2014.
[32] ADESO, Global Centre on Cooperative Security, and OXFAM 2015, 7, 15.
[33] Federal Government of Somalia 2017, 1, 20.

also reduce risk concerns among international banks, allowing them to reinstate their financial transactions with Somalia.[34]

However, remittances from Somali migrants are not alternatives for national revenues or for international aid to develop the country. They play dissimilar roles promoting development: remittance incomes attend to precise goals, being subject to the choices of recipients and the diaspora, while foreign direct investments (FDI) may affect national infrastructure and Official Development Assistance addresses the people's social needs at a more national level. While some analysts may find informal systems' fragmented nature advantageous because they can help undocumented migrants and people in rural areas to access services, others believe informal channels assist criminal activities due to their degree of fragmentation and anonymity.[35]

South Africa

In SA, in 2017 the Financial Intelligence Centre Amendment (FICA) Act was promulgated, with the purpose of supporting the legislation in force, fighting against the financing of terrorism and money laundering by introducing a risk-based approach to customer due diligence.[36] The most significant amendment consists in the introduction of the risk-based method to the identification and assessment of terrorist financing and money laundering risks. Instead of setting absolute minimum requirements, the risk-based approach enables a responsible institution to adopt risk-informed choices regarding the management of its unique risks.[37] It puts the risk-based method at the centre of SA's AML/Counter Financing Terrorism regime, recognizing that the risks of terrorist financing and money laundering differ between and within sectors.[38] The FICA Act also requires an understanding of terrorist financing and money laundering threats at different stages, including within institutions in private sectors and the national Government.

Counting on customer due diligence measures, the scope of the FICA Act is to improve clarity in the financial system. In this way, it is easy to understand who deals with both non-financial and financial

---

[34] It defines as offences money laundering (article 2) and terrorism financing (article 3). Article 6 prohibits the opening of bank accounts anonymously or under a fictitious name.
[35] European Parliament 2013, 21, 28–29, 36.
[36] Republic of SA 2017. In this regard, see: Bester, Hougaard, and Chamberlain 2010, 17–19.
[37] Hugo, and Spruyt 2018, 236–237.
[38] Government of SA 2017, 1.

institutions and to establish the background of the corresponding business.[39] This is imaginable if suitable data are taken by the financial institutions in order to back up any ensuing investigation of terrorist financing and money laundering. From this it follows that institutions in the South African financial system are doing business with well-known entrepreneurs. Additionally, they can identify customers who are doing illegal business, reporting them to the authorities.[40]

Governments are more and more adopting a firm attitude of attack towards economic crimes. This is because non-compliance impacts on their capacity to secure foreign loans, necessary for their development, at the same time excluding them from global financial markets.[41] In this effort, they are also helped by the entry into force of the 2003 African Union (AU) Convention on Preventing and Combating Corruption[42] whose Article 6 is dedicated to the 'cleaning' of the profits made through corruption. The Convention has the potential to reduce opportunities for States' top officials to use the international banking system to 'clean' the earnings from corruption.[43] A similar article is present also in the United Nations (UN) Convention against Corruption (Art. 23 'Laundering of Proceeds of Crimes'). This convention also has an article (Art. 14) entirely dedicated to measures to prevent money laundering. The UN Convention has been widely ratified in Africa, with the only two exceptions represented by Eritrea and Somalia.[44] In particular, SA is putting in place several strategies in order to more completely fight against the plight of corruption in the country.[45]

Currently, SA legislation intended to counter money laundering obliges banks to implement several processes and controls to detect and investigate suspicious activities.[46] It also compels customers to provide proof of the source of their funds and proof of residence before they can have access to financial services. Banks must verify the identities of clients before opening accounts, keeping transaction records, and reporting suspicious transactions.[47] This procedure excludes honest migrants who are paid in cash and those living in informal

---

[39] Financial Intelligence Centre undated (Draft Guidance), 2.
[40] Government of SA 2017, 1.
[41] Lawrence 2017.
[42] AU 2003.
[43] Olaniyan 2004, 84. Generally, see: Udombana 2003.
[44] UNGA 2003.
[45] E.g. Budhram and Gueldenhuys 2018, 57.
[46] Lawrence 2017.
[47] Financial Intelligence Centre undated (Guidance Note 4), 2.

settlements.[48] Local banks, often used in the past by migrants – both documented and undocumented – to send remittances home, have started to realize that, in order to conduct business in global markets, they need to more strictly comply with anti–money laundering legislation. Foreign banks are hesitant to register African financial institutions as correspondent banks because this provokes too many risks if the African partner bank is insolvent. For this reason, for example, Deutsche Bank has terminated several partnerships with banks in Africa.[49]

These regulations have repercussions on the lives of migrants, especially on costs of remittances. While South Asians pay $6 for every $100 they send home, Africans pay twice that amount. SA has the highest remittance costs in Africa and approximately 21 per cent of money saved for relatives in SA is spent in shipping charges.[50] The average fees for transferring remittances to Africa were 9.3 per cent in the first quarter of 2019, the World Bank found. This figure is significantly higher than the Sustainable Development Goal (SDG)[51] target of 3 per cent. Banks were the most expensive network to transfer remittances, at an average cost of 10.9 per cent.[52] The high cost of remittances in Africa occurs for several reasons. First, regulations require MTOs to ensure that they are not supporting terrorists by sending them money or helping them in money laundering. The administrative costs associated with these payments may discourage people with bad intentions. However, these costs also increase the charges for people legally receiving money. The result is that many of them turn to informal markets. Yet, transactions of small amounts will benefit from less onerous regulations. Lack of choice by consumers is another reason why costs of remittances may be high in Africa. For example, the South African Post Office (SAPO: the national postal service of SA) for many years has cooperated with only one MTO – Telkom. Until 1991, SAPO and Telkom formed one company, in fact. As the post office is an accessible place to collect money sent from abroad, especially in rural areas, post offices hold a virtual monopoly in many

---

[48] Carter 2011, 530.
[49] Lawrence 2017.
[50] IRIN News 2013.
[51] The SDGs are a collection of seventeen global goals set by the UNGA in 2015 for the year 2030. The SDGs are part of the 2015 Resolution of the UNGA 'The 2030 Agenda for Sustainable Development', A/RES/70/1.
[52] KNOMAD 2019, vii.

African regions. Monopolies entail higher costs on those transfers and, consequently, smaller amounts of money received by Africans.[53]

Taking as an example remittances from SA to Zimbabwe, in June 2018 the average cost to send $100 via bank was about $23 while using an MTO (such as Western Union or MoneyGram) the average cost was about $10. MTOs can deliver the money within hours while banks can take from 2 to 5 working days.[54] At the same time in 2018, to remit $500 from Kenya to Uganda cost, on average, about $21 via bank, about $17 via post office, but only $9 via MTOs, with delivery always made within hours of sending.[55] In another context, Malians in Senegal remit money exclusively through MTOs with an average fee of $6 on about $150.[56] A different example is given by Nigerians in SA, which have never followed a strategy of development led by remittances as, on the contrary, has been the case in countries with higher rates of emigration. This is due to the notion that international migration only exposes developing countries to brain drain and capital flight.[57]

The industry innovates in offerings from retailers and financial services companies, along with other challenges to be considered. Since Shoprite's (Africa's largest food retailer) introduction of money transfer at its money market counter in 2006, retailers, banks, and mobile operators targeting remittance users have significantly augmented they offerings.[58]

Today, major South African banks offer services focused on money transfers and allowing holders of accounts to transfer money to any South African cell phone. Then, the beneficiary can collect the money from an ATM through an access code.[59] Alternatively, Zimbabwean migrants in SA rely on informal paths to transfer their money home, for example giving it to friends or even bus drivers. As a matter of fact, this method is often not much cheaper than using banks, while also being considerably riskier. Many migrants report negative experiences, including long delays in remittances reaching the recipients, loss of their goods, and theft of their money.[60]

---

[53] Kopf 2018.
[54] AU undated, from SA to Zimbabwe.
[55] AU undated, from Kenya to Uganda.
[56] AU undated, from Senegal to Mali.
[57] Oyebamiji, and Asuelime 2018, 226.
[58] Techno Service 2016, 2.
[59] McGovern 2011.
[60] PASSOP 2012, 23–24.

While developments have effectively permitted low-cost and secure channels for South Africans to receive and send money within the country, opportunities persist to improve financial inclusion. Existing domestic remittance products do not adequately build up bonds to a wider variety of financial products. Many beneficiaries collect remittance receipts instantly. The result is that this configuration is detached from the general growth in electronic payments and developing connections across the financial system.[61] In effect, this situation can entail fraud and money laundering risks to providers who do not have visibility into the financial histories of their customers.[62]

Contrary to international remittances, managing issues have not arisen as a significant obstacle to the introduction of low-cost offerings. Yet, two significant requirements make up the market. First, users are obliged to show a proof of identity (South African Smart ID Card). Second, non-banks need to cooperate with a financial institution in order to offer effective money transfer products. For instance, Shoprite's money transfer service functions via Standard Bank. These two requirements represent a barrier for new market candidates to overcome, particularly if they cannot rely on a physical footprint (to verify IDs in person) or if they do not have relationships with any South African banks.[63]

Kenya

In Kenya, the Proceeds of Crime and Anti-Money Laundering (Amendment) Act 2017 (POCAMLA 2017) inflicts rigid penalties on those guilty of economic crimes.[64] Although Kenya has had an AML legislation in force since 2009 – and revised in 2012[65] – the country has remained exposed to financial fraud and money laundering.[66] The scantiness of the previous legal context to implement an area that has experienced substantial developments in traditional as well as in non-traditional financial services has generated several breaches, exploited by a variety of actors.[67] In order to fight money laundering and guarantee

---

[61] Techno Service 2016, 2.
[62] Radcliffe, and Voorhies 2012, 4.
[63] Techno Service 2016, 10.
[64] Government of Kenya 2017; Section 24B, not exceeding 5 million shillings – about $50,000 – for a natural person and not exceeding 25 million shillings – about $250,000 – for a corporate body.
[65] Government of Kenya 2009, section 3.
[66] Barasa 2018, 4.
[67] Africa Practice 2017, 1–3.

privacy on remittances, in 2018 a Data Protection Bill was introduced, which would require banks, telecommunications operators, and other businesses to obtain consent before collecting and processing personal data.[68] Still, flaws in the legal regulation and in how to enforce it have been emphasized in several bribery scandals that have shaken Kenya recently.[69]

Kenya has seen a rise in innovative finance start-ups, in addition to the ever-growing under-regulated network of unlicensed money remittance systems.[70] So, although rigour in the application of POCAMLA 2017 is yet to be observed, it may be that organizations in this space – hosting platforms that are potential havens for money laundering – will be most severely affected.[71] Nonetheless, the spirit of the new legislation is right to tackle a regulatory system that has been lacking in many areas, and it represents a strong step in the right direction in this regard.

Diaspora remittances to Kenya from Kenyans abroad have been growing. Remittances for December 2018 amounted to $243.6, million, being 19.5 per cent higher than the inflows registered in December 2017. Remittances from North America accounted for 45 per cent ($109.7 million) of total inflows in December 2018, while inflows from Europe and other continents accounted for 31.8 per cent ($77.4 million) and 23.2 per cent ($56.5 million), respectively. The total remittance inflows in 2018 amounted to $2,697 million, which was 39 per cent higher than the $1,947 million recorded in 2017.[72] Presently, diaspora remittances are Kenya's highest foreign exchange beneficiary, with euros, US dollars, and British pounds sterling having overtaken tea and coffee exports and tourism.[73]

What's Next?

In previous decades, attempts to back financial systems and remittances in Africa have alternated between periods of gratification and crisis management.[74]

---

[68] United Nations High Commissioner for Refugees (UNHCR) 2019, 45.
[69] Wambui 2018, 44–45.
[70] Africa Practice 2017, 3.
[71] Africa Practice 2017, 3.
[72] Central Bank of Kenya 2018.
[73] Amadala 2019.
[74] ADESO, Global Centre on Cooperative Security, and OXFAM 2015, 15.

Money transfers helped to broaden the dimensions of the financial market in Africa but also led to a reduction in fixed charges and net interest margin. While the flow of remittances is also at the origin of the growth of the financial sector in African countries where governments own the majority (if not the totality) of banks, an even greater growth in their financial sector is experienced by countries where the government owns very few banks. The ownership of banks by government is more relevant in African countries with poor protection of property rights, an underdeveloped financial system, an interventionist (in the national economy) government, and a low level of per head income.[75]

Merits of migration in developing countries are still debated. On one side, migration can drain financial and human assets from the countries of origin of migrants, helping the growth of the personal income of the migrant. However, from this standpoint, remittances represent an enticement for migration, in this way contributing to falling domestic production and revenues.[76]

The perception, corroborated by the reality illustrated in the previous paragraphs, that Africa is the epitomic last stop to launder money has changed in recent years. Better technology, stronger legislation on the matter, and a greater commitment by banks represent three aspects that should allow Africa to become a compliance environment. The AU is actively participating in this effort by considering 'money laundering' as one of the crimes for which the African Court of Justice and Human Rights has competence.[77]

The international community's research efforts should address the termination of the bank accounts of market speculators as well as the consolidation of financial institutions in Africa. Some proposals to address long-standing subjects are undisputed, for example, the creation of the conditions for a more transparent banking sector on the continent and greater capacity for supervision within the financial institutions.[78] On the other hand, some questions that are similarly not conducive to a more sustainable African financial system would necessitate supplementary analysis because they are not understood. In addition, the effects of the growing dependence on mobile money for international

---

[75] Cooray 2012, 955.
[76] Orozco, and Wilson 2005, 376.
[77] AU 2014. Art. 28I bis of the Malabo Protocol. To date, 15 November 2020 not yet into force.
[78] E.g. Quintyn, and Taylor 2007.

remittances as well as regular payments, with a special look at marginalized communities, women, and elderly populations, should be studied.[79]

Based on the fact that remittances are important in favouring economic growth, governments in Africa should put in place policies to ensure that remitting is attractive for Africans living abroad. The flow of remittances should not be hindered and should preferably flow through formal or official channels.[80] Such policies should concentrate on increasing the consistency and effectiveness of international money transfer mechanisms as well as on making the cost of international money transfers cheaper.[81] In this regard, African governments should avoid the temptation to tax remittances. Any levy would be not fruitful given the low wages of many senders.[82] In fact, countries will obtain greater social and economic gains from remittances through institutional and regulatory changes that will allow more viable options for Africans when leveraging their money.[83]

Finally, while the global political system has adopted mechanisms to simplify international communication, investment, and trade *and* instruments to combat money laundering, less has been done for people moving abroad as part of the globalization process. The UN Global Compact is soft law and has yet to show its worth. In many African countries nothing concrete is being done to curb illegal migration: too many economic sectors would be adversely affected by such a decision. Immigration laws, especially in those particular host African countries favouring tighter immigration rules on both national security and economic grounds, are not reflective of the actuality provided by the new labour markets.[84] The increase of remittances calls for a broader discussion of immigration policies in the African context.

References

Adenutsi, Deodat E. 2011. 'Financial development, international migrant remittances and endogenous growth in Ghana'. *Studies in Economics and Finance* 28, no.1: 68–89.

---

[79] Okello 2015, 41.
[80] Nyamongo et al. 2012, 258–59.
[81] Adenutsi 2011, 82.
[82] Piper, and Basaran 2018.
[83] Orozco, and Wilson 2005, 391.
[84] Terry 2005, 13.

ADESO, Global Centre on Cooperative Security, and OXFAM. 2015. *Hanging by a Thread: the Ongoing Threat to Somalia's Remittance Lifeline*. At https://reliefweb.int/sites/reliefweb.int/files/resources/bn-hanging-by-thread-somalia-remittances-190215-en.pdf

Africa Practice. 2017. *A Perspective on Kenya's Proceeds of Crime and Anti-Money Laundering (Amendment) Act, 2017*. At www.africapractice.com/wp-content/uploads/2017/05/africapractice-A-perspective-on-Kenyas-Proceeds-of-Crime-and-Anti-Mon....pdf

AfDB. 2007. 'Making finance work for Africa partnership'. At www.afdb.org/en/topics-and-sectors/initiatives-partnerships/making-finance-work-for-africa-partnership/economic-financial-governance

2016. 'The African Development Bank to partner with Standard Chartered Bank and tackle financial crime'. At www.afdb.org/en/news-and-events/the-african-development-bank-to-partner-with-standard-chartered-bank-and-tackle-financial-crime-16213/

AIR. 2018. *Progress Report*. At https://au.int/sites/default/files/newsevents/workingdocuments/34086-wd-air_progress_report_-_stc_finance_2018_english.pdf

2018. *Statute*. At https://au.int/sites/default/files/treaties/35831-treaty-statute_african_institute_for_remittances_e.pdf

Amadala, Victor. 2019. 'Diaspora inflows at all-time high in June as tax amnesty ends'. *The Star*. At www.the-star.co.ke/business/kenya/2019-07-22-diaspora-inflows-at-all-time-high-in-june-as-tax-amnesty-ends/

Anonymous. 2014. 'African Institute for Remittance'. *Africa Research Bulletin* 51, no. 1: 20275A.

AU. Undated. *Send Money Africa* (different countries). https://sendmoneyafrica-auair.org/#:~:text=Send%20Money%20Africa%20is%20a,%2C%20Faster%2C%20Safer%20and%20Easier

2002. *High-Level Inter-Governmental Meeting on the Prevention and Combating of Terrorism in Africa. Plan of Action of the African Union High-Level Inter-Governmental Meeting on the Prevention and Combating of Terrorism in Africa*. Mtg/HLIG/Conv.Terror/Plan (I).

2003. *African Union Convention on Preventing and Combating Corruption*.

2014. *Protocol on Amendments to the Protocol on the Statute of the African Court of Justice and Human Rights*.

Barasa, Tiberius. 2018. *Illicit Financial Flows in Kenya: Mapping of the Literature and Synthesis of the Evidence*. Partnership for African Social and Governance Research (PASGR). At www.pasgr.org/wp-content/uploads/2018/09/Kenya-Illicit-Financial-Flows-Report.pdf

Bester, Hennie, Christine Hougaard, and Doubell Chamberlain. 2010. *Reviewing the Policy Framework for Money Transfers*. University of Stellenbosch. At https://cenfri.org/wp-content/uploads/2017/12/Regulatory-framework-for-money-transfers_South-Africa.pdf

Bokosi, Fanwell K. and Tafadzwa Chikumbu. 2015. *Tackling Illicit Financial Flows from and within Africa*. African Civil Society Circle. At http://iffoadatabase.trustafrica.org/iff/afrodad.pdf

Broadway, Philippa. 2015. *De-risking; Assessing the Consequences of Enhanced Anti-Money Laundering and Counter Terrorist-Financing Regulation on Access to Finance*. LLM Dissertation, University of London. At https://sas-space.sas.ac.uk/6346/

Budhram, Trevor and Nicolaas Gueldenhuys. 2018. 'Corruption in South Africa: The demise of a nation? New and improved strategies to combat corruption'. *South African Journal of Criminal Justice* 31, no. 1: 26–57.

Carter, Erin. 2011. 'Remittances should not break the bank: South Africa's exchange control regulations, anti-money laundering identity requirements, and protecting cross-border remitters'. *George Washington International Law Review* 43, no. 3: 529–554.

Central Bank of Kenya. 2018. *Remittances Inflows*. At www.centralbank.go.ke/uploads/diaspora_remittances/665341324_December%202018.pdf

Cooray, Arusha. 2012. 'Migrant remittances, financial sector development and the government ownership of banks: Evidence from a group of non-OECD economies'. *Journal of International Financial Markets, Institutions and Money* 22, no. 4: 936–957.

European Commission. 2019. 'European Commission adopts new list of third countries with weak anti-money laundering and terrorist financing regimes'. At http://europa.eu/rapid/press-release_IP-19-781_en.htm

European Parliament (Directorate-General for External Policies of the Union). 2014. 'The impact of remittances on developing countries', EXPO/B/DEVE/2013/34 March 2014 PE 433.786. At www.europarl.europa.eu/meetdocs/2009_2014/documents/deve/dv/remittances_study_/remittances_study_en.pdf

Federal Government of Somalia. 2017. *Financial Government Report*. At https://somaliampf.net/files/Financial_Governance_Report_(English).pdf

Federal Republic of Somalia. 2016. *Anti-Money Laundering and Countering the Financing of Terrorism Act*. At www.centralbank.gov.so/index_html_files/Anti-Money-Laundering-and-Countering-the-Financing-of-Terrorism-Act-2016-English-Version.pdf

Financial Intelligence Centre. Undated. *Draft Guidance on the Implementation of New Measures to Be Introduced by the Financial Intelligence Centre Amendment Act, 2017*. At www.fic.gov.za/Documents/DRAFT%20GUIDANCE%20ON%20THE%20IMPLEMENTATION%20OF%20THE%20AMENDMENT%20ACT%20as%20of%2014%20June%202017.pdf

Financial Intelligence Centre. Undated. *Guidance Note 4 on Suspicious Transaction Reporting*. At www.fic.gov.za/Documents/101012%20Guidelines%20on%20STR%20Manual%20Form.pdf

Government of Kenya. 2009. *The Proceeds of Crime and Anti-Money Laundering Bill, no. 9 (revised in 2012)*.

Government of Kenya. 2017. *The Proceeds of Crime and Anti-Money Laundering (Amendment) Act*.

Government of SA. 2017. *New Approach to Combat Money Laundering and Terrorist Financing*. At www.fic.gov.za/Documents/A%20NEW%20APPROACH%20TO%20COMBAT%20MONEY%20LAUNDERING%20AND%20TERRORIST%20FINANCING%20(2).pdf

Hugo, Charl and Vynand M.A. Spruyt. 2018. 'Money laundering, terrorist financing and financial sanctions: South Africa's response by means of the Financial Intelligence Centre Amendment Act 1 of 2017'. *Journal of South African Law* 2018, no. 2: 227–255.

IRIN News. 2013. 'African migrants pay high prices to send money home'. *Mail and Guardian*. At https://mg.co.za/article/2013-02-28-african-migrants-pay-high-prices-to-send-money-home

KNOMAD. 2019. *Migration and Remittances: Recent Developments and Outlook*. Migration and Development Brief no. 31. At www.knomad.org/sites/default/files/2019-04/Migrationanddevelopmentbrief31.pdf

Kopf, Dan. 2018. 'Remittances to Africa cost far too much – more competition would change that'. *Quartz Africa*. At https://qz.com/africa/1272445/remittances-sending-cash-to-africa-is-most-expensive-says-world-bank/

Lagarde, Christine. 2014. 'Empowerment through financial inclusion'. Address to the International Forum for Financial Inclusion. At www.imf.org/en/News/Articles/2015/09/28/04/53/sp062614a

Lawrence, William. 2017. 'Money laundering compliance for Africa?' *Business Brief*. At www.bbrief.co.za/2017/06/09/money-laundering-compliance-africa/

McGovern, Anna. 2011. 'Dialing for cash: Mobile transfers expand banking'. *African Renewal*. At www.un.org/africarenewal/magazine/december-2011/dialing-cash-mobile-transfers-expand-banking

MFW4A. Undated. *Islamic Finance*. At www.mfw4a.org/our-work/islamic-finance

Mwega, Francis M. 2014. *Financial Regulation in Kenya: Balancing Inclusive Growth with Financial Stability*. Overseas Development Institute (ODI), Working Paper no. 407. At www.odi.org/sites/odi.org.uk/files/odi-assets/publications-opinion-files/9279.pdf

NEPAD Secretariat. 2003. *Sixth Summit of the NEPAD Heads of State and Government Implementation Committee: Objectives, Standards, Criteria and Indicators for the African Peer Review Mechanism*. At www

.aprmtoolkit.saiia.org.za/documents/official-documents/44-atkt-osci-aprm-2003-en/file
Nyamongo, Esman M. et al. 2012. 'Remittances, financial development and economic growth in Africa'. *Journal of Economics and Business* 64, no. 3: 240–260.
OAU. 1999. *OAU Convention on the Prevention and Combating of Terrorism*.
OHCHR. 2016. *Counter-terrorism Measures Threaten Money Sent Home by Somali Diaspora, UN Rights Experts Warn*. At www.ohchr.org/EN/NewsEvents/Pages/DisplayNews.aspx?NewsID=16959&LangID=E
Okello, Julius. 2015. *Effectiveness and Challenges of Using Mobile Money Service in the Implementation of the Social Assistance Grants for Empowerment Program in Uganda*. African Institute for Strategic Research Governance and Development (AISRGD). At www.imtfi.uci.edu/files/docs/2015/Julius%20Okello%20-%20FINAL%20REPORT.pdf
Olaniyan, Kolawole. 2004. 'The African Union Convention on Preventing and Combating Corruption: A critical appraisal'. *African Human Rights Law Journal* 4, no. 1: 74–92.
Orozco, Manuel and Steven R. Wilson. 2005. 'Making migrant remittances count'. In Terry, Donald F. and Steven R. Wilson (eds.). *Beyond Small Changes: Making Migrants Remittances Count*. Washington, DC: Inter-American Development Bank: 375–394.
Oyebamiji, Sunday I. and Raquel A. Asuelime. 2018. 'Transnational families in migration and remittances: The case of Nigerian migrants in South Africa'. *Journal of African Union Studies* 7, no. 1: 211–231.
PASSOP. 2012. *Strangling the Lifeline: An Analysis of Remittance Flows from South Africa to Zimbabwe*. At www.passop.co.za/wp-content/uploads/2012/04/Strangling-the-lifeline-PASSOP-Report-on-Remittances-to-Zimbabwe.pdf
Piper, Nicola and Tugba Basaran. 2018. 'GCM Commentary: Objective 20: Promote faster, safer and cheaper transfer of remittances and foster financial inclusion of migrants'. *RLI Blog on Refugee Law and Forced Migration*. At https://rli.blogs.sas.ac.uk/2018/10/04/gcm-commentary-objective-20/
Plaza, Sonia. 2014. 'Anti-Money laundering regulations: Can Somalia survive without remittances?' *Blog of the World Bank*. At http://blogs.worldbank.org/peoplemove/anti-money-laundering-regulations-can-somalia-survive-without-remittances
Quintyn, Marc and Michael W. Taylor. 2007. *Building Supervisory Structures in Sub-Saharan Africa–An Analytical Framework*. IMF Working Paper WP/07/18. At www.imf.org/external/pubs/ft/wp/2007/wp0718.pdf
Radcliffe, Daniel, and Rodger Voorhies. 2012. *A Digital Pathway to Financial Inclusion*. At https://ssrn.com/abstract=2186926

Republic of SA. 2017. *Financial Intelligence Centre Amendment Act*, Act No. 1, no. 396.

Staff Writer. 2016. 'How money remittance has leapfrogged Africa's financial industry'. *SME South Africa*. At www.smesouthafrica.co.za/16622/How-fintech-is-disrupting-money-transfer-in-Africa/

Techno Service. 2016. *Domestic Remittances in South Africa: Leveraging the Dynamic Marketplace to Boost Financial Inclusion*. At www.technoserve.org/files/downloads/South-Africa-domestic-remittances-report.pdf

Terry, Donald F. 2005. 'Remittances as a development tool'. In Terry, Donald F. and Steven R. Wilson (eds.). *Beyond Small Changes: Making Migrants Remittances Count*. Washington, DC: Inter-American Development Bank: 3–19.

Terry, Donald F. and Steven R. Wilson (eds.). 2005. *Beyond Small Changes: Making Migrants Remittances Count*. Washington, DC: Inter-American Development Bank.

Udombana, Nsogurua J. 2003. 'Fighting corruption seriously? Africa's anti-corruption convention'. *Singapore Journal of International and Comparative Law* 7, no. 2: 447–488.

UN. Undated. *United Nations and the Rule of Law: World Bank*. At www.un.org/ruleoflaw/un-and-the-rule-of-law/world-bank/

UNGA. 2003. *UN Convention against Corruption*, A/RES/58/4.

UNGA. 2018. *Global Compact for Safe, Orderly and Regular Migration*, A/RES/73/195.

UNHCR. 2019. *Displaced and Disconnected (Country Reports)*. At www.unhcr.org/innovation/wp-content/uploads/2019/04/Country-Reports-WEB.pdf

USAID. 2016. *The Strategic Framework for Somalia: 2016–2019*. At www.usaid.gov/sites/default/files/documents/1860/Public_Strategy_USAID.Somalia_03.29.2017_3.pdf

USAID. 2017. 'Somalia and US sign landmark Development Objective Assistance Agreement (DOAG)'. At www.usaid.gov/somalia/press-releases/dec-5-2017-somalia-and-us-sign-landmark-development-objective

US Government Publishing Office. 2014. *Public Law no 113–156*. www.congress.gov/113/plaws/publ156/PLAW-113publ156.pdf

Waemustafa, Waeibrorheem and Azrul Abdullah. 2015. 'Mode of Islamic bank financing: Does effectiveness of Sharia Supervisory Board matter?' *Austin Journal of Basic & Applied Sciences* 37, no. 9: 458–463.

Wambui, Maina G. 2018. *Breaking the Cycle of Corruption in Africa*. Masters Dissertation in Diplomacy, University of Nairobi. At http://erepository.uonbi.ac.ke/bitstream/handle/11295/105870/Wambui_Breaking%20The%

20Cycle%20Of%20Corruption%20In%20Africa%20A%20Case%20Study%20Of%20Kenya.pdf?sequence=1&isAllowed=y

World Bank. 2015. *Remittances Prices Worldwide*. At https://sendmoneyafrica.worldbank.org/

World Bank Group. 2017. *Migration and Remittances*. At www.worldbank.org/en/topic/labormarkets/brief/migration-and-remittances

PART III

Citizenship

14

Millionaires and Mobility: Inequality and Investment Migration Programs

KRISTIN SURAK

For the past several years, *Highlife*, the British Airways inflight magazine, has carried a set of rather unexpected advertisements. A thick pull-out section in the middle bearing the title "Belong" introduces "the most trusted citizenship by investment programs in the world." Images of golf, yachts, and idyllic families on pristine beaches head sections touting programs that naturalize those who invest or donate at least $100,000 in a country. At no small sum, what's the allure? The wealthy often appear to be privileged cosmopolitans, members of an elite globetrotting class for which borders have little meaning. Indeed, the very rich are an unusually mobile set. One survey of over 2,000 affluent individuals in six world regions found that nearly half had lived in more than one country[1] – a staggering proportion given that migrants account for only 3 percent of the world's population. Yet there are limits: wealthy individuals from outside the West still face the same visa controls as their less privileged compatriots. A prosperous Bangladeshi citizen cannot simply board a plane to Canada as a prosperous American can. What options are available for such moneyed movers? And what are the implications for inequality today?

This chapter examines the intersection of *inter*national inequality in what citizenship secures and *intra*national inequality in wealth. It introduces the basic contours of elite wealth at a global level, as well as the operation of investment migration programs. It then addresses the trajectory of capital accumulation in the major regions of demand, as well as the key motives of buyers. It concludes by assessing the ways that inequality in what citizenship secures produces demand for such options, though it is largely those who have won in a new capitalist system who

---

[1] Barclays 2014 at 11.

can afford the opportunities. It also addresses whether or not investment migration programs significantly exacerbate inequality in the countries of origin.

Inequalities: Intra-country and Inter-country

Global wealth is increasingly concentrated the hands of a small set of elites. By 2016, the world's richest 1 percent held over half of all global wealth – a 40 percent increase over the previous five years.[2] Within this privileged class, the most affluent segment boasts even greater wealth accumulation. By 2014, around 16.5 million high net worth individuals (HNWIs) – people with assets valued between USD1 million and $30 million – held 20 percent of global wealth. And above them, ultra-high net worth individuals (UNHWIs), with assets over more than $30 million, numbered just 210,000 yet possessed 13 percent of global wealth.[3]

The greatest number of millionaires and billionaires continue to hail from the West. Yet the past thirty years have seen steady growth in new wealth beyond its borders, in countries outside the global core. In 2000, only 7 percent of UNHWIs came from emerging economies, yet they accounted for nearly a quarter of the group's growth in the following fifteen years.[4] The trend is symptomatic of the diversification of the geographic origins of new wealth. According to researchers at Capgemini, non-Western countries account for nearly half of the top twenty markets giving rise to HNWIs: Japan, China, India, South Korea, Saudi Arabia, Russia, Brazil, Kuwait, and Hong Kong.[5] With the exception of Japan, most of these states regularly appear on "emerging market" lists that rank places offering enormous profit potential. Indeed, when

---

[2] Credit Suisse Global Wealth Report 2014 at 2, Credit Suisse Global Wealth Report 2016 at 4.
[3] Wealth-X and Arton Capital 2014 at 10. Asset figures used for calculating HNWIs and UNHWIs typically underreport wealth by excluding primary residences and collectables such as art. They also do not report wealth that has moved through offshore structures. According to one estimate, already a decade old, HNWIs protected around USD12 trillion in tax havens. See Palan, Murphy, and Chavagneux 2010 at 5.
[4] Credit Suisse 2016 at 20. Credit Suisse classifies individuals with wealth between USD1 million and USD50 million as "high net-worth."
[5] Capgemini 2016 at 9. Hong Kong issues its own passports that allow for much greater visa-free access than those of the Mainland. The statics I quote offer only general contours of a more complex situation. Most professionally produced wealth reports do not make clear how the nationality of their respondents is assessed, nor do they take into account multiple nationalities or residences.

figured in local currency terms, emerging economies contribute more to the increase in global wealth than high-income European and Asian economies.[6]

Notably, the Capgemini list contains a number of countries that offer relatively limited mobility. While a German can show up on the doorstep of 177 countries and be allowed in, a passport from Russia grants visa-free access to only around 100. This may be low, yet it is far better than Kuwaiti papers, which guarantee visa-free access to only 82 countries, let alone Chinese ones, which gain their holder immediate entry into only 50. The arbitrariness of admission serves as a reminder that not all citizenships are the same when it comes to the package of rights and benefits they guarantee. The result creates hitches for the moneyed classes in developing countries and emerging markets who are unable to access the mobility options available to counterparts from wealthier and more Western countries. Indeed, examining Human Development Index (HDI) scores reveals that countries with very high HDI averages tend to grant visa-free access to citizens of similarly well-positioned countries, but not to those with low HDI rankings. Conversely, those from countries that score low on HDI are more likely to enter similar countries visa free, and very unlikely to get visa-free access for places with very high HDI. As such, even the limited mobility that citizenship in a lower-ranked country secures tends to be to similarly low-ranked places.

Wealthy individuals from outside the West who seek improved mobility are motivated by risk management and business opportunities.[7] Though investment migration can be a story of immigration, most often it is not. A Chinese national acquiring a second citizenship in a Caribbean country may simply be looking for a means to travel from the UK to France, on to Germany, and then through Switzerland to Italy without having to send her passport to five separate embassies to secure entrance visas. A stateless Bidoon businessman in the Middle East may use investments to secure his first passport for international travel, and one for his daughter to join her class on a school trip abroad. A retired pilot from South Africa, formerly a labor migrant in Dubai, may look to

---

[6] Credit Suisse 2016 at 16.
[7] See Surak 2020b. Between 2015 and 2018, I conducted over 100 formal and over 350 informal interviews with government officials, service providers, investor migrants, locals in countries hosting investment migration programs, and others connected to the spread of investment migration programs. The fieldwork was funded in part by the Leverhulme Foundation.

live out his years by splitting his time between resorts in the Mediterranean and the Pacific. A Russian national may acquire an additional citizenship merely as an insurance policy against an unpredictable government, a hedge against uncertain prospects. Indeed, during the height of the COVID-19 lockdown, Russian citizens were not allowed to leave the country – only those with an additional citizenship elsewhere were given the green light to cross the border. As such, mobility – or future mobility – rather than migration per se, is typically at stake.[8]

Investment Migration

This mix fuels demand for investment migration. Money alone does not buy entry into the global jet set; political borders must be navigated as well. A range of options are available to those with means who seek papers from Global North countries. Student visas are one common route.[9] "Birth tourism" is possible in countries with jus soli provisions.[10] Most states have entrepreneurial provisions within their migration laws that facilitate the residence of foreigners who start and run businesses capitalized at a minimum level.[11] And a number of countries facilitate naturalization or residence for people with ancestors from the territory.[12]

Supply

Investment migration programs fall within this broad set of options and are in some ways the most straightforward. They enable residence, permanent residence, or citizenship to be acquired in exchange for an investment or monetary contribution. Unlike the entrepreneurial channels described above, the investment is passive: that is, the investor simply provides a cash injection and does not need to be involved in the day-to-day management of the business or prove business qualifications. As such, the country screens for only economic capital, not human capital. The schemes also stand apart from discretionary grants of

---

[8] Nonetheless, I continue to use the term "investment migration" as it is in common currency and does not risk conflation with "investment mobility," which refers more narrowly to financial flows, without the possibility of human mobility attached to it.
[9] Liu-Farrer 2009; Fong 2011.
[10] Balta and Altan-Olcay 2016.
[11] de Lange 2018, 2019.
[12] Tintori 2012; Cook-Martin 2013; Harpaz 2015, 2019.

citizenship or residence, made on an exceptional basis, such as when New Zealand naturalized Peter Thiel after he purchased a few luxury properties and donated to an earthquake relief fund. In contrast, investment migration programs set out a formal application procedure. The applicant must invest a clearly defined minimum amount into an approved investment option, go through due diligence checks, and supply health certificates and private health insurance documentation. The application process, often involving a few levels of government and various background checks, can take anywhere from several weeks to several months.

Investment migration schemes come in two types: residence by investment programs and citizenship by investment programs. Of these, residence by investment programs are far more plentiful, with over sixty countries offering schemes. These may eventually lead to citizenship, but only after a significant period as a resident. Yet this may not require actually living in the country. Residence in many legal systems is metaphysical rather than physical,[13] and not all countries require physical presence to maintain residence status. Those with a Portuguese "Golden Visa" are required to visit the country for only two weeks every two years. Latvia obliges its investment migrants to spend only one day per year in the country.[14] Prices, investments, and statuses can vary too. In the case of the US EB-5 program, most applicants invest the minimum – which went from $500,000 to $900,000 in 2019 – into a designated real estate project and receive in return a temporary Green Card which becomes a standard Green Card after two years. The UK requires an investment of at least £2 million in bonds or UK-listed companies to qualify for residence and eventually permanent residence and citizenship, though it also imposes a physical presence requirement of at least 180 days every year to renew the permit. In Quebec, applicants may invest CAD800,000 into a company or simply pay CAD220,000 up front – a more popular option – to receive permanent residence.[15] Though the investment sizes are large, caps on the programs in Canada and the United States limit numbers: at the time of writing, around 5,000 people become residents of Canada and 10,000 become residents of the United States annually through these channels.

As of 2020, thirteen countries – Antigua, Dominica, Grenada, Saint Kitts, and Saint Lucia in the Caribbean, plus Malta and Cyprus in the

---

[13] Ford 1999.
[14] On the demographic uptake of such programs, see Surak 2020c; on the economic outcomes, see Surak and Tsuzuki 2021.
[15] In November 2019, the program was suspended pending review.

Mediterranean, as well as Turkey, Jordan, Montenegro, North Macedonia, Cambodia, and Vanuatu – offered formal citizenship by investment programs. Applicants in these schemes donate or invest between USD100,000 and €2.5 million, in addition to processing fees, to secure citizenship for themselves, or also their families, within an average of three to six months.[16] The minimum costs and possible forms of investment are clearly specified. Typically, the programs are run by a designated unit within the government, and the government also licenses the companies that are allowed to file applications and sets standards for due diligence. Residence requirements, too, are kept to a minimum, if they exist at all. Indeed, the demand for physical presence – even if only to pick up the passport – can be considered an unwelcome burden that may limit the competitiveness of the "product." Around 10,000 individuals naturalize through these channels each year.[17]

Though often glossed in the literature, the difference between the two options is significant. At the procedural level, residence programs may lead into citizenship, but not necessarily; if citizenship is acquired, it is through a separate and subsequent qualifying procedure.[18] At the substantive level, residence can be lost more easily than citizenship: if one fails to maintain the conditions of the investment, one can expect to lose the residence status. Citizenship, by contrast, is far harder, though not impossible, to revoke. As citizenship is usually for life, the investment can typically be sold after a specified period, while "golden visa" programs usually extend residence only as long as the investment is retained. Furthermore citizenship is inheritable, whereas residence is not, raising the stakes of its acquisition for future generations. Of course, citizenship is not the end-goal for all: residence may be more desirable to investors

---

[16] See Surak 2016 and Surak 2021.
[17] The size of the phenomenon is also dependent on the availability of alternatives. For example, demand for second passports in Latin America has been muted due to the easy access to Spanish or Italian citizenship through ancestry routes (see Cook-Martin 2013). Investor citizenship is also a phenomenon of the *nouveaux riches*. Often families with inherited wealth have already worked out citizenship or residence options for their descendants.
[18] As such, Bulgaria's investment residence program does not operate as an independent citizenship by investment program (cf. Scherrer and Thirion 2018) since applicants move first through residence, held for at least one year, and then submit a separate qualifying investment to apply through an additional channel for citizenship. This stands in contrast to the Maltese and Cypriot regulations, which grant residence as a procedural matter within the process of applying for investor citizenship.

from countries, such as China, where dual citizenship is forbidden, which affects risk calculations when acquiring a second passport.

Furthermore, individuals may combine citizenship and residence options. International wealth planners advising clients on how best to structure their assets and personal mobility may pair Caribbean passports with investor visa options in places such as the United Kingdom, Canada, or the United States, where their clients prefer to live or spend time.[19] For example, a Vietnamese investor hoping to become a Canadian may, alongside an investor visa for Canada, also purchase a Caribbean citizenship to secure visa-free access to the Schengen Area during the five years she waits to qualify for her target citizenship. In step with this demand, Antigua now issues its investor citizens an initial passport valid for five years – the amount of time typically required to apply for citizenship elsewhere. Those who wish to maintain their citizenship thereafter must visit the country for at least five days and swear an oath of allegiance.

Demand

Demand for both channels comes largely from three areas: China, Russia and the CIS countries, and the Middle East.[20] Not only have these regions seen remarkable generation of HNWIs, but the Freedom House ranks nearly all of the relevant countries as "not free," which can lead to great concerns among the wealthy about the rule of law and protection of assets. Examining the origins of the wealth in these cases, however, suggests that often such individuals did not simply draw a bad straw in the birthright lottery. On the contrary, for many it was birth in these countries at a particular historical juncture that enabled them to amass great wealth in the first place. That is, political borders contained the political-economic transformations that facilitated the creation and accumulation of capital. Effectively, they produce structural differentiation that can offer economic opportunities, advantages, and disadvantages, generating or reinforcing class boundaries. Working with and around these barriers, wealthy elites use citizenship by investment programs to convert their accumulated economic capital into benefits provided by states.

---

[19] Surak 2016.
[20] Surak 2020b.

In China, entrepreneurs constitute the bulk of billionaires.[21] Yet – as is often the case across the world – their achievements cannot be boiled down to hard work and boot-strap pulling alone, particularly in a place defined by connections. The deregulation of state-owned enterprises in the 1980s came through insider privatization, which enabled cadres and well-placed managers to gain preferential access in what would become the world's largest experiment in marketization. By the 1990s, large private businesses were legalized, and "foreign" investment from Taiwan and Hong Kong flowed in to boost the development of China's Special Economic Zones. But the Communist Party kept the market tightly controlled. Crucially, it limited foreign ownership and required ventures led by foreigners to be carried out jointly with nationals, while maintaining a strong hand over foreign exchange. The result was a windfall for well-connected citizens who reaped spectacular gains. By 2001, Jiang Zemin renamed the increasing – and increasingly wealthy – business class a fundament of socialism, now with "Chinese characteristics." Over these years, private wealth skyrocketed. Where it accounted for slightly more than the national income in 1980, it rose to 500 percent of the national income in 2016.[22] Marketization and privatization also drove down the share of public property within the national wealth figures: it dropped from about 70 percent in 1978 to 30 percent in 2015.[23] Inequality has been stoked as well. Where China once boasted levels similar to the egalitarian Nordic countries in the 1970s, it approaches US levels today. As of 2015, the top 10 percent hold about 67 percent of the wealth.[24]

Yet most entrepreneurs continue to be dependent on the state for capital and business opportunities. Personal connections with officials and other businesspeople remain essential for getting ahead, while these network effects erect high barriers to entry for those without links.[25] In turn, officials remain dependent on their connections to successful entrepreneurs to reach the development targets assigned by the central government. Meanwhile, Beijing continues to protect its market against foreign ownership. This combination has meant that the greatest opportunities emerging from the market transformations in China have been monopolized by nationals, and it is the Chinese business elite who have

---

[21] Freund 2016 at 28.
[22] Novokmet et al 2017 at 25.
[23] Piketty et al 2017 at 4.
[24] Piketty et al 2017 at 6.
[25] Osburg 2013; See also Goodman 2008.

benefited most. Where China accounted for only 4 percent of global wealth in 2000, by 2016 it accounted for 15 percent.[26]

Post-Soviet cases tell a similar story of well-placed nationals reaping the benefits of market transformation. The fall of communism offered the IMF, World Bank, and US Treasury the opportunity to implement neoliberal market reforms, which came in the form of the so-called shock therapy. Boris Yeltsin pushed through, in many cases by decree, the rapid privatization of state assets, which enabled well-placed bosses and apparatchiks to accumulate vast quantities of wealth. In a context of unstable property rights, insider status allowed the most dexterous to win government contracts and licenses, and later the shares of firms and natural resources, in a rigged bidding system. As publicly held goods were privatized, a handful of the well-connected gained substantial ownership of key firms at rock-bottom prices. Energy, telecommunications, oil, and metals fed a new generation of oligarchs. Caroline Freund estimates that at least half, if not all, billionaires in Russia, Ukraine, Georgia, and Kazakhstan gained their fortunes by using political connections to gain hold of natural resources.[27]

Inequality skyrocketed within a region where political ties determined who had access to the spoils. In the transition from communism to capitalism, the share of the income held by the top 10 percent increased from 25 percent in 1991 to more than 45 percent in 1996. The top 1 percent saw even greater dividends: their increase in the share of income rocketed from around 5 percent in 1989 to over 26 percent by 2008.[28] As in China, goods once held in the name of the people became the private holdings of a few. According to Filip Novokmet, Thomas Piketty, and Gabriel Zucman, the marked rise in private wealth within Russia has come largely at the expense of public wealth.[29]

In the Middle East, too, fortunes are made within states. Outside the region, money is most closely associated with oil, but typically those in the high net worth brackets amassed their wealth through entrepreneurial activities and investments in real estate, banks, and construction. Indeed, only 3 percent of UNHWIs in the UAE accumulated their wealth through oil or gas.[30] In the GCC, the diversification of the economy in places like Dubai and Doha offered new opportunities for financial gain

---

[26] Credit Suisse 2016 at 16.
[27] Freund 2016 at 28.
[28] Novokmet et al 2017 at 33.
[29] Novokmet et al 2017 at 26.
[30] Wealth-X 2014 at 90.

as vast cities were erected in deserts. They became magnets for the superrich in the region as well. The number of people holding at least $30 million in assets has increased from about 4,500 people 2011 to 6,000 in 2014, who now hold more than half of the wealth in the UAE. Even if mobility within the Middle East is common, over 90 percent of the superrich in the region maintain their core businesses in their country of birth.[31] National connections still matter.

Comparing across the cases makes evident that the state limits which many investment migrants attempt to work around are often the very ones that enabled them to accrue great wealth in the first place. That is, borders lie at the heart of the accumulation of substantial economic resources in the first instance. In many cases, the entrepreneurial or oligarchic elites would not have the vast financial resources to seek out other options had they not been born in their country of origin at a particular historical conjuncture – one marked by mass privatization, marketization, and increasing economic inequality within them.

Yet for the winners, the accumulated capital becomes a resource for transcending political borders that are a liability, now or in the future. Investment migration options help secure these routes. In many cases, the *nouveaux riches* are looking for improved mobility options, superior schooling for their children, or an "insurance policy" if an authoritarian government cracks down or turns against them.[32] As such, if economic inequality within states enables some to make use of these options, inequality between states in what citizenship secures ensures that demand remains strong.

Outcomes

What is the impact on economic inequality? Though the empirical outcomes of these programs are several, only two issues will be discussed here. It might be presumed that elites, as they circumvent the state boundaries that enabled them to accumulate great wealth, may thereby impede economic growth within their countries of origin. Notably, many investor migrants come from countries with foreign exchange controls that they must illegally circumvent to make their qualifying investment for residence or citizenship. The result is that resources are drained from a country that might otherwise be reinvested in it. Thus in the process of

---

[31] Wealth-X 2014 at 76–77, 91.
[32] Surak 2020b.

skirting national borders, it might be thought that the wealthy exacerbate class boundaries.

However, a real effect is not evident because the numbers of investor residents and citizens are miniscule. Even if 3,000 Chinese nationals invest $900,000 in the United States each year to obtain Green Cards through the EB-5 program, the total amount hardly registers against the estimated $1 trillion that leaves China annually, despite stringent currency control laws. Among Russians, oligarchs hold about as much wealth outside the country as the rest of the population does within Russia.[33] The rich in the Middle East and Africa and Eastern Europe, including Central Asia, hold between 23 and 27 percent of their wealth offshore. Relative to these sizeable figures that characterize the nature of wealth-protection strategies in general,[34] citizenship by investment programs tip no balances in class inequality in the countries from which participants hail.

What about the economic impact on the countries offering the programs? States with more popular schemes will see between one thousand and two thousand new citizens naturalizing through the programs annually. Smaller programs will welcome merely a few hundred. For a microstate like Saint Kitts, with a resident population of only 55,000, the proportions are significant. According to official statements, nearly 11,000 investors naturalized between 2006 and 2016, the time when the program took off. Individuals working with the scheme suggest that the figure may be even higher. What are the implications for the countries offering citizenship by investment programs?

For small states, the potential economic benefits are substantial. Malta collected over €1 billion from its citizenship by investment programs in its first four years. Cyprus, home to a formal program since 2007, has accrued over €2 billion. The size of the figures can be compared with the countries' GDP of approximately €10 billion and €20 billion respectively. In the Caribbean, Antigua and Grenada accrue around 10 percent to 15 percent of their GDP through the programs. But they are no match for Saint Kitts, with its "legacy product," which has traditionally accounted for much of the sales in the Caribbean. In some years, the state obtained nearly 40 percent of its GDP through citizenship by investment. A number of questions might be asked about how these injections have benefited the local economies. Travel around the islands reveals

---

[33] Novokmet et al 2017 at 18, 26.
[34] See, for example, Cooley and Heathershaw 2018.

a number of trophy projects, like the solar panels at the airport in Antigua. Funds have also been used for social initiatives such as scholarship programs and entrepreneurial training. In some cases, the schemes have supported the construction of popular resorts that employ hundreds of locals and attract tourist dollars to the islands, furthering economic development. In other cases, pledged hotels and port projects have never materialized or proceed at the slow pace of a white elephant, and questions remain as to where the money has gone. Several Caribbean countries have used part of the proceeds to pay off international loans, an expenditure that improves the economic health of a country but leaves no visible traces. Malta is accruing its revenues in a fund, though little of the money has been spent, and a number of the public works projects promised at the launch of the program are yet to get off the ground.

Clearly, these outcomes have the greatest impact on the local residents,[35] who live in countries where tax revenues are low, import needs are high, and – especially in the Caribbean – cruise ships, hurricanes, and most recently COVID-19 have taken a toll on the tourism sector. In places like Saint Kitts and Cyprus, which have longer histories of formal programs, local support for citizenship by investment is widespread, if interspersed by dissenting voices. New programs are more controversial, particularly if the government is perceived as corrupt.[36]

These outcomes can matter for investor citizens, for they may see themselves as having a stake in their new country. Those who qualify through investing in real estate or businesses will be concerned about economic prospects and the return on their investment. Even those who apply through donation channels still retain an interest in the country's foreign relations, for external states – and the visa-free access they grant – determine the value of investor citizenship.[37] When Saint Kitts lost visa-free access to Canada in 2014, its annual figures for investor naturalizations fell too. Yet the membership acquired through CBI represents

---

[35] The population of resident foreigners in most countries offering citizenship by investment is substantial, topping 20 percent in Cyprus, Jordan, and Antigua, and is likely to reach similar levels in other Caribbean countries where intra-Caribbean mobility is common and facilitated by free mobility within CARICOM, and where governments are reluctant to take censuses and officially recognize the sizeable foreign populations. Emigration is also sizeable, and again the effects are magnified for small island countries. For example, the 2017 American Community Survey counted 34,000 Grenada-born residents in the United States alone – about a third of the population of the country, which numbers 107,000.

[36] See Surak 2020a.

[37] Surak 2016; Surak 2021.

citizenship in its thinnest form, what Christian Joppke has termed "citizenship light."[38] Gone are concerns with identity and a sense of belonging. Absent are expectations of social welfare benefits, social protection, and resource redistribution. The obligations of political membership, already on the decline across the board,[39] are nonexistent too. No military service, no jury duty, and of course no substantial taxes are expected of the new citizens. Its substance inheres in a legal status verified through documents: it is access to the passport that matters.

Conclusion

Demand for additional citizenships will remain as long as countries outside the global core continue to produce wealthy citizens looking to improve their mobility or for an insurance policy against their own government. Microstates too, with few alternative revenue sources, will continue to turn to citizenship options, particularly as international pressure on financial products and tax services mounts. Even a small state has jurisdiction to capitalize on. But because the value of citizenship as a commodity is set outside the country selling it, regional or bilateral alliances, in addition to the sanction of core states, are essential for these channels to retain their value. These relations are not irreversible, as Saint Kitts learned in its dealings with Canada. Now that the United Kingdom has exited the European Union or should the Schengen Zone break up, the use-value of investment citizenship in small countries linked to them will drop. Of course the loss of visa-free access is not just a problem for the viability of such programs; it directly affects all citizens, investor or not. In Caribbean countries, with large diaspora communities in the Global North, international travel is common, but the risk and expense of applying for visas can be forbidding for many. As such, the costs for the local population can also be high if visa-free access is compromised. Recognition of external – geopolitical and politico-economic – determinants of the appeal of citizenship as a commodity, as well as their attendant risks, is crucial for understanding the limits and dynamics of the market for citizenship products. After all, citizenship, as both an instrument and an object of social closure,[40] is a means of exclusion. It is inequality, rather than equality, that defines the worth of citizenship – whether economic or not.

---

[38] Joppke 2010.
[39] See Spiro 2008.
[40] Brubaker 1992.

References

Alstadsaeter, Annette, Niels Johannesen, and Gabriel Zucman. 2017. "Tax Evasion and Inequality." National Bureau of Economic Research Working Paper 23805. www.nber.org/papers/w23772

Balta, Evren and Özlem Altan-Olcay. 2016. "Strategic Citizens of America: Transnational Inequalities and Transformation of Citizenship." *Ethnic and Racial Studies* 39, no. 6 (May 2): 939–957.

Barclays Wealth and Investment Management. 2014. "Wealth Insights: The Rise of the Global Citizen?" *Barclays Wealth Insights* 18.

Beardsley, Brent, Bruce Holley, Miriam Jaafar, Daniel Kessler, Federico Muxi, Matthias Naumann, Jürgen Rogg, Tjun Tang, André Xavier, and Anna Zakrzewski. 2017. "Global Wealth 2017: Transforming the Client Experience." *The Boston Consulting Group.*

Brubaker, Rogers. 1992. *Citizenship and Nationhood in France and Germany.* Cambridge: Harvard University Press.

Capgemini. 2016. "World Wealth Report 2016." www.caproasia.com/2016/10/21/capgemini-world-wealth-report-2016/

Cook-Martín, David. 2013. *The Scramble for Citizens: Dual Nationality and State Competition for Immigrants.* Stanford: Stanford University Press.

Cooley, Alexander and John Heathershaw. 2018. *Dictators without Borders: Power and Money in Central Asia.* New Haven: Yale University Press.

Credit Suisse. 2014. "Global Wealth Report 2014." *Credit Suisse Group.*

    2016. "Global Wealth Report 2016." *Credit Suisse Group.*

de Lange, Tesseltje. 2019. "Intersecting Policies of Innovation and Entrepreneurship Migration in the EU and the Netherlands." In S. Carrera, L. den Hertog, M. Panizzon, and D. Kostakopoulou (eds.), *EU External Migration Policies in an Era of Global Mobilities: Intersecting Policy Universes*, pp. 224–243. Leiden: Brill.

    2018. "Welcoming Talent? A Comparative Study of Immigrant Entrepreneurs' Entry Policies in France, Germany and the Netherlands." *Comparative Migration Studies* 6 no. 27: 1–18.

European Commission. 2019. "Investor Citizenship and Residence Schemes in the European Union." Report from the Commission to the European Parliament, the Council, the European Economic and Social Committee, and the Committee of the Regions. COM(2019) 23 final.

Fong, Vanessa. 2011. *Paradise Redefined: Transnational Chinese Students and the Quest for Flexible Citizenship in the Developed World.* Stanford: Stanford University Press.

Ford, Richard. 1999. "Law's Territory (A History of Jurisdiction)." *Michigan Law Review* 97, no. 4: 843–930.

Freund, Caroline. 2016. *Rich People Poor Countries: The Rise of Emerging-Market Tycoons and Their Mega Firms*. Assisted by Sarah Oliver. Washington, DC: Peterson Institute for International Economics.

Goodman, David, ed. 2008. *The New Rich in China: Future Rulers, Present Lives*. 1st edition. London and New York: Routledge.

Harpaz, Yossi. 2015. "Ancestry into Opportunity: How Global Inequality Drives Demand for Long-Distance European Union Citizenship." *Journal of Ethnic and Migration Studies* 41, no. 13 (November 10): 2081–2104.

——— 2019. "Ancestry into Opportunity: How Global Inequality Drives Demand for Long-Distance Citizenship." *Journal of Ethnic and Migration Studies*. 41(13): 2018–2104.

Joppke, Christian. 2010. "The Inevitable Lightening of Citizenship." *European Journal of Sociology / Archives Européennes de Sociologie* 51, no. 1 (April): 9–32.

Liu-Farrer, Gracia. 2009. "Educationally Channeled International Labor Mobility: Contemporary Student Migration from China to Japan." *International Migration Review*. 43(1): 178–204.

Novokmet, Filip, Thomas Piketty, and Gabriel Zucman. 2017. "From Soviets to Oligarchs: Inequality and Property in Russia, 1905–2016." National Bureau of Economic Research Working Paper 23712.

Osburg, John. 2013. *Anxious Wealth: Money and Morality Among China's New Rich*. Stanford: Stanford University Press.

Palan, Ronen, Richard Murphy, and Christian Chavagneux. 2009. *Tax Havens: How Globalization Really Works*. Cornell Studies in Money. Ithaca: Cornell University Press.

Piketty, Thomas, Li Yang, and Gabriel Zucman. 2017. "Capital Accumulation, Private Property, and Rising Inequality in China, 1978–2015." WID.world Working Paper Series 2017/6.

Reuters. 2015. "China's Outward Investment Tops $161 Billion in 2016: Minister." www.reuters.com/article/us-china-economy-investment/chinas-outward-investment-tops-161-billion-in-2016-minister-idUSKBN14F07R.

Scherrer, Amandine and Elodie Thirion. 2018. "Citizenship by Investment (CBI) and Residency by Investment (RBI) Schemes in the EU." www.europarl.europa.eu/thinktank/en/document.html?reference=EPRS_STU(2018)627128

Spiro, Peter J. 2008. *Beyond Citizenship: American Identity After Globalization*. Oxford, New York: Oxford University Press.

Surak, Kristin. 2016. "Global Citizenship 2.0: The Growth of Citizenship by Investment Programs." Investment Migration Working Papers 2016/3.

——— 2020a. "What Money Can Buy: Citizenship by Investment on a Global Scale." In *Deepening Divides: How Borders and Boundaries Drive Our World Apart*, Didier Fassin, ed. London: Pluto Press.

2020b. "Millionaire Mobility and the Sale of Citizenship." *Journal of Ethnic and Migration Studies.* DOI: 10.1080/1369183X.2020.1758554

2020c. "Who Wants to Buy a Visa? Comparing Residence by Investment Programs in the European Union." *Journal of Contemporary European Studies.* DOI: 10.1080/14782804.2020.1839742

2021. "Marketizing Sovereign Prerogatives: How to Sell Citizenship." *European Journal of Sociology.* Forthcoming.

Surak, Kristin and Yusuke Tsuzuki. 2021. "Are Golden Visas a Golden Opportunity? Assessing the Economic Outcomes of Residence by Investment Programs in the European Union." *Journal of Ethnic and Migration Studies.* DOI: 10.1080/1369183X.2021.1915755

Tintori, Guido. 2012. "More than One Million Individuals Got Italian Citizenship Abroad in Twelve Years (1998–2010)." *RSCAS Citizenship News* (blog), http://eudo-citizenship.eu/news/citizenship-news/748-more-than-one-million-individuals-got-italian-citizenship-abroad-in-the-twelve-years-1998-2010%3E.

Wealth-X, and Arton Capital. 2014. "A Shrinking World: Global Citizenship for UNHW Individuals." www.artoncapital.com/documents/publications/Arton-Capital-Wealth-X-Report-web.pdf

15

Are Citizenship by Investment Programs Legitimate? Suggesting Some Assessment Methods

ELENA PRATS

Introduction

Programmes granting citizenship in exchange for economic transactions, also known as citizenship by investment programmes (CIPs), have been the object of much reflection during the last decade. Unsurprisingly due to the nature of its main object – citizenship – scholars from disciplines as diverse as political science, sociology, or economics have written about the programmes from both a descriptive and a normative approach. Despite the enormous interest on the programmes by scholars, notably since the launch of the Maltese programme, which granted on grounds of money not only the national but also the European citizenship, I have not identified anyone assessing the legitimacy of the programmes in a systematic manner. This chapter represents the first approach to fill this gap. For that purpose, I focus on the following tasks. First, I present a definition of CIPs that will help to delimit the object of study and add some conceptual clarification to the study of the phenomenon. Second, I make a distinction between the several conceptions of the term 'legitimacy' in order to show that depending on the meaning followed, different methods of assessment arise. I then argue in favour of following the meaning of 'legitimacy' as tantamount to 'lawful', and finish by doing the theoretical exercise of deploying in detail a method of assessment – contract law – grounded on the mainstream characterization of CIPs as programmes commodifying and *selling* citizenship. Thus, if the mainstream description of CIPs as programmes selling citizenship is correct, and if the states are acting as private actors on the sale of citizenship – as seems to be the case for those arguing that states are *selling* citizenship – then contract law appears as an appropriate method to assess the lawfulness of the programmes.

Citizenship by Investment Programmes: Laying the Foundations

The number of programmes and policies that could be included in the category of *ius pecunia*[1] is enormous and increasing rapidly. All sorts of Immigrant Investor Programmes and Policies (IIPs)[2] follow the mode of acquisition of citizenship by naturalization through *ius pecunia*. Policies and programmes in this category offer a residence-related right to applicants, whose motivations to apply can differ greatly from one to another.[3]

A particular sort of IIP are citizenship by investment programmes (CIPs). Although multiple arguments have been deployed in favour and against[4] these and related programmes, several scholars taking a normative stance towards them have not defined the programmes either in a positive manner, by saying *what* the programmes indeed are, or in a negative form, by differentiating them from other sorts of related programmes. I consider that in order to understand properly the phenomenon of CIPs it is essential to delimit its scope by offering a definition that distinguishes the programmes from other sorts of IIPs. My suggested definition of CIPs is:

> CIPs are laws that in a *systematic* way grant or create state authority to grant citizenship in exchange for *economic transactions*, which *waives or significantly reduces requirements* that other naturalization applicants need to fulfil.[5]

---

[1] Citizenship has both an inclusion and an exclusion dimension. The term *ius pecunia* was first used by J. Stern (2011) and later by J. Džankić (2012); however, each of them departed from a different dimension of the concept of citizenship. Although both authors used it to refer to a mode of acquiring citizenship (naturalization), Stern used it to point out a situation where money represented an element of *exclusion*, while Džankić used it to refer to the situation where money worked as an element of *inclusion*. In this text, the term *ius pecunia* is used in its inclusive meaning. For a brilliant insight on the duality of money as an element of exclusion and inclusion related to citizenship, see Sachar's contribution in this book.

[2] Here, I include diverse sorts of programmes, which can go from the EB-5 Investor programme granting permanent residence to those investing in a new commercial enterprise in the United States or creating or preserving ten permanent full-time jobs for qualified US workers, to the Maltese Individual Investor Program granting residence rights and allowing acquisition of citizenship after one year of residence to those investing in the country.

[3] For an insight into the different motivations of applicants see Surak's contribution in this book, Džankić (2015), and Frank (2011).

[4] The soundest arguments in favour of and against *ius pecunia* will be presented in the next section.

[5] To my understanding, the difference between IIPs and CIPs resides in the fact that the former grant visas or residence permits, which potentially can end in allowing the subject to naturalize, while the purpose of CIPs is principally the bestowing of citizenship by

Although programmes differ enormously from one to another, this definition allows us to pinpoint some of the common features of the programmes. First, CIPs use citizenship as a tool to attract a certain type of applicant[6] whose contribution to the country would be done by economic means. Second, these programmes are elaborated in a systematic way, that is to say, that bestowing citizenship is not done in an utterly discretional manner on an individual basis but according to some procedure pre-established following certain formal requirements. Third, the programmes divert the naturalization route to a fast lane by waiving or significantly reducing requirements required of other naturalization applicants. Although in some cases the programmes cut any other requirements, very often they keep a reduced period of residence in the country as a mandatory requirement in an attempt to prove the 'genuine link' between applicant and state of naturalization.

The number of existing programmes in the world according to this definition is still unclear and difficult to scrutinize due to the huge quantity of policies. Reducing the scope to European Union member states results in a more feasible as well as interesting task, since in the case of programmes established by EU member states, bestowing national citizenship simultaneously bestows European citizenship, which entails access to supranational and transnational rights and the imposition of some duties to other EU member states. By applying the above-mentioned definition to the several policies established by EU member states I conclude that there are clearly CIPs in Bulgaria, Cyprus,[7] and Malta.[8]

---

waiving or cutting naturalization requirements that in other cases would apply (like the period of residence, civic and language tests, etc.). That is to say, the reason for the general IIPs is to grant migration rights as well as to *open a route* to acquiring citizenship, while the reason for the particular programmes called CIPs *is to end it* by granting *status civitatis*.

[6] Although this is a feature of CIPs, it is certainly not exclusive of these programmes. All over the world exist laws (or by discretional decisions) facilitating the acquisition of citizenship through naturalization to sportspeople, scientists, spouses, etc. In this case, the favourite applicant is a wealthy person.

[7] It is necessary to mention that Cyprus has recently established the end of the programme from November 2020 due to the corruption scandal related to the CIP unveiled by Al Jazeera, 'The Cyprus papers'. For more information, see www.aljazeera.com/news/2020/10/12/cypriot-politicians-implicated-in-plan-to-sell-criminals-passport (accessed October 20, 2020)

[8] For a view of the reasoning for reaching this conclusion as well as a detailed explanation of the three CIPs at the EU, see the Report from the Commission to the European Parliament, the Council, the European Economic and Social Committee and the Committee of the Regions *Investor Citizenship and Residence Schemes in the European Union*, released on the 23rd of January 2019, the EU Commission, and also read Prats (2019).

Scholarly Debate

Sound arguments on the economic benefits for states or even on the 'ethics and efficacy of selling national citizenship' (Borna & Stearns, 2002) have been offered by those defending the idea of 'selling citizenship rights' as something beneficial.[9] Arguments and claims against what has been labelled as the 'selling' or 'commodification' of citizenship and citizenship rights are mainly based on political or sociological grounds. The most welcomed claims by academia can be grouped into four types. The first considers that IIPs (including CIPs) exacerbate inequality, either internally or globally.[10] The second considers that the programmes imply an intrusion of the market into the political sphere, which can be detrimental for democracy.[11] The third, related to the former, is that IIPs corrupt democracy.[12] Last but not least, the fourth type gathers claims pointing out that the programmes undermine the character of citizenship.[13]

Although all four types of claims against the implementation of IIPs are strong, these are conceptual claims usually unsubstantiated by data[14] and in some cases not applicable on a generalized basis.[15] Moreover, two more facts need to be noted. First, despite the several claims against the implementation of CIPs, no theory or method has been suggested to assess the legitimacy of the programmes. Second, most of the claims in favour of or against have been made from the perspectives of sociology, economics, or political science. Yet, few scholars have approached the phenomenon from a legal point of view and offer legal arguments to assess the legitimacy of the programmes. This is particularly surprising if we consider the legal nature of the phenomenon – from the procedure of enacting the laws giving birth to the programmes, to

---

[9] For an insight of the arguments in favour of 'selling citizenship' see Shachar, Bauböck, Bloemraad, and Vink, 2017, pp. 797–804 (chapter 35).

[10] This claim has been defended, among others, by Boatca (2015); Shachar (2014, 2018); Shachar et al. (2017).

Bauböck offers a similar argument. He argues that 'Turning the status of citizenship itself into a marketable commodity *would tear down a wall of protection* that keeps social class from becoming, once again, a formal marker of inequality of citizenship rights and status' Bauböck (2014).

[11] Defended, among others, by Bauböck (2014); Shachar (2018).

[12] Claimed, among others, by Bauböck (2014).

[13] Presented, among others, by Džankić (2012); Shachar (2018). See also Shachar, Chapter 16 in this book.

[14] This is due to the fact that states very often do not release data related to naturalized applicants through particular CIPs and general IIPs.

[15] As an example, the claim that CIPs corrupt democracy is unconvincing when referring to countries that maintain physical presence requirements for electoral participation, as is the case of several, according to Surak (2016, pp. 5 and 6).

the outcome of their implementation. In the coming pages, I will attempt to fill this gap by presenting several methods for assessing the legitimacy of the CIPs, some of which offer a pure legal intra-systemic view. Since the selection of one or another method will be based on the conception of legitimacy followed, it is essential to present the several meanings of the term legitimacy before suggesting the different methods related to each of them.

On Legitimacy

A conceptual clarification on the meaning of legitimacy needs to be made before presenting the existing methods. Commonly understood, legitimacy has two meanings: validity and lawfulness.[16] There is a third typical meaning that introduces some sorts of non-legal arguments (such as moral arguments and arguments of justice) as opposed to a legal situation. Thus, the meanings are: (i) Legitimacy equals formal validity,[17] (ii) Legitimacy equals lawfulness,[18] and (iii) Legitimacy beyond the law.

Under the first meaning, legitimacy as formal validity, an assessment of the legitimacy of the programmes would be done merely by intra-systemic formal legal reasons. This meaning equates legitimacy with a narrow understanding of validity that conceives formal validity as a necessary and sufficient condition for the law to be legitimate. Thus, following this meaning:

> For a Law to be legitimate is for it to be formally valid.

For a person following this meaning, a plausible method to assess the legitimacy of the programmes would be to check if the CIPs are formally valid by assessing if the enactment procedure of the laws establishing them has been according to the formal rules of Act of Enactment in the Parliament. If a programme which has been assessed following this method fails in proving its legitimacy, logically it will also fail an assessment following the second meaning of legitimacy, as lawfulness.

---

[16] https://en.oxforddictionaries.com/definition/legitimacy

[17] Someone could argue that under this meaning legitimacy is treated as a synonym for formal legality.

[18] A method following this second meaning would add legal intra-systemic substantial content and therefore be more demanding than a method following the meaning of validity. Thus, while those following the first meaning would consider formal validity as a necessary and sufficient condition to argue that a particular law is legitimate, those following the second meaning would consider formal validity a necessary, but not a sufficient, condition to characterize a law as legitimate because they would argue that legal substantial content would also need to be included.

The second meaning, legitimacy as lawfulness, understands formal validity as a necessary, but not sufficient, condition. This meaning is more demanding because it requires for a law to be legitimate not only to be formally valid but also respectful to certain intra-systemic legal substantive content. The intra-systemic legal substantive content may emanate from a national, supranational, or international organ. Thus, following this meaning:

> *For a Law to be legitimate is for it to be formally valid and conformed to intra-systemic legal substantive content.*

Thus, an assessment following this meaning will require enquiry into not only formal aspects but also on substantive content. This substantive content will be limited to the one belonging to the legal system under consideration, which may integrate content emanating from national, supranational, or international organizations. An example of a method following this meaning would be the one opposing CIPs against the substantive principles stated in the constitutions of the particular states establishing programmes, which would be acting as benchmarks. If arguments could be made proving that the programmes are acting against those constitutional principles, arguments against the legitimacy understood as lawfulness of the CIPs could be made. By way of example, if the constitution of state X states as a principle equality before the law regardless of economic capacity, and an argument could be made proving that CIPs violate equality before the law by virtue of limiting acquisition of citizenship on grounds of economic capacity, then the CIP would fail the assessment of legitimacy understood as lawfulness. It is necessary to mention here that an assessment on a national level following this second meaning does not need to invoke necessarily the substantive content appearing in the constitution. National laws may refer to substantive content (here, moral) shaped, interpreted, and integrated into the legal system by legal institutions. This is the case, for instance, for the Maltese Civil Code, which establishes, in its article 985, that objects that are contrary to morality may not be the object of a lawful contractual agreement. In the next section, I deploy in detail the contract law method, a method that follows this second meaning, as an example of an assessment method.

An assessment on a supranational level would require assessing whether a law establishing a CIP in a country which has committed to a supranational organization (such as the EU) violates any of these commitments. For the case of Bulgaria, Cyprus, and Malta, although citizenship is a *domaine réservé* of the states, EU member states are still obliged to fulfil their commitments towards other member states.[19] If arguments can be made proving that the establishment of CIPs violates such commitments (for instance, violating the duty of sincere cooperation)[20] then the result of an assessment following this second meaning will fail on the grounds of this method focusing on the supranational intra-systemic legal substantive content.

Similarly, it is possible to make an assessment using some principles of international law. Although not without controversy, some principles affecting the understanding of citizenship have been stated by international courts. Among the most relevant may be the 'genuine link' principle, stated by the International Court of Justice (ICJ) in the *Nottebohm* case in 1955.[21] In that case, the ICJ stated that nationality is:

> a legal bond having as its basis a social fact of attachment, a genuine connection of existence, interests and sentiments, together with the existence of reciprocal rights and duties. It may be said to constitute the juridical expression of the fact that the individual upon whom it is conferred, either directly by the law or as the result of an act of the authorities, is in fact more closely connected with the population of the State conferring nationality than with that of any other State.

A method assessing the programmes on the grounds of respect for the international principle of 'genuine link' should focus on answering the following question: 'Can an economic investment in the form of X in a country be sufficient to prove the social fact of attachment to that country?' In turn, even the most enthusiastic people keen to reply with a positive answer would need to differentiate among the candidates' wealthy status and the total impact that such an investment has to their fortunes. If satisfactory arguments cannot be made proving that merely an economic investment is enough to develop a genuine link towards the

---

[19] That EU member states are obliged to fulfil their commitments towards other member states when granting national citizenship has been declared, among other sentences, in Case C-135/08, Janko Rottman v Freistaat Bayern, Judgment of the Court of Justice of the EU (Grand Chamber) of 2 March 2010 and Case C-369/90 Mario Vicente Micheletti and others v Delegación del Gobierno en Cantabria (1992) ECR I-04239. In this last one, the Court stated that 'It is for each Member State, *having due regard to Community law*, to lay down the conditions for the acquisition and loss of nationality'. For a brilliant insight of European governance of national citizenship laws see Maas (2016)

[20] The duty of sincere cooperation laid down in Article 4(3) TEU. An excellent approach to the hypothesis that CIPs may entail a breakthrough for sincere cooperation in citizenship in the EU is presented by Sergio Carrera (2014).

[21] Nottebohm case (Liechtenstein v. Guatemala) [1955] ICJ 1.

country that established a CIP, then the programmes would be considered illegitimate following the meaning of lawfulness by failing to satisfy requirements of international principles affecting citizenship, particularly the requirement of a genuine link.

The third meaning presented, which has been named *legitimacy beyond the law,* allows detaching legitimacy from legality, making it possible to argue for the illegitimacy of a legal provision on moral or justice grounds. Under this third meaning, assessing the legitimacy of X would be done by being coherent with an extra-legal system (for instance, a moral system). This is the meaning of legitimacy that seems to be followed by most authors researching CIPs when offering moral and justice arguments to argue against the legitimacy of the programmes. As an example, the argument that CIPs increase global inequality and therefore are illegitimate implicitly entails a conception of the good that requires a certain level of equality. Yet, the problem with most people following this third meaning is that they presuppose a certain degree of moral objectivism that is not at all demonstrated by their arguments. Thus, their claims and arguments based on a certain moral conception come out sparsely underpinned if unaccompanied by a justification proving the moral objectivism about which many others – in which I include myself – are sceptical. For that reason, it seems evident that any person interested in following this third meaning for assessing the legitimacy of CIPs should first make an effort to prove that the moral or justice claims upon which they base their assessment of the programmes are sufficiently objective to be accepted by – at least – the society establishing the programme.

This greatly insurmountable difficulty makes the case for the convenience of starting the evaluation of the legitimacy of the CIPs by following the meanings as legally valid or as lawfulness. Yet, the limited value obtained by assessing the programmes following the meaning as formal validity leads me to conclude in favour of following the second meaning, lawfulness.

For that reason, and as an example of how to develop a method following this second meaning as lawfulness, I deploy in the next section the contract law method. My job here is not to evaluate the legitimacy of any specific CIP, but to present an available method that may be employed to evaluate the programmes so as to show that this question of methods of evaluation or assessment, which *prima facie* may strike some as a very theoretical question, actually yields very different and potentially contrasting results interesting for scholars, lawmakers, and practitioners. Yet this chapter will not deploy the method extensively, since this task would exceed the purposes of the chapter.

An Assessment Method: Applying Contract law

CIPs are programmes that grant citizenship in exchange for economic transactions. This practice has been described on many occasions as 'selling of citizenship', not only by academics[22] and the media[23] but also by the EU Parliament.[24] When characterizing the phenomenon of CIPs as a 'selling of citizenship', one is simultaneously implying that citizenship is the object of *negotium juridicum*, and therefore, that the legal regulation on contracts can be applicable to it. Although the characterization of CIPs as a 'sale of citizenship' is eye-catching, there are reasons not to accept it as a given, which made me argue against this labelling on previous occasions.[25] *Prima facie*, it may be considered at least partly inaccurate and at odds with our understanding of the legal phenomenon, and as such it is not risk-free: keep in mind that in law, describing phenomena accurately is critical to ascribe correct legal consequences. Under a legal perspective, arguing that CIPs are *selling* citizenship implies that the programmes represent a contractual form and thus that one would expect to follow the rules set up by (1) law, (2) legal doctrine (especially where it is source of law), and (3) legal science, as to what can be object of such a transaction.

In the coming paragraphs, I nonetheless argue from the assumption that the mainstream characterization of *selling* citizenship is correct. If this were the case, i.e. that states are selling citizenship, then a contract among state and applicants should be presumed, and the general conditions of validity of contracts should be applicable for each particular CIP,

---

[22] Among several others, the following are essays that describe the phenomenon of CIPs as the 'selling of citizenship': Bauböck and Shachar (2014), Surak (2016), Tanasoca (2016), and Shachar's chapter in this book.
[23] Among several others, some examples are: 'Passports for sale' (January 17, 2018 in CBS News), 'Cyprus "selling" EU citizenship to super-rich of Russia and Ukraine' (September 17, 2017 in The Guardian), 'Malta free to sell EU citizenship, Commission says' (November 14, 2013 in EU Observer).
[24] During the debate in the EU Parliament that took place on January 15, 2014 to discuss the Maltese CIP, the unanimous description of the effect of the Maltese programme was the 'selling of citizenship'.
[25] In my talk 'Conceptual misunderstandings on *ius pecunia*', presented at the Academic Workshop of the Investment Migration Council, June 5, 2017, Geneva, Switzerland, I deployed several arguments against this characterization.

being the contract susceptible to invalidity under certain legally determined circumstances.

The method I am suggesting here, the contract law method, would operate on this basis, that is, on assuming that CIPs establish a contractual relationship between states and candidates to which the general conditions of contract validity are applicable. In this scenario, assessing the legitimacy of the programmes would be done by looking through the conditions of validity of contracts existing in the legal system of the particular state that established a CIP. If no ground for invalidity applies, the contract would *eo ipso* be valid, and the programme that gave rise to this contract would be considered legitimate from the point of view of contract law. On the contrary, were we to find that the contract does not respect a condition of validity, the contract would be invalid either *ex tunc* (from the outset) or *ex nunc* (from now on) – depending on the condition and the particular legal system.

Consequences of being declared invalid *ex tunc* or *ex nunc* differ significantly. If a contract is declared invalid *ex nunc*, it will no longer be enforceable; while if a contract is declared invalid *ex tunc*, it is considered never to have been entered upon, and the parties would lose any rights or obligations imposed by the contract.

Under the assumption that we are working under, i.e. that CIPs entail a selling of citizenship, by using the contract law method in order to assess the legitimacy of the programmes, one scenario in which one could eventually end is that the implicit contract to which applicants sign when applying to naturalize could be judicially declared either invalid *ex nunc* or *ex tunc*, if there are venues to access the judiciary. The consequences would differ greatly from one scenario to the other.

If the contract were declared invalid *ex nunc* the result would be the discontinuation of the particular CIP by invalidating the contracts from now on. More interesting and disturbing would be a scenario in which the contract were judicially declared invalid *ex tunc*. Following legal doctrine, in that conceivable, but unlikely, scenario the parties would have to retrieve their supplies, that is to say, states would have to pay back to the applicants the investments while applicants would have to give back their passports.[26] Obviously, several legal questions would rise in this scenario. What would happen to those naturalized investors who lost

---

[26] This is obviously a very unlikely scenario but not an impossible one according to the logic guiding contract law. Nonetheless, it would depend on which legal consequences were attached and in case of trial the evaluation of these by the judge.

their former citizenship by naturalizing in Malta? Would some of them become stateless?[27] Would agents[28] be sentenced to return their profits in relation to a service pertinent to the contract invalidated *ex tunc*? What costs would be we looking at and what would these costs exactly represent for the state?[29]

Though data on the impact of CIPs is usually scarce or unavailable, Malta releases an annual report on its Individual Investor Programme.[30] I will use the data derived from this report in order to illustrate what consequences could follow from an invalidation *ex tunc*. The point of this is to show that the impact of a possible court ruling declaring the contract between the two parties invalid *ex tunc* would be significant. This, in turn, can be taken either as a reason to further investigate the 'contract law' assessment method; or as an indicator that the assumption on which the analysis is grounded is unlikely, so we might not really be dealing with 'selling citizenship' after all. But before venturing into the possible meanings of the results, let me present them.

In the fourth annual report from Malta[31] we read that

> During the period under review by this Report (1st of July, 2016 – 30th June, 2017), the contributions collected by the Identity Malta Agency (IMA) amounted to €290,225,000, equating approximately to 2.74% of the GDP relative to the same period.

The report also indicates the distribution of the funds, for the specific period, and since the launch of the IIP, as well as the economic benefits for Malta. The numbers are the following: for the National Development and Social Fund, €249,328,799; for the Consolidated Fund, €106,855,199;

---

[27] According to art. 8 of the Convention on the reduction of statelessness, 'A Contracting State shall not deprive a person of its nationality if such deprivation would render him stateless.' However, the same article establishes that it is permissible that a person loses her nationality '(b) where the nationality has been obtained by misrepresentation or fraud'. In the case of applicants naturalizing through CIPs, could it be argued that acquiring citizenship by investing in a country is equivalent to fraud in absence of other connections between the naturalized person and the country?

[28] According to the Fourth Annual Report of the Office of the Regulator (page 19), the total number of Accredited Agents as in June 2017 stands at 141. Available at https://oriip.gov.mt/en/Pages/Documents-and-Links.aspx (accessed on May 10, 2018).

[29] We have reason to believe the sums might be conspicuous as 'in small countries, the impact of citizenship by investment schemes can be substantial. At public conferences, the Prime Minister of Saint Kitts has declared that the receipts from its citizenship by investment program accounted for 37% of its GDP in 2015' (Surak, 2016, p. 25). See also Surak's contribution in this book.

[30] See footnote 28.

[31] Page 19 of the Report.

for Identity Malta Agency, €23,701,500; and for the scheme's private and only concessionaire, Henley&Partners, €19,054,000. As the numbers show, these economic benefits have indeed been significant. The numbers also give an insight into the proportion that the invalidation *ex tunc* of the contract at hand would entail – of course, were we (1) dealing with a contract that (2) would not meet the validity conditions of the contracts in the particular legal system.

Sticking to the same example, and just with the purpose of showing how the method would work, let us pay attention now to the conditions of validity of contracts in Maltese law.

Conditions of Validity of Contracts in Maltese Law

The conditions of validity of contracts in Maltese law are found in Chapter 16 of the Civil Code (Cc). Article 966 Cc establishes that the conditions essential to the validity of a contract are: (a) capacity of the parties to contract; (b) the consent of the party who binds himself; (c) a certain thing which constitutes the subject-matter of the contract; (d) a lawful consideration. Conditions (c) and (d) on subject-matter and consideration[32] deserve special attention here.

Regarding the subject-matter (c), article 982 Cc indicates that only things that are not *extra commercium* are susceptible to be the subject-matter of an agreement. Article 1370 Cc specifies that 'all things which are not *extra commercium* may be sold, unless the alienation thereof is prohibited by any special law'. Let us now specify what *extra commercium* would imply. In Roman law, three kinds of *res* (things) were considered *extra commercium*: (1) *res divini iuris*, (2) *res publicae*, and (3) *res communes*. *Res publicae* included things belonging to the state. The Civil Code of Malta also leaves the *res publicae extra commercium* in its Tittle III (of domain public) of the Fourth Schedule of the Civil Code.[33]

---

[32] Subject-matter refers to the object of the contract while consideration to the cause (Mahasneh, 2014).

[33] The Tittle III (of domain public) of the Fourth Schedule of the Civil Code only mentions three things to be considered as property in the public domain: the coastal perimeter, the internal waters and seabed, and the subsoil (article 4(1)). One may wonder whether the category of objects belonging to the *res publicae* could be extended to include citizenship (*status civitatis*) as well; here defined as the legal status granting the individual a particular position before the state. Arguments on this line have not been provided yet. An attempt to follow this path could be done by selecting the features of objects included in the category that justify its maintenance outside commerce by checking its relevance according to the intention of the legislator. If the features that motivated the legislator to exclude

Thus, in the event we would be in front of a *numerus apertus* list allowing that an argument is done sustaining that *status civitatis* would be found to be an object of *res publicae extra commercium*, it would follow that it could not be lawfully sold: it would entail a *prohibition on alienation* of the kind that *negotium juridicum* allows. It remains to be tested whether such a prohibition would, on this line of argument, extend to any seller. So, if it were the case that *status civitatis* were found to fall into the *extra commercium* category, it would most certainly mean that citizens would be prohibited from 'selling' their own status. Yet, it remains to be seen if it would also imply that the State could not lawfully *sell* the status. If we were to find that the legal category of *extra commercium* to be such that not even the State could lawfully 'sell' *status civitatis*, we would most probably need to conclude that states are engaging in unlawful alienation. No arguments along this line of reasoning have yet been developed. Mine here is a first tentative step along the way of clarifying what it would mean for *status civitatis* to be classified into the category of *extra commercium*. Any attempt to follow this path of reasoning should insist on the features that things need to have in order for them to be adequately classified as *extra commercium*.

Another limit to the objects that are susceptible of being subject to contract law can be found, in the case of Malta, in the Civil Code's article 985, which establishes that objects that are impossible, prohibited by law, *contrary to morality*, to public policy, may not be the object of a lawful contractual agreement. On the grounds of this article, another set of questions arise: for instance, should we say that *status civitatis* is an object the alienation of which, or the contractual disposition of which at least, can be *contrary to morality*? To answer this question, we would need to know more about the *contrary to morality* – requirement in Maltese contract law. Let us just assume for the moment that this requirement would be frustrated by the object at hand (citizenship). That is to say, if it could be argued that selling citizenship is prohibited since its very object cannot be sold because its disposal and purchase would be 'contrary to morality', then an argument against the validity of the contract could be made.

Let me now turn to requirement (d) of Article 966 in chapter 16 of the Civil Code establishing the lawful conditions to the validity of a contract.

---

them from commerce could be attributed to citizenship, then an argument in favour of considering citizenship an object *extra commercium* could be made. It is outside the scope of this chapter to make arguments following this line.

Regarding the requirement that an object may be sold only if it can be made into a contract having 'a lawful consideration', article 987 establishes that an obligation without a consideration, or founded on a false or an unlawful consideration, shall have *no effect*, while article 990 establishes that the consideration is unlawful if it is prohibited by law or *contrary to morality* or to public policy. Again, the Civil Code of Malta introduces elements that would allow testing whether CIPs – were these a contractual form – would be allowed/legitimate under the laws of Malta. If it were somehow proven that the consideration on which the contract in question relies would be *contrary to morality* – whatever that would mean pursuant to valid law in Malta – the consideration would be unlawful, and the contract then would be invalid.

The example of the laws of Malta shows that it cannot be excluded *a priori* that the legitimacy of CIPs may be tested on *intra-systemic* legal grounds. This means that it might be possible to argue against the legitimacy of CIPs (were these a kind of selling of citizenship) by providing arguments on (i) the fact that citizenship is an object *extra commercium* or on (ii) that the sale would be 'contrary to morality'.[34] And this would be so, not in virtue of the political or any particular normative opinion of the assessor, but in virtue of *intra-systemic* friction in the Maltese legal system.

Concluding Remarks

In this chapter, I have suggested some methods to assess the legitimacy of CIPs depending on the particular meaning of legitimacy followed. I have also developed in detail a method for assessing CIPs' legitimacy based on contract law doctrine. This method hinges upon the common and recurrent characterization of CIPs as 'selling citizenship', an undisputed and underchallenged characterization. Anyone willing to use this method to assess the legitimacy of the programmes will, therefore, need to argue that CIPs are indeed selling citizenship. Were these arguments non-existent, both the method and the characterization of the phenomenon as 'the selling of citizenship' should be neglected, and ideally another method among those presented should be used. Were scholars and practitioners interested in using the contract law method to assess the legitimacy of the programmes, then solid arguments proving that CIPs are *selling* citizenship need to be made first. In the event that strong arguments proving

---

[34] Here understood as the conception of *morality* embedded in the Maltese legal system.

that the programmes represent a form of 'selling of citizenship' are provided, then this economic policy tool to collect and make money with citizenship and migration rights as its enticement would represent the ultimate way in which money matters in migration: it would not simply enable migration, but also alter the citizenry of the states.

References

Bauböck, R. (2014). What is wrong with selling citizenship? It corrupts democracy! In Should citizenship be for sale? *EUI Working Paper RSCAS, 2014/1*. Available at: https://cadmus.eui.eu/bitstream/handle/1814/29318/RSCAS_2014_01.pdf?sequence=1&isAllowed=y

Boatca, M. (2015). Commodification of citizenship. Global inequalities and the modern transmission of property. In I. Wallerstein, C. Chase-Dunn, and C. Suter, eds., *Overcoming Global Inequalities*, London: Routledge, Taylor & Francis Group, 3–18.

Borna, S., and Stearns, J. M. (2002). The ethics and efficacy of selling national citizenship. *Journal of Business Ethics*, 37, 193–207.

Carrera Núñez, S. (2014). How much does EU citizenship cost? The Maltese citizenship-for-sale affair: A breakthrough for sincere cooperation in citizenship of the union? *CEPS Paper in Liberty and Security in Europe*, 64, 1–54.

Džankić, J. (2012). *The Pros and Cons of Ius Pecuniae: Investor citizenship in comparative perspective* [Working Paper]. http://cadmus.eui.eu//handle/1814/21476

Džankić, J. (2015). *Investment-based citizenship and residence programmes in the EU.* http://cadmus.eui.eu/bitstream/handle/1814/34484/RSCAS_2015_08.pdf

Frank, R. (November 3, 2011). Surge in Rich Chinese Who 'Invest' in U.S. Citizenship. *The Wall Strate Journal*. https://blogs.wsj.com/wealth/2011/11/09/surge-in-rich-chinese-who-invest-in-u-s-citizenship/

Maas, W. (2016). European governance of citizenship and nationality. *Journal of Contemporary European Research*, 12(1), 532–551.

Mahasneh, N. (2014). Subject matter and consideration of the contract: The approaches of the 2010 UNIDROIT PICC, the 1980 CISG, and the 1976 Civil Code of Jordan. *Uniform Law Review – Revue de Droit Uniforme*, 19(3), 390–410. https://doi.org/10.1093/ulr/unu025

Mindus, P. and Prats, E. (2018). La cittadinanza «a pagamento» nell'Unione europea. *Quaderni costituzionali*, 1, 246–252. https://doi.org/10.1439/89202

Prats, E. (2019). Citizenship by investment programmes: Express naturalisation for bulky wallets. An arbitrary de jure stratification? *Revista de Derecho Político*, 106, 347–377.

Shachar, A. (2014). Dangerous liaisons: Money and citizenship. In Should citizenship be for sale? *EUI Working Paper RSCAS, 2014/1*. Available at: https://cadmus.eui.eu/bitstream/handle/1814/29318/RSCAS_2014_01.pdf?sequence=1&isAllowed=y

Shachar, A. (2018). The marketization of citizenship in an age of restrictionism. *Ethics & International Affairs, 32*(01), 3–13. https://doi.org/10.1017/S0892679418000059

Shachar, A., Bauböck, R., Bloemraad, I., and Vink, M. P. (eds.). (2017). *The Oxford Handbook of Citizenship* (1st ed.). New York: Oxford University Press.

Stern, J. (2011). Ius pecuniae—Staatsbürgerschaft zwischen ausreichendem Lebensunterhalt, Mindestsicherung und Menschenwürde. In *Migration und Integration – wissenschaftliche Perspektiven aus Österreich* (pp. 55–74).

Surak, K. (2016). *Global citizenship 2.0. The growth of citizenship by investment programs. Investment migration working paper 2016/3.* http://investmentmigration.org/download/global-citizenship-2-0-growth-citizenship-investment-programs/

Tanasoca, A. (2016). Citizenship for sale. *European Journal of Sociology, 57*(01), 169–195. https://doi.org/10.1017/S0003975616000059

16

Wealth as a Golden Visa to Citizenship

AYELET SHACHAR

In recent years, restrictive immigration and naturalization policies have become the dominant response to the pressures of worldwide mobility.[1] Governments are erecting ever higher walls – physical, symbolic, material – to impede access to their territories and delineate membership boundaries.[2] At the same time, a growing number of countries are selectively opening their gates to those with deep pockets – known in wealth management jargon as "high net worth individuals" – offering them expedited, simplified, easy-pass naturalization in return for sizeable monetary transfers. Under such "citizenship or residence by investment" programs, as they are called, capital becomes a gateway to fast-tracked membership, providing exemptions from requirements that are strictly enforced for would-be immigrants of more modest means, such as extended residence, civic integration, and linguistic proficiency.[3] My fascination with the role of wealth as *both* barrier *and* accelerator to citizenship, the topic of this chapter, is part of a broader exploration of the versatile toolbox of line-drawing techniques deployed by governments the world over. The goal of these tools may at times appear contradictory,

---

[1] Following a period of liberalization, the "restrictive turn" is typically dated back to the early 2000s.
[2] Shachar 2020a; Shachar 2020b.
[3] Citizenship by investment ("golden passport") programs create a direct link between money transfers – in large quantities, ranging in the European Union, for example, between €1 million and €2.5 million – and expedited and simplified bestowal of citizenship. These programs are directed at wealthy individuals who can transfer substantial amounts of money across borders; the investors themselves are not required to move to the new home country. They are not even required to manage the investment upon which the transaction rests. Residence by investment ("golden visas") programs also rely on the same transactional logic, but the investors gain only temporary or permanent residency status, not citizenship. In the European Union, the value of such residence by investment programs is significantly increased by the fact that the golden-visa holder also gains free movement throughout the entire European Schengen zone.

at once "tightening" and "lightening," restricting and relaxing, constricting and loosening the requirements of access to membership.[4]

The Property Qualification

Wealth as a criterion for citizenship – not so long ago thoroughly discredited in post-revolutionary democratic societies – is making a come-back. "Earning a living" has become an official precondition for naturalization in a growing number of countries, merging economic and cultural perceptions of membership that distinguish between those who "deserve" (or have "earned") the right to stay, and those who are perceived as "too different" or simply too burdensome. By contrast, migrants with substantial quantities of mobile capital now benefit from access to a "golden passport" of their choice. Literally, they may buy their way in.[5]

Placing money-based barriers to passage through the gates of admission adds another major obstacle to citizenship, even for long-term residents. Beyond practical difficulties, it indirectly reactivates the historical connection – a system long ago ascribed to the realm of inegalitarian and anti-democratic – between property and citizenship. Derek Heater observes that treating wealth qualifications as a precondition for membership is "as old as the status of citizenship itself."[6] It was not until the French Revolution that conceptions of citizenship emphasizing equality among members of the body politic began to play a significant role on the historical stage, offering an alternative to up-until-then prevalent structures; "legal *inequality*, not simply factual inequality, was the basis of the social order."[7] The abolition of the ancien-régime's privileges, estates, and "distinctions, whether useful or honorific ... enjoyed by certain [persons] and denied to others,"[8] gave rise to a competing revolutionary vision of rights-based membership, whereby *citoyens/citoyennes* constitute the political community of equals. We may refer to this as the invention of a modernist conception of citizenship.[9] Speaking of

---

[4] Shachar 2020b; Joppke 2010
[5] While definitions vary, I refer to wealth, net worth, and mobile capital interchangeably as representing the total sum of assets, minus liabilities and debts, owed by the respective individual.
[6] Heater 2004, 66.
[7] Brubaker 1992, at 35.
[8] Brubaker 1992, at 35 (quoting Behrens 1967, 46).
[9] The term "rights-based conception of citizenship" is drawn from Hammersley 2015, 471. The transition from ancient to modern conceptions of citizenship did not arise out of thin air in the French Revolution. It followed centuries of debates and alterations to ancient

"ancient" and "modernist" in this context is obviously an oversimplification as there have been many gradations and competing interpretations of each model, especially when it comes to defining *who* can gain access to citizenship, and according to *what* criteria.[10] Even if we treat citizenship (as I think we should) as an essentially contested concept, this acknowledgment does not take away from the theoretical insights that can be drawn from contrasting modernist and ancient conceptions of citizenship.[11]

Greek and Roman citizenship were built on structural inequality whereby the majority of residents, not to mention slaves, were excluded from access to citizenship. This title that was reserved for a male head of household, born to not only an Athenian father but also an Athenian mother, representing an early form of what some scholars would call "racialized citizenship."[12] Whereas the Greek model of citizenship viewed the citizen as a "political animal," defined by ruling and being ruled in turn, the Roman model focused more on legal status and rights, but nevertheless remained hierarchical.[13] The Romans did not fear extending citizenship to a variety of individuals, including foreigners, freed slaves, and plebians, "without any pretention to make them join in the business of rule."[14] This hierarchy was not free from exclusion: women, slaves, and non-Romans were barred from citizenship, and the accompanying rights and protections attached to it.[15] As Ryan Balot observes, although Roman citizens were formal equals, it was the wealthy, elite Roman order who ultimately ruled and dominated "political life, which in turn meant that ordinary citizens had to fight in order to assert and extend their rights."[16]

---

conceptions of citizenship which historians date back to as early as the end of the sixteenth century and early seventeenth century.

[10] Hammersley 2015.
[11] Brubaker 1992; Bruchell 2002; Hammersley 2015; Ballot 2017; Joppke 2019; Of course, there are additional differences between ancient and modernist conceptions of citizenship. While I emphasize the dimension of equality, other important distinctions refer to questions of scale – anchoring back to ancient Athens, Sparta, and Rome, a citizen was an inhabitant of a city (not a nation-state) – as well as modes of political participation.
[12] FitzGerald 2017; Joppke 2019, 861.
[13] I thank Helena Lank for this formulation. For further discussion, see Bruchell 2002; Ballot 2017.
[14] Joppke 2019, 861.
[15] Over time, the ranks of Roman citizens throughout the empire had increased, a process that culminated in AD 212 with the Edict of Caracalla (the Constitutio Antoniniana), which granted citizenship to all free inhabitants of the empire.
[16] Ballot 2017.

The French Revolution offered a critical moment of breakage between citizenship and property. The collapse of the ancien régime with its once-entrenched structural inequality engendered a reimagination of the social order in which *citoyens* replaced *privilégiés*.[17] The revolutionary emphasis on rights-based and equality-centered citizenship promoted the questioning of the property qualification, just as it pushed to the fore the claims for inclusion of religious minorities, women, free men of color, and slaves in the colonies, offering justification for *expanding* the boundaries of membership. We know from the historical record that this promise of equal citizenship – even merely as a formal legal status, let alone a lived experience – was only partly implemented, and even today remains unfulfilled in many parts of the world.[18] But the failure to wholly implement a principle does not detract from its normative attraction. Unlike the ancient model, the modernist conception provides us not only with a lexicon for claiming equality *among* members, but also the syntax for challenging "the grounds on which certain inhabitants could be excluded *from* it."[19] This trajectory is far from unidirectional, however, and it has always faced competing counternarratives and provoked calls for *constricting* access.[20] Fast forward from the past to the present. Today's restrictive turn fits squarely into this pattern. States have proven more enterprising than most theories would have predicted in finding new ways to control migration and mobility, developing a sophisticated kaleidoscope of territorial, cultural, and economic line-drawing techniques that can be deployed selectively against different target groups,[21] and according to different baselines, including means, privilege, and power.[22]

---

[17] On these major conceptual changes, see, e.g., Smith 2002, 105–115; Brubaker 1992, 35–49. The modernist conceptions of citizenship incorporated elements of democratic, national, and bureaucratic, or statist innovations. The tensions among these narratives have played out ever since, leading to different constellations in different locations and different time periods.

[18] For a host of legal and political reasons, these exclusions are today more implicit than explicit but remain harmful nonetheless.

[19] Hammersley 2015, at 476.

[20] For an influential account, see Smith 1997.

[21] Shachar 2020a; 2020b

[22] In recent years, important strides have been made in revealing the impact of considerations of race, culture, ethnicity, gender, sexuality, and, increasingly, religion too in de facto shaping the prospects of migration and integration – despite being formally prohibited and discredited. For an excellent review of these developments, see Ellermann 2020. While enriching and nuancing previous accounts, surprisingly little attention has been paid to the persistence of wealth in creating, or replicating, unequal

I will highlight throughout my discussion the tensions and paradoxes revealed by the newfound "alchemy" of turning wealth into a golden passport to citizenship. I begin, however, by exploring the dazzling range of economic barriers that make entry, settlement, and naturalization ever more difficult for almost all categories of immigrants, save those entering by virtue of their bank accounts. Both developments – restrictive closure and selective openness – represent different facets of the same trend. Without explicitly stating as much, programs that turn wealth into a core criterion for admission conceptually reignite an older, exclusive, and exclusionary vision according to which one would have to hold property (in land, resources, or in relation to one's "dependents," including women, slaves, and children) in order to qualify as a citizen. This raises profound challenges to rights-based accounts of political membership that place equality at their core.

Economic Thresholds as Barriers

After many years of neglect, the function of wealth (or lack thereof) as a criterion for membership is regaining scholarly attention. Sociologists, philosophers, and legal scholars have turned their gaze toward considerations of how different types of capital play into the politics of selection in "shaping possibilities and impossibilities of migration."[23] Passage through the bolted gates of admission is open to some, but shut to others. Whereas the specific details may vary from country to country – an obligation to participate in the economy or proof that a would-be immigrant has never applied for, or collected, welfare benefits – these policies share the basic premise that immigrants must exhibit self-sufficiency. Schematically, there are three main gates: entry (gaining lawful admission upon territorial arrival); settlement (securing a long-term residence permit in European legal parlance, equivalent to a "green card" in the United States); and naturalization (acquiring citizenship in the new home country).[24] Exceptions to this generic process may be made at the discretion of state authorities – and indeed such exemptions are plentiful when it comes to those benefiting from golden visas and golden passports. For everyone else, the journey toward naturalization is an

---

admission to territory and membership. My analysis in this chapter contributes to recent efforts to begin to close this glaring gap.

[23] Bonjour and Chauvin 2018, 5.
[24] Hammar 1990, 16–18.

unremitting "filtering process,"[25] widely regarded as the "most densely regulated and most politicized aspect of citizenship laws."[26]

Inquiries into a prospective citizen's economic self-sufficiency may take place at the naturalization stage (the third and traditionally final gate), or may be backtracked to the earlier stage of establishing permanent residency (the second gate), and potentially even prior to gaining lawful admission in the first place (the initial gate). In Europe, economic requirements are proliferating; these requirements complement, rather than replace, proof of civic integration. For example, in Austria, applicants for permanent residency must show proof of "adequate means of subsistence," which must exceed the minimal income level below which they would fall into reliance on social assistance. When applying for naturalization, they must show proof of their disposable income, which is the amount they have in hand *after* paying rent or any other fixed expenses. In Belgium, "proof of economic participation" is required, which translates into a record of at least 468 working days. The self-employed are obliged to provide proof of payment of six trimesters of social security contributions. In Denmark, a condition for obtaining Danish citizenship requires that the applicant has never drawn on welfare benefits, and has no "debt to the public."[27] This last is not a metaphysical concept but a material one: the person must have paid off any child allowance paid in advance by the public sector, daycare payment, or repayment of a home loan. Finland requires a declaration of the origin of the migrant's income, which must include a "reliable account of current and past sources of income," for the entire period of residence prior to naturalization. Germany defines the conditions for self-sufficiency even more meticulously. These include minimum income requirements and proof of sufficient funds to support self and family without reliance on government assistance. Applicants are also obliged to carry adequate health insurance and must have diligently paid into the social security and pension system for a period of at least sixty months. They must also provide evidence of adequate living quarters in compliance with mandated requirements – set at 13 square meters per person, to be precise. A 2018 comparative study of economic criteria for naturalization has estimated, remarkably, that "about 60 to 70 percent of Austrian female blue-collar workers would *not* be able to meet the income

---

[25] Legomsky 1994, 291.
[26] Bauböck and Goodman 2010.
[27] For discussion of the intersection of income requirements in immigration regulation and broader debates about the sustainability of the welfare state in Nordic countries, see Eggebø and Staver 2021.

requirements for naturalization in Austrian citizenship law. Consequently, if an 'average' female blue-collar worker had not acquired citizenship by descent – being born to Austrian parents – she would be excluded from citizenship and the rights that come with it."[28] If this is true for local-born and -bred members of the community, imagine the economic barriers that newcomers face.[29]

In the United States, new restrictions to adjustment of status took effect in 2020, expanding the definition of "public charge" to new programs such as food stamps – a federal program providing assistance to low- or no-income households with young children to purchase staple items such as bread and milk.[30] Applicants must further demonstrate household income of at least 125 percent of the federal poverty guidelines. Factors that may count against the applicant include insufficient savings, financial liabilities, previous approval to receive a public benefit, low credit score, absence of health insurance, education, or language skills, and having a sponsor who is unlikely to provide financial support. Each of these factors has clear socioeconomic underpinnings. Increasingly, the idea of *earning* membership takes on a dual meaning of proving one's "deservingness" – complying with tighter civic integration and naturalization procedures, and economic self-sufficiency.[31]

The bolted gates of admission, so carefully guarded when it comes to the many, are swung open when it comes to the propertied few. *Their* journey to membership is paved with golden visas and golden passports. Across the globe, a growing number of governments are proactively promoting expedited, simplified pathways to citizenship for the rich and affluent, in exchange for a substantial investment or donation. Here, wealth-based criteria do not restrict mobility and migration, but rather *facilitate* it.

Wealth as Facilitator of Privileged Access

For those with an abundance of capital, the gates of admission seem to dissolve like a mirage. Governments go out of their way to proffer

---

[28] Stadlmair 2018, 48 (citing Joachim Stern's data findings) (emphasis added).
[29] Such economic barriers tend to disproportionately harm women and members of minority communities. For an overview of the literature, see Hacker 2017, 149–196. See also de Jong and de Hart 2021; Eggebø and Staver 2021; Mantu 2021 in this volume.
[30] The food stamps program is officially known as the Supplemental Nutrition Assistance Program (SNAP). These policy changes were later suspended by the Biden administration.
[31] For a recent survey on increased barriers to naturalization in the United States, see Capps and Echeverría-Estrada 2020.

accelerated and abridged entryways for the rich. Prime ministers and other governmental officials regularly attend glitzy industry-organized conferences to "market" their countries' respective citizenship – and residence by investment programs to potential wealthy purchasers, or third-party agents acting on their behalf. These programs target über-rich individuals who are willing to pay millions to diversify their "citizenship portfolio," granting them expeditious naturalization or residency in exchange for real estate purchase, government bonds, flat-fee investment, or direct donation.[32] The latter, as one participant in this booming industry undiplomatically observed, manifests explicitly the transactional logic undergirding the citizenship trade: "You write a check to the government and they give you a passport."[33] In certain cases, millionaire migrants need not even set foot in the new home country.

On the most recent count, as of 2020, close to twenty countries offer full-blown cash-for-passport schemes that create a direct link between money transfers and expedited bestowal of citizenship. An additional sixty jurisdictions confer residency permits in accelerated fashion in return for monetary investments. The sums involved are significant, ranging from the near US$2 million mark in the United States (edging closer to US$1 million for specially designated areas) to a minimum of £2 million in the United Kingdom for a leave of remain (the greater the investment, the shorter the wait time for settlement). In Australia the "significant investor" visa is open to those who are willing to invest more than AU$5 million, while the super wealthy can apply for a "premium" visa that will fast-track them to residency within twelve months in exchange for AU$15 million. Portugal's golden visa program grants residency to global investors in exchange for €500,000 in property or capital investments, coupled with "extremely reduced minimum stay requirements." Millionaire migrants can acquire "passports of convenience" from the island nations of the Caribbean and the Pacific without a requirement for residence in, or even visit to, the passport-issuing country. It should be clear by now that access is made *easier* for those at the top echelon, even if their ties to the admitting country are tenuous

---

[32] Programs vary in the specifics of the investment and donation routes they offer. For a concise overview, see Scherrer and Thirion 2018, Annex 2.
[33] Sovereign Man, September 21, 2020 Newsletter. www.sovereignman.com/international-diversification-strategies/our-sovereign-woman-explores-turkeys-citizenship-by-investment-program-28903/ In the case of Cyprus, for example, close to half of the purchasers hail from Russia and its oligarchic social strata who are in search of access to EU citizenship.

at best; by contrast, it becomes ever harder for those with established links but modest means.

While the details of the various programs vary, they all rely on a shared premise: allowing the well resourced, even those with only tenuous ties to the passport-issuing country, a fast track to citizenship. Here, private wealth becomes a tool to determine the quintessentially *public* act of defining whom to admit to membership.[34] This is a new and troubling variation on the old theme of property as a prerequisite for citizenship, a virtual "velvet rope" dividing the haves and have-nots that must be crossed before a given individual may become eligible to join the ranks of members.[35] By allowing the intrusion of money matters into the *demos*-sculpting sphere, governments not only permit but actively facilitate queue jumping for the well resourced; these individuals gain entry ahead of others who might have a more pressing need, rather than want, to enter the destination country.[36] Whereas uninvited migrants, including asylum seekers and refugees, are blocked long before they reach the actual borders of the desired destinations (they are in effect preemptively barred passage through the first gate of admission), "desired" high net worth individuals are propelled to the front of the admission line.[37] Wealth becomes an added barrier to entry, an extra "protective coating" that states put in place to ensure that the undesired remain outside the gates while the prosperous glide through them.

In addition to exacerbating global inequality in access, this more instrumental, flexible, and market-oriented interpretation of the grounds for inclusion or exclusion not only extends a red-carpet to the rich and affluent, it may also impact the situation of those who have already settled in the new home country. Long-term residents are at a disadvantage, especially if they cannot meet the mounting economic barriers I have recounted above. Here, those who have established meaningful links to the new home country may remain on its territory, but their passage through second and third gates of admission is at risk. This creates an unfair competition between those who have already settled in the country and those for whom a stack of cash becomes a surrogate for membership.[38]

---

[34] For further discussion, see Shachar 2018; Surak 2020.
[35] Schwartz 2020.
[36] Surak 2020 discusses the wealth industry's prediction that substantial wealth accumulation will occur in emerging markets beyond the traditional global core.
[37] Shachar 2020a.
[38] The "real and effective" standard is applied in many jurisdictions, affirming a notion of citizenship as social membership; it is most famously drawn from the *Nottebohm Case*, 22.

An example may help illustrate this last point. The United States has established its variant of the golden visa, formally known as the employment-based fifth preference category (EB-5), allowing the superrich a pathway to a green card, effectively enabling them to jump to the front of the line. The price of admission? As of 2019, it stood at US$1.8 million (up from US$1 million). A "discounted" investment of US$900,000 (up from US$500,000) will suffice if the monies are funneled to target employment areas, which are defined as distressed.[39] The Trump administration had taken a belligerently restrictive, tough-on-immigration approach: young children have been separated from their parents, refugee admission has been limited to a trickle, and authorized immigration has largely dried up. But at the same time, the Trump administration continued to exercise a policy of selective openness for "desirable" (read: millionaire) migrants. In 2017, the Deferred Action for Childhood Arrival (DACA) was revoked; this legislation had allowed young men and women (known as the Dreamers) brought to the country as infants to remain in the United States. In the same year, the administration *renewed* and *expanded* the EB-5 program, allowing an easy-pass to citizenship for footloose members of the global 1 percent, or "Parachuters," for whom the transfer of funds acts as a substitute for the arduous, if not near-impossible, processes of naturalization – as in the case of the Dreamers.

Such inequality in the treatment of different categories of would-be members – those who bask in money, but have few actual ties to the polity versus those with deep, genuine links but little money – tests our intuitions about the meaning and attributes of the relationship between the individual and the political community to which she belongs. To date, despite perennial legislative proposals to address their situation, the Dreamers have no legal pathway to establish a secure status in the only country they know as home. Meanwhile, the Parachuters gain a green card in an accelerated fashion, often exempt from the screening "tests" such as language proficiency that other immigrants must clear. A sword of deportation hangs over the heads of the Dreamers. A gilded pathway awaits the Parachuters.

This decision focused on the claims for diplomatic protection and recognition of citizenship by other members of the international community.

[39] It is worth noting here that in the past such monies for "distressed" areas have been funneled to finance exclusive real estate projects in urban centers or ritzy ski and golf courses. This has raised the ire of critics on both sides of the aisle.

This inconsistency is hard to square with notions of fairness and equality that are central to democratic, civic republican, liberal, and radical conceptions of state and society: it allows passage through the gates of admission to be determined by privilege, power, and financial might. This is a reincarnation of the property qualification, which was supposed to have been stamped out of the realm of membership definition with the rise of modernist conceptions of citizenship. Allowing the transfer of monies to serve as the basis for membership, completely detached from any kind of connection to the said polity – residence, commitment, even presence – is far more than just a change in form. It touches on the very fiber of membership in a way that may impact the substantive content and expressive value of the good being transacted. The surge in golden visas and golden passports contributes to broader processes of commodification that prioritize credit lines over civic ties, eroding the promise of equal citizenship. It intervenes in domestic debates about the rise and fall of citizenship solidarity as a bulwark against social, political, and economic deprivation, just as it illuminates processes that mar inequalities in access to membership globally.[40]

The American golden visa program has many counterparts in other desirable destinations. To the surprise of many, today it is Europe – the progenitor of modern statehood and the contemporary inventor and facilitator of the world's most comprehensive model of supranational citizenship – that is leading the trend toward pecuniary-centered membership transactions. The most recent data reveal that more than half of EU member states have designated immigrant-investor routes. Of these countries, some offer fast-tracked entry visas, many of which allow for later application for permanent residence, while others offer easier access or direct access to golden visas or permanent residence status. Yet others have gone further, offering express access to citizenship for direct cash transfers. In 2013, Malta, the smallest member state of the European Union, put its citizenship up "for sale": the country offered expedited naturalization in return for a non-recoverable donation to government coffers to the tune of €1.15 million. This effectively opened a gilded back door to European citizenship. At the time, such a transaction did something that none of the European countries – including those with golden visas and residency permits – were willing to do: it waived territorial and

---

[40] I do not address here the interests of those who stay in the country of origin, although questions of justice may arise here if the millionaire migrant is using the new citizenship to avoid public disclosure rules or tax obligations in the home country.

residency presence requirements altogether. Following a storm of criticism, culminating with a special session held in the European Parliament (during which the then Vice-President of the European Commission declared that "citizenship must not be up for sale!"), Malta eventually amended its policy.[41] These revisions included a nominal one-year residency requirement, which, in practice, can be fulfilled by simply having an address in the country, not necessarily physically residing in it. However, the Maltese government did not back down from its bolder scheme: placing a price tag on Maltese (and by extension European) citizenship. Until 2020, Cyprus offered the costliest golden passport in Europe (the price tag price is €2 million), but in return it granted the speediest route to citizenship of only three months. This program came under heavy scrutiny after leaked governmental documents revealed that Cypriot golden passports were sold to convicted criminals, money launderers, and individuals entrusted with prominent public functions in their respective home countries, known as "politically exposed persons" at higher risks of corruption.[42] Following these revelations, officials from the European Commission vowed to explore the options for legal action against Cyprus over its citizenship by investment scheme. Ultimately, the Commission launched infringement procedures against Cyprus and Malta, holding that their golden passport programs breached EU law on several counts, including the principle of sincere cooperation (Article 4(3) of the Treaty on the European Union).[43] By turning citizenship into a luxury good for those who can afford the exorbitant price, these countries are de facto defining the rules to obtain EU citizenship and undermining the integrity of this status. In response to the infringement proceedings, the Cypriot government announced that it will suspend its program, causing frenzy among the world's wealthiest who were looking to gain fast and easy access to Europe; they rushed to fill in their applications before the program's close date. Malta also declared that its investor citizenship scheme had reached its cap and consequently will not accept new applications, although both countries announced their intention to modify their programs rather than phase them out altogether.

[41] For discussion of the impact of the EU multilevel system on the Maltese case, see Maas 2016.
[42] Cyprus Papers 2020 (referring to data concerning the purchase of golden passports in the period between 2017 and 2019). In 2019, under pressures from the EU, Cyprus tightened the rules governing its citizenship by investment scheme.
[43] Commission 2020.

The financial stakes are high for both countries. A report released in 2018 estimated that Cyprus raised €4.8 billion through its scheme. Malta reaped approximately €718 million.[44] The Maltese "business model" was imported to Europe by transnational intermediaries (global law firms specializing in the citizenship trade), drawing upon the experiences of Caribbean nations which have developed a specialty in offshore banking, wealth-planning services, and, increasingly, the purveying of citizenship-for-sale programs. In some of these countries a freshly minted passport will be issued in as little as ninety days in exchange for roughly $150,000 – a bargain compared to the cost of a Cypriot passport, although the latter, unlike the former, granted (until the European Commission's legal challenge) access to a coveted prize: EU citizenship.

The Clientele and the Intermediaries

For-profit intermediaries play a key role in linking well-heeled individuals to governments offering a new desired commodity. One such intermediary promotes its enterprise by claiming it "empowers high net worth individuals and families to become global citizens by investing in a second residence or citizenship and helps transform their dreams into a reality through highly personalized products and services."[45] The targeted clientele are an exclusive club of "hundreds of wealthy individuals" – mostly rich elites hailing from emerging economies or politically volatile countries[46] – who are in a position to utilize their wealth to acquire a new passport "quickly and simply, without major disruption to [their] life."[47] The motivation for purchasing citizenship may range from seeking greater visa-free travel by acquiring a "stronger" passport (several global indexes nowadays rank the "power" of a passport relative to other competitors or counterparts) to paving an escape route in case life circumstances change in the home country. Less sanguine causes have been identified by a comprehensive report released by the European Commission in 2019 as raising "security gaps resulting from granting citizenship without prior residence, as

---

[44] Transparency International and Global Witness 2018, at 3.
[45] Arton Capital, "High Net Worth Investor," www.artoncapital.com/ (accessed September 14, 2020).
[46] For illuminating analysis, see Surek 2021, in this volume.
[47] Henley and Partners 2020, "Introduction to the World of Citizenship-by-Investment," www.henleyglobal.com/citizenship-by-investment (accessed September 14, 2020)

well as risks of money laundering, corruption and tax evasion associated with citizenship or residence by investment."[48] These concerns are further aggravated by the lack of transparency that characterized many of these programs, to say nothing of their opaque governance and accountability structures.[49] Add to this the fact that the growing transnational industry of "citizenship and residence planning," as it is known, is only sparingly if at all regulated by national, regional, or international rules. This provides the said intermediaries tremendous latitude to appeal to "seven- or eight-figure entrepreneurs" with offers to "reduce their tax bill, grow wealth overseas, and become global citizens."[50] In contrast with cosmopolitan accounts emphasizing our shared humanity or personhood, global citizenship here puts on a pedestal a vision of "nomad capitalists" and "sovereign men," who, freed from the shackles of mono-citizenship, gain the freedom to write their own rules.[51] They may well put to use their diversified citizenship portfolio to evade tax everywhere or to grow their wealth anywhere by escaping the claws, real or imagined, of "nanny states." In the wake of COVID-19, the libertarian streak of this vision has become even more pronounced. In the midst of a period of considerable uncertainty, intermediaries capitalize on insecurity, marketing golden visas and golden passports as hedging off the unpredictable, as a Plan B for diversifying one's citizenship portfolio. These agents offer their prosperous clientele a strategy to ensure "they will always be in a position of strength, no matter what happens (or doesn't happen) next."[52]

Concluding Remarks

The requirements governing access to membership tell us a great deal about a given society's vision of citizenship, the expressive function of law, and the power dynamics revealed when one stands on the cusp of admission. Money matters in shaping entry, settlement, and naturalization prospects – generating tremendous new opportunities for the few, while

---

[48] EU Commission 2019, at 2.
[49] EU Commission 2019.
[50] Nomad Capitalist 2020 https://nomadcapitalist.com/
[51] Nomad Capitalist and Sovereign Man are names of two such intermediary firms catering wealth management and citizenship and residence by investment services to high net worth individuals.
[52] Sovereign Man, "The Two Critical Requirements of a Perfect Plan B," available at www.sovereignman.com/plan-b/real-life-example-of-a-perfect-plan-b-22101/ (visited September 24, 2020).

closing doors for the many.[53] Laws and regulations do not simply define categories and guide action; they also constitute that which they purport to describe.[54] The cocktail of laws and regulations that combine economic barriers for long-term residents with fast-tracks for a wealthy transnational elite contributes to processes of global and domestic sorting.[55] These processes amplify inequalities of access, *both* within states *and* across borders. Golden visa and golden passport schemes lay bare the interconnection between the internal and external impacts of the erosion of the promise of equality springing from modernist, rights-based conceptions of citizenship. Taken to its logical conclusion (*ad reductio*), were citizenship allocation to become reliant on a price mechanism as a matter of course, to the exclusion of other important considerations, not only would the vast majority of the world's population be prevented from ever gaining a chance to access citizenship in well-off polities, but over time it might lead to a dystopian world in which *anyone* included in the pool of members has to pay to retain their membership status or risk being priced out.[56] If such a scenario were to unfold, wealth criteria, along with heighted civic integration requirements, may reshape the greater class of those who are likely to enjoy full membership, providing a pretext for anti-emancipatory narratives that could *deny* citizenship to those who cannot afford or "earn" it.

Such stratification cuts against the ideal of modernist conceptions of membership as a bulwark against structural inequality, especially along lines of heritage or status hierarchy. While officially discredited, such policies also revive in new clothes the old specter of property-based qualifications. Turning wealth into a golden passport for citizenship betrays not only the ideal of political equality but also the struggle to expand the boundaries of membership to include those once excluded on account of race, gender, ethnicity, religion, sexuality, and – all too often – economic line-drawing as well.

Acknowledgments

I had the honor of delivering the keynote lecture at the "Show Me the Money! Money Matters in Migration Policy and Practice" conference held at the University of Amsterdam, which was the precursor to this

---

[53] This is the premise of this volume, and the conference which led up to it.
[54] Sunstein 1996.
[55] Harpaz 2019.
[56] For further discussion, see Shachar 2017.

volume. I am grateful to the organizers, Tesseltje de Lange, Annette Schrauwen, and Betty de Hart, for their generous invitation and hospitality during my visit to Amsterdam, and to Willem Maas for helpful comments on this chapter. My contribution offers an abbreviated and modified version of an argument that originally appeared as "Unequal Access: Wealth as Barrier and Accelerator to Citizenship," *Citizenship Studies* 25 (2021).

References

Ballot, Ryan. 2017. "Revisiting the Classic Ideal of Citizenship." In Ayelet Shachar, et al. eds., *The Oxford Handbook of Citizenship*. Oxford: Oxford University Press.
Bauböck, Rainer and Sara Wallace Goodman. 2010. "Naturalisation," *EUDO Citizenship Policy Brief No. 2* https://perma.cc/SU3W-SKDP
Behrens, Catherine Betty Abigail. 1967. *The Ancien Régime*. London: Thames and Hudson.
Bonjour, Saskia and Sebastien Chauvin. 2018. "Social Class, Migration Policy and Migrant Strategies: An Introduction," *International Migration* 56, no. 4, 5–18.
Brubaker, Rogers. 1992. *Citizenship and Nationhood in France and Germany*. Cambridge, MA: Harvard University Press.
Burchell, David. 2002. "Ancient Citizenship and its Inheritors," In Engin F. Isin and Bryan S. Turner eds., *Handbook of Citizenship Studies*. London: Sage.
Capps, Randy and Carlos Echeverría-Estrada. 2020. *A Rockier Road to U.S. Citizenship? Findings of a Survey on Changing Naturalization Procedures*. Washington, DC: Migration Policy Institute.
Eggebø, Helga and Anne Staver. 2021. "Follow the Money: Income Requirements in Norwegian Immigration Regulations." In this volume.
Ellermann, Antje. 2020. "Discrimination in Migration and Citizenship." *Journal of Ethnic and Migration Studies* 46, no. 12, 2463–2479.
European Commission 2019. *Report from the Commission to the European Parliament, the Council, the European Economic and Social Committee and the Committee of the Regions*. Brussels, COM (2019) 12.
European Commission 2020. Press Release, *Investor Citizenship Schemes: European Commission Opens Infringements Against Cyprus and Malta for "Selling" EU Citizenship*. Brussels, 20 October 2020.
FitzGerald, David Scott. 2017. "The History of Racialized Citizenship." In Ayelet Shachar, et al. eds., *The Oxford Handbook of Citizenship*. Oxford: Oxford University Press.

Hacker, Daphna. 2017. *Legalized Families in Era of Bordered Globalization*. Cambridge: Cambridge University Press.

Hammar, Tomas. 1990. *Democracy and the Nation State: Aliens, Denizens, and Citizens in a World of International Migration*. Avebury.

Hammersley, Rachel. 2015. "Concepts of Citizenship in France during the Long Eighteenth Century." *European Review of History* 22 no. 3, 468-485.

Harpaz, Yossi. 2019. *Citizenship 2.0: Dual Nationality as a Global Asset*. Princeton: Princeton University Press.

Heater, Derek. 2004. *A Brief History of Citizenship*. New York: NYU Press.

Joppke, Christian. 2017. "The Inevitable Lightening of Citizenship," *European Journal of Sociology* 51, no. 1, 9-32.

Joppke, Christian. 2019. "The Instrumental Turn in Citizenship." *Journal of Ethnic and Migration Studies* 45, no. 6, 858-878.

Legomsky, Stephen H. 1994. "Why Citizenship?" *Virginia Journal of International Law* 35, 279-300.

Maas, Willem. 2016. "European Governance of Citizenship and Nationality," *Journal of Contemporary European Research* 12, 532-551.

Nottebohm Case (*Liechtenstein v. Guatemala*). International Court of Justice 1955. I.C.J. Reports 1.

Ong, Aihwa. 1999. *Flexible Citizenship: The Cultural Logic of Transnationality*. Durham, NC: Duke University Press.

Scherrer, Amandine and Elodie Thirion. 2018. *European Parliamentary Research Service: Citizenship by Investment (CBI) and Residency by Investment (RBI) Schemes in the EU*. Brussels: European Union.

Schwartz, Nelson D. 2020. *The Velvet Rope Economy: How Inequality Become Big Business*. New York: Doubleday.

Shachar, Ayelet. 2017. "Citizenship for Sale?" in Shachar et. al eds., *The Oxford Handbook of Citizenship*. Oxford: Oxford University Press.

Shachar, Ayelet. 2018. "The Marketization of Citizenship in Age of Restrictionism." *Ethics and International Affairs* 32, no. 1, 3-13.

Shachar. Ayelet. 2020a. *The Shifting Border: Legal Cartographies and Migration and Mobility*. Critical Powers Series. Manchester University Press.

Shachar, Ayelet. 2020b. "Beyond Open and Closed Borders: The Grand Transformation of Citizenship." *Jurisprudence* 11, no. 1, 1-27.

Smith, Rogers M. 2002. "Modern Citizenship" In Engin F. Isin and Bryan S. Turner eds., *Handbook of Citizenship Studies*. London: Sage.

Smith, Rogers M. 1997. *Civic Ideals: Conflicting Visions of Citizenship in U.S. History*. New Haven: Yale University Press.

Stadlmair, Jeremias. 2018. "Earning Citizenship: Economic Criteria for Naturalisation in Nine EU Countries." *Journal of Contemporary European Studies* 26, no. 1, 42-63.

Sunstein, Cass. 1996. "On the Expressive Function of Law." *University of Pennsylvania Law Review* 144, 2021–2053.

Surak, Kristin. 2021 "Millionaires and Mobilities: Inequality and Migration Investment Programs." In this volume.

Transparency International and Global Witness. 2018. *European Getaway: Inside the Murky World of Golden Visas,* www.transparency.org/en/publications/golden-visas

17

Divided Families and Devalued Citizens: Money Matters in Mixed-Status Families in the Netherlands

JUDITH DE JONG AND BETTY DE HART

Introduction

This contribution is informed by our research interest in *mixed-status families:* one family member has no residence status – illegalized migrant – while the other family members are legal residents or citizens.[1] Although a familiar issue in American literature, such mixed-status families are seldom studied in the European context.[2] By means of a case study in the Netherlands, we explore how the precarious residence status of one of the family members affects the others who are not directly illegalized themselves.

We focus, specifically, on the financial consequences of being a mixed-status family. In the Netherlands, such financial consequences chiefly result from the Dutch Linkage Act 1998 (*Koppelingswet*), which excludes illegalized migrants from social welfare and benefits. A subsequent Act also extended this exclusion to the legal, permanent resident, or citizen partner in mixed-status families. The latter are now excluded from certain social benefits paid by the tax services, e.g. benefits for housing,

---

[1] Following Kalir and Wissink 2016 we use the term 'illegalized' to underscore the process by which states move to categorize and treat certain people as being 'illegal'. These people can be failed asylum seekers, undocumented migrants, visa over-stayers, and/or migrants with a criminal record. Our selection of respondents also included migrants with 1F-status and migrants who lost an earlier residence status. According to the Geneva Refugee Convention, people who are in danger of prosecution in their country of origin cannot be deported. However, exclusion clause 1F states that if a migrant is suspected of having committed crimes against humanity or human rights, he or she can be denied asylum. This leaves '1F migrants' in the Netherlands with no possibility of acquiring rights, but also no way of returning to their country of origin.

[2] Bernhard et al. 2007; Schueths 2012; Castañeda and Melo 2014; López 2015; Kanstroom and Lykes 2015; Romero 2015.

health, or child care. Hence, although not illegalized themselves, the legal partners, especially those who depend on social benefits to make ends meet, are both directly and indirectly affected by the illegalized status of their partner.

This chapter is structured as follows. We first explore the position of the legal partner in mixed-status families from a theoretical perspective. Building on Bridget Anderson's work on 'failed citizenship', we demonstrate how inclusion and exclusion intersect in mixed-status families, resulting in the exclusion of the 'insider' legal partners from the normative community of value. Furthermore, Saskia Sassen's work on the 'logics of expulsions' directs our focus to the financial consequences of illegalized migrant status and their impact on mixed-status families.[3] Taken together, we provide new insights into the meaning of citizenship, and illustrate how financial instruments linked to migration policies draw borders within families, relegating them to the margins of society.

Following on from this, we sketch the political and legal background of excluding legal partners from social benefits in mixed-status families, as it applied in the period of our fieldwork in 2017 and 2018. We show how their exclusion ensued without any substantial political debate, making mixed-status families and their precarious financial situation effectively invisible. Thereafter, we address the impact of being in a mixed-status family on the partners with legal residence status, based on interviews with members of mixed-status families, lawyers, and NGOs. We demonstrate how the invisibility of mixed-status families in the political debate is exacerbated in the highly specialized field of 'legal aid' in the Netherlands. We argue that the financial consequences not only heavily influence the family resources, but also threaten to divide the family. Couples have to make a choice between staying together and economic survival. Finally, we draw conclusions on how the case of mixed-status families enhances theoretical understandings of citizenship, migration, and the welfare state.

Mixed-Status Families, Deportability, and Exclusion from 'Good' Citizenship

Although 'migrant' and 'citizen' are commonly thought of as separate categories, such categorization does not reflect the lives of many families who are composed of both citizens and illegalized migrants.[4] The

---

[3] Sassen 2014.
[4] López 2015.

increasing but limited amount of literature on these so-called mixed-status families demonstrates the profound ways in which the illegalized migration status of one family member influences the lives of all family members, including those with legal status or citizenship.[5] Hence, migration laws have repercussions at the family level, including financially.

As mentioned earlier, academic literature on mixed-status families is mainly from the United States and largely absent from the European academic context.[6] European scholarship focuses on how illegalized migrants are affected by citizenship boundaries that complicate their everyday lives by producing limited access to proper working conditions, social welfare, and security.[7] However, this literature mainly treats illegalized migrants as isolated individuals, to an extent aligning with a state logic that posits 'citizens' and 'migrants' as binary opposites, in which exclusion of migrants from social welfare serves to protect citizens.[8] This restricted focus on migrants as isolated individuals provides few insights into their embeddedness in society through family links or how relatives are affected by the precarious status of the migrant; family members are mentioned as 'support networks' offering housing at most.[9] Instead, we look specifically at the experiences of these permanent resident or citizen family members. Their mere existence and intimate links with illegalized migrants challenge understandings of restrictive migration and social welfare policies, supposedly 'protecting' the resident citizen population who 'deserve' social benefits by keeping the 'others' out.

Thus, the position of legal partners in mixed-status families is best understood by building on Bridget Anderson's argument that immigration and citizenship are not simply about legal status but fundamentally about status in the sense of worth and honour, i.e. membership of the community of value.[10] While the Foreigner/Non-Citizen can demarcate who belongs to the nation from the outside, the community of value can also be defined from the inside, by the 'Failed Citizen'.[11] Citizens can be excluded from 'good citizenship' as Failed Citizens: they are imagined as incapable of achieving national ideals, or failing to live up to them.[12]

---

[5] Castañeda and Melo 2014; Romero 2015, among others (see above footnote 2).
[6] See, however, Bhabha 2004; Chauvin et al. 2019; Bonjour and de Hart 2020; Griffiths 2019.
[7] Kritzman-Amir and Spijkerboer 2013.
[8] Koning 2020.
[9] Engbersen et al. 2003.
[10] Anderson 2013.
[11] Anderson 2013.
[12] Anderson and Bauder 2014, 4.

Failed Citizens are imagined as the undeserving poor, e.g. in the figure of the 'welfare queens' or 'benefit scoundrels'. Hence, Non- and Failed Citizens are fundamentally normative categories.

While in Anderson's understanding a fuzzy line can still be drawn between Failed Citizens and Non-Citizens, mixed-status families bring together both categories into one family, placing this divide even further into question. Rather than bringing migrants up to the level of the permanent resident or citizen partner, the legal partner is pulled down towards the position of illegalized migrant, both legally and normatively, and is placed outside the community of value, as a 'Failed Citizen'. Therefore, it is useful to see the permanent resident or citizen family members as Failed Citizens, who are no longer considered members of the community of value and no longer deserve protection due to their family ties with illegalized migrants.[13]

Anderson's work fits very well with that of Sassen on the 'logics of expulsions'.[14] Mixed-status families are pushed from the core social and economic orders of the community of value to its margins, where they cease to be of value as workers and consumers. This is the result of the shrinking neoliberal state that leaves regulating social issues to the market, withdrawing support from groups of people who are considered vulnerable and exploitable due to their own misfortune: in this case, being part of a mixed-status family. Their punishment is financial: withdrawal of social benefits and fines for 'fraudulently' making use of such benefits which they were no longer entitled to as Failed Citizens in a family relationship with an illegalized migrant.

Mixed-status families are also dynamic units: they can be made up of any combination of illegalized migrants and (naturalized) citizens. They are subject to change: legal residents may lose their residence permit, citizens may lose their citizenship, and previously 'illegalized' migrants may gain residence or citizenship rights.[15] Thus, partners in mixed-status families find themselves in legally uncertain, liminal categories.[16] This is confirmed by our interviews: in some cases the family relationship started when the migrant partner had a legal status, but was subsequently re-categorized as 'illegal', e.g. due to loss of a job, which implied that social benefits were also retroactively considered incorrectly obtained.

---

[13] López 2015, 94.
[14] Sassen 2014.
[15] Fix and Zimmerman 1999, 397.
[16] Fix and Zimmerman 1999, 397.

A Short Overview of Mixed-Status Families and the Dutch Welfare State

In Esping-Anderson's typology of welfare states based on the relationship between state, family household, and market, the Netherlands has been typified as a pro-family caring state.[17] Such states are typified as viewing care as primarily located in the family, but increasingly provide public resources and support care. Eggebø has pointed out that typologies of welfare states do not take into account immigration policies, the inclusion of which may provide a different picture.[18] Indeed, the Netherlands is one of the more restrictive states in terms of social welfare for migrants.[19] Such welfare policies, intersecting with migration polices (the migration control–social policy nexus), affect mixed-status families in profound ways.[20]

The Dutch erosion of the relatively strong post-war welfare state model started in the 1980s, instigated by the economic crisis. It continued during the 1990s, defended with a normative discourse of individual responsibility to provide for oneself. At the same time, public awareness of fraud in the context of social security law increased and more people were subjected to assessment checks of their personal lives.[21] Also during the 1990s, migration law became increasingly restrictive, as migrants came to be seen as a burden on the welfare state. As a result of these developments, Bonjour and Duyvendak have noted how being Dutch in government policies came to be increasingly defined in middle-class terms, as citizens living up to an ethos of hard work, excluding lower-class Dutch citizens and equating them to migrants.[22]

Against this background, illegalized migrants became an increasingly problematized category, targeted by several means of exclusion. In 1998, the so-called Linkage Act [*Koppelingswet*] excluded illegalized migrants from social benefits, welfare benefits, and healthcare (Article 10, Aliens Act). This Linkage Act aimed to make a direct link between migrants' residence status and their rights to social welfare and benefits provided by the state. Moreover, it became more difficult for illegalized migrants to regularize their residence. The consequence of the Linkage Act was not

---

[17] Esping-Andersen 1990; Daly 2000.
[18] Eggebø 2010.
[19] Koning 2020.
[20] Ataç and Rosenberger 2019.
[21] Walsum 2008, 69, 80.
[22] Bonjour and Duyvendak 2018, 894.

that residence was terminated by actual expulsions but that residence was made more difficult.[23] Policymakers hoped that illegalized migrants would leave the country independently. Following the increasingly strict citizen–migrant dichotomy in this period, policymakers did not take into account that families may consist of (illegalized) migrants as well as permanent residents or citizens. Policymakers conceived of illegalized migrants mainly as single, economically motivated males. Families were merely mentioned as 'offering housing' to illegalized migrants, not as sharing households and family life.[24] In reality, many of them established families and had children with partners who were legal residents or citizens.

Hence, how did the illegalized residence status of one of their members affect mixed-status families? Fix and Zimmerman discern three ways in which migration and citizenship policies impact mixed-status families.[25] First, through *differentiation* between family members, excluding some members from access to public institutions, while including others. Second, *spillover effects* of restrictions targeting illegalized migrants may impact the life of the permanent migrant and citizen family members. Finally, couples may be divided by keeping families physically apart across borders. What these authors did not envision, and what is central in this contribution, is the direct legal exclusion of the permanent resident or citizen partner from social welfare and benefits because of the family relationship with the illegalized partner.

This was exactly what happened in 2005, with the introduction of the AWIR (General Act Income-dependent Benefits). This Act aimed to provide social benefits for low-income families. It excluded the legal partner of an illegalized migrant from social benefits paid by the tax services for rent, healthcare, and child care.[26] Additionally, the partner in the Netherlands has no right to benefits granted for child daycare if the other partner resides outside the EU, or is illegalized.[27] In 2015, the Participation Act maintained the exclusion of the illegalized partner from social welfare, but still included this partner in determining the

---

[23] Van Eijl 2012, 185.
[24] Second Chamber 2003–2004, 29 537, nr. 2, p. 11 and 13. In the Memorandum of Clarification families were mentioned several times, mainly as a hindrance to expelling irregular migrants. Second Chamber 1994–1995, 24 233, nr. 3, p. 10.
[25] Fix and Zimmerman 1999, 401.
[26] Highest Administrative Court Council of State. 22 October 2014, ECLI NLRVS2014:3788. *Jurisprudentie Vreemdelingenrecht*, 2014/393, annotation Paul Minderhoud.
[27] Art. 1.6 Child Daycare Act.

level of welfare allocated to the permanent resident or citizen partner, resulting in substantial financial reductions. The effects of these exclusions from social benefits are exacerbated by the fact that in Dutch migration law, residence permits are withdrawn with retroactive effect to the moment when the right of residence was lost.[28] In such cases of retroactive withdrawal, not only the right to benefits may be lost, but the family may also have to pay back the benefits that were received during this period. Additionally, they may be fined for not informing the immigration or other authorities properly and on time, e.g. about the break-up of a family relationship or loss of employment.[29]

As Sassen argues, the expelled become invisible by being pushed to the margins and this certainly counts for mixed-status families.[30] Political debates on illegalized migrants failed to even acknowledge their existence. Consequently, the exclusion of the legal partner in the 2005 AWIR took place without any political or public debate. The political debates on the Linkage Act were already predominantly technical in nature, rendering invisible the underlying moral and normative implications.[31] The Memorandum of Clarification to the 2005 AWIR merely stated:

> Without such a stipulation, an alien without legal residence could profit indirectly from benefits that are granted to the interested party [the legal partner, authors]. This would be contrary to what was aimed at by the Linkage Act.[32]

This justification of exclusion of the legal partner was not further explained, or questioned in parliament. However, the consequences of this provision have become increasingly apparent, although most attention has been directed at the position of children and children's rights.[33] Part of the invisibility of mixed-status families resulting from these

---

[28] Boeles 2019.
[29] Only if the family is in a legal procedure against the withdrawal of a residence permit, some of the financial benefits may stay in place if this procedure is started immediately after the decision to withdraw (73 lid 1 Aliens Act).
[30] Sassen 2014.
[31] Pluymen 2008.
[32] Second Chamber, 2004-2005, 29764, nr. 3, p. 44. Only on one occasion did the Labour Party enquire about the exclusion of citizen children with an illegalized parent from funding for school books. Proceedings 20 January 2005, p. 46–2952. The amendment put forward by the Labour Party did not obtain the required majority. Second Chamber Proceedings 3 February 2005, p. 49–3183.
[33] E.g. Children's Ombudsman, *Nederlandse kinderen ontkoppeld. Als de verblijfsstatus van je ouders je levensstandaard bepaalt* 2017. www.ombudsmanrotterdam.nl/web/uploads/2017/12/2017.KOM014-Nederlandse-kinderen-ontkoppeld.pdf. Last visited 10 February 2019.

policies is that their numbers are unknown, and that they cannot be found in statistics. Estimates made by the Children's Ombudsman in 2017, on the number of mixed-status families with children excluded from social benefits, indicate it may involve around 4,000 families with children in 2015.[34]

Both national and international courts have accepted the justification of the exclusion of the legal partner as being in line with Article 8 (right to family life) and 14 ECHR (non-discrimination) and necessary for effective migration control. Exceptions were thought necessary only in exceptional circumstances, such as in case of a chronically ill partner and young baby.[35] Nevertheless, the Dutch Highest Administrative Court acknowledged that, although not the aim, the effect of the Act may be dividing families.[36]

Methodology

In order to explore how the above legal framework affects mixed-status families' everyday lives, we conducted seventeen semi-structured interviews between May 2017 and March 2018: nine with experts in the field, lawyers and NGOs, and two with state agencies: one interview with the social benefit taxation authorities and one with the office 'Title and Identity' of the Immigration and Naturalisation Service (IND).[37] We subsequently conducted six interviews with couples in a mixed-status relationship.[38] The limited number of interviews with families is not only due to the explorative nature of our research, but also due to the vulnerability of mixed-status families; they sometimes declined participation, or we decided to not pursue the interview ourselves because of ethical

---

[34] Children's Ombudsman, 2017.
[35] ABRvS 22 October 2014, ECLI NLRVS2014:3788, *JV* 2014/393 annotation Minderhoud.
[36] ECtHR, *Yeshtla v. the Netherlands*, 7 February 2019. (Appl.No. 37115/11); ECtHR *Aghmadi en Jaghubi – Nederland*, 4 April 2019, (Appl. Nos. 70475/14, 70530/14), ECLI: CE:ECHR:2019:0312DEC007047514, EHRM, Dorani en Khawati – Nederland, 4 April 2019, (Appl. Nos. 71815/14, 71827/14) ECLI:CE:ECHR:2019; *Bah v. United Kingdom*, ECtHR 27 September 2011, 56328/07 (Bah), *JV* 2012/33, annotation Slingenberg.
[37] This department was established following the Linkage Act. It registers or changes codes referring to different residence statuses, which then become visible for municipalities and taxation authorities.
[38] We would like to thank all our interviewees, especially the families, for sharing their stories with us.

considerations. Still, taken together, the seventeen interviews provided important insights into the lives of mixed-status families.

We recruited respondents through lawyers and NGOs that offered support to illegalized migrants. In the family interviews, we spoke to partners together. Although this may have influenced what they shared with us, we made this decision because of the precariousness of their situation. Partners often provided mutual support during the conversation. We asked them about their relationship; the legal process; the implications for marriage and legal establishment of paternity of children; the impact on their family life; the financial, psychological, and emotional consequences; their support system; and their perspectives for the future. To guarantee anonymity of respondents, pseudonyms were used and retraceable personal characteristics were removed. Each interview was transcribed and analysed in Atlas.Ti. We used a directed content analysis, in which we coded and grouped the different consequences for mixed-status families. We paid close attention to how other variables, such as income, disabilities, or illness, affected the identified effects.

(In)visibility of Mixed-Status Families

The invisibility of mixed-status families in the political debates discussed above can also be found in the social field of legal aid and NGOs supporting illegalized migrants. This is the result of strong specialization of this field in the Netherlands, meaning that most lawyers are experts either in migration law or in social security law, but not both. Migration lawyers are mostly in contact with the illegalized migrant, while lawyers specialized in social security support the legal partner. Couples are often engaged in multiple legal procedures, sometimes with different lawyers and relevant NGOs, looking at various aspects of their family situation. Consequently, the 'mixed-status family' is rarely seen as a whole. The legal partners frequently act as 'gatekeepers', as their knowledge of the Dutch system and language make them the main actor in dealing with state institutions.[39] However, they are not always on the radar of the authorities, lawyers, or NGOs who deal with the illegalized partner.

This invisibility results in a lack of awareness of the impact of decisions made in the field of migration law for social security rights and vice versa. A lawyer specialized in social security law mentioned an example:

---

[39] De Hart 2003.

> The [illegalized] father [...] wanted to live with his family, but if the municipality finds out they will get into trouble with social welfare. So, we tell them: you really shouldn't live with them, and now he wanders around, so that at least the woman is not cut back on benefits. But that is difficult.

The husband being homeless not only affected the family situation, but also seriously imperilled his chances of regularizing his legal status, which requires sharing a household.

Hence, the specialization of legal aid can result in an orientation towards the interests of one of the partners and not the family as a whole. Even in their access to aid, mixed-status families can become invisible and divided.

Making Ends Meet: Economic Precariousness

The following is an explanation how the legal partner's exclusion from social benefits in a mixed-status family has severe financial consequences for the family as a whole: making it difficult for them to make ends meet, often over a longer period of time and without much prospect of solving the financial problems. In many cases, the economic situation of the legal partner was already precarious before the relationship with the illegalized partner. This was largely due to an inability to work caused by medical or psychological problems; or a disadvantaged position in the labour market.

Frequently, these financial consequences are unexpected: on occasion significant benefit cuts were imposed by surprise even after following advice from authorities or the legal professionals to solve a particular legal issue. For some couples this resulted in a sense of loss of rights, making them take on their 'un-deservingness', by not claiming financial rights to which they were legally entitled. Exclusion from social benefits constituted a major problem in their lives. This included mixed-status couple Nicole and Robert. Robert was a Dutch citizen and had worked all his life until he became chronically ill. As he was no longer able to work, he received social benefits. After the birth of their children, Robert and Nicole decided to start a procedure to regularize Nicole's residence, during which they continued to receive benefits. Nicole narrates what happened after her request for residence was rejected:

> Our lawyer said: don't give up, we persevere, we can appeal on the basis of your chronic disease and minor children. So we started. But I had to register [at Robert's address] and then the misery really started. Because I registered, not knowing that my partner's income would be stopped, no

more benefits. We only received €666 in benefits, and our rent is €619. So we didn't have anything to live on.

The Linkage Act's official aim of preventing the illegalized partner from 'profiting' from social welfare had the opposite effect of depriving the legal partner and children of any liveable income. Mixed-status couples come to rely on churches, food banks, municipalities, and loans from family and friends. Furthermore, the continuing stress, health, and psychological problems severely affected Robert and Nicole's family. Although they describe these years as a hell, they continued to make the most of their situation, supporting each other and focusing on making ends meet to keep their home and have food on the table:

> Nicole: We didn't have any money, we had to borrow money to survive or to do some groceries. He [Robert] always said: even if we only receive 600 euros, I have to pay my rent, because if we don't, where can we stay? So, he always said: even if we have to sit in the dark, we will light candles but we have to pay rent. And so we did.

After years of living in poverty, Robert and Nicole's lawyer was able to arrange for some extra benefits from the municipality, until Nicole finally received her residence permit. For Nicole and Robert, the financial trouble came as a surprise: they did not know in advance that registering Nicole would result in social benefit cuts. For another mixed-status couple, Fatana and Ahmed, the social benefit reduction was the unexpected consequence of following the municipality's advice to register Ahmed at Fatana's address, to make it easier to arrange for a Dutch passport for their son without Ahmed having the required identity papers.

> Fatana: The civil register said, why isn't [your husband] registered at your address? I said, yes it was never possible because he couldn't identify himself. Then this civil servant said: well, since I have just ascertained his identity, I could register him if you would like that. [...] Then they registered him and I had something in the back of my mind like, I hope I won't get into trouble. So then they stopped everything [social benefits] upward from the date that he was registered with me. Meanwhile, with a lot of effort, I managed to unsubscribe him again. [...] Now we are still left without these social benefits, because they say, he is your allowance partner. I say: yes, he has been that for fifteen years. But, apparently, I stirred up the hornet's nest.

As already mentioned, not all families started out as mixed-status families, but became so *retroactively*, after a residence permit was withdrawn.

A NGO worker recalls how a husband became illegalized after losing his residence permit as a labour migrant because his employer went bankrupt, retroactively invalidating his contract. The family had to pay back the healthcare and rent benefits they had received during his employment period, starting at the moment he lost his residence permit. In some cases, authorities recover months or even years of paid benefits, causing families to end up with debts which they cannot possibly pay off. It is especially this retroactive recovery of benefits that may make families lose any sense of legal certainty, as a social security lawyer explains:

> With people who have a changing residence status, you can see that constantly new decisions are made and amounts recovered. With one of these families, there was a big recovery of money and she [the citizen partner] paid this. But then later I said: you are now entitled to benefits, because at that moment the [illegalized] partner had submitted a request for residence and, thus, they were entitled for a while. But they did not dare to request it because they were afraid of recoveries. And I said: no, that is impossible, because you are entitled at least for these months, but they didn't dare risk it.

Thus, the financial consequences of the illegalized status of the migrant partner for the legal partner pushes mixed-status families to the margins of society, to the extent that they are silenced, made invisible, and do not claim the rights to which they are entitled. It does not make the illegalized partner leave, but families are divided all the same, as we demonstrate in the next section.

Dividing Families

As explained above, the Linkage Act and subsequent Acts are measures of deterrence and discipline: they do not effectuate the direct expulsion of illegalized migrants, but make their life in the Netherlands difficult, so that they decide to leave on their own account. In none of our cases was actual deportation at stake, but families were in danger of being divided in other ways. The financial consequences may be such that the illegalized partner is pushed out of the family home as a form of self-surveillance, a forced living apart together, to safeguard at least some income to the legal partner. A lawyer commented on the consequence of dividing families:

> I find it an unlawful stretch of the Linkage Act. Equally from a legal perspective. What happens is that someone who has a residence permit

> is equated with someone who doesn't have a residence permit. Nobody can explain this. Certainly with the effects it has, it's just perverse. [...] The government says: that's your own choice, your own problem that you can solve by applying for divorce or a legal separation. [...] My objection as a lawyer is that it's a violation of art 8 [the right to family life of the ECHR]. To provide in your minimal livelihood you just have to divorce your husband.

However, contrary to this lawyer's statement, as explained in par. 3, national and international courts have ruled that Art. 8 ECHR is not violated, as states have the authority to regulate migration and may use exclusion from social welfare and benefits to do so, even if it excludes the legal partner. Consequently, an intimate relationship with an illegalized family member is constructed as a *choice,* the 'wrong' choice for which legal partners, as Failed Citizens, are held responsible and become punishable. Their self-surveillance, staying together or not, means that they may even hold themselves responsible.[40]

In the interviews, we learned of one case in which what started out as a 'paper' separation to maintain benefits ended up in an actual breakup of the family relationship. However, in the family interviews, partners persisted in keeping the family together against such severe pressures (which is obviously also due to our selection of interlocutors). Staying together thus may be seen as a form of resistance, a 'weapon of the weak'[41], against policies that are meant to keep them apart. Legal partner Aisha says:

> Yes, if he [her husband Farid] is deregistered, we do receive [benefits], but I don't want to deregister him, he belongs with us. Our financial problems do not play a major role in the relationship itself. We sleep badly and worry a lot, that he doesn't have a job or this or that. But it's not like I expect him to leave.

Aisha strongly dismisses the scenario that Farid leaves the household. However, her statement also reflects that staying together is no longer self-evident and requires an explanation; this further demonstrates the precariousness of family life of mixed-status families. In response, couples emphasize their perseverance in overcoming their problems together as a family:

---

[40] Van Houdt, Suvarierol, and Schinkel 2011, 411.
[41] Scott 1985.

> Robert: She is always there for me. When I see her and if she sees me and the children, that is mental support, we didn't give up. So, the support is... just when you see each other and listen and talk to one another.
>
> Nicole: If he wasn't at home, I always wandered around on the street, I didn't have anything else to do but walking on the street. But if he got home he called me: where are you? [...] But if he wasn't at home, I didn't feel comfortable, I never wanted to stay at home alone until now.

Other respondents reported taking in and caring for the illegalized partner as a 'civic duty', as a matter of good citizenship, which directly runs counter to the exclusionary definition of 'good citizenship' as implied in the Linkage Act. This indicates that the financial precarity affects families differently: while some families no longer perceive living together as a given, others instead become closer as they feel the need to support one another and step in where the state has taken a step back.

Deportability and Anxiety in Everyday Life

Obviously, financial precariousness and the pressure of dividing families impact the psychological and physical well-being of mixed-status family members. As De Genova[42] posits, migrant 'illegality' is experienced as a palpable sense of *deportability*. Even if risks of deportation are low, as is the case in the Netherlands, the fear of deportation is always lingering in the background and prevents families from making long-term plans. This 'revocability of the promise of the future' hinders partners in building a durable life.[43] Consequently, stress, anxiety, and insecurity are an intrinsic part of daily life. Mariam, a Dutch citizen who fled Afghanistan twenty years ago, tells us:

> I came to the Netherlands and I thought that everything would get better. [...] but instead of my life improving, it is getting worse. When I was in Afghanistan, the situation was almost the same. Then, I was worrying about the future, and I do so now. There, I thought that I wasn't going to get any food. I also do here too, and if I can't pay my bills, I will have to live on the street. While, when you leave your country, to better countries – you expect that you will have a good life or a good future, but where is that future?

Mariam's partner has been illegalized for nine years. The authorities were alerted to their situation when they moved to another home, and withdrew her benefits in response. Shortly after that, she also lost her job as

---
[42] De Genova 2002, 439.
[43] De Genova 2002, 427.

a financial administrator. The stress kept her awake at night; she was unable to make long-term plans, postponing even seemingly simple ones such as buying a cupboard.

> When we moved here, I wanted to buy a cupboard, but I didn't do it. I didn't know whether he [her illegalized husband] would stay here or not. [...] Until now I haven't bought the cupboard. This was the effect of [not having] his residence permit. All these things that happen in our life, they do have effect. What will happen tomorrow?

In mixed-status families, deportability is extended to the legal or citizen partner. As gatekeepers, legal partners are caught up in a dual responsibility: one towards the state to keep the migrant out and one towards the family, to maintain their unity and keep the illegalized partner in. NGO workers asserted that legal partners experience the anxiety of deportation even more, as they fear whether they will see their partner at the end of the day and may have to raise their family alone. Mariam notes how this responsibility includes curtailing her emotions:

> I have to arrange everything. I always have to go to the authorities. I can't discuss everything. [...] I don't say that I slept badly, or that I didn't sleep all night. Such a thing I won't tell my children or husband, because it is something for myself. [...] I am already broken; I don't want to break someone else. What if the entire family breaks, what would that accomplish? And if I would say something, they wouldn't be able to help. If I would tell him, I can't pay the rent, he can't help me, right? Besides, he probably has a lot of problems himself.

This gatekeeping extended to the interview situation, during which Mariam was talking about her responsibility for managing the household, with her husband sitting next to her. He did not understand Dutch and Mariam did not involve him in the conversation. It exemplifies how even *within* families partners can become divided, in not always sharing their experiences and protecting each other from their fear and emotions.

Mixed-status families' abilities to handle the economic, social, and emotional impacts can depend on their social network. A lawyer explained how he catered to one specific nationality client group, who work illegally within a closed, tight-knit community, in which they offer each other support, thus reducing some of the direct financial effects of the Linkage Act. Robert and Nicole were able to maintain a living because they borrowed from family and friends. Such social networks may mitigate the consequences of the Linkage Act for one family, but it also shifts the burden of providing for families' welfare to entire communities.

Conclusions

Migration control is deemed necessary to protect citizens' access to the welfare state. The welfare state is seen as a system that organizes citizens and Non-Citizens into multilayered hierarchies in which immigration status and non-status open or close doors to access welfare benefits.[44] In such discourses, 'citizens' or permanent residents, on the one hand, and illegalized migrants, on the other hand, are constructed as separate categories, making families that include both categories invisible, escaping political, public, and academic attention.

Laws that function as a form of post-entry migration control by blocking access to social benefits have, unsurprisingly, largely *failed* to make the illegalized migrant leave.[45] Instead, legal partners in mixed-status families are pushed into poverty, putting them in a tight spot with at least a dual role as (failed) gatekeeper for the state, while also struggling to keep the family together. Our findings contribute to understandings of citizenship as well as the welfare state. As to citizenship, Anderson already notes that distinctions between Failed Citizens and Non-Citizens are blurred.[46] Mixed-status families complicate this picture further by uniting Failed Citizens and Non-Citizens in one family. Legal partners turn into Failed Citizens, not only because they depend on social benefits to have a liveable family income and are seen as not living up to the neoliberal workers ethos, but also because of their choice for a migrant partner. Civic membership as automatically acquired through residence is transformed into a process in which the citizen has to prove to be a worthy bearer of rights by fulfilling economic and cultural requirements.[47] As restrictive migration policies result in 'status mobility'[48] the consequences of being a mixed-status family are *not* the result of permanent resident or citizens starting a relationship with an illegalized partner, as in many cases the migrant partner started as a legal migrant. This 'backdoor' of restrictive migration policies deserves more academic attention.

Mixed-status families raise pressing questions about the increasingly blurred moral judgements associated with both poverty and illegality as axis of Othering. Under a neoliberal 'workfarist' regime, employment

---

[44] Sabates-Wheeler and Feldman 2011, xii.
[45] Ataç and Rosenberger 2019.
[46] Anderson 2015, 73.
[47] van Houdt, Suvarierol, and Schinkel 2011, 419.
[48] Schuster 2005.

becomes a civic obligation.[49] Moreover, their case points to the state as central to setting normative standards about what an 'appropriate' family relationship looks like.

The available European research on social rights of migrants starts from the migrant–citizen binary and consequently does not pay any attention to mixed-status families. Hence, we do not know whether the Dutch case is unique, or exemplary of what happens in other European states. European case law gives some indication that exclusion of family members in mixed-status families from social rights also occurs in other European states.[50] Despite the fact that European Court of Justice judgements in *Ruiz Zambrano* and *Chávez-Vílchez* have increased opportunities for illegalized migrants to regularize their residence, at least if the family includes an EU citizen child (art. 20 Treaty of the Functioning of the European Union), the situation of legal uncertainty continues because of restrictive enforcement practices and the lack of a clear legal framework.[51] The legal and normative justification of the exclusion of permanent residents and citizens in mixed-status families remains a pressing issue.

References

Anderson, Bridget. 2015. *Migration, Precarity, and Global Governance. Challenges and Opportunities for Labour*. Oxford: Oxford University Press: 68–82.

Anderson, Bridget. 2014. 'Exclusion, Failure, and the Politics of Citizenship'. RCIS Working Paper 2014/1.

Anderson, Bridget. 2013. *Us and Them? The Dangerous Politics of Immigration Control*. Oxford: Oxford University Press.

Anderson, Bridget. 2011. 'Citizenship, Deportation and the Boundaries of Belonging'. *Citizenship Studies* 15, no. 5: 547–563. At https://doi.org/10.1080/13621025.2011.583787.

Ataç, Ilker and Sieglinde Rosenberger. 2019. 'Social Policies as a Tool of Migration Control'. *Journal of Immigrant and Refugee Studies* 17, no. 1 Routledge: 1–10. At https://doi.org/10.1080/15562948.2018.1539802.

Berneri, Chiara. 2018. 'Family Reunification between Static EU Citizens and Third Country Nationals: A Practical Way to Help Families Caught in the Current

---

[49] Chauvin, Garcés-Mascareñas, and Kraler 2013, 81.
[50] See the *Bah* case mentioned in note 35, in which a permanent resident mother in the United Kingdom was excluded from public housing because her illegalized son lived with her.
[51] CJEU Case C-34/09, *Gerardo Ruiz Zambrano v. Office national de l'emploi (ONEm)*, 8 March 2011; CJEU Case 133/15, H.C. *Chavez-Vilchez and Others v. Raad van Bestuur van de Sociale verzekeringsbank and Others*, 10 May 2017. Berneri 2018, Maas 2008.

Immigration Crisis'. *European Journal of Migration and Law* 20, no. 3: 289–313. At https://doi.org/10.1163/15718166-12340028.

Bernhard, K. Judith, Luin Goldring, Julie Young, Carolina Berinstein, and Beth Wilson. 2007. 'Living with Precarious Legal Status in Canada: Implications for the Well-Being of Children and Families'. *Refuge: Canada's Journal on Refugees* 24, no 2: 101–115. At https://doi.org/10.25071/1920-7336.21388.

Bhabha, Jacqueline. 2004. 'The "Mere Fortuity" of Birth? Are Children Citizens?' *Differences: A Journal of Feminist Cultural Studies* 15, no 2: 91–117. At www.muse.jhu.edu/article/170544.

Boeles, Pieter. 2019. 'Wat Is de Ruimte Voor Intrekking van Verblijfsvergunningen Met Terugwerkende Kracht?' [What is the Room for Withdrawing a Residence Permit with Retroact?] *Asiel & Migrantenrecht* 3: 95–109. At https://research.vu.nl/en/publications/what-is-the-room-for-withdrawing-a-residence-permit-with-retroact, accessed 27 November 2020.

Bonjour, Saskia and Betty de Hart. 2020. 'Intimate Citizenship: Introduction to the Special Issue on Citizenship, Membership and Belonging in Mixed-Status Families'. *Identities* 1–17. At https://doi.org/10.1080/1070289X.2020.1737404.

Bonjour, Saskia and Jan Willem Duyvendak. 2018. 'The "Migrant with Poor Prospects": Racialized Intersections of Class and Culture in Dutch Civic Integration Debates'. *Ethnic and Racial Studies* 41, no. 5: 882–900. https://doi.org/10.1080/01419870.2017.1339897.

Bosniak, Linda. 2006. *The Citizen and the Alien. Dilemmas of Contemporary Membership*. Princeton and Oxford: Princeton University Press.

Castañeda, Heide and Milena Andrea Melo. 2014. 'Health Care Access for Latino Mixed-Status Families: Barriers, Strategies, and Implications for Reform'. *American Behavioral Scientist* 58, no. 14: 1891–1909. At https://doi.org/10.1177/0002764214550290.

Chauvin, Sébastien, Blanca Garcés-Mascareñas, and Albert Kraler. 2013. 'Employment and Migrant Deservingness'. *International Migration* 51, no. 6: 80–85. At https://doi:10.1111/imig.12123.

Chauvin, Sébastien, Manuela Salcedo Robledo, Timo Koren, and Joël Illidge. 2019. 'Class, Mobility and Inequality in the Lives of Same-Sex Couples with Mixed Legal Statuses'. *Journal of Ethnic and Migration Studies* 1–17. At https://doi.org/10.1080/1369183X.2019.1625137.

Daly, Mary. 2000. *The Gender Division of Welfare*. Cambridge: Cambridge University Press.

De Genova, Nicholas P. 2002. 'Migrant "Illegality" and Deportability in Everyday Life'. *Annual Review of Anthropology* 31: 419–447. https://doi.org/10.1146/annurev.anthro.31.040402.085432.

De Hart, Betty. 2003. *Onbezonnen Vrouwen. Gemengde Relaties in het Nationaliteitsrecht en het Vreemdelingenrecht.* Amsterdam: Aksant.
Eggebø, Helga. 2010. 'The Problem of Dependency: Immigration, Gender, and the Welfare State'. *Social Politics* 17, no. 3: 295–322. https://doi.org/10.1093/sp/jxq013.
Engbersen, Godfried, Joanne van der Leun, Richard Staring, and Jude Kehla. 2003. *De Ongekende Stad 2: Inbedding En Uitsluiting van Illegale Vreemdelingen.* Amsterdam: Boom.
Esping-Andersen, Gosta. 1990. *The Three Worlds of Welfare Capitalism.* Cambridge: Polity Press and Princeton, NJ: Princeton University Press.
Fix, E. Michael and Wendy Zimmerman. 1999. 'All Under One Roof: Mixed-Status Families in an Era of Reform'. *International Migration Review* 35, no. 2: 397–419. At https://doi.org/10.1111/j.1747-7379.2001.tb00023.x.
Griffiths, Melanie. 2019. '"My Passport is Just My Way Out of Here." Mixed-Immigration Status Families, Immigration Enforcement and the Citizenship Implications'. *Identities*, 1–19.
Kalir, Barak and Lieke Wissink. 2016. 'The Deportation Continuum: Convergences Between State Agents and NGO Workers in the Dutch Deportation Field'. *Citizenship Studies* 20, no. 1: 34–49. At https://doi.org/10.1080/13621025.2015.1107025.
Kanstroom, Daniel and M. Brinton Lykes, eds. 2015. *The New Deportations Delirium: Interdisciplinary Responses.* New York: New York University Press.
Koning, Edward A. 2020. 'Accommodation and New Hurdles: The Increasing Importance of Politics for Immigrants' Access to Social Programmes in Western Democracies'. *Social Policy and Administration*, https://browzine.com/libraries/320/journals/9184/articles-in-press?showArticleInContext=doi%3A10.1111%2Fspol.12661
Kritzman-Amir, Tally and Thomas Spijkerboer. 2013. 'On the Morality and Legality of Borders: Border Politics and Asylum Seekers'. *Harvard Human Rights Journal* 26, no. 24: 0–39.
López, Jane Lilly. 2015. '"Impossible Families": Mixed-Citizenship Status Couples and the Law'. *Law and Policy* 37, no. 1–2: 93–118. At https://doi.org/10.1111/lapo.12032.
Maas, Willem. 2008. 'Migrants, States, and EU Citizenship's Unfulfilled Promise'. *Citizenship Studies* 12, no. 6: 583–596.
Nicholls, J. Walter. 2016. 'Producing-Resisting National Borders in the United States, France and The Netherlands'. *Political Geography* 51: 43–52. At https://doi.org/10.1016/j.polgeo.2015.12.001.
Pluymen, Manon. 2008. *Niet Toelaten Betekent Uitsluiten: Een Rechtssociologisch Onderzoek naar de Rechtvaardiging en Praktijk van Uitsluiting van Vreemdelingen van Voorzieningen.* Den Haag: Boom Juridische Uitgeverij.

Romero, Mary. 2015. 'Foreword'. In April Schueths and Jodie Lawston, eds., *Living Together, Living Apart: Mixed Status Families and US Immigration Policy*. Seattle: University of Washington Press.

Sabates-Wheeler, Rachel and Rayah Feldman. 2011. 'Introduction: Mapping Migrant Welfare onto Social Provisioning'. In Rachel Sabates-Wheeler and Rayah Feldman, eds., *Migration and Social Protection: Claiming Social Rights Beyond Borders*. Basingstoke: Palgrave Macmillan.

Sassen, Saskia. 2014. *Expulsions: Brutality and Complexity in the Global Economy*. Harvard University Press.

Schueths, M. April. 2012. '"Where Are My Rights?" Compromised Citizenship in Mixed-Status Marriage: A Research Note'. *Journal of Sociology and Social Welfare* 39, no. 4: 97–109.

Schuster, Liza. 2005. 'The Continuing Mobility of Migrants in Italy: Shifting between Places and Statuses'. *Journal of Ethnic and Migration Studies* 31, no. 4: 757–774. At https://doi.org/10.1080/13691830500109993.

Scott C. James. 1985. *Weapons of the Weak: Everyday Forms of Peasant Resistance*. New Haven: Yale University.

Van Eijl, Corrie. 2012. *Tussenland: Illegaal in Nederland, 1945-2000*. Hilversum: Verloren.

Van Houdt, Friso, Semin Suvarierol, and Willem Schinkel. 2011. 'Neoliberal Communitarian Citizenship: Current Trends towards "Earned Citizenship" in the United Kingdom, France and the Netherlands'. *International Sociology* 26, no. 3: 408–432. At https://doi.org/10.1177/0268580910393041.

Van Walsum, Sarah. 2008. *The Family and the Nation: Dutch Family Migration Policies in the Context of Changing Family Norms*. Cambridge: Cambridge Scholars Publishing.

18

Money in Internal Migration: Financial Resources and Unequal Citizenship

WILLEM MAAS

Oh, if you ain't got the do re mi, folks, you ain't got the do re mi
Why, you better go back to beautiful Texas, Oklahoma, Kansas, Georgia, Tennessee
California is a garden of Eden, a paradise to live in or see
But believe it or not, you won't find it so hot
If you ain't got the do re mi

– Woody Guthrie, chorus of "Do Re Mi" from *Dust Bowl Ballads*[1]

At the height of the Dust Bowl that precipitated the largest ever internal migration in the United States, Los Angeles Police Department chief James Edgar Davis organized a "bum blockade" in 1936 by sending 136 officers to all major entry points on California's borders with Arizona, Nevada, and Oregon, with orders to turn back migrants who had "no visible means of support."[2] Described in John Steinbeck's celebrated novel *The Grapes of Wrath*, the migrants, mostly American citizens from Oklahoma, Texas, Missouri, New Mexico, and Arkansas, were labeled with the derogatory term "Okies" and blamed for an economy already devastated by the Great Depression. Political candidates accused them of shiftlessness, lack of ambition, school overcrowding, and stealing jobs from Californians, and supporters of the blockade included *The Los Angeles Times*, the city's Chamber of Commerce, sheriff, prosecutor's

---

[1] "Dough" is slang for money. Verse 1 of the song ends with "the police at the port of entry say / 'You're number fourteen thousand for today'," and after the chorus, verse 2 starts with "You want to buy you a home or a farm, that can't deal nobody harm / Or take your vacation by the mountains or sea / Don't swap your old cow for a car, you better stay right where you are" – alluding to the economic uncertainty of internal migration, the high number of internal migrants, and the police officers patrolling the California state border to turn back internal migrants who were poor. Thanks to Sara Saidi for research assistance and Tesseltje de Lange and Annette Schrauwen for suggestions.

[2] Maas 2013a; Rasmussen 2003. Parts of this chapter build on a piece which appeared in a forum about urban citizenship: Maas 2020a. The word "bum" connotes a lazy or homeless person; the "bum blockade" took place in February 1936.

office, some judges and public officials, railroads, the county Department of Charities, and hard-pressed state relief agencies.[3] Responding to criticism that the blockade was an outrage, *The Times* editorialized "Let's Have More Outrages" and praised it as a way to keep out "imported criminals ... radicals and troublemakers," while others lauded the police for "providing much-needed protection against such swarms of two-legged locusts," meaning unemployed fellow Americans from states affected by the drought.[4]

Californians feared not only economic competition but also illness from their immigrating fellow citizens, and disease-fearing Californians burned to the ground one riverbank shantytown, home to some 1,500 Dust Bowl migrants.[5] The blockade ended after two months, prompted by the negative publicity caused by the police refusing entry to a celebrity Hollywood director whose hobby was mining in Arizona and who had tried to return home wearing his dirty work clothes. The director sued Davis and the LAPD for not letting him back into California, quickly dropped the suit when the police threatened him and his family, but too late to turn public opinion.[6] The end of the blockade seemed to safeguard freedom of movement across state borders, but in 1939 the district attorneys of several counties most affected by Dust Bowl migrants began using California's 1933 Indigent Act to reduce migration into California by poor people. The Indigent Act outlawed bringing indigent persons into the state, and the district attorneys indicted, tried, and convicted more than two dozen people who helped their poor American relatives move into California. But the American Civil Liberties Union challenged the prosecutions and pushed the issue all the way to the US Supreme Court, which ruled in 1941 (in the case *Edwards v California*) that states had no right to restrict interstate migration by poor people or any other Americans.[7] Despite that ruling, prioritizing local citizenship over national citizenship continues, not only in the United States but also in other societies.

---

[3] Rasmussen 2003.
[4] Conner 2016; Maas 2020b; Rasmussen 2003.
[5] Kiger 2019.
[6] Davis had sent his right-hand man, LAPD Lieutenant Earle Kynette (later sent to prison for planting a bomb to discourage an investigation into a different matter), to forcibly persuade director John Langan to drop the suit, who quickly complied, but it had already generated too much negative publicity. Rasmussen 2003.
[7] Weiser 2020.

As shown below with illustrations not only from the United States, but also from China, India, Canada, Europe, and beyond, money plays a part in all kinds of migration, both as facilitator and as barrier. This is true not only of international migration, the movement of people across international borders, but also of the movement of people within a political system, known as internal migration. Although the vast bulk of academic attention focuses on international migration, internal migration is a much more prevalent form of the movement of people; even counting only movements between a country's largest administrative units, there are over three times more internal migrants than international migrants worldwide.[8] Yet as the Dust Bowl migrations demonstrate, the movement of citizens across internal boundaries is not always free; central governments must strive to guarantee the rights of internal migrants.[9] As the other chapters in this book make clear for international migrants, rich or otherwise desirable migrants are generally valued, while poor or undesirable migrants are generally feared or shunned. More often than not, money makes the difference between being wanted or unwanted – and this holds true even when the prospective migrants are internal migrants with shared rights and citizenship. Housing restrictions, efforts to attract well-off residents, and limits on mobility for those needing public assistance are only some ways in which money acts as barrier or incentive to internal migration. These various roles of money in internal

---

[8] Most current is the UNDP's "conservative" estimate that in 2009 there were some 740 million people who had moved between the largest administrative units in their country (states in the United States or India, provinces in Canada or China, etc.) compared with about 210 million people who had moved internationally (International Organization for Migration 2019, 19; Skeldon 2018, 1); by 2019 the number of international migrants had increased to 272 million, there were 41.3 million people displaced internally due to conflict and violence (with Syria 6.1 million, Colombia 5.8 million, and the Democratic Republic of Congo 3.1 million accounting for the largest numbers), with no updated estimate of the total number of internal migrants. In counting internal migrants, the territorial unit matters significantly: the smaller the unit, the greater the number of "migrants": as Skeldon notes, in India in 2001 some 42.2 million people were classified as having moved across a state boundary; but 76.8 million people had moved from one district to another within their state, and some 181.8 million people had changed residence within their district. To take a US example, someone moving from Manhattan across the river to New Jersey might be classified as an internal migrant (moving states from New York to New Jersey) while someone moving from Manhattan to Buffalo NY (600 kilometers away but still within New York State) might not – unless the chosen unit is the city, in which case the number of internal migrants becomes much larger.
[9] Bruzelius and Seeleib-Kaiser 2020; Maas 2008; Maas 2009; Maas 2013a; Maas 2017; Maas 2020c.

migration demonstrate the ways in which financial disparities and conditions exist in tension with ideas of equal citizenship.

Socioeconomic Status and the Limits of Equal Citizenship

Socioeconomic status is a key marker of disparity in societies, and contemporary societies place a high premium on people who are healthy, highly educated, and able to navigate the demands of a capitalist economy, with its values of competitiveness, merit, and individual achievement – values that are in tension with ideas of democracy and equal citizenship.[10] Of course the idea of democratic equality is a relatively recent invention, in historical terms.[11] Until the middle of the twentieth century, for example, Americans "were defined by law and custom as local citizens, and local laws determined whether they could receive benefits or even move from one place to the next"; by the 1970s, however, public opinion and policies had converged on the view that the "federal government bore some responsibility for migrants and that migrants, as national citizens, were entitled to the same rights and privileges as long-time residents. The contemporary welfare state and conception of national citizenship emerged out of these debates over internal migration."[12]

Among many other effects, the premium placed on desirable citizens makes subsidized housing unattainable for poor prospective internal migrants. For example, the New York City Housing Authority specifies that while non-residents may apply for subsidized housing, "due to NYCHA's long waiting list, available apartments will be offered to applicants who live or work in New York City first" – effectively barring low-income non-residents. Furthermore, only people who already live or work in New York City can qualify for priority assignment as victims of domestic violence, "working families" who "do not live or work in New York City will not be assigned any working family priority," and even homeless people must have previously resided in NYC to qualify for priority. The result is that only those with the means to afford market rates can move to NYC unless they want to risk becoming homeless; other cities have similar policies.[13]

---

[10] Parts of this section expand on the forum discussion in Maas 2020a; see also Seubert 2020.
[11] Dahl 1998.
[12] Minoff 2014.
[13] In England, local councils decide who is eligible for "council housing," and commonly exclude people without local connections. Furthermore, many councils require applicants to have lived or worked in the area for a certain time before they can even apply to be placed on the waiting list. For example, one London council states that applicants must "have lived

Of course people without the means to afford market rates do move to new cities in search of economic opportunity or to escape bad situations in their place of previous residence, but any public assistance they receive tends to come from national or regional governments rather than municipal authorities. Even politically progressive bastions such as San Francisco and New York deport poor and homeless people to other jurisdictions.[14] This is nothing new. Indeed, cities were engaging in cost–benefit analysis of migrants and residents even before there were states.[15] For example, the Dutch Republic's economic success depended on a constant stream of migrant workers, sailors, soldiers, servants, as well as transmigrants to the Dutch colonies in Asia and America. Cities such as Amsterdam, Haarlem, Leiden, Rotterdam, Gouda, and Middelburg attracted highly skilled and wealthy migrants by reimbursing moving costs, extending capital to (re)start businesses, making available manufacturing space, and offering tax rebates – benefits that often sparked the locals' envy. Leading families monopolized political positions while individuals could be stripped of citizenship for irresponsible behavior. Citizenship was usually acquired through birth or marriage but could also be purchased, which was attractive because of the municipal social welfare provisions reserved for citizens.[16]

As in the Dutch Republic, today's "world cities" seek to attract the "best and brightest" – but they sort potential residents by socioeconomic status either through the operation of market forces (which may appear neutral but are shaped by many factors that are far from neutral) or through active intervention. Echoing Seubert (cities are "increasingly less a home for ordinary people who want to live in the city"[17]), a Toronto Region Board of Trade report notes that housing in Toronto is "increasingly unaffordable, unsuitable and unavailable"; existing homes "often do not meet the needs of lower- and moderate-income people. Employers are finding it harder to recruit and retain employees, and workers are facing tough choices between more expensive housing and longer commutes. Left unchecked, these forces will drive Toronto in the same direction as

---

in the London Borough of Havering for six continuous years." Councils cannot exclude people serving in the UK armed forces, those fleeing domestic abuse, or those who are "legally homeless." Council housing transfers from another area should be possible – but as always there are gaps between law and practice. https://england.shelter.org.uk/housing_advice/council_housing_association/who_is_eligible_to_apply_for_council_housing

[14] Maas 2020b.
[15] Prak 2020.
[16] Maas 2013b, 396.
[17] Seubert 2020, 25.

San Francisco, New York and other global cities where only a select class of professionals can afford to live."[18]

The report cites as one model the University of British Columbia, which offers "more than 10% of its campus housing portfolio [...] to full-time faculty and staff for 25% below market rates," is "piloting a rent geared to income (RGI) program for lower-income staff," and offers low-interest-rate loans and grants for down payments. Another model is Whistler, which requires developers of new properties "to either build accommodation for their future workers or provide cash-in-lieu for the [Whistler Housing Authority] to build workforce housing. The WHA can also negotiate with private residential developers to grant higher density rights if that increase is used for affordable housing for the workforce." The report notes: "Qualified occupants must work a minimum 30 hours per week at a local business and must occupy their unit full-time as their primary residence. WHA enforces these rules by an annual attestation and a complaints-based investigation and enforcement process." Such models are a remarkable instrumentalization of housing for workers (only good workers qualify for subsidized housing, and they must leave once they stop working), yet they are far from unique; qualification for local privileges varies based on socioeconomic status and is unrelated to the supposed equality of citizenship status.[19]

Both public and private housing markets increase inequality in cities by excluding those who cannot afford high housing costs. Public housing authorities tend to increase exclusion through qualifying criteria that keep out newcomers or socially undesirable people. The WHA has a waiting list just like the NYCHA and like public housing authorities elsewhere, which all apply cost–benefit calculations. They may evict residents for using illegal drugs or abusing alcohol; entire households may be evicted if any member of the household or even a guest engages in drug-related criminal activity.[20] In the private market, the affordability crisis discussed in the Toronto report is not unique: young university graduates are flocking to cities, and living in smaller and smaller spaces,[21] but less educated people are leaving. Cities are increasingly populated by

---

[18] Toronto Region Board of Trade, 27
[19] There is of course a long history of housing provided by companies in so-called company towns; the difference is that the WHA and similar associations are public rather than private.
[20] "Know Your Rights: Housing and Arrests or Criminal Convictions | The Bronx Defenders" 2021
[21] Barría 2021

young, rich workers, while older and poorer people or families who want children move out[22] – and homeless people are forced out.[23]

Money and Internal Migration in the United States, China, India, and Europe

There is much concern about internal migrants being attracted by higher levels of social benefits within federal states or other free movement systems such as the European Union, yet the evidence that significant numbers of migrants are motivated by higher benefits is slim to nonexistent. An oft-cited study based on data from the early 1990s found that poor US residents were much more likely to move to another state because of the "push" of increased competition for jobs from immigrants moving to their state of origin than they were influenced by the "pull" of higher social assistance benefits in their state of destination.[24] One newspaper article about several families who had moved from Chicago, Illinois, to Madison, Wisconsin, quoted the co-author of a book on so-called "welfare magnets," who said that most academic studies found that migration to higher-benefit states "is real, but is quite modest" because decisions to move are "as complicated for poor people as they are for rich people" and are rarely mono-causal – but that state legislators would often trim benefits to ensure they were not more generous than neighboring states, despite the lack of evidence for significant benefit-induced migration.[25] Other studies repeat the finding that the level of welfare benefits has no or only marginal effect on decisions to move between states in the United States, despite increasing disparities in levels of social assistance.[26]

As a non-democracy, China can curtail the internal migration of its citizens by allowing provinces and cities to impose residence requirements and restrictions. Despite official restrictions, millions of people move from rural to urban areas and from central provinces to the industrialized coast, leading to China having the largest number of "illegal" migrants in the world: as of 2019 there were an estimated 288 million people in the so-called floating population. An earlier study estimated that fully one-fifth of China's population consists of migrant

---

[22] Thompson 2019
[23] https://nlchp.org/wp-content/uploads/2018/10/Housing-Not-Handcuffs.pdf
[24] Frey et al. 1996
[25] Johnson 1995; Peterson and Rom 1990.
[26] De Jong, Graefe, and Pierre 2005.

workers, drawn by higher earnings but also (with sharp gender differences) non-economic motivations such as personal development.[27] One detailed study of internal migrants in China found that three main concerns of local governments determined their willingness to extend local citizenship rights to internal migrants: economic development (demand for workers), fiscal protectionism (limiting outsider access to scarce resources), and social stability (fear of outsiders). Local citizenship rights are more valuable to poorer migrants, because they rely on public services and cannot afford private options. When writing new policies, "local bureaucrats try to 'guess who has money', to attract people who 'will not depend on the government'."[28] More generous welfare policies and government services are correlated with stricter policies, protectionist trends are strongest for low-skilled labor migration, and news media reports often conflate internal migrants, crime, and social disorder.[29] Such disparities and discrimination for Chinese citizens seeking to move within China run counter to the idea of equality.

Because China is not a democracy and does not guarantee freedom of movement to its citizens, India is a better illustration of the limits of equal citizenship and free movement rights within democracies. As in China, internal migration within India is seen as key for economic development.[30] And like almost all democratic societies, India guarantees freedom of movement within the territory to all citizens. Yet every one of the Indian states has policies that favor that state's residents in access to education, employment in the public sector, and social assistance programs. "Migrants have little or no state-level support and are often scapegoated by local law enforcement and politicians for any trouble. They are underpaid, underserved and unable to be fully productive. Interviews with interstate migrants across India revealed widespread despondency about their quality of life and a yearning to go back home eventually."[31] The result is that migrant status in India is strongly correlated with socioeconomic status, as reflected in a 2017 report by the Indian government's Working Group on Migration, which recommended that hostel facilities need to be provided to accommodate migrants from marginalized communities. Social security provisions are usually not portable across state boundaries, so migrants lose access when they

[27] Chiang, Hannum, and Kao 2015.
[28] Vortherms 2017, 113.
[29] Vortherms 2017, 115.
[30] Deshingkar and Grimm 2005.
[31] Aggarwal et al. 2020.

leave their home states, and also cannot gain access at their destinations. The Working Group concluded that "is important to confront discrimination whenever it appears and reinforce the contributions that migrants make to their places of residence and reaffirm the rights of Indians to settle and work anywhere in India."[32] An independent report characterized internal migrants in India and neighboring countries Nepal, Sri Lanka, Pakistan, Bhutan, Bangladesh, and the Maldives as being "stateless without losing the state's legal recognition"; lack of proper "nutrition, health hazards, illiteracy and the tag of outsiders within their own countries make them run from one place to another to live a life without rights and dignity" – with the result that "citizenship has no meaning" for internal migrants.[33]

Meanwhile, the evolving system of free movement guaranteed for citizens of EU member states by EU citizenship faces similar challenges. Departing from the earlier dynamic of ever more open and mobile societies, recent years have seen a turn toward more restrictive welfare policies in Europe.[34] Similarly, the 2003 Long-term Residents Directive was hailed by some as a new form of membership related to EU citizenship but is available, after five years of continuous residence, only to third-country nationals who can "prove that they have adequate resources and sickness insurance to avoid becoming a burden"; even after individuals acquire long-term resident status, member states may "limit equal treatment in respect of social assistance and social protection to core benefits."[35] As the chapters in this volume by Schrauwen and Mantu confirm, the basic political dynamic is one of the European Commission and Court generally supporting increased rights while member state governments generally advocate restrictive measures for both third-country nationals (who do not have automatic rights to live and work in the EU) and EU citizens (for whom EU citizenship had long promised that ideal).[36] Other research has found that intra-EU migration is generally seen as a positive phenomenon in contrast to a generally negative perception about immigration from outside the EU.[37] Yet EU mobility may also strengthen the primacy of national citizenship for stayers.[38] And in Europe – as in the United States,

---

[32] Government of India 2017, 66, 67.
[33] South Asia Alliance for Poverty Eradication 2020.
[34] Mantu 2021; Martinsen and Werner 2019; Schrauwen 2021.
[35] Council Directive 2003/109/EC. For discussion, see Bonjour 2018.
[36] Maas 2007.
[37] Salamońska 2017.
[38] Siklodi 2020.

China, and India – there is discrimination against the poor and others of low socioeconomic status. Increasingly, the Court of Justice of the European Union in Luxembourg and the European Court of Human Rights in Strasbourg emphasize social affiliation with the host society, thereby cautiously embracing moderately communitarian narratives of membership that temper the traditional emphasis on equal treatment and residence security across borders.[39] Such moves represent a departure from the ideals of equal citizenship and fit with a political dynamic in which governments engage in cost–benefit analysis of prospective immigrants and emigrants.

Governments Distinguishing Desirable from Undesirable People

Governments of all kinds and at all levels – whether national, regional, or local – engage in cost–benefit analysis to determine which migrants or residents to encourage and which to discourage from moving. Governments seek to attract or retain desirable people, while blocking undesirable people from moving in or encouraging them to leave.[40] This means that proposals such as Maarten Prak's to view citizenship as a club with initiation dues can seem appealing: considering local rights in economic terms could open up "local citizenship to a conversation about ownership and access, including the compensation that the established feel they are entitled to from the new members of their community."[41] Yet such economic conversations are inherently exclusionary, because they limit access to those who are able to afford it.

Since the rise of national citizenship, one role for national governments has been to counter the discriminatory tendencies of "mean cities" discussed by Enrico Gargiulo and Lorenzo Piccoli. In Italy, as in many other countries, registering one's residence is necessary to access social assistance, public housing, public health, and more. But sometimes local voters, urban movements, and municipal administrations deliberately make registration difficult, thereby restricting the rights not only of immigrants but also those of fellow citizens deemed undesirable, such as people who move a lot, Roma, and homeless people.[42] This role is mirrored by EU citizenship, which provides that citizens of EU Member States may live anywhere within the territory of the Union only as long as

---

[39] Thym 2020.
[40] Maas 2020b.
[41] Prak 2020.
[42] Gargiulo and Piccoli 2020.

they do not "burden" the host society (though the Citizenship Directive provides permanent residence without preconditions after five years of legal residence). European cities have not been particularly welcoming toward Roma, for example, and some governments have similarly sought to limit access for retirees, students, or members of other marginalized groups.[43]

Dissuading or Banning Undesirable Residents

Very few governments voluntarily extend rights to people perceived, correctly or incorrectly, as a threat or burden. Anyone who doubts the proclivity of cities to ban undesirable people has not followed the news about low-level sex offenders with decades-old convictions being banned from public areas[44] (and often being unable to work as a result); or about people with mental health, addiction, or disability issues getting a criminal record for being homeless[45] (and hence becoming ineligible for public housing); or any of the numerous petitions to expel high-profile (or low-profile[46]) criminals. President Trump's executive order requiring both states and localities to consent before refugees can be resettled[47] could be considered a move toward urban citizenship because it gives cities a role in determining who may reside, but it also sets exclusion as the default.[48]

The transition from the Trump to the Biden administration in the United States recasts the discussion about immigration, but both international and internal migrations have a local dimension. Although the national-level political rhetoric in the United States often tends to be restrictionist, the actual actions of local governments are often more accommodating, often because of the economic contributions that immigrants make coupled with overarching civil rights norms.[49] Historically informed research demonstrates that US states restrict or expand rights for Americans in an enduring tension between state and national citizenship – including for free movement between the states.[50] The upshot is that some

---

[43] Gehring 2013; Lafleur and Mescoli 2018; Maas 2020c; Parker and López Catalán 2014; Schenk and Schmidt 2018.
[44] Lovett 2012.
[45] Healy 2017.
[46] Newell 2020.
[47] "Executive Order on Enhancing State and Local Involvement in Refugee Resettlement" 2021.
[48] Weinberg 2021.
[49] Graauw 2021; Williamson 2018.
[50] Colbern and Ramakrishnan 2020

states and localities are more welcoming than others, either for international migrants or for internal migrants, or both. Although significant numbers of internal migrants moving to Canada's westernmost province of British Columbia access social welfare,[51] the province's Housing Minister affirmed that "We don't have border security here that says you can't come into British Columbia. If you arrive at a shelter here, we don't judge you by where you come from. We try to help you."[52] At the same time, many Canadian provinces and US states impose strict residency requirements on individual receiving social assistance, effectively limiting their mobility within the federation. For example, Quebec and Ontario specify a seven-day maximum period of absence per month before assistance payments are stopped; such policies make it difficult, if not impossible, for individuals receiving public assistance to search for employment opportunities in other jurisdictions.[53]

Access to housing acts as a barrier (for the poor) or facilitator (for the rich) to free movement. Comparative research confirms that individuals who live in public housing are less mobile than those who do not.[54] This is nothing new, as governments have long been attempting to ameliorate living conditions for the poor. The US federal Department of Housing and Urban Development's HOPE IV program, created in 1992, allowed cities to replace low-income housing projects with mixed-income housing. In the process, the program dispersed tens of thousands of low-income residents, who lost their existing communities.[55] One study found that even those low-income residents who had received vouchers to move to higher-income areas tended to cluster in poor African-American neighborhoods, reinforcing a stratified housing market.[56] Even well-intentioned programs may thus dissuade free movement. As another example, the federally funded

---

[51] "Nearly one in seven new welfare recipients in B.C. last year were from out-of-province," affirmed *The Province* newspaper in 2016, arguing that, as "more homeless and unemployed people continue to arrive here, British Columbia should make it clear to other provinces that offloading their poor on B.C. is not acceptable."

[52] Quoted in Maas 2020b

[53] The government of Ontario specifies that a "person who is absent from Ontario for a period greater than seven days is not eligible for assistance unless the absence is approved by the Administrator as necessary for reasons of health or exceptional circumstances": www.mcss.gov.on.ca/en/mcss/programs/social/directives/ow/9_2_OW_Directives.aspx) while a similar policy in Quebec has been decried as violating human rights: www.cbc.ca/news/canada/montreal/quebec-welfare-travel-court-1.5379695

[54] Lui and Suen 2011.

[55] Manzo, Kleit, and Couch 2008.

[56] Oakley and Burchfield 2009.

Medicaid program is the largest source of medical and health benefits for almost one-quarter of the US population (primarily low-income Americans); yet Medicaid benefits vary significantly from state to state, and moving between states often results in confusion and disempowerment.[57]

Attracting Desirable Residents

Social class and inequality separate those able to migrate from those lacking the means.[58] This is true not only for international migration but also for internal migration. Surveying a burgeoning literature on local citizenship, Bauböck is right to worry that "the integrity and inclusiveness of local democracy would be jeopardised if those born in the city or descending from parents established in the city enjoy special privileges – as they do under the Chinese hukou system,"[59] but similar privileges exist in democratic states. The ideal resident is wealthy, healthy, and employed rather than poor, sick, or needing assistance. Underpaid teachers or nurses have a higher socioeconomic status than an unemployed person or someone with a criminal record or mental illness – indeed, many cities try to attract young workers by offering incentives[60] – but if they do not have enough money, they are often relegated to less desirable neighborhoods. Wealth, rather than any other element of socioeconomic status, is increasingly the sole criterion for being able to afford city life.

By 2018, over 200 US cities had a median home value over $1 million – clearly unaffordable on the median national household income of $61,937; meanwhile, even though over 46 million people (over 14% of the overall US population) lived in "non-metro" areas, these areas accounted for less than 10 percent of overall GDP.[61] Perhaps Bauböck is right that "cities should determine who their citizens are independently of how states do this" – but increasing the capacity of cities to grant citizenship rights would not necessarily ameliorate the problem of inequality and might in fact aggravate it, as cities act like other governments and engage in overt or covert selection processes that privilege some people over others. In a system in which state and local governments provide social welfare,

---

[57] Michener 2018.
[58] Bonjour and Chauvin 2018.
[59] Bauböck 2020.
[60] Maas 2020a, 71, mentions incentives such as the one by Tulsa, Oklahoma, offering $10,000 for tech workers moving to Tulsa.
[61] Maas 2020a, 71, and calculations from U.S. Census Bureau.

encouraging the out-migration of people who are "burdens" and encouraging the in-migration of people who are "contributors" make financial sense; San Francisco buses over 1,000 homeless people out of the city annually, while New York City also pays for destitute residents to "return home" to other parts of the United States, most notably Puerto Rico.[62]

Meanwhile Puerto Rico and other states actively recruit the rich. Puerto Rico has special tax incentives to attract millionaires and billionaires from the rest of the United States: zero tax on dividends, interest, and capital gains. Florida's lack of state income tax often succeeds in attracting wealthy Americans from other states: in 2016, the relocation of a single taxpayer (hedge-fund billionaire David Tepper) from New Jersey to Florida caused New Jersey's income to fall by hundreds of millions of dollars.[63] Such examples simply scratch the surface of the political and economic consequences of internal migration, and the role that money plays in persuading or dissuading such movements.

Conclusion: Money versus Citizenship in Internal Migration

Just as the 1936 "bum blockade" on California's borders was popular when it kept out migrants perceived as undesirable but lost support when a celebrity was denied readmission, so too similar political dynamics are at play with internal borders in contemporary societies, both democratic and not. Examples raised in this chapter from Canada, China, Europe, India, and the United States demonstrate that money facilitates or inhibits internal migration. Tax policies, access to housing, differences in job opportunities between cities and rural areas, and other disparities make it difficult for central governments to safeguard free movement. When protectionism seeking to limit access to scarce resources, or fear of outsiders as threatening social stability, competes with economic motivations (e.g., demand for workers) or identity claims (common citizenship), central governments must intervene if they wish to guarantee free movement. When social security provisions in federal states such as India are not portable across state boundaries, migrants lose access when they leave their home region while being unable to gain access in their destination region, a scenario that is comparable to debates about the possibilities and limits of citizenship of the European Union in facilitating free movement among the EU member states. Though the analysis above has been on natural

---

[62] Maas 2020b.
[63] Maas 2020b.

persons, it could easily be extended to companies and other legal persons: as local governments seek to attract "desirable" residents and dissuade or ban "undesirable" residents, central governments must mitigate the financial and other inequalities that threaten the ideal of equal citizenship.

References

Aggarwal, Varun, Giacomo Solano, Priyansha Singh, and Saniya Singh. 2020. "The Integration of Interstate Migrants in India: A 7 State Policy Evaluation." *International Migration* 58, no. 5 Wiley: 144–63.

Barría, Cecilia. 2019. "The Tiny Flats Taking over Latin America." At www.bbc.com/worklife/article/20190703-the-tiny-flats-taking-over-latin-america

Bauböck, Rainer. 2020. "Cities vs States: Should Urban Citizenship Be Emancipated from Nationality?" In Rainer Bauböck and Liav Orgad, eds. *Cities vs States: Should Urban Citizenship Be Emancipated from Nationality?* Fiesole: EUI RSCAS Working Paper 2020/16.

Bonjour, Saskia. 2018. "Family Reunification and Migrant Integration Policies in the EU: Dynamics of Inclusion and Exclusion." *The Routledge Handbook of Justice and Home Affairs Research*, 215–226.

Bonjour, Saskia and Sébastien Chauvin. 2018. "Social Class, Migration Policy and Migrant Strategies: An Introduction." *International Migration* 56, no. 4: 5–18.

Bruzelius, Cecilia and Martin Seeleib-Kaiser. 2020. "Social Citizenship in Federations: Free Movement and Social Assistance Rights in the EU and Beyond." *West European Politics* 0, no. 0: 1–23. www.tandfonline.com/doi/full/10.1080/01402382.2020.1826189

Chiang, Yi-Lin, Emily Hannum, and Grace Kao. 2015. "It's Not Just About the Money: Gender and Youth Migration from Rural China." *Chinese Sociological Review* 47, no. 2: 177–201.

Colbern, Allan and S. Karthick Ramakrishnan. 2020. *Citizenship Reimagined: A New Framework for States' Rights in the United States.* Cambridge: Cambridge University Press.

Conner, Thomas. 2016. "The Anti-Okie Panic." At https://thislandpress.com/2016/11/10/the-anti-okie-panic/

Dahl, Robert A. 1998. *On Democracy.* New Haven: Yale University Press.

De Jong, Gordon F., Deborah Roempke Graefe, and Tanja St. Pierre. 2005. "Welfare Reform and Interstate Migration of Poor Families." *Demography* 42, no. 3, 469–96.

Deshingkar, Priya and Sven Grimm. 2005. "Internal Migration and Development: A Global Perspective." International Organization for Migration. https://publications.iom.int/books/mrs-ndeg19-internal-migration-and-development-global-perspective

"Executive Order on Enhancing State and Local Involvement in Refugee Resettlement." 2021. *The White House*.

Frey, William H., Kao-Lee Liaw, Yu Xie, and Marcia J. Carlson. 1996. "Interstate Migration of the US Poverty Population: Immigration 'Pushes' and Welfare Magnet 'Pulls.'" *Population and Environment* 17, no. 6: 491–533.

Gargiulo, Enrico and Lorenzo Piccoli. 2020. "Mean Cities: The Dark Side of Urban Citizenship." In Rainer Bauböck and Liav Orgad, eds. *Cities vs States: Should Urban Citizenship Be Emancipated from Nationality?* Fiesole: EUI RSCAS Working Paper 2020/16.

Gehring, Jacqueline. 2013. "Free Movement for Some: The Treatment of the Roma after the European Union's Eastern Expansion." In Willem Maas, ed. *Democratic Citizenship and the Free Movement of People* Leiden: Martinus Nijhoff.

Government of India. 2017. "Report of the Working Group on Migration." Government of India. Ministry of Housing and Urban Poverty Alleviation.

Graauw, Els de. 2021. "City Government Activists and the Rights of Undocumented Immigrants: Fostering Urban Citizenship within the Confines of US Federalism." *Antipode* n/a, no. n/a.

Healy, Jack. 2017. "Rights Battles Emerge in Cities Where Homelessness Can Be a Crime (Published 2017)." *The New York Times*, January 9, sec. U.S.

International Organization for Migration. 2019. "World Migration Report 2020." International Organization for Migration.

Johnson, Dirk. 1995. "Rethinking Welfare: Interstate Migration." *The New York Times*, May 8.

Kiger, Patrick J. 2019. "How the Dust Bowl Made Americans Refugees in Their Own Country." *History*. www.history.com/news/dust-bowl-migrants-california

"Know Your Rights: Housing and Arrests or Criminal Convictions | The Bronx Defenders." 2021. At www.bronxdefenders.org/housing-and-arrests-or-criminal-convictions/

Lafleur, Jean-Michel and Elsa Mescoli. 2018. "Creating Undocumented EU Migrants through Welfare: A Conceptualization of Undeserving and Precarious Citizenship." *Sociology* 52, no. 3: 480–96.

Lovett, Ian. 2012. "Public-Place Laws Tighten Rein on Sex Offenders." *The New York Times*, May 30

Lui, Hon-Kwong and Wing Suen. 2011. "The Effects of Public Housing on Internal Mobility in Hong Kong." *Journal of Housing Economics* 20, no. 1: 15–29.

Maas, Willem. 2007. *Creating European Citizens*. Lanham: Rowman & Littlefield.

2008. "Migrants, States, and EU Citizenship's Unfulfilled Promise." *Citizenship Studies* 12, no. 6: 583–95.

2009. "Unrespected, Unequal, Hollow?: Contingent Citizenship and Reversible Rights in the European Union." *Columbia Journal of European Law* 15, no. 2: 265–80.

2013a. "Equality and the Free Movement of People: Citizenship and Internal Migration." In Willem Maas, ed. *Democratic Citizenship and the Free Movement of People.* Leiden: Martinus Nijhoff.

2013b. "Immigrant Integration, Gender, and Citizenship in the Dutch Republic." *Politics, Groups, and Identities* 1, no. 3: 390–401.

2017. "Boundaries of Political Community in Europe, the US, and Canada." *Journal of European Integration* 39, no. 5: 575–90.

2020a. "Does Urban Citizenship Promote Inclusion for the Poor, Sick, and Outcast?" In Rainer Bauböck and Liav Orgad, eds. *Cities vs States: Should Urban Citizenship Be Emancipated from Nationality?* Fiesole: EUI RSCAS Working Paper 2020/16.

2020b. "Citizenship and Free Movement in Comparative Federalism." In Jae-Jae Spoon and Nils Ringe, eds. *The European Union and Beyond: Multi-Level Governance, Institutions, and Policy-Making.* London: Rowman & Littlefield, 75–93.

2020c. "European Citizenship and Free Movement after Brexit." In Scott Greer and Janet Laible, eds. *The European Union after Brexit.* Manchester: Manchester University Press, 95–112.

Mantu, Sandra. 2021. "Women as EU Citizens: Caught between Work, Sufficient Resources, and the Market." In Tesseltje De Lange, Willem Maas, and Annette Schrauwen, eds. *Money Matters in Migration. Policy, Participation, and Citizenship.* Cambridge: Cambridge University Press.

Manzo, Lynne C., Rachel G. Kleit, and Dawn Couch. 2008. "'Moving Three Times Is Like Having Your House on Fire Once': The Experience of Place and Impending Displacement among Public Housing Residents." *Urban Studies* 45, no. 9: 1855–78.

Martinsen, Dorte Sindbjerg, and Benjamin Werner. 2019. "No Welfare Magnets – Free Movement and Cross-Border Welfare in Germany and Denmark Compared." *Journal of European Public Policy* 26, no. 5: 637–55.

Michener, Jamila. 2018. *Fragmented Democracy: Medicaid, Federalism, and Unequal Politics.* Cambridge: Cambridge University Press.

Minoff, Elisa M. Alvarez. 2014. "The Age of Internal Migration: Destitute Migrants, Liberal Reformers, and the Transformation of American Citizenship, 1930–1972." book proposal on file with author.

Newell, David. 2020. "Cottrell's Cove Residents Start Petition to Kick Alleged Thief out of Town | CBC News." *CBC*. www.cbc.ca/news/canada/newfoundland-labrador/cottrells-cove-petition-kick-man-out-1.5439023

Oakley, Deirdre and Keri Burchfield. 2009. "Out of the Projects, Still in the Hood: The Spatial Constraints on Public-Housing Residents' Relocation in Chicago." *Journal of Urban Affairs* 31, no. 5: 589–614.

Parker, Owen and Óscar López Catalán. 2014. "Free Movement for Whom, Where, When? Roma EU Citizens in France and Spain." *International Political Sociology* 8, no. 4: 379–95.

Peterson, Paul E. and Mark C. Rom. 1990. *Welfare Magnets: A New Case for a National Standard.* Washington, D.C.: Brookings Institution.

Prak, Maarten. 2020. "The 'Sunk Costs' of Local Citizenship." In Rainer Bauböck and Liav Orgad, eds. *Cities vs States: Should Urban Citizenship Be Emancipated from Nationality?* Fiesole: EUI RSCAS Working Paper 2020/16.

Rasmussen, Cecilia. 2003. "LAPD Blocked Dust Bowl Migrants at State Borders." *Los Angeles Times*, March 9.

Salamońska, Justyna. 2017. "Mobilities against Prejudice: The Role of Social Transnationalism in Europe in Sentiments towards Immigration from Other EU Member States and from Outside the EU." In Anna Triandafyllidou, ed. *Multicultural Governance in a Mobile World.* Edinburgh: Edinburgh University Press, 87–107.

Schenk, Angelika and Susanne K. Schmidt. 2018. "Failing on the Social Dimension: Judicial Law-Making and Student Mobility in the EU." *Journal of European Public Policy* 25, no. 10: 1522–40.

Schrauwen, Annette. 2021. "Pushing out the Poor: Unstable Income and Termination of Residence." In Tesseltje De Lange, Willem Maas, and Annette Schrauwen, eds. *Money Matters in Migration. Policy, Participation, and Citizenship.* Cambridge: Cambridge University Press.

Seubert, Sandra. 2020. "'Zombie Urbanism' and the Search for New Sources of Solidarity." In Rainer Bauböck and Liav Orgad, eds. *Cities vs States: Should Urban Citizenship Be Emancipated from Nationality?* Fiesole: EUI RSCAS Working Paper 2020/16.

Siklodi, Nora. 2020. *Politics of Mobile Citizenship in Europe.* New York: Palgrave.

Skeldon, Ronald. 2018. "International Migration, Internal Migration, Mobility and Urbanization: Towards More Integrated Approaches." International Organization for Migration(IOM). https://publications.iom.int/system/files/pdf/mrs_53.pdf

South Asia Alliance for Poverty Eradication. 2020. "Migration in South Asia: Poverty and Vulnerability." Kathmandu. https://saape.org/news/migration-in-south-asia-poverty-and-vulnerability-report-2020-launched-globally/

Thompson, Derek. 2019. "The Future of the City Is Childless." *The Atlantic.* www.theatlantic.com/ideas/archive/2019/07/where-have-all-the-children-gone/594133/

Thym, Daniel. 2020. "Supranational Courts in Europe: A Moderately Communitarian Turn in the Case Law on Immigration and Citizenship." *Journal of Ethnic and Migration Studies* 0, no. 0: 1–18. www.tandfonline.com/doi/full/10.1080/1369183X.2020.1750353

Toronto Region Board of Trade. "Housing a Generation of Workers." At www.bot.com/Portals/0/PDFs/BOARD_Woodgreen_WorkforceHousing.pdf.

Vortherms, Samantha. 2017. "Between the Center and the People: Localized Citizenship in China." PhD dissertation, Madison, WI: University of Wisconsin Madison.

Weinberg, Tessa. 2021. "Refugees Will No Longer Be Allowed to Resettle in Texas, Governor Abbott Tells Feds." *Star-Telegram*. www.star-telegram.com/news/politics-government/article239118873.html

Weiser, Kathy. 2020. "The Bum Blockade – Stopping the Invasion of Depression Refugees – Legends of America." www.legendsofamerica.com/ca-bumblockade/

Williamson, Abigail Fisher. 2018. *Welcoming New Americans?: Local Governments and Immigrant Incorporation*. Chicago: University of Chicago Press.

INDEX

advocacy groups, 56
Africa, 4, 47, 56, 76, 223, 231, 257
   African Institute of Remittances (AIR), 226
   Making Finance Work for Africa (MFW4A), 225
agencies
   development, 58
   European Asylum Support Office ('EASO'), 44, 46, 49, 50
   European Border and Coast Guard, *See* Frontex
Algeria, 60
armed non-state actors, 74, 81, 85
asylum
   application/claim, 43, 44, 169, 172, 178
   asylum seekers/ claimants, 6, 30, 130, 133, 136, 175, 210, 218, 287
   laws/legislation, 130, 173
   policies, 101
   procedure, 218
Australia, 29, 30, 31, 286
Austria, 29, 113, 284

bank account, 12, 205, 210, 212, 216, 228, 236, 283
bargaining power, 100, 101, 164
Baumol effect, 3, 152
Belgium, 29, 284
Benelux, 173
Birth tourism, 250
birthright lottery, 253
border(s)
   border control, 40, 42, 49, 56, 65, 101, 130, 169, 174, 207
   border externalization, 56, 68
   bordering process, 38
   Euro-Moroccan, 55
   Frontex, *See* Frontex
   inclusive or exclusive border drawing, an, 39
   Operations Sophia and Irini, 47
   unlawful deportation, 60
British Columbia, 322, 328
budget
   Aeneas regulation, 64
   Asylum, Migration and Integration Fund ('AMIF'), 49
   donors, 19, 27, 32, 55, 63, 66
   EU budget, 6, 9, 46, 48, 49
   European Emergency Trust Fund for Africa, 47
   Internal Security Fund ('ISF'), 47
   make-or-buy decisions, 160, 164
   Multiannual Financial Framework ('MFF'), 45
   personal care, 154, 155
bureaucracy, 23, 65, 67, 68, 206

California, 317, 318, 330
Canada, 10, 29, 247, 251, 319, 330
capital
   economic, 250
   human, 250
   mobile, 280
capitalist, 102, 192, 247, 292, 320
care
   24/7 care, 157
   family carers, 150, 156, 159, 162
   Haushaltshilfen (home helps), 153
   healthcare coverage, 62
   LIMC placement agencies, 150, 153, 156, 157, 162, 165
   live-in migrant carer, 11, 149, 163
   long-term care (LTC), 11, 149
Caribbean, 74, 79, 215, 249, 257, 286

INDEX

Central and Eastern Europe (CEE), 120, 152, 165, 176
children, 31, 68, 81, 138, 192, 198, 256, 283, 302, 323
China, 248, 253, 257, 319, 323, 330
  floating population, 323
cities, 55, 75, 113, 256, 320, 330
citizenship
  as commodity, 259
  by investment, 13, 247, 251, 257, 263, 290
  dual, 253
  earned citizenship, 114, 126
  equal, 3, 282, 289, 320, 324, 331
  EU citizenship – citizenship of the Union, 6, 12, 114, 125, 188, 200, 290, 325
  failed, 298
  for sale/selling, 143, 263, 266, 271, 275, 276
  genuine link, 265, 269, 270, 288
  Greek/Roman, 281
  market, 188
civil society
  organisations, 63, 66
  partnerships, 62, 66
Colombia, 29, 74, 77, 81, 86, 88
  Caminantes, 76, 81, 83, 85
  Colombian-Venezuelan borderlands, 74, 77, 81, 83, 85, 88
commodification of citizenship, *See* Citizenship, as commodity
communities, marginalized, 237
contract law, 13, 263, 268, 272, 275, 276
corruption, 225, 231, 290, 292
cost
  considerations, 150, 156, 159, 160
  containment strategy, 155, 159
Costs and benefits of migration, *See* Migration, costs and benefits
COVID-19, 50, 82, 205, 211, 250, 258, 292
crisis
  Covid-19, *See* COVID-19
  economic, 113, 114, 301
  migration, 38, 39, 46, 47, 49
  refugee, 130, 131, 134, 142
Cyprus, 251, 257, 265, 268, 290

debt
  bondage, 94, 104, 105
  cycle of, 94
Denmark, 133
deportability, 310, 311
drug trade, *See* Trafficking, Drugs
Dust Bowl, 317, 318, 319

elite, 13, 247, 254, 281, 291
employer
  involuntary, 199
  sanctions, 7, 169, 171, 172, 178, 183
equality/inequality
  gender, 130, 188, 201
  legal, 280
European Court of Human Rights, 208, 326
European Union
  Council of the European Communities, 173
  duty of sincere cooperation, 269
  enlargement, 153, 165, 172, 175, 178
  European Commission, 23, 122, 176, 227, 290, 325
  European Council, 64, 175, 177
  European Court of Justice, 11, 208, 313, 326
  European Parliament, 179, 210, 290
  Free Movement Law, 123, 165, 189, 192, 199, 201
  intra-EU mobility, *See* Migration, intra-EU mobility
  Treaty of Amsterdam, 176
  worker, *See* Worker, EU
European Union Legislation [EU legislation]
  Directive 2003/109/EC – Long-term Residents Directive, 325
  Directive 2003/86/EC – Family reunification Directive, 133
  Directive 2004/38/EEC – Citizens' Rights Directive [Residence Rights Directive], 117, 118, 190, 194, 198
  Directive 2009/50/EC – Blue Card Directive, 124
  Directive 2009/52/EC – Employer Sanctions Directive, 181, 183

European Union Legislation (cont.)
  Directive 2014/92/EU – Payment account Directive, 205, 209, 211, 212
  Directive 2015/849/EU – Anti-Money Laundering Directive, 205, 209, 210
  Directive 96/71/EC – Posted workers Directive, 153, 165
European Union Policy
  2020 New Pact on Migration and Asylum, 112
  Common European Asylum System ('CEAS'), 43
  European Agenda on Migration, 40, 41, 43, 44
  Facility for Refugees in Turkey, 48
  Global Approach on Migration (GAM), 64
  Migration Partnership Framework, 48, 50
  return, 40
  Talent Partnerships, 112
exploitation
  exploitation of LIMCs, 161
expulsion, 3, 6, 41, 121, 191, 205, 216, 298, 308

fees
  recruitment fees, definition of, 94, 103
financial development, 223
financial inclusion, 205, 210, 217, 224, 226, 234
financial services, 211, 223, 224, 228, 231, 234
Finland, 284
flexible contracts, *See* Labour Contracts
Florida, 330
France, 172, 173, 177, 249
  French Revolution, 280, 282
Frontex [European Border and Coast Guard], 41, 42, 46, 49
funds, *See* Budgets

Germany, 29, 114, 118, 133, 149, 152, 155, 172, 193, 249, 284
Gibraltar, 56

Global Compact for Safe, Orderly and Regular Migration, 93, 205, 213, 220, 225, 237
golden passport, *See* Passport
golden visa, *See* Visa
Greece, 49, 175

homelessness, 113, 121, 217, 320, 330
housing, 13, 75, 113, 214, 297, 319, 328

identity
  claims, 330
  documents, 207, 234, 307
  national, 112
immigration
  control, 117, 130, 169, 170, 182, 213
  enforcement, 3, 170, 173, 181
immigration conditions
  financial resources, 2, 27, 56, 80, 197, 256
  income requirement, 9, 130, 132, 135, 139, 284
immigration decision
  deportation, 102, 117, 288, 308, 310
  first admission, 124
  removal, 41, 117, 121, 183
income threshold, *See* Immigration conditions
India, 248, 319, 324, 330
informal economy, 9, 75, 83, 126, 179
integration
  civic, 279, 284, 285, 293
  measures, 49
  objectives, 44
  of third-country nationals, 40
  policies, 45, 130
  strategy, 61, 62
International Labour Organization (ILO), 25, 26, 93, 96, 103, 173
International Monetary Fund (IMF), 228, 255
international organizations, 19, 55, 56, 136, 268
intersectionality, 144, 197
intra-EU mobility, *See* Migration, intra-EU mobility

Italy, 26, 172, 175, 179, 249, 326
ius pecunia, 264

Kenya, 214, 223, 233, 234

labour
   (im)migration, 5, 9, 25, 93, 112, 123, 124, 131, 140, 152, 324
   informal (grey or black market), 86, 154
   unauthorized, 172, 181
labour contracts
   employment mode, 150, 155, 158, 161, 164
   flexible, 115, 119
   forced, 94, 103
   temporary, 124
labour inspectorate, 178, 179, 182
labour market
   controls, 177, 182, 183
   enforcement, 173, 179, 180, 181
   European, 112, 176
   inspection, 178, 179
   participation, 131, 136, 140, 142, 151, 192
   violations, 179, 183
legality, 11, 164, 270

Malta, 13, 218, 251, 257, 265, 273, 289
   Civil Code, 268, 274
Middle East, 56, 76, 176, 249, 253, 257
migrant care workers, 3
migrant workers
   Asian, 96, 99
   unauthorized, 169, 172, 176, 181
migration
   control cooperation, 56, 58, 64
   costs and benefits of, 8, 112
   family reunification, 5, 44, 131, 135, 142
   financing, 98
   illegalized, 299
   industry, 56, 57
   intra-EU mobility, 113, 115, 125
   investment, 12, 249, 250, 256
   irregular, 30, 40, 45, 58, 64, 101, 220
   labour (im)migration, *See* Labour, (im)migration

   legal, 40, 44, 49, 64, 105
   post-colonial, 172
   routes, 58
   undocumented, 170, 175, 176
mixed-status families, 13, 297, 301, 307, 311
mobility
   social, 96
money laundering, 11, 205, 218, 223, 292
money transfer operators, 214, 217
Morocco, 9, 55, 59, 63, 66
   Mohammed VI, 60
   National Strategy of Migration, 61
   Regime of Medical Assistance, 62

naturalization, 8, 12, 250, 264, 279, 283
Netherlands, 4, 13, 29, 113, 121, 150, 172, 206, 217, 297
   Dutch Republic, 321
   Linkage Act, 174, 297, 301, 307, 308, 311
New Jersey, 330
Nomad capitalist, 292
Norway, 131, 137, 142

Ontario, 328

passport, 74, 98, 249, 259, 272, 280, 283, 286, 291, 307
payment card, 211
permits
   residence, 124, 131, 139, 210, 283, 303, 307, 311
   work, 96
Poland, 30, 152, 156, 165
population
   ageing, 151
Portugal, 286
problem representation, 142
prostitution, 85, 86, 88
Puerto Rico, 330

Quebec, 251, 328

regularization, 61
remittances, 2, 11, 205, 211, 213, 217, 223, 228, 235

residence
  by investment, 251, 279, 292
  extended, 279
  long-term, 283
  permanent, 10, 130, 139, 191, 194, 250, 289, 327
rights
  human, 5, 61, 94, 208
  labour, 94, 103
Roma, 197, 326
Russia, 218, 248, 253, 257

San Francisco, 321, 322, 330
sanctions
  employer, *See* Employer, Sanctions
  freezing assets, 208
Schengen, 169, 173, 253, 259
self-sufficiency, 136, 138, 189, 198
Slovakia, 156, 158
smuggling
  activities, 42
  anti-smuggling operations, 47
  networks, 40
  of migrants, 42
social assistance/social benefits, 13, 61, 116, 174, 190, 196, 284, 297, 323
social cohesion, 112
social security, 1, 162, 178, 217, 284, 301, 305, 324
solidarity, 114, 132, 138, 194, 289
Somalia, 224, 228, 231
South Africa, 224, 233, 249
Spain, 172, 175, 178, 179
stateless, 207, 249, 273, 325
sufficient (financial) resources/ financial threshold, *See* Immigration conditions
Switzerland, 29, 55, 63, 249
  Swiss Development Agency, 65

targeting migrants, measures, 219
terrorism/terrorist
  financing, 208, 224, 230
  War on Terror, 58
Toronto, 321, 322
trafficking
  arms, 88
  drugs, 64, 78, 88
  human, 94, 224
  sex, 84
transit countries, 58, 64

unbanked, 205, 211, 216, 218
UNHCR, 24, 26, 29, 55, 67
United Kingdom, 29, 117, 133, 175, 253, 286
  2016 Immigration Bill, 180
  Gangmasters' Licensing Authority, 178
  Morecambe Bay, 178
  Windrush scandal, 215, 216
United Nations, 19, 93, 231
  Security Council Resolution 1373 (2001) countering financing of terrorism, 207
United States, 26, 30, 229, 285, 317, 323, 327
  DACA/ Dreamers, 288
  Green Card, 251, 257, 283, 288
  US Supreme Court, 318

Venezuela, 74, 77, 80, 83, 85, 88
violence, 60, 75, 141, 182, 320
visa
  golden, 251, 283, 286, 292
vulnerability, 67, 76, 94, 102, 105, 115, 143, 304

welfare
  benefits, 113, 135, 139, 191, 283, 301, 323
  distribution, 112
  state, 4, 12, 131, 136, 152, 298, 301, 320
  system, 122, 138, 151, 189, 194
  tourism, 120
welfare policy
  cash-for-care benefits, 153
welfare state, *See* Welfare, State
work
  illegal, 174, 176, 181
  unauthorized, 171
  undeclared work, 170, 176, 181
worker
  atypical workers, 122
  EU, 113, 120, 124, 157, 190, 194

illegal, 178
migrant care workers, 150, 152, 161
posted, 153, 165
self-employed, 85, 123, 153, 157, 191
undocumented, 174, 178

working conditions
   exploitative, 95
   fair working conditions, 150, 161
worksite raids, 171, 181

www.ingramcontent.com/pod-product-compliance
Ingram Content Group UK Ltd.
Pitfield, Milton Keynes, MK11 3LW, UK
UKHW030637171224
452390UK00008B/77